Transnational Societies, Transterritorial Politics

Migrations in the (Post-)Yugoslav Region, 19th–21st Century

SÜDOSTEUROPÄISCHE ARBEITEN

Für das

SÜDOST-INSTITUT

herausgegeben von

ULF BRUNNBAUER

und

KONRAD CLEWING

2009

R. OLDENBOURG VERLAG MÜNCHEN

SÜDOSTEUROPÄISCHE ARBEITEN

141

Transnational Societies, Transterritorial Politics

Migrations in the (Post-)Yugoslav Region 19th–21st Century

Edited by

Ulf Brunnbauer

2009

R. OLDENBOURG VERLAG MÜNCHEN

For Georgia Kretsi (1972–2009)

Bibliografische Information der Deutschen Nationalbibliothek
Die Deutsche Nationalbibliothek verzeichnet diese Publikation in der Deutschen Nationalbibliografie; detaillierte bibliografische Daten sind im Internet über <http://dnb.d-nb.de> abrufbar.

ISBN: 978-3-486-59163-7

Satz: Kraus PrePrint, Landsberg am Lech
Druck und Bindung: AZ Druck und Datentechnik GmbH, Kempten

Table of Contents

Ulf Brunnbauer

Editorial

The rationale of the book

On 8 March 1972, nineteen-year-old Vera Rimski arrived in Munich from Yugoslavia; at the train station she was met by an official German delegation headed by the Minister of Labour Affairs of the Free State of Bavaria, Fritz Pirkl, and the head of the Federal Agency of Labour, Josef Stingl (see picture on the cover page). Vera Rimski was greeted as the "two millionth *Gastarbeiter*" in the FR Germany and received flowers and a portable TV set as gifts. The main Bavarian newspaper, *Süddeutsche Zeitung*, reported on the occasion:

> *Josef Stingl thanked the Yugoslav woman and all other Gastarbeiter for their significant contribution to the gross national product, which in the first place, had made the high living standard in the Federal Republic possible.*[1]

Very few of the many Yugoslav citizens, who came to the FR Germany in the 1960s and 1970s in search of work or as family members, were greeted in a similar way. The typical experience for most of them was depicted by filmmaker Krsto Papić in his 1971 documentary "Special Trains" (*Specijalni vlakovi*).[2] The film begins by showing the rather humiliating medical checks performed by German doctors, which wishful Yugoslav workers already had to undergo in Yugoslavia, before they could receive permission to go to Germany. Then, the film accompanies the migrants from Yugoslavia on their train journey to Germany. They are complaining about the need to go abroad to earn enough money to feed their family, and with tearful eyes express feelings of sorrow for being divided from their family and of their fear about living in a foreign country. In Munich, where they disembark from the "Special Train", i.e. the trains specifically organised to transport *Gastarbeiter* from Yugoslavia to Germany, they are brought to the basement of the central station, which had served as an air-raid shelter during World War Two. There, the workers, exhausted from the journey from Yugoslavia, are told that they would not be called by their name any more but by number.

1 *Süddeutsche Zeitung*, 9 March 1972.
2 The film (length: 15' 21") was produced by Zagreb Film. Papić had already dealt with *Gastarbeiter* migration to the FR Germany in his 1967 short film "*Halo, München*", which shows the impact of emigration on the poor karst regions of Dalmatia.

They have to wait until the people from the Federal Labour Agency announce their number through the loudspeaker and tell them their final point of destination.

These two radically different experiences upon arrival in Munich belong to the same story: the migration of hundreds of thousands of people from socialist Yugoslavia to Western Europe after labour migration had been allowed by the Yugoslav government in the 1960s. Subsequently, Yugoslavia became one of the main sources of migrant labour in Europe. Yet the wave of labour migration that came to be known as *Gastarbeiter* migration was neither the first nor the last mass migration movement from this region in modern times. Many parts of what in the twentieth century twice belonged to a Yugoslav state (1918–1941, 1945–1991) had seen significant emigration and seasonal migration in the 'long' nineteenth century until World War One. If immigration opportunities were available, people of working age from the 'Yugoslav' territories regularly sought their chances abroad, where wages were higher and economic opportunities more accessible. In many cases, however, these hopes proved illusionary and migrant workers ended up being exploited and having to endure terrible working and living conditions, yet the stream of workers would not be cut as long as a liberal migration regime prevailed.

Social change, economic and career considerations is only one cluster of reasons why so many people were on the move in this region during the last two centuries. The other reasons relate to violence, war, repression and expulsion: population movements during wars, refugees from war and political persecution, and "ethnic cleansing" constitute another salient part of the history of migration in the Balkans, separate from labour migration. Nation- and state-building in this region in the nineteenth as well as the twentieth century often resulted in the expulsion, or even killing of those who did not fit into the notion of the harmony between the ethnically defined nation and the state. The expulsion of Albanians from the *sancak* (district) of Niš by Serbian troops, when Serbia annexed the area in 1877/8 was an early example; more well-known are the cases of expulsion of the ethnic 'other' during the Balkan Wars, especially in Macedonia. The Second World War was a time of unprecedented forced migration and refugee movements in occupied Yugoslavia as well. The forced migration of ethnic Germans and Italians from Yugoslavia in 1945 is another case in point. The expulsion of ethnic 'others' during the wars of the 1990s in Bosnia-Herzegovina, Croatia and Kosovo not only gained particular international attention – and was one of the reasons for the establishment of the International Criminal Tribunal for the former Yugoslavia in Den Haag – but also produced the generic term for this type of forced migration: "ethnic cleansing".

Leaving one's home country voluntarily in order to make money abroad or pursue university studies, and being expelled from home at gun-point by heavily armed, blood-thirsty militiamen are two radically different experiences. Nevertheless, both can be retold and analysed within the prism of migration history, without ignoring the fact that "ethnic cleansing" has much more to it than 'just' migration – it must be placed in the context of genocide. However, voluntary and forced migrants also share many experiences and often face similar problems in the accepting society. Both labour migrants and victims of forced migration can become transnational actors maintaining multi-stranded links with their former home, so that they are involved in two societies and states. Refugees, who have become settled, provide support to newcomers from their home countries, regardless whether these are forced to leave or whether they come as economic immigrants. Both the 'economic' emigrants and the victims of forced migration are often actively involved in the political and organisational life of the 'diaspora', working together or struggling for hegemony. Hence, from the point of view of immigration and the ensuing migrant practices, the linkages and intersections between 'voluntary' and 'forced' migration are manifold. Also from the perspective of those who leave, the distinction between 'voluntary' and 'forced' is often a blurred one. Apart from the fact that all human behaviour is constrained and 'voluntary' emigration is thus determined by structural forces such as economic want, there are also cases of migration that are neither forced in the narrow sense nor really voluntary. Take for example the pressure that the government of Yugoslavia put on its Albanian population in the 1930s, so that the latter would leave the country without having to be expelled by outright violence.

Hence, the area of the former Yugoslavia provides a real laboratory for important research questions in migration studies. Case studies from this region allow the discussion of pertinent problems in contemporary migration research, such as the role of transnational links and diaspora nationalism, the effects of emigration on sending societies, the role of emigration policies and the linkages between them and nation-building, and the changes in migration patterns and their long-term development. On the other hand, many of these important questions have not been sufficiently studied neither for the area of Yugoslavia nor the Balkans in general. There is a real disproportion between the significance of migration for the region in the past and present and the state of its research. Of course, the research situation is not uniform: Yugoslav migrants in Germany and other Western countries, for example, have been studied extensively since the 1960s. Sociological migration research started to develop quickly, particularly in Zagreb, in close connection to the *Gastarbeiter* migration. The history of overseas emigration from Slovenia and Croatia found frequent treatment as well. More recently, various studies have considered the post-Yugoslav diasporas and their role in national politics at 'home'. However, there remain gaps in the research. One particular problem is the lack of comparative approaches; another is of historical research that has long-term perspectives.

In order to present the current state of research on migration from the area of the former Yugoslavia and to stimulate a dialogue between scholars from different disciplinary backgrounds, who work on various aspects of Yugoslav and post-Yugoslav migration, the conference "*(Post-)Yugoslav Migrations. State of Research, New Approaches, Comparative Perspectives*" convened at the Berlin College for the Comparative History of Europe in December 2006. Funded by the *Fritz Thyssen Stiftung* and organised by Georgia Kretsi and the editor of this volume (then both researchers at the Institute for East European Studies at the Free University of Berlin), the conference aimed to give an overview of current research on (post-) Yugoslav migration as well as to stimulate discussions about the potential contribution of this research to migration studies in general. The present edited volume comes out of the conference. Its goal is to establish this region, which is now divided into the independent countries of Bosnia-Herzegovina, Croatia, Kosovo, Macedonia, Montenegro, Serbia, and Slovenia, as a laboratory of historical and contemporary migration research.

Another goal of this volume is to highlight the intense links between the societies of the former Yugoslavia and the world – linkages also created by a long history of migration. Hence, if we want to understand this region in the past and present we need to consider the multi-faceted consequences of migration. Successive waves of emigration, return, and remigration thoroughly transformed the (post-)Yugoslav societies and integrated them into global connections. As a consequence, political regimes in the region pursued distinctive emigration policies in reaction to the fact that the social practices of their populations, as a result of emigration, did not coincide with the limits of state sovereignty. Hence, transnational social practices gave birth to transterritorial policies predicated on the perception of emigrants as being part of the nation. The region under consideration, thus, is perfectly suited for the discussion of the analytical potential, but also limits of the paradigm of transnationalism. Case studies, such as those presented in this volume, point to the necessity to research transnationalism from below, i.e. to establish transnational practices empirically from the outset, before conceptual conclusions are drawn. Concrete research shows that, on the one hand, many migrants did have social involvements in their former home country and that transnational links were also existent more than a century ago; on the other hand, many migrants did not pursue transnationalism at all, so the paradigm would not help to understand their experiences.

Chapter outline

The book falls into two main parts. The first is historical; the second focuses on recent developments and is based on ethnological and sociological methods. An overarching topic that connects both parts is the study of transnational links and their significance.

The first chapter by Ulf Brunnbauer discusses continuities and changes in the history of emigration from the region of the former Yugoslavia during the nineteenth and twenty-first centuries. The chapter describes the changing patterns of economic emigration, such as the shift from seasonal migration to temporary and eventually permanent emigration, as well as changes in the destination countries. It provides statistical information on emigration processes from the late nineteenth century up to the 1980s, also citing newly found data from archival sources. Brunnbauer aims to provide systematic explanations for the recurrent nature of emigration from the region, pointing to economic forces, the role of networks and the emergence of "cultures of migration". He also delineates the different emigration policies in this area since the late nineteenth century, stressing the importance of the state in the process of emigration and the close relations between emigration policy and nation-building.

In the second chapter, Marjan Drnovšek explores the patterns in emigration from Slovenia during the last two centuries. He points out the importance of emigration from Slovenia and its long history, identifying various waves of emigration from the Slovenian lands since the nineteenth century. Many Slovenians went overseas before World War One, turning their back on an underdeveloped region faced by the agrarian crisis. During the interwar period, when large parts of the lands inhabited by Slovenians were part of fascist Italy, Slovenians also fled political pressure and assimilation attempts. Slovenia additionally recorded significant emigration processes after World War Two, for example during the *Gastarbeiter* migration. The chapter traces these various forms of historical emigration processes from Slovenia, differentiating between their determining factors, providing quantitative data on the number of emigrants, and discussing relevant economic and political contexts. It also presents some peculiar instances of emigration, such as that of Slovenian women who went to Egypt as wet nurses and the forced emigration of Germans from Slovenia.

The connection between nation-building and emigration policies is emphasised in Edvin Pezo's discussion of interwar Yugoslavia's migration policy and the emigration of non-Slavic Muslims to Turkey (1918–1941). The author explores the policies of the Serb dominated first Yugoslav state towards the non-Slavic speaking Muslim minorities in what was called 'Southern Serbia' (today's Kosovo and Macedonia). The government aimed at changing the ethnic make-up of these regions, which were heavily populated by Muslim Albanians and Turks, who were considered by the political elite as 'strangers', because they did not fit into the concept of a Yugoslav, i.e. South Slavic, or Serb nation. Among the policies were attempts to facilitate the emigration of these 'strangers', mainly to Turkey. The author discusses the political decision making by government authorities and their negotiations with the Turkish government on a minority exchange treaty. Such an agreement was eventually concluded in 1938 but not put into practice. In the 1930s the government also explored ways of how to put pressure on the Albanians and Turks in Southern Serbia, so they would leave.

The emigration policies of the first Yugoslavia are also the subject of the third chapter, in which Aleksandar R. Miletić analyses its relevant legal framework and actual institutional practices, mainly during the period 1918–1928. The Kingdom of Serbs, Croats, and Slovenes, established in 1918, pursued active emigration policies based on the Law of Emigration (1921) and other legislation. For that purpose, special government institutions were created in Zagreb and Belgrade. The emigration policies served various goals: they sought to bring cross-border movement under the authority of the state, to maintain the emotional attachment of 'Yugoslav' emigrants to their home, to support emigrants and returnees in need, and to prevent members of the dominant nation(s) from emigrating, while minority members were not allowed back, even if they held Yugoslav citizenship. Hence, there were close links between policies of emigration, citizenship and nation-building, which became evident also in the state's efforts to facilitate the emigration of ethnic minorities. However, the analysis also reveals that many regulations remained on paper only due to the extensive corruption and red tape in the emigration authorities.

Another important example of emigration policies in this region is discussed by Karolina Novinšćak, who analyses the decision making processes of the Yugoslav and West-German governments prior to the conclusion of the recruitment agreement between the SFR Yugoslavia and the FR Germany in 1968. The author emphasises the contradiction between ideological demands and convictions on the one hand, and economic and political needs on the other. Yugoslavia was the only socialist country to allow labour migration to Western countries since the 1960s, systematically 'exporting' surplus labour in order to ease tensions in the domestic labour market. At the same time, the booming economies of Western Europe were in demand of cheap manual labour. The FR Germany soon became the most important destination country for *Gastarbeiter*. Using original archival material from German and Yugoslav sources, the author discusses the stony path of negotiations between the Yugoslav and the West-German government for a recruitment agreement. A huge obstacle was the fact that diplomatic relations between the two countries no longer existed because Yugoslavia recognised the GDR. The author shows, however, that the substantial interest of both governments to regulate and facilitate the recruitment of Yugoslav workers for the German economy finally helped to overcome the ideological considerations.

One common trait of the emigration policies of various regimes in the area of the former Yugoslavia, including the socialist state, was their attempt to render emigrants loyal 'diasporas'. This policy is discussed in detail by Francesco Ragazzi in his chapter on Croatian 'diaspora politics' in the 1990s. The chapter begins by pointing out that these Croatian politics, which in the 1990s received international attention when members of the diaspora supported nationalist mobilisation and Croatia's war efforts, were not new at all. The author reveals that Croatian politicians had already developed ways to retain the loyalty of emigrants during the overseas migration before World War One. The discussion shows that as a reaction to emigration and the state's fear of losing control over its citizens, transterritorial concepts of nationhood and citizenship were developed so that emigrants could be imagined as part of the nation. The state designed special policies to address its presumed members abroad, thus extending its claims to sovereignty across its borders. Ragazzi has established a clear continuity between such efforts beginning in the late nineteenth century, through the first and second Yugoslavia, to the now independent Republic of Croatia, where the diaspora has become an important political subject, even being granted a vote in national elections. However, the paper also points to significant discrepancies between (official) rhetoric and political practice.

Emigration from Croatia, generally, belongs to the best researched cases of emigration from the region of the former Yugoslavia. Of all parts of the former Yugoslavia, it is the Croat lands that have been most affected by emigration processes, so it was not by chance that Zagreb became a centre for migration research. The chapter written by Dubravka Mlinarić discusses this tradition of emigration research in Croatia and its main paradigms. The author presents the development of emigration research in that country, looking at contributions from different disciplines such as history, ethnology and sociology. One of her main points is that research on emigrants and *Gastarbeiter* stood apart for a long time, mainly for ideological reasons. During socialism, the ruling communists associated the pre-1945 emigration with anti-communist, nationalist sentiments; this was also reflected in research, so many migration specialists avoided the topic of the diaspora. Mlinarić also points to some salient patterns in the interpretation of emigration by Croatian scholars, such as the framing of emigration as a demographic 'loss' to the nation, and she raises problematic issues, such as nationalistic approaches to studies on overseas emigrant communities.

The second cluster of chapters places its main focus on the links between emigrants and their former 'home'. Mirjam Milharčič Hladnik analyses the migration story of a family from Slovenia, discussing issues of family links across the ocean and adaption to a new home in the USA. Based on the detailed analysis of correspondence between this Slovenian family unit, some of whose members emigrated to the USA before and after World War Two, the author discusses individual perceptions of migration, gendered experiences and the creation of new subjectivities. She points out the role that notions of the 'homeland' played for those family members who had gone to the USA. In this particular case, the 'home' region belonged to different states during the twentieth century, which also affected the family members' identification. The chapter further reveals the practical effects of family links across the Atlantic, e.g. sending money and aid to Slovenia. In the final section, the author describes the political mobilisation of the Slovenian emigrants, especially the female ones, in the USA, during Slovenia's struggle for independence and international recognition in the early 1990s. She shows how images of the former 'homeland' were re-invented and how political mobilisation had an emancipative effect on the migrant community.

Transnational links are also the centre of attention in Robert Pichler's discussion of emigration, rural development and images of the home(land) in an Albanian village in the Republic of Macedonia. The chapter discusses the particular migration patterns of Albanians from the Republic of Macedonia during the socialist period and their effects today. The first part of the article explains the reasons why, since the 1960s, the Albanian minority in the Republic of Macedonia had a much higher proclivity for migration – especially to Austria, Switzerland and Germany – than members of the majority population. The author argues that this was the result of under-investment by the socialist state in the economic development of minority areas, together with the structural marginalisation of the Albanians in Macedonia, who had less access to state jobs than ethnic Macedonians. The second part of the chapter analyses the impact of emigration on the village of Veleshtë and its architecture. Migrant investments have thoroughly transformed the landscape of the village and also led to improvements in its infrastructure. The author points to the particular role of new houses which are usually very big though for most of the year uninhabited; they are manifestations of migrants' claims to also be part of their 'home' community despite their physical absence.

Patterns of emigrants' self-identification constitute the focus of Aleksandra Pavićević's contribution. She discusses the changing modes of identification of emigrants from Serbia living in the Americas and in European countries. The author develops an original and innovative perspective by looking in particular into the issue of death, as an evidently important event in the lives of individuals and communities. Death can also become a manifestation of ethnicity and of community. Funerals, cemeteries, gravestones and obituaries present valuable empirical material, which the author uses for her ethnographic account of the processes of identification of Serbian emigrants. The chapter introduces a very peculiar form of transnationalism: death is often closely linked with images of the 'home' and sometimes the dead bodies even travel 'home', while at the same time death threatens to dissolve social networks that cross borders.

Janine Dahinden develops a critical perspective on the paradigm of transnationalism in her discussion of (post-)Yugoslav migrations through the lens of current concepts in migration research. Her chapter analyses the transnational practices of Kosovo-Albanian and Serbian immigrants in Switzerland, focussing on the evaluation of the extent and role of transnational networks. After reviewing the theoretical literature on transnationalism, the author asks how far these concepts can be applied to the two above-mentioned emigrant groups from the former Yugoslavia. She concludes that the intensity of transnationalism has to be differentiated for the various social groups within the migrant community. Actually, only relatively few of the observed migrants are really involved in sustained and dense transnational networks. The intensity of involvement in the home, e.g. by remitting money, is a function of the migrant's success in their new environment and also of time. For many of the observed migrants, the concept of transnationalism does not make much sense when describing their social networks and collective identities, despite the expressions of long-distance nationalism found among these migrant communities.

Transnational practices within families are studied by Jasna Čapo Žmegač in her analysis of Croat migrant families in Bavaria (FR Germany) who have been dispersed across national borders. The author first describes the bi-local lives of the families that she interviewed in their temporal dynamics. She then sketches different family strategies for coping with the problem of working abroad and the rearing of children; the question of where to raise the children – whether to take them to Germany or leave them with relatives in Croatia – was a crucial one for the migrant parents. In many cases children spent part of their youth with their parents and part of it in Croatia and Bosnia. The author also explains how difficult it was for Croat migrants to realise their initial wish to return from Germany after a few years of working there. Instead, they had to devise flexible family strategies, in which family members often lived here and there. Hence, transnational family practices emerged which impacted on family cohesion, the education of children, and life perspectives. The chapter makes clear that family strategy, plans for the future, kin relations and decision making within the family have to be scrutinised in order to understand transnational practices.

The last chapter continues the discussion of the role of networks for migrant families. Pascal Goeke evaluates the potential of network analysis for exploring family change among migrants, focusing on Bosnian immigrants in the FR Germany. The author also discusses the development of network analysis in sociology and in particular systems theory, and its applicability to migration studies. He argues that networks are a secondary social form resulting mainly from the increasing functional differentiation of society. With respect to families, this can be exemplified by the transformation of the traditional complex Balkan family household (*Zadruga*), which was a close-knit social segment of agnatic male kin, into nuclear families. Network analysis has to adapt to these changes and must not take the family as a primordial network. The author concludes that families have lost their potential as an all-embracing social form, and individuals increasingly depend on individual networking, which aims at crossing boundaries.

Acknowledgments

This publication would not have been possible without the generous support of the *Fritz Thyssen Stiftung*, which funded the conference and also the publication of the book. The Berlin College for the Comparative History of Europe (*Berliner Kolleg für Vergleichende Geschichte Europas*), and especially its managing director Arnd Bauerkämper, deserve my gratitude for helping to organise the conference out of which this book stems.

The person who deserves most of the credit for this book, however, is sadly no longer among us. The conference "(Post-)Yugoslav Migrations" was the brainchild of Georgia Kretsi, who was pursuing a project about the role of the Kosovar diaspora in the political development of Kosovo. Georgia's intellectual curiosity and fondness for questions of theory were essential for designing a conference where different epistemologies and methodologies could be presented and evaluated for their potential application in the case studies under consideration. Thanks to her insistence the conference became a very multi-disciplinary one, looking at migration from various perspectives. Georgia did not have the chance to present her own groundbreaking research at the conference because she fell ill beforehand. Nevertheless, she did attend its proceedings. For more than two years she fought an uphill struggle against a terrible sickness. Nobody who met her during this time will ever forget her strength, her power and her sheer will to live. At the age of 37, Georgia tragically passed away. She will always be remembered as an excellent researcher and emphatic personality, whose joie de vivre was so contagious. This book is therefore devoted to the memory of Georgia Kretsi, social anthropologist and good friend.

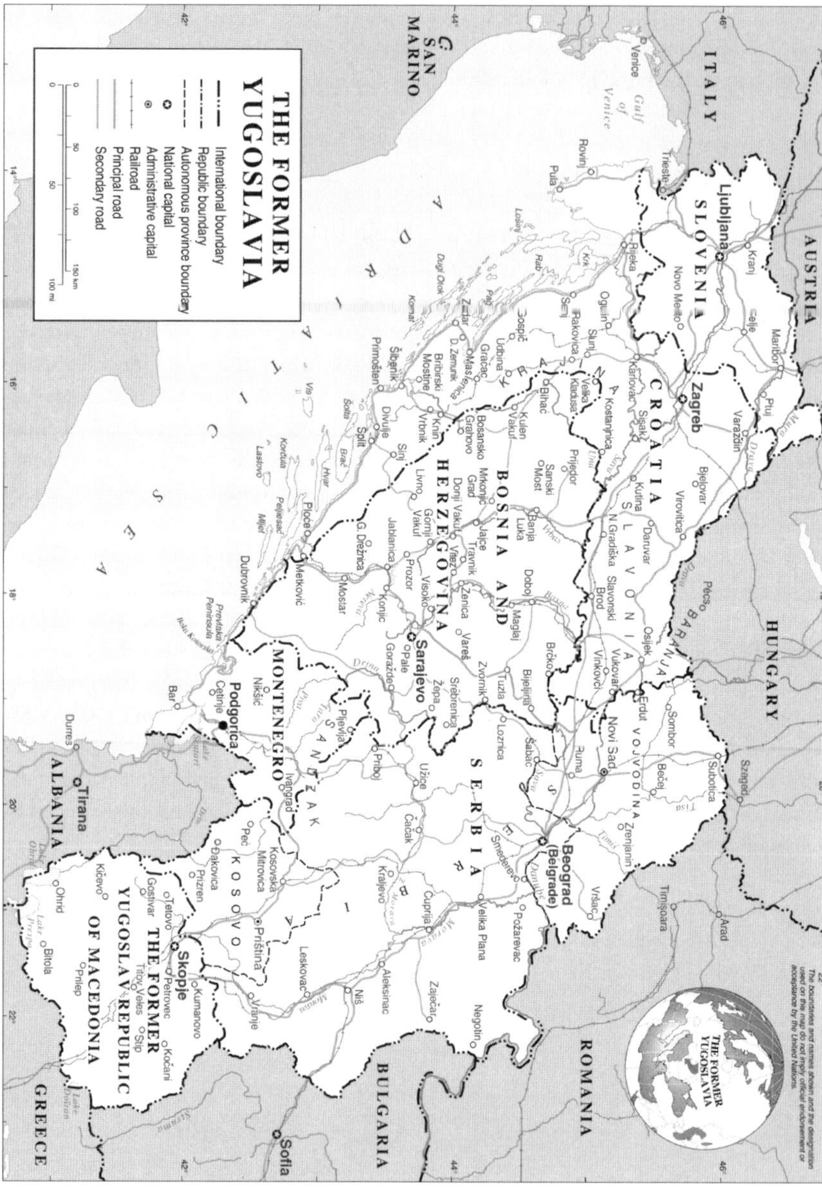

Map: The former Yugoslavia as of 2007 (based on UN Map No. 3689)

Ulf Brunnbauer

Labour Emigration from the Yugoslav Region from the late 19th Century until the End of Socialism: Continuities and Changes

Introduction

On 19 April 1910, deputy Ante Pinterović took the floor of the assembly of the Kingdoms of Croatia and Slavonia, the *Sabor*, and read his interpellation to the provincial government, claiming, "The emigration question has been occupying our public." Today, "half a million of our people" already live in America and most of them are "lost for Croatia". Many emigrants "suffer from poor working and living conditions". The most able work force is lost to America and will be missed at home. The emigrants do send money home but these means "are often not used for the purposes useful for our people and our land". In the region of Lika, from which most of the emigrants come, a lot of migrant money is spent for buying alcohol, "even champagne". Pinterović claims that many patriotic organisations had urged the government to introduce a law on emigration so that it would benefit the country, if indeed it could not be stopped; the money from the emigrants should be used for the improvement of their regions of origin.[1]

This quote introduces several problems discussed in this volume. First of all, it reveals that emigration constitutes a *longue durée* social phenomenon in the area, which in the twentieth century was occupied by Yugoslavia but also the Balkans in general. It also illustrates the concerns of political elites about the consequences of emigration, and in particular their critique of the ways emigrants spent their savings. These concerns were a recurrent topic in the domestic debates over emigration, which started in the late nineteenth century. This was not accidentally the time when the South Slav regions experienced intensified efforts at nation-building: political elites often made a connection between nationalism and emigration, pointing to the dangers of emigration for the nation-building project but also seeing its potential for the creation of ethnically pure nations. Hence, various political regimes in the region tried to police emigration and bring it in concordance with the state's development goals. From the point of view of society, however, emigration constituted an important social practice which was triggered first by economic needs but soon became a much more complex phenomenon, predicated upon networks and cultural patterns that turned migration into a typical stage of the life cycle.

1 Stenografički zapisnici 1908–1913, 807–10.

In this introductory chapter I will discuss three main problems concerning 'Yugoslav' emigration from the late nineteenth century until the end of socialist Yugoslavia (1990–91): first, I will give an overview of the quantitative dimension; the numbers can also help to illustrate important changes in the patterns of migration, such as from regional to overseas destinations or from temporary to permanent emigration. In the second part of the chapter I will look into possible explanations for the persistence of emigration from this region. Here, economic factors do play an important role but they cannot make up the whole story. Networks, patterns of social stratification, and cultural attitudes are just as important here. In the last part, I discuss the emigration policies of the different states in the area and their various political regimes. The hypothesis here is that political elites were worried about the fact that due to emigration, the societies over which they ruled became transnational and extended across state borders; therefore, governments attempted to extend the limits of state sovereignty to include the emigrants into their polities. In more practical terms, governments regularly aimed at using emigration for their economic policies and addressed its social consequences.

The discussion of these topics will concentrate on labour migration, which is of course a rather arbitrary limitation, given the fact that this region's history was also shaped by forced migrations and political exile. For certain problems, such as the discussion of transnationalism or remittances, the distinction between 'voluntary' and 'involuntary' emigration does not make much sense either – as the respective chapters in this volume show – because refugees also maintained intense contacts with their families at home. This distinction is relevant, however, for other problems, such as the economic reasons for emigration as well as state policies towards emigration, and of course for the migrants themselves. Although all human behaviour is limited by certain constraints, it makes a difference whether one leaves his or her country because militiamen point a gun at oneself, or because one hopes to earn more money abroad, balancing the expected gains from emigration against its costs.

This article aims to provide not only an introduction to the history of 'Yugoslav' emigration in the nineteenth and twentieth centuries but also a framework for the following chapters. It is based on archival documents and other primary sources as well as secondary literature. A note on the latter is required here: the state of research on emigration from the former Yugoslavia, and from Southeastern Europe in general, is very uneven in geographic, topical and methodological terms. There is on the one hand a lot of literature, in particular by sociologists, economists and other social scientists, on the so-called *Gastarbeiter* migration of the 1960s and 70s. On the other hand, the historical inquiry is limited to certain regions or suffers from ethno-centrism. There is in particular a lack of historical treatises that cover the whole region, portray emigration as a *longue durée* phenomenon and put it into a comparative perspective. Some aspects of the history of emigration, such as from Croatia to Serbia and Bosnia-Hercegovina in the nineteenth century, or the emigration policies of interwar Yugoslavia and socialist Yugoslavia until the early 1960s, have hardly been touched at all. An overview such as the present one, therefore, must be deficient in those areas, where it can raise questions for future research rather than give definite answers.

Given the extent of the archival material available for the study of the history of migration in and from this region, some of which has not been used at all until now, much remains to be done. In view of the exemplary nature of migrations from Yugoslavia – understood as geographical denomination – this task seems fruitful not only for the social history of this particular region but for migration studies in general.

Quantitative dimension of emigration

Statistical data for the number of emigrants from the Yugoslav area had begun to be published by the end of the nineteenth century. Of course these figures have to be critically assessed, since even today states are unable to count all migration movements. Undocumented migrants in particular were not included in the official numbers. Nevertheless, the published data do provide reasonable estimates. Aside from this, we do not possess more adequate sources for the establishment of aggregated quantitative trends. The first published aggregated figures come from the Kingdoms of Croatia and Slavonia, then part of the Habsburg Monarchy, which started to publish annual numbers for emigration in 1899 (Table 1).

Table 1: Emigration from Croatia and Slavonia, 1899–1913

	Total emigration	**To North America**
1899	4,195	2,954*
1900	4,176	3,452*
1901	8,854	6,717
1902	12,046	9,833
1903	14,224	11,907
1904	5,591	3,524
1905	28,059	22,196
1906	25,592	21,818
1907	26,079	22,808
1908	5,689	2,805
1909	14,069	11,363
1910	16,779	13,872
1911	8,215	6,604*
1912	15,979	14,239*
1913	13,000	11,868*
Total	**202,547**	**165,960**

* Numbers are for "America".
Sources: Statistički godišnjak Kraljevina Hrvatske i Slavonije 1905, 244; 1906–1910, 200; for 1899–1900 and 1911–13, Lakatoš, Narodna Statistika, 64.

The total number of emigrants from Croatia and Slavonia might well have been higher, given that in the same period almost 250,000 passports were issued and many emigrants certainly did not bother to let the state know about their intentions.[2] Also strongly affected by emigration was Dalmatia, which constituted a separate administrative entity in the Austrian part of the Dual Monarchy. According to demographic calculations by Manfred Makale in 1912, some 58,000 persons emigrated from Dalmatia between 1881 and 1910.[3] To give numbers for the pre-1914 period, for the other countries that would make up Yugoslavia, is difficult because of the lack of statistical data. The independent state of Serbia and Montenegro did not produce aggregated statistical information on emigration. Permanent emigration was insignificant for Serbia anyway. Most of the estimated 10,000–18,000 labour migrants who went abroad from 1890 to 1912 were seasonal ones who did return.[4] The situation was different in Montenegro, which had a high rate of overseas emigration. The state, which in Montenegro enjoyed rather ephemeral powers over society, did not produce aggregated numbers, but reasonable estimates claim that by the eve of the Balkan Wars (1912–13), out of a total population of about 222,000 people, between 11,000 and 20,000 Montenegrins had emigrated abroad, most of them to the USA.[5] The number of emigrants from Bosnia-Hercegovina (occupied by Austria-Hungary after 1878 and eventually annexed in 1908) as well as Macedonia (until 1912 part of the Ottoman Empire) cannot be established in any reasonable way, but for the latter, significant overseas emigration from the beginning of the twentieth century can be concluded from archival evidence.[6]

Another way of establishing approximate numbers for emigrants from the South Slav areas is to consult statistics produced by the destination countries. These, however, come with not only the usual difficulties when counting migrants, such as the neglect of un-documented migration, but also with the problem of national categorisation. Migrants from the Habsburg Empire to the USA (Table 2), for example, were counted as Austrian and Hungarian citizens but also classified according to ethnic criteria, which, however, did not always match the indigenous views. Serbs, Bulgarians and Montenegrins were, for example, sometimes put together, and in other US statistics "Dalmatians, Bosnians and Hercegovinians" appear, which obviously reflects the regional identifications of emigrants at their interviews with immigration officers on Ellis Island.

Interwar Yugoslavia (Kingdom of Serbs, Croats and Slovenes until 1929; Kingdom of Yugoslavia 1929–41) published detailed numbers on emigration with regional, ethnic, confessional, demographic and social breakdowns – on emigration to European destinations, however, only since 1927 (Table 3). Emigration to the Americas significantly declined after

2 Croatian State Archive (hence abbreviated as HDA), f. 101, Modruško-riječka županija, kn. 1–9 (1886–1904).

3 Makale, Zadnji popis, 14.

4 Petrović, Pečalbari, 4.

5 Pejović, Iseljavanje Crnogoraca, 449; Radusinović, Stanovništvo Crne Gore, 133.

6 See reports by Bulgarian trade agents in Macedonia between 1904 and 1910, in the Bulgarian Central State Archive (CDA), Sofia, f. 331, op. 1, a.e. 110.

Table 2: Immigration to the USA from Austria-Hungary, 1900–1909

Fiscal year	1900/1	1901/2	1902/3	1903/4	1904/5	1905/6	1906/7	1907/8	1908/9	Sum
Germans	7,816	16,249	23,597	22,507	33,642	34,848	40,497	27,576	21,096	227,828
Czechs	3,766	5,589	9,577	11,838	11,593	12,635	13,363	9,899	6,609	84,869
Poles	20,288	32,429	37,499	30,243	50,785	43,803	59,719	26,423	36,483	337,672
Ruthenians	5,276	7,533	9,819	9,415	14,250	15,880	23,751	12,298	15,468	113,690
Serbs	717	1,004	1,723	2,023	2,552	4,424	7,263	7,444	3,628	30,778
Italians	1,463	1,714	2,170	1,984	2,355	1,962	1,506	1,121	1,151	15,426
Magyars	13,310	23,609	27,113	23,851	45,871	42,848	59,593	23,826	27,941	287,962
Croats	17,815	30,223	32,892	21,105	34,932	43,157	47,125	19,782	19,473	266,504
Rumanians	557	1,735	4,173	3,851	7,261	10,811	18,429	8,791	7,484	63,092
Slovaks	29,243	36,931	34,410	27,895	52,282	36,550	41,815	15,979	22,374	297,479
Jews	13,006	12,848	18,759	20,211	17,352	14,885	18,885	15,293	8,431	139,670
Other	43	2,668	4,277	2,235	2,848	3,489	6,561	97	53	22,271
Sum	**113,300**	**172,532**	**206,009**	**177,158**	**275,723**	**265,292**	**338,507**	**168,529**	**170,191**	**1,887,241**

Source: Annual Reports of the General Commissioner for Immigration; quoted in Makale, Zadnji popis, 20–1.

World War One because of immigration restrictions. The 1924 Johnson-Reed Act set an annual quota of 671 for Yugoslav immigrants to the US.[7] Between 1921 and 1939, 65,060 Yugoslav citizens were recorded as leaving for the USA. The second most popular overseas destination was Argentina, where the immigration regime was less restricted in the 1920s, with 44,423 recorded emigrants; third came Canada with 33,606. As Table 3 shows, the world economic crisis of 1929 and the ensuing global recession almost stopped overseas emigration from Yugoslavia. Instead, European destinations became more important: the most significant one for the whole interwar period was France (56,511 recorded emigrants from Yugoslavia for 1927–39), followed by Germany (38,275 emigrants in the same period), which by the end of the 1930s became the most important destination for labour migrants from Yugoslavia due to the Nazi policies of recruiting foreign labour (*Fremdarbeiter*) for the German economy. This policy was continued after the destruction of Yugoslavia in April 1941 by Nazi Germany: between May 1941 and January 1945, for example, more than 150,000 workers were recruited from the "Independent State of Croatia"[8], which had concluded a recruitment agreement with Germany in May 1941, i.e. only one month into its existence.[9]

During almost the first twenty years after World War Two, socialist Yugoslavia pursued closed door policies for economic migration. However, despite restrictions on the issuing of

7 Čizmić, Mikačić, Neki suvremeni problemi, 266.

8 The "Independent State of Croatia" (Croatian acronym NDH) was established by Nazi Germany after its defeat of Yugoslavia in the April War of 1941. The NDH comprised most of today's Croatia plus Bosnia and Hercegovina and became infamous especially for its mass murder of Serbs, Jews and Roma.

9 Sundhaussen, Wirtschaftsgeschichte Kroatiens, 181.

Table 3: Emigration from interwar Yugoslavia, 1920–1939

	To Overseas	To Europe	Total
1920	6,279		6,279
1921	12,965		12,965
1922	6,086		6,086
1923	11,473		11,473
1924	19,575		19,575
1925	17,643		17,643
1926	18,230		18,230
1927	21,976	6,560	28,536
1928	21,789	12,538	34,327
1929	18,189	19,425	37,614
1930	13,560	25,409	38,969
1931	4,808	10,560	15,368
1932	2,454	6,642	9,096
1933	2,221	7,508	9,729
1934	2,907	11,004	13,911
1935	3,345	10,120	13,465
1936	3,860	8,625	12,485
1937	5,378	14,287	19,665
1938	5,686	14,376	20,062
1939	3,789	23,613	27,402
Total	**202,213**	**132,144**	**334,357**

Sources: Statistički godišnjak kraljevine Jugoslavije 1929, 122; 1938/39, 137–9.

passports and a strict border regime, a growing number of Yugoslav citizens left the country from the late 1950s in search of work abroad. Once economic emigration was liberalised in 1963–4 (see Novinšćak in this volume) and Yugoslavia concluded the first bilateral recruitment treaties with Western countries (1965), the number of 'temporary' migrants rapidly grew (Table 4). As a result of this wave of emigration, the 1971 Yugoslav census counted almost 775,000 citizens living "temporarily" abroad. Despite the stop on recruitment of foreign workers by most Western countries because of the global recession in 1973–74, the number of Yugoslavs abroad grew, mainly thanks to family reunification, to more than 836,000 by 1981 (Table 5). Yugoslav migration specialists, such as Ivo Baučić, estimated the real number of Yugoslav citizens living abroad at more than one million in the 1970s.[10] In 1971, 3.8 percent of the total population of Yugoslavia lived as "workers" in foreign countries and one in five of all employed Yugoslavs worked abroad. Yugoslavia was second in Europe as concerns the emigration rate, after Portugal (5.7 percent) and before Italy (3.4 percent).

[10] Baučić, Neka suvremena obilježa, 89; cf. Mesić, External Migration, 180.

Table 4: Annual number of Yugoslav citizens taking work abroad, 1960–1970[11]

Until 1960	15,342
1961	4,288
1962	8,131
1963	8,682
1964	10,204
1965	20,373
1966	25,855
1967	26,920
1968	57,238
1969	123,639
1970	239,779

Source: Savezni zavod za statistiku, Lica na privremenom radu, 9.

Table 5: Yugoslav citizens living abroad, 1971 and 1981

Republic of origin	**1971**	**1981**
Bosnia and Hercegovina	147,742	173,940
Montenegro	11,258	17,720
Croatia	257,975	210,330
Macedonia	70,104	101,393
Slovenia	55,001	51,090
Serbia	232,000	282,231
Serbia proper	135,383	185,118
Vojvodina	71,466	60,991
Kosovo	25,151	36,122
Yugoslavia total	**774,080**	**836,704**

Source: Savezni zavod za statistiku, Lica na privremenom radu, 9; Schierup, Migration, Socialism, 111.

The single most important destination country for labour migrants from Yugoslavia was the Federal Republic of Germany, which had concluded a recruitment agreement with Yugoslavia in 1969. By 1971, 61 percent of all Yugoslavs working abroad lived there (411,503 persons). The second most popular destination country was Austria (twelve percent) followed by Australia (six percent), France (five percent), and Switzerland (three percent).

11 These numbers have to be taken with considerable reservation because they are not based on annual reports but on the replies given by labour migrants counted in the 1971 census. Other data point to much higher numbers of annual moves abroad already before 1970. Hence, people who had returned by 1971 are not included in these figures. According to information by the Central Committee of the League of Communists of Croatia, for example, almost 50,000 people had already left Croatia by the end of 1964 (HDA, f. 1220, 7.23, D–1114).

Return migration and changes in the nature of migration

Statistical information can also reveal information about the characteristics of migration. For the region and period under consideration, data are available that allow differentiation of migration according to gender, age, educational and occupational status, confessional and ethnic affiliation, regional origin and destination, etc. These data provide not only a relatively detailed picture of the emigrants but also insights into changes in the patterns of emigration.

One of the significant changes revealed by statistical data concerns the destination countries and, in particular, the transformation of temporary into permanent emigration. The geographical area of Yugoslavia had been characterised by high levels of seasonal migration, mainly within the region, already prior to the nineteenth century, similar to other parts of the Balkans.[12] While seasonal migration is statistically especially hard to grasp, because most of it happened within a particular country and no border crossing was involved, it nevertheless left traces in official records. There was, for example, significant temporary migration from Habsburg Croatia to independent Serbia in the nineteenth century and, after 1878, also to Bosnia-Hercegovina, which was occupied by Austria-Hungary but technically still part of the Ottoman Empire until 1908. According to passport protocols from the 1880s for Croatian counties, most passports were issued for Serbia and Bosnia-Hercegovina, but from the late 1880s, the number of passports issued for "America" increased until America became by far the most popular destination. In 1887, 576 (10.3 percent) out of a total of 5,592 passports issued in the district of Modruš-Rijeka, for example, were for "America"; by 1902 this had risen to 11,088 (86.1 percent) out of 13,002.[13]

These changes in direction, however, did not automatically mean that emigration became permanent because many migrants did return, also from overseas. Michael Palairet, in his comparison of the "new" Balkan immigration to America in the late nineteenth century and the "newest" emigration of *Gastarbeiter* from Yugoslavia, asserts that most overseas migrants believed that they would return after a couple of years.[14] Their plan was to stay three to four years abroad and return with savings that would help to improve the living standards of their family, for example by buying additional land and livestock. Many of the Yugoslav migrants realised this plan as shown by their relatively high rates of return. Between 1908 and 1923 the rates of return from the USA (calculated as the difference between immigration to and emigration from the USA of the particular groups) was 87 percent for "Bulgarians, Serbs and Montenegrins", 51 percent for "Croats and Slovenes" and 29 percent for "Dalmatians, Bosnians and Hercegovinians".[15] Re-emigration in the years before World War One had been only slightly lower, indicating that almost half of the South Slav

12 Palairet, The Migrant Workers.
13 HDA, f. 101, Modruš-riječka županja, kn. 1–9 (1886–1904).
14 Palairet, The 'New' Immigration, 44.
15 US government figures quoted in Čizmić, Emigration from Croatia, 156.

immigrants to the USA eventually returned. In 1908, an economically difficult year in the US, more people returned to Croatia and Slavonia from the USA than immigrated into the country.[16] Incomplete numbers for migration from Montenegro in 1911 indicate that more people returned from America than went overseas (529 returnees vs. 497 emigrants); the majority of the returnees to Montenegro had spent three to four years in America.[17] In the interwar period, around 107,000 return migrants from overseas were counted in Yugoslavia and in the 1930s some 83,000 returnees from European countries.[18]

The majority of labour migrants who left Yugoslavia in the 1960s and 70s also intended to return after a couple of years spent working abroad. Their aim was to save enough money to use their savings for the improvement or construction of homes, purchase of durable consumer goods and, in the case of farmers, of land and agricultural machinery. This intention corresponded to the stated aims of the Yugoslav government, which considered labour migration a temporary phenomenon and urged migrants to come back. Many did, but to establish the exact numbers of returnees is impossible due to the lack of coherent statistical data. One has also to consider that many returnees emigrated again once they were faced with the difficulties of re-integration in Yugoslav society, especially in terms of finding a job. The quota of returned migrants in the 1964–72 period was estimated at between nineteen and thirty-four percent.[19] A significant number of migrants went back in the mid-1970s as a result of the economic crisis and growing unemployment in the Western economies. Živan Tanić speaks of 170–200,000 returnees in 1974 and 1975.[20] Other Yugoslav estimates claim that in the 1970s, more than 600,000 labour migrants returned and a further 110,000 in the first half of the 1980s.[21] The Yugoslav census of 1981, however, recorded only 282,873 returned migrants for 1965–81.[22]

The migrant perspective of return is also revealed by the fact that only a minority of emigrants sold their property. In the interwar period, less than ten percent of emigrants with property had sold it before departure.[23] The predominantly male character of overseas migration was also an indicator that migrants wanted to come back because only a few of them actually brought their family with them. Of the 128,000 recorded overseas emigrants from Croatia and Slavonia between 1901 and 1910, only fourteen percent were female.[24] Many of the women emigrants also left for work and not to join a family or accompany their husband. From interwar Yugoslavia, 43,000 women emigrated classified according to occupation and 15,000 as a "dependent family member". Hence, migrants appear to

[16] HDA, f. 790, Benko Grado, k. 3, br. 54.
[17] Archive of Montenegro (ACG), Ministarstvo unutrašnjih djela, fasc. 111–123 (1911–12).
[18] Statistički godišnjak kraljevine Jugoslavije 1929, 122; 1938/39, 137–9.
[19] Marković, Milenović, Neka pitanja vezana zu reintegraciju radnika, 29.
[20] Tanić, Povratak radnika iz inozemstva, 947.
[21] Malačić, Labor Migration, 213.
[22] Ibid.
[23] Statistički godišnjak Kraljevine Jugoslavije 1929, 126–7; 1938/9, 140–1.
[24] Statistički godišnjak Kraljevina Hrvatske i Slavonije 1905, 244–5; 1906–1910, 199–200.

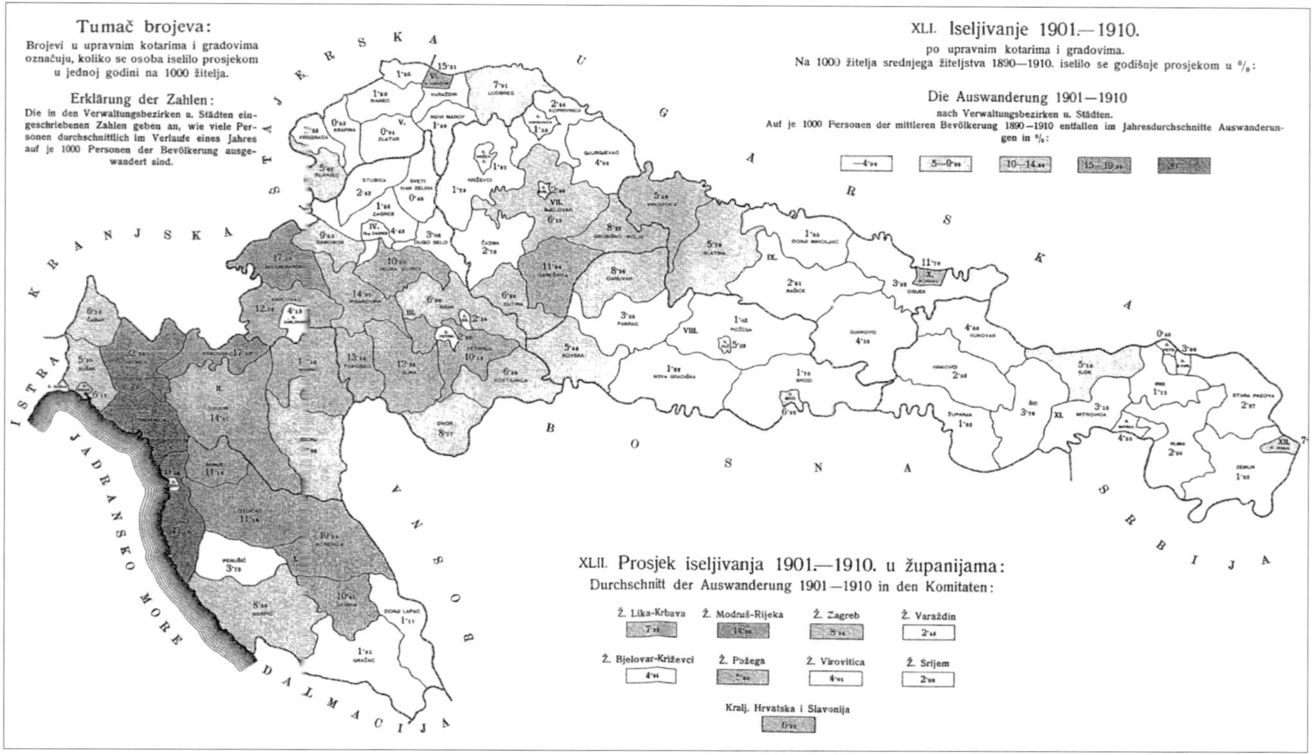

Map 1: Intensity of overseas emigration from Croatia and Slavonia by districts and towns, 1901–1910. *Note:* Darker colours mark higher emigration intensity. The figures indicate the average annual number of emigrants per 1,000 population. The highest value ist for the municipality of Delnice in the west (32 emigrants per year per 1,000 inhabitants), the lowest for the district of Krapina (0.63 per 1,000) north of Zagreb.. *Source:* Archive of Yugoslavia.

have regarded overseas migration as a geographic and temporal extension of traditional practices of seasonal migration, made possible by cheap and fast transport on steamships to America. This attitude was already observed by contemporaries. The administrator of the Croatian coastal district of Sušak, for example, wrote in a report in 1897 that there was no need to worry about the high number of migrants from his district. The typical migrant from *Pomorie*, the coastal region, did not leave for good but returned to his family after spending two or three years working in America. The practice of temporary migration to far-away destinations was old in this region and, therefore, regulations on the restriction on emigration should not apply to this region because they would obstruct the traditional way of life.[25] Another good example for the temporary migration from the coastal regions of Croatia was the high number of labourers who went to Egypt to work on the Suez Canal in the 1860s, and came back.[26]

The statistical information also clearly depicts from which regions migrants came. Generally, there was a west-east gradient in terms of intensity of emigration: the Adriatic islands, the coastal, and the Dalmatian mountain regions being most affected. But even within regions characterised by strong emigration, there were significant differences. In the Kingdom of Croatia and Slavonia before World War One, the coastal regions had the highest rates of emigration (Map 1). Between 1901 and 1910, almost fifteen percent of the total population of the district of Modruš-Rijeka emigrated, as against less than three percent in the districts of Srijem and Varaždin in the interior. This is explained by local economic and ecological factors, the existence of prior emigration and thus migration networks, as well as the proximity of ports, although the latter played an ever-diminishing role when the Balkans were connected to the European railways network. It became more convenient for migrants to take the train from Croatia to one of the North Sea ports, such as Cherbourg, Hamburg or Bremerhaven, from where transport to America was faster and cheaper. In 1910, 5,128 emigrants from Croatia and Slavonia travelled from Bremerhaven and 2,993 from Rijeka.[27] From 1921 to 1933, only about 14,000 emigrants from Yugoslavia embarked in Split or (Italian) Trieste, the closest ports with overseas links; the majority left from North Sea ports. In the interwar period, Croatia, Slovenia and Dalmatia continued to provide the most emigrants from Yugoslavia – almost two thirds of all overseas emigrants between 1920 and 1929.

These regional differences would reappear in the *Gastarbeiter* migration of the 1960s and 70s, when again Croatia was the part of Yugoslavia with the highest rate of emigration. In 1971, 33.4 percent of all Yugoslavs working abroad came from Croatia, whose share in the total population was 21.6 percent. Serbia proper, without the autonomous provinces of Kosovo and Vojvodina, made for 25.6 percent of the total population but only 17.1 percent

[25] HDA, f. 79, OUZV, Kraljska hrvatsko-slavonsko-dalmatinska zemaljska vlada, odjel za unutarnje poslove, k. 1935 (1897), br. 2517.

[26] To give an example: Between 9 September and 31 October 1865, the Rijeka district administration issued 414 passports for Egypt. HDA, f. 99, Riječka županija, k. 100 (1865), br. 502–950.

[27] Statistički godišnjak Kraljevina Hrvatske i Slavonije 1906–1910, 203.

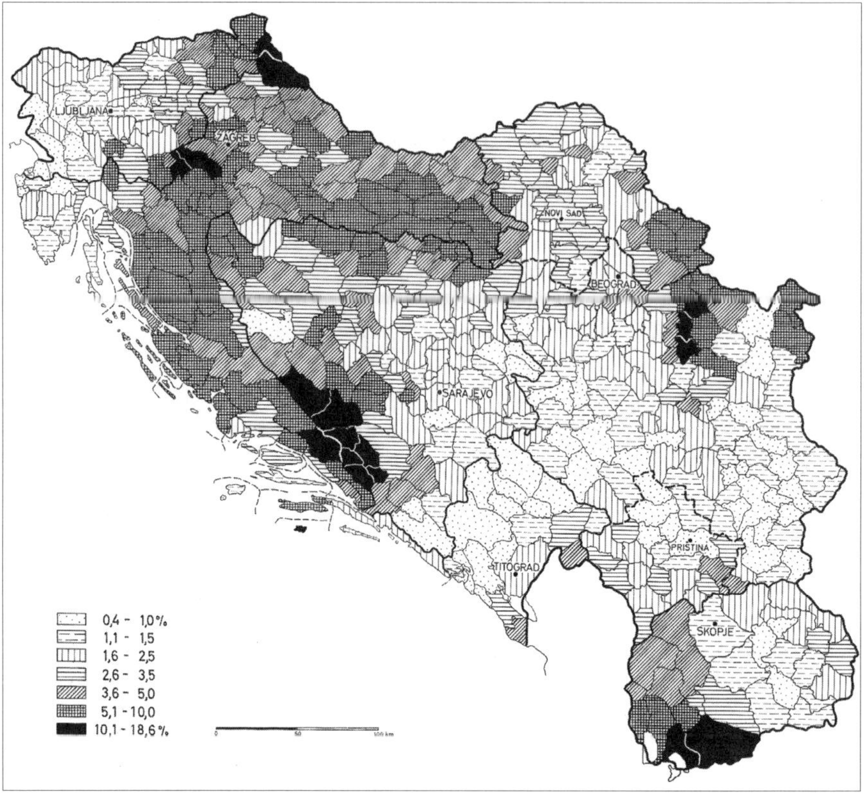

Map 2: Percentage of population living abroad by municipalities, 1971 (as % of total population of the municipality). *Source:* Baučić, Radnici u inozemstvu, suppl. 6.

of the "workers temporarily employed abroad". There was, however, a significant change in the geographic distribution of emigration from Yugoslavia in the 1960s and 70s. While initially most emigrants came from Croatia, the wave of emigration moved increasingly to the eastern and southern areas of the country, which were known as the lesser developed parts of Yugoslavia. In general, however, the regions of Yugoslavia remained very differently affected by emigration (see Map 2). On the municipality level the differences could be striking: in 1971, the community with the highest rate of emigrants was Imotski in Croatia, where nineteen percent of the population lived abroad. Four more municipalities in Yugoslavia had a rate of registered emigration of more than fifteen percent, whereas six municipalities in Yugoslavia counted only half a percent of their inhabitants or even less to be abroad in 1971.[28]

[28] Savezni zavod za statistiku, Lica na privremenom radu.

Explanations: economy, networks and culture

Economic factors

Labour emigration from the Balkans constitutes a *longue durée* social phenomenon. This raises the question of which explanations can be found for the fact that generation after generation, people went abroad in search of work, better pay and increased life chances. Traditional research on migration would look at the push and pull factors. But such a simplified model which views social processes in homeostatic terms and humans as rational choice actors cannot account for the complexity of migration patterns and their persistence. Leslie Page Moch asserts that:

> *Within large-scale economic frameworks that circumscribed the limits of the possible, European men and women chose to move, or not to move, in the context of their own village, family, and belief systems. If we focus on the macroeconomic level alone, we lose the actors who are essential to this drama, dismissing their agendas and denying the factor of human agency.*[29]

Nevertheless, the economy cannot be discounted as an important factor, especially at the beginning of each emigration wave. Migrants themselves often pointed to economic needs that forced them to search for labour abroad. In the many hundreds of applications for passports to Egypt in order to work on the Suez Canal, for example, prospective migrants in the Rijeka area in the mid 1860s pointed out that because of the decline in the shipbuilding industry and the lack of construction work, they had to search for work abroad in order to feed their families. Most of these men were either repairmen on shipyards (*kalafat*) or builders.[30] A century later, *Gastarbeiter* would initially leave Yugoslavia because they could not find a job or they could earn much more in Western Europe – average salaries in German industry were more than three times higher than in Yugoslavia.[31]

The economy of emigration, however, is complicated. Macroeconomic factors interplay with microeconomic ones and the decision to leave, or stay, is also strongly influenced by family, culture, peer groups, and individual choices. Macroeconomic factors can be said to lay the structural foundation of the proclivity to emigrate from a particular region; these structures become particularly evident in the case of crises in the business cycle. In the most general terms, economies in the Balkan region and also most parts of Yugoslavia have been weak in creating non-farming jobs. Industrialisation came late, only really breaking through after World War Two; even under socialism it remained incomplete. Scarce employment outside agriculture, combined with a predominantly smallholder farming pattern, consequentially meant low wages. In all periods under observation, farmers constituted the majority of emigrants. 50 percent of emigrants from Croatia and Slavonia in 1901–1910 were

29 Moch, Moving Europeans, 7.

30 HDA, f. 99, Riječka županija, k. 88 (1864), br. 86–469; k. 100 (1865), br. 502–950.

31 Nikolić, Neke karakteristike jugoslovenske migracije, 5–6; Baučić, Socijalno-ekonomske posljedice, 31.

classified as farmers and 24 as agricultural labourers; 54 percent of the overseas emigrants from Yugoslavia in 1923–39 fell into the same category; 47 percent of the *Gastarbeiter* as of 1971 had been engaged in farming, forestry and fishery before leaving the country. Hence, this area experienced the processes of de-agrarisation, industrialisation and urbanisation also in the form of emigration, given that the overwhelming majority of migrants would work in industry.

The combined impact of structural weaknesses of the economy and crises in the business cycle is evident both in the initial phase of overseas and *Gastarbeiter* migration. Large-scale emigration to the Americas began in the 1890s, when the coastal regions of the Adriatic, which belonged to the poorest parts of the Habsburg Empire, were hit by the phylloxera, which almost destroyed one of the few cash-earning pursuits of this region, i.e. wine-making. In Croatia and Slavonia the average annual production of wine declined from 1.4 million hectolitres in 1886 to less than 200,000 hectolitres in the 1890s and did not fully recover until World War One.[32] Non-farming economic outlets were hardly developed: in 1910, around 80 percent of the population of Croatia, Slavonia and Dalmatia were engaged in farming. The averages for Austria and Hungary were 48 and 62 percent respectively.[33] The unfavourable economic structure resulted in an increasing debt load on the peasant population. The total amount of debt in Croatia and Slavonia increased by ten times from 1880 to 1910, pressing households to look for cash incomes.[34]

A particular economic crisis also spurred labour migration from socialist Yugoslavia in the 1960s. The Yugoslav economy still had a huge farming sector, which in 1961 engaged half of the active population. At the same time, industry had been rapidly expanding throughout the 1950s. However, the economic reforms of the mid-1960s, which aimed at a more balanced economic development and pushed enterprises to more efficiency, led to a temporary decline in overall employment, as industries shed the redundant workforce and few new jobs were created (Table 6). From then on, unemployment would become a characteristic feature of the Yugoslav socialist economy and would reach dramatic proportions in the 1980s.[35]

The period in-between these two waves of economic emigration was not rosy in economic terms either, but large-scale emigration was made impossible because of restrictions on immigration by the traditional destination countries or because of the initially very restrictive exit policies of socialist Yugoslavia. Thus in the interwar and early socialist years, potential emigration was partially redirected towards domestic destinations. Interwar Yugoslavia pursued active colonisation policies, especially in areas where non-Slavic minorities lived (Vojvodina, Kosovo, Macedonia); socialist Yugoslavia was characterised by intense domestic migration, related also to the creation of new industries and jobs in the service sector in the 1950s and 60s. Between 1946 and 1960, 4.2 million domestic migration movements

[32] Statistički godišnjak Kraljevina Hrvatske i Slavonije 1906–1910, 344.

[33] Kreser, Gustoća žitelstva, 74.

[34] Ibid., 115.

[35] Woodward, Socialist Unemployment.

were counted in Yugoslavia and 3.4 million between 1961 and 1971; 5.1 million people left their village between 1946 and 1971.[36]

Table 6: Development of employment in Yugoslavia, 1960–1970

	Total employment	Activity rate (in %)	Unemployed	Job vacancies	Vacant jobs (per 100 unemployed)
1960	2,972,000	16.2	159,230	59,092	37.1
1961	3,242,000	17.4	191,283	57,136	29.9
1962	3,318,000	17.6	236,563	57,805	24.4
1963	3,390,000	17.8	230,272	78,605	34.1
1964	3,608,000	18.7	212,486	83,067	39.1
1965	3,662,000	18.8	236,969	53,304	22.5
1966	3,582,000	18.2	257,607	43,677	17.0
1967	3,561,000	17.9	269,067	33,531	12.5
1968	3,587,000	17.8	310,997	35,505	11.4
1969	3,706,000	18.2	330,626	43,202	13.1
1970	3,850,000	18.9	319,586	46,293	14.5

Source: Baučić, Socijalno-ekonomske posljedica, 29.

Macroeconomic developments, thus, had a significant impact on migration; but to determine exactly which, one has to leave the macro-level and look into local contexts and factors underlying individual and collective decision making. In the Yugoslav territories, such as in many other cases, there was no clear-cut connection between poverty and emigration. Actually, it was usually not the poorest that left, and emigration continued even after the initial economic reasons had subsided. Take for example the development of wages in Croatia before World War One: average wages for agricultural labourers in the district of Modruš-Rijeka, which was most affected by emigration, were constantly above the Croatian average in the first decade of the twentieth century, while in the district of Varaždin, which saw very little emigration, wages were only half or less of these and the lowest in Croatia.[37] That there was no immediate link between destitution and emigration would also come as a surprise to the Yugoslav communists, when they decided to open the borders for labour migrants in the 1960s. They had envisaged this as a temporary measure to reduce unemployment. Eventually, only a minority of *Gastarbeiter* came from the unemployed and from the least developed regions. According to the census of labour migrants in 1971, only 7.2 percent of the migrants had been unemployed before they left Yugoslavia.[38] It was the most prosperous republics of Yugoslavia, Slovenia and Croatia, from which a disproportionally high number of migrants came in the 1960s.

[36] Tanić, Seljaci na evropskim raskrsnicama, 9–10.
[37] Statistički godišnjak Kraljevina Hrvatske i Slavonije 1906–1910, 350.
[38] Savezni zavod za statistiku, Lica na privremenom radu, 11.

The economy of migration, of course, cannot be understood if the receiving side is left unconsidered. The expression *pull*-factors might be an unfortunate one, but the search for cheap and unorganised labour – as provided by immigrants in the industrial economies of North America and Western Europe, and also the mining and farming industries in South America before the global depression of the 1930s – did provide a powerful stimulus; in particular because these opportunities were known to potential migrants or at least they believed that such opportunities existed. The three US states with the highest numbers of immigrants from Slovenia, Croatia and Serbia before World War Two were the industrialised states of Pennsylvania, Ohio and Indiana; more than 70 percent of the Yugoslav immigrants to the US lived in urban areas according to Gerald Govorchin's 1961 study.[39] The *Gastarbeiter* of the 1960s found work in the expanding industries and service sectors of the booming economies of Western Europe, especially in the Federal Republic of Germany, where domestic supply of labour for poorly paid manual jobs was declining and employers were considering immigrants from Southern Europe a convenient source of cheap labour.

A particular economic factor for emigration was the activities of emigration agents. The archival records since the late nineteenth century are filled with reports on agents and officials of steamship companies who agitated for emigration in Croatia, Dalmatia and Slovenia and later also other parts of the region, despite the prohibitions on advertising for emigration. Agents were active in all regions with significant emigration, and major towns boasted branch offices of international steamship companies. As the contribution of Aleksandar Miletić in this volume shows, state regulations concerning the transportation of emigrants were often bypassed by corruption and red tape, as steamship companies bribed officials in order to get licences, etc. For them, emigration was huge business and Southeastern Europe a market with huge demand. Some agents were also involved in illegal migration or human trafficking. However, the impact of the agents' activities on the motivation to leave is difficult to assess. Even contemporaries did not agree whether emigration agents created a new urge for emigration or rather satisfied existing demand. It appears that emigration agents in general acted more like travel agencies, even though a certain number of emigrants were stimulated to leave by the promises of the agents.[40]

Networks and emerging cultures of migration

These macroeconomic factors neither explain why particular individuals decided to move nor why emigration was such a persistent phenomenon in the region. The memoirs of Louis Adamic, who went to the USA in 1913, provide an idea about the actual dynamics of the migrant's decision:

> *As a youngster, eighteen or twenty years ago, back in my native village in Carniola I experienced a thrill every time a man returned from the United States. Four or five years before he had*

[39] Govorchin, Americans from Yugoslavia, 69–70.

[40] See Just, Ost- und südosteuropäische Amerikaauswanderung, 56–7.

quietly left for America, a poor peasant clad in homespun, with a bundle on his back; now, an Amerikanec, he usually sported a blue serge suit, buttoned shoes, with India rubber heels, a derby, a celluloid collar, and a loud necktie, made even louder by a dazzling horseshoe pin, while his two suitcases of imitation leather bulged with gifts from America for his relatives and friends in the community ... Thus in my boyhood the idea that the United States was a sort of paradise on earth – the Golden Country, the Land of Promise – was kept vigorously alive by the Amerikanci in our village, and, of course, by tens of thousands of returned emigrants in other villages and towns in Eastern, Central and Southern Europe, from which, until lately, American industries (notably mining and steel) drew much of their labor power. Thus the ambition to go to the United States was kindled in boys by men who had been there.[41]

The influence of letters from emigrants and returnees had also been noted in a report by the administration of the Lika-Krbava district of Croatia in 1890, which stated that:

From this region people go to America mainly because they are persuaded by local people, who have returned from America, or by the beautiful promises of their co-villagers, who write from America and cannot but praise their high salaries.[42]

Emigrants did not only send letters but often also pre-paid tickets. From interwar Yugoslavia more than a quarter of overseas emigrants travelled on a pre-paid trip; two thirds of emigrants had relatives in the country of destination.[43] Migrant networks provided information about migration opportunities, sent money or tickets for the trip, and significantly eased the material and psychological stress for immigrants after arrival, helping with accommodation, adaptation to the new environment and access to the labour market. Migration, thus, produced a self-generating momentum.[44]

Very similar processes were at play in case of the *Gastarbeiter* migration despite the socialist state's effort to be its primary organiser. According to reports from Yugoslav migration specialists, most of the labour migrants left on their own initiative without involvement of the state.[45] Carl-Ulrik Schierup, in his study on emigration from the Serbian municipality of Kladovo in the 1960s and 70s, concluded that kin and friendship networks were more important channels of emigration than professional recruiters sent by foreign companies and the Yugoslav state labour agency, *Savezni zavod za poslove zapošljavanja*.[46] Very often people used to go where the first *Gastarbeiter* from their community had gone, establishing fairly stable patterns. In the village of Ljubičevac investigated by Schierup, for example, 337 out of 391 migrants in the age group 20–50 years had gone to Denmark, which otherwise

41 Adamic, The Land of Promise, 618–9. Louis Adamic (Alojz Adamič) was born in 1899 in current-day Slovenia and died in 1951 in Milford, N.J. He came to the US in 1913, where, after working in manual jobs, he worked as left-wing journalist and professional writer after World War I. His 1934 book "The Native's Return", based on his visit to the Kingdom of Yugoslavia, became a bestseller.

42 Quoted in Čizmić, O iseljavanju iz Hrvatske, 37.

43 Statistički godišnjak Kraljevine Jugoslavije 1929, 126; 1938/9, 140.

44 Cf. Åkerman, Towards an Understanding, 300.

45 Tanić, Seljaci na evropskim reskrsnicama, 87.

46 Schierup, Houses, Tractors, Golden Ducats, 28.

was not the destination of choice for migrants from Yugoslavia.[47] The links could even span generational divides: many labour migrants from the parts of socialist Yugoslavia that had been left by numerous overseas emigrants before World War One, would go to the same overseas countries in the 1960s. This explains, for example, why 9,168 out of the 13,415 migrant workers from the municipality of Bitola in Macedonia in 1971 were to be found in Australia, where many an emigrant from Macedonia in the early twentieth century had gone. For labour migrants from some Adriatic islands and Montenegro, the USA was one of the most important destination countries in the 1960s, reproducing a similar pattern as in the late nineteenth/early twentieth century. Migrants obviously received support from their co-ethnic immigrant communities there.[48]

Apart from networks as a social force for stimulating and reproducing migration, cultural dynamics also played an important role in maintaining the flow of migrants. The letters of emigrants, usually full of praise for their new environment, returns and visits by emigrants who showed off, and the goods brought home by migrants or bought by their families changed local social and cultural dynamics. Consumerism, especially in the socialist Yugoslavia, also crept in thanks to labour migration, creating needs that would be satisfied only if one went abroad and earned the necessary money. A Mercedes was out of reach for the ordinary Yugoslav worker and villager, but it became an important symbol of social status and prestige. In Krsto Papić's 1968 short film "*Halo München*", students of a grammar school in the impoverished Dalmatian hinterland leave class in order to chase a Mercedes with a German registration plate; Papić used this as a critical comment on the cultural alienation produced by migration, but for many a Yugoslav citizen, the ability to purchase consumer goods became an important part of their work efforts and consequently, the possession of these items by others triggered emulation. These goods were also a means of enduring local prestige and status competition. A particular symbol of both success abroad and of the continued belonging to the native community were impressive houses built in many a Yugoslav migrant town and village (Pictures 1–3). These houses frequently had more than 200 square meters of living space but were often not used or only inhabited by part of the family.[49] In rural areas, modern tractors of Western vintage also became an important status symbol, so that many rural households acquired tractors, even if these could not efficiently be employed because they owned little land. The eastern Serbian peasants in Tanić's study even spoke of "tractorisation", the purchase of tractors and other farming machinery being among the most important motives for emigration.[50]

The purchase of modern durable consumer goods, the erection of huge houses and the successful competition for local prestige put pressure on Yugoslavs to search for work abroad because domestic jobs, especially in rural areas, would not pay enough to meet consumer expectations. Schierup's 1973 study on Yugoslav rural migrants to Denmark, therefore, car-

47 Ibid., 26.

48 Savezni zavod za statistiku, Lica na privremenom radu, 79–93.

49 Bratić, Malešević, Kuća kao statusni simbol, 145–9; see Pichler in this volume.

50 Tanić, Seljaci na evropskim reskrsnicama, 83; see Schierup, Houses, Tractors, Golden Ducats.

ries the evocative title "Houses, tractors, golden Ducats. Prestige game and migration." The eminent Yugoslav migration researcher Ivo Baučić summarised these dynamics:

> *In the emigration regions, employment abroad is often the result of* collective decisions and emulation. *Due to the* demonstrative effects, *neighbours want to achieve the same standard of living that the migrants had reached because of working abroad. Employment abroad becomes a factor in the struggle for* social prestige.[51]

Yugoslav specialists also pointed to the negative consequences of these developments because migration became so engrained in the individual's perspectives that many, especially in rural areas, would rather forgo better education and leave Yugoslavia as soon as possible to earn more money in manual jobs abroad than in a qualified one in Yugoslavia. This would de-value education and lead to new stratification in Yugoslav villages: previously, families with the most land had enjoyed the highest prestige and their sons were the most looked for as bridegrooms; now, it was families with incomes from migration, who often originally belonged to the poorer classes of the village.[52] Tanić also asserts that the "traditional cohesion of the village collective is being destroyed because the competition for wages furthers the egoistic ambitions and the atomisation of solidarity".[53] From the household perspective, however, the access to migrant incomes became an essential element for the improvement of material living conditions. Already in the late nineteenth century, many 'passive', i.e. poor regions in the Balkans depended on migrant remittances and savings of returnees, a pattern which re-emerged during the *Gastarbeiter* migration. These incomes were not only used for status items but especially for the building of new houses or the reconstruction of old ones and for the meeting of daily expenses.

The social pressures underlying migration were closely linked to these expected incomes. Village communities, for example, expected migrants to send money back not only to their families but also to give for the improvement of the village infrastructure. Many a school building, sewage and water system, local road but also church in villages in socialist Yugoslavia were built or renovated with money donated by migrants. Hence local communities had an interest in emigration and facilitated exit even at times when the state tried to restrict it. This was one reason why the elaborate emigration policies of the federal government of Yugoslavia did not work (see below). Many households also had an essential interest in migration and sent one or more of their members abroad. This practice would also help the preservation of 'traditional' family patterns. In some parts of the former Yugoslavia, especially its rural ones in the south and east, the pattern of multi-generational, patriarchal households in which married sons would continue to live with their father survived until the second half of the twentieth century. For these households, income from migration was important for the maintenance of 'traditional' cultural and social practices, such as the pay-

51 Baučić, Socijalno-ekonomske posljedice, 37; italics in the original.
52 Schierup, Migration, Socialism, 37.
53 Tanić, Seljaci na evropskim reskrsnicama, 127.

Picture 1–3: Migrants' houses in eastern Serbia, 2006. *Source:* Ulf Brunnbauer.

ment of bride prices. The "ducats" mentioned in Schierup's study were gold coins bought from migrant incomes and used as donations to the family of the bride.[54]

The connection between household structure and emigration was particularly evident among the Albanians of Yugoslavia, who preserved the multiple patriarchal household longer and to a greater extent than other populations in the country. The survival of these structures was also predicated on migration. Albanians in Kosovo but also Macedonia faced severe job shortages: the Kosovo economy remained underdeveloped and in Macedonia, state jobs were preferentially given to the ethnic Macedonians, while the Albanian minority remained dependent on farming and migration. Therefore, Albanians were disproportionally represented among the *Gastarbeiter* from Macedonia, and in Kosovo almost a third of the active population worked abroad in the 1970s. Many of the multi-generational households sent one or more of their sons abroad to earn money for the whole household. The migrants remitted most of their earnings, where they were managed by the father. These incomes also made it possible to continue to exclude women from the wage economy, as reflected also in their marginal share among the labour migrants: 95.3 percent of those who had left Kosovo before 1971 were male (this number also includes the Serb population in Kosovo), while

[54] Schierup, Houses, Tractors, Golden Ducats, 47.

in Slovenia, for example, 40 percent of all labour migrants were women.[55] Hence, migration – apart from other factors, such as insecurity – facilitated the survival of the patriarchal multi-generational household. It is significant that complex household structures in Kosovo have been dissolving more quickly over the last decade when the opportunities for emigration became more restricted and the remittances from the migrants declined.[56]

Emigration and the state

Charles Tilly in his essay on Migration in Modern European History stresses that the modern state and its bureaucrats are deeply suspicious of moving populations and prefer sedentary subjects because these can more easily be counted, taxed, drafted into the army, sent to school and controlled.[57] The modern state, therefore, not only developed the administrative category of emigration as a particular form of human mobility which involves the crossing of state borders, but also a rich arsenal of measures to control, direct and restrict human movement. This concerned domestic migrations, immigration and emigration as well. The policies of exit, i.e. the regimentation of emigration, however, have found far less attention by scholars than the policies of entry, i.e. immigration.[58] Only recently has this field become more popular among scholars investigating migration processes.[59] The region under consideration can make a valuable contribution to the reactions of states to emigration and their attempts to regulate it; all the more so, because during the last century, the different political regimes in the territory of the former Yugoslavia pursued very different emigration policies and, therefore, provide for an inherently comparative discussion.

Emigration policies were an issue in all the countries and political systems in this area: the Kingdoms of Croatia and Slavonia (as part of the Dual Monarchy), the independent Principalities/Kingdoms of Serbia and Montenegro (before 1918), the Ottoman Empire (controlling Macedonia and Kosovo until 1912), the Kingdom of the Serbs, Croats and Slovenes/Yugoslavia (1918–41), the "Independent State of Croatia" (1941–45), and the Federal People's Republic of Yugoslavia/Socialist Federal Republic of Yugoslavia (1945–91). The independent states emerging from the dissolution of Yugoslavia also pursued active policies towards their emigrants. These policies displayed the full range of potential emigration regulations: facilitation of emigration (for economic and ethnic reasons), laisser-faire exit regimes, selective restrictions on emigration, prohibition of voluntary emigration, facilitation of return/repatriation, and the creation of diasporas. The main rationales behind these

55 Savezni zavod za statistiku, Lica na privremenom radu, 99–112.

56 European Stability Initiative, Cutting the Lifeline.

57 Tilly, Migration in Modern European History, 48.

58 A Google search for "immigration policy/policies" gave more than 13 million hits as of July 2008, while "emigration policy/policies" produced only 4 million results, asking, "Did you mean 'immigration' policies?"

59 Cf. Green, Weil, Citizenship and Those who leave.

measures were related to economic policies, concerns about the well-being of the emigrants, and nation-building.

The first consistent efforts to regulate emigration were made in the Kingdoms of Croatia and Slavonia before World War One. The legal situation as concerns emigration was complex with regard to this polity because emigration was also part of the legislation of Hungary, to which Croatia and Slavonia belonged, although the Croatian authorities would issue their own regulations. Dalmatia, the Slovene Lands, and Istria, being parts of Austria, were subject to a laisser-faire exit regime until 1913, when emigration of recruits was prohibited in the Austrian part of the Dual Monarchy; the publication of adverts and brochures which propagated emigration had already been outlawed in Austria in 1852.[60] In Croatia and Slavonia emigration especially to overseas destinations was of concern to the authorities from at least the early 1880s.[61] The government kept records about the issuing of passports and gathered information from the local administration about emigration. Of particular concern were the activities of emigration agents, whose influence on the population was considered harmful because they persuaded people to leave their country by lying about conditions in the destination countries; they also often cheated them. In February 1890, the Croatian government prohibited the business of emigration agents for the first time; this regulation was repeated several times thereafter.[62] Similar concerns were also shared by the Hungarian government, which had outlawed the advertising of emigration in its first emigration law of 1881.[63] Between 1885 and 1891 the Hungarian government issued decrees ordering postal officers not to deliver brochures advertising emigration and to return post which appeared to include tickets for overseas; the names of the addressees were to be disclosed to the local authorities.[64] Particular efforts were made in 1897 by the Croatian government and also authorities in other provinces of the Habsburg Monarchy to stop emigration to Brazil, where emigrants usually ended as ruthlessly exploited labourers on large estates.[65]

Efforts at regulating emigration increased in Croatia when mass overseas emigration set in and emigration increasingly became the subject of public debate. The government established a special office for emigration in its internal affairs department and in 1899 began to release annual data on the number of migrants. In 1901 it issued a decree for the regulation of the transportation of emigrants, requiring all pertinent businesses to acquire a licence from the government and imposing rules to protect emigrants on their trip. In 1905 the government also established the "Emigration Fund" (*Iseljenički fond*), which was used for the needs of emigrants and financed by fees from steamship companies, penalties,

60 Just, Ost- und südosteuropäische Amerikaauswanderung, 46.

61 See HDA, f. 78, Vlada, k. 172 (1881).

62 Stenografički zapisnici 1897–1902, 99.

63 Just, Ost- und südosteuropäische Amerikaauswanderung, 50.

64 HDA, f. 79, OUZV, Kraljska hrvatsko-slavonsko-dalmatinska zemaljska vlada, odjel za unutarnje poslove, k. 1935 (1897).

65 See the many documents in HDA, f. 79, OUZV, Kraljska hrvatsko-slavonsko-dalmatinska zemaljska vlada, odjel za unutarnje poslove, k. 1935 (1897) and k. 2962 (1898).

and the emigration tax that emigrants had to pay.[66] Newspapers regularly reported on the fate of emigrants, public activists propagated against emigration, and the Croatian Diet, the *Sabor*, discussed this issue several times. The most commonly held position by politicians in Croatia and Slavonia was that emigration was harmful for the individuals and their families as well as the nation, which would lose members. A typical illustration of this attitude is a speech by Lazar Horvat, secretary of the "Union of Serbian Agrarian Societies" (*Savez srpskih zemljoradničkih zadruga*) in Croatia, held in September 1912. He warned his "brothers not to believe the lies of various agents, who sweeten to you America and describe it, as if honey and milk would flow there. [...] Be aware, when I tell you: *America is the grave of our people, its new Kosovo, its abyss and not its salvation.*"[67] In the Croatian Diet, several deputies urged the government to act against emigration or at least to effectively stop agitation for emigration. Croatian representatives in Vienna and Budapest criticised the Austrian and Hungarian government for not doing enough to stop emigration.[68] Only a few voices in Croatia asserted the positive effects of emigration for the poor regions of the country, where it provided an exit from rural overpopulation and access to urgently required cash incomes.[69]

In 1910, the government of Croatia and Slavonia introduced a bill on emigration in the *Sabor*, which was modelled after the restrictive Hungarian emigration law of 1903, described by James Davenport Whelpley in 1905 as "up to the present time the most drastic of its kind".[70] This bill defined the "emigrant", put the business of transporting emigrants under strict control by the government, stipulated detailed rules on the transportation and rights of passengers, forced potential emigrants to inform the authorities about their leaving the country in advance, and prohibited emigration for certain population groups, such as criminals and recruits without approval by the military authorities.[71] The bill included a proposition which would have allowed outlawing emigration "if the economic existence, morale and physical well-being of the emigrant" was threatened. Another interesting proposition concerned the attitude of the government towards its emigrants, indicating future policies to create diasporas: the state should find ways and take measures to "keep the love and affection of [the emigrants] for their home country alive". The bill eventually did not become law, because legislation on emigration matters was out of the competencies of the *Sabor* but had to be decided in Budapest. The draft bill, however, would provide a model for legislation in Yugoslavia after World War One.

66 Benko Grado, Razvitak naše državne iseljeničke službe, 21.

67 Horvat, Naše iseljeničko pitanje, 6, 12; italics in the original.

68 Čizmić, O iseljavanju iz Hrvatske, 39–40.

69 Ibid., 40.

70 Whelpley, The Problem of the Immigrant, 37.

71 The Croatian bill is published in *Stenografički zapisnici Sabora kraljevina Hrvatske, Slavonije i Dalmacije 1910–1915*. XXV svečane zaključne saborske sjednice od 7. studenoga 1911. Sv. II. 1911, Prilog 7, k. 1–10. An English translation of the Hungarian Law of 1903 is provided in Whelpley, The Problem of the Immigrant, 252–269.

While Croatia and Slavonia – and the Habsburg Monarchy in general – as well as Montenegro pursued essentially liberal exit regimes despite efforts to regulate emigration, the independent Kingdom of Serbia took a much more restrictive course.[72] In Serbia, the economic situation was very different compared to the coastal areas at the Adriatic, and peasants had benefited from policies which safeguarded their holdings. In nineteenth century Serbia, which was sparsely populated, the government had even invited settlers from Montenegro and the Habsburg Monarchy to move to Serbia, where they were promised land, so that the area under plough would be extended.[73] Overseas emigration from Serbia in any significant dimension only started in 1908, caused by economic problems. The government reacted quickly and imposed prohibitive fees for passports, which forced most of the – albeit few – emigrants from Serbia to leave without documents (thus without leaving a trace in the statistics). Jelenko Petrović estimated the overall number of emigrants to America from Serbia before World War One at only 3,000.[74] The Ottoman Empire, which until 1912 still controlled Macedonia and Kosovo, also prohibited emigration, although these rules were not strictly enforced because government officials either were indifferent to emigration or took bribes for providing would-be emigrants with identity documents.[75]

In 1918 the new Kingdom of Serbs, Croats and Slovenes, which in 1929 would be renamed the Kingdom of Yugoslavia, was established, comprising the territories of the previously independent states of Serbia and Montenegro and large parts of the South Slav areas of the former Habsburg Monarchy. The new state pursued very active emigration policies, which resulted in distinctive legislation and the establishment of specialised institutional bodies.[76] Emigration policies addressed different concerns: the state wanted to make emigration beneficial for the national economy; emigration was to be used as a means of nation-building;[77] emigration regulations had to adapt to the immigration rules of destination countries; and the state wanted to protect and support its emigrants. Aside from this, there was additionally an at least conceptual link between emigration policies and the intense domestic colonisation policies, which also followed an economic and 'national' rationale: members of the constitutive nations were settled in minority areas, whereas members of the large minorities were pressurised to leave. As a result, the state attempted to control and to direct the movement of its population and to wield sovereignty over those who had left the country.[78]

72 The Serbian policies were similar to those of Bulgaria, which in 1908 passed a most restrictive emigration law immediately after the first significant emigration movement to overseas. The law all but cut legal emigration for economic reasons.

73 It was the Serbian king's temporary halt on colonisation from Montenegro in 1882, which gave the initial trigger for overseas emigration from that country.

74 Petrović, Pečalbari, 6.

75 See Karpat, The Ottoman Emigration, 186–9.

76 See Miletić in this volume.

77 See Pezo in this volume.

78 See Ragazzi in this volume.

The basic means of regulation was the emigration law of 1922 and the implementing provisions of 1923; the law bore obvious similarities to the Croatian draft bill of 1910. It defined the emigrant and declared emigration "free", pending special provisions by the government in emergency situations. At the same time it imposed strict regulations on the transportation of emigrants (actually, most of its articles dealt with the transportation of emigrants). All companies wanting to transport migrants from Yugoslavia had to acquire a licence from the government and to pay a fee. Financial penalties in case of violation of these rules would go into the emigration fund, as well as the fees paid by each emigrant. The fund supported emigrants in despair who wanted to return, and financed a home for destitute emigrants in Yugoslavia. The law prohibited agitation for emigration; agents were allowed only to inform about the practicalities of travel. The law also envisaged identity policies towards the emigrants: in places with significant 'Yugoslav' émigré communities, migrant organisations should be established with liaison secretaries to work with the Yugoslav diplomatic services. In these countries, special envoys to work with the emigrants were to be stationed at the diplomatic representations, sent by the emigration department of the Ministry for Social Policies.[79] The state also established specialised institutions, in order to place emigration under state control: at the Ministry for Social Policies, the Department for Emigration was created in 1920. In Zagreb, the General Emigration Commissariat was established in 1922, evolving from the former emigration department of the Croatian provincial government. Although it lost its autonomy in 1923 and was attached to the Ministry for Social Policy, the Commissariat remained the most important emigration institution, especially with regard to providing information on emigration and caring for the needs of emigrants.[80] The Commissariat, for example, published the brochures *Iseljenički vijesti* ("Emigration News") and *Iseljenički propisi* ("Emigration Regulations") for official use, which informed about emigration rules, emigration possibilities, immigration legislation and various practical matters.[81]

The policies of the state were supported and accompanied by the activities of emigration organisations in Yugoslavia, which lobbied for the needs of the emigrants and developed recommendations on how emigration would be made beneficial for the economy. In 1928 these organisations established the "Union of the Organisations of the Emigrants" (*Savez organizacija iseljenika,* SORIS) in Zagreb. The largest of these organisations was also based in Zagreb and published the monthly journal "The Emigrant" (*Iseljenik*), which in 1928 was renamed "The New Emigrant" and turned into the mouthpiece of the Union of the Organisations of the Emigrants; other periodicals devoted to emigration appeared as well. In Zagreb there was the "Emigrants' Museum", which provided information on the Yugo-

79 Zakon o iseljavanju, *Službene novine,* no. 39, 21 February 1922.

80 Hranilović, Iseljenička politika i služba; Antić, Iseljenička politika stare jugoslavenske države.

81 The Commissariat's archive has not been preserved but parts of its documentation are kept in the archive of the Interior Ministry of the Kingdom of Yugoslavia in the *Arhiv Serbije i Crne Gore* (formerly *Arhiv Jugoslavije*) in Belgrade (ASCG, f. 4), and in the personal archive of Arthur Grado Benko in the Croatian State Archive in Zagreb (HDA, f. 790).

Picture 4: Title covers of interwar emigration periodicals. *Sources:* National Library of Serbia, Croatian State Archive.

slav émigré communities.[82] Emigration activists, such as Milotislav Bartulica, urged the state to strengthen the "whole body of the people", which also included those living abroad. Emigration policy must defend and protect the interests of those emigrants, who "according to their moralistic attachment and economic interests belong to the home country", in order to prevent these feelings "from drying out or taking root in another state or national organism".[83] Co-ethnic emigrants, thus, were imagined as being part of the nation even if they had never been citizens of the new Yugoslavia. This was clearly reflected in the expression "tenth *banovina*" used for the emigrant communities (*banovina* was the name given to administrative units after the constitutional re-alignments of 1929).

The state also made a clear link between emigration policy and nation-building; for that purpose, the government took 'positive' as well as 'negative' measures. Among the former was propaganda among 'Yugoslav' emigrants, especially in the Americas, who should develop feelings of attachment to the new state and eventually return or at least continue sending money home. The government supported emigrant organisations with a 'Yugoslav' orientation and the Kingdom's diplomatic service acted in the same direction. This was an urgent task given the fact that most of the emigrants on which Yugoslavia laid claim had left their home before the new Yugoslav state even existed, i.e., before 1918. This was reflected in the émigré organisations in America as well: most of them had been founded either on a confessional or a regional basis, although there were 'Yugoslav' ones as well, which especially during World War One supported the idea of Yugoslav unification. A 1921 article in the progressive journal "*Nova Evropa*" deplored the "division of [the emigrant organisations] into twenty or more according to tribe; that way they are much weaker and of less use".[84] The 'negative' measures, which clearly gave emigration policy a national angle, addressed non-Slavic populations, which did not fit the idea of the 'tri-unite' nation of Serbs, Croats, and Slovenes. The Serb dominated government in particular put pressure on the Albanians and Turks in southern Serbia (Kosovo and Macedonia) to leave the country. The Ministry of Foreign Affairs also ordered the Yugoslav embassies not to issue return documents to emigrants from Yugoslavia who belonged to the German and Magyar minorities: in 1929, for example, it wrote to the embassy in Buenos Aires that "applications for repatriation to the Kingdom by our citizens of Magyar and German nationality must be declined". The embassy was ordered to go "to the extremes" to prevent these "a-national elements" from returning.[85]

In 1941 the first Yugoslavia was destroyed by German attack; in 1945 Yugoslavia was re-established but as a socialist state ruled by the victorious communists under Josip Broz Tito. The new regime initially pursued radically different emigration policies compared to the pre-1941 governments; these were in accordance with the pattern set by other commu-

[82] For information about the *Iseljenički muzej*, see its archive in HDA, f. 1619. On *SORIS*, see HDA, f. 967.

[83] Bartulica, Iseljenička politika, 4–5.

[84] Lazarević, Jugoslovenske potporne organizacije, 20.

[85] ASCG, f. 385, Ambasada Kraljevine Jugoslavije Buenos Aires, fasc. 4, a. jed. 29.

nist regimes. Until the early 1960s voluntary emigration was prohibited, with the exception of ethnic Turks from Macedonia, who were allowed to leave the country in the 1950s after an agreement with Turkey had been concluded; tentative steps towards the liberalisation of labour emigration began in the first years of the 1960s. The policies towards those emigrants, who had left the country before the communist takeover or during its course, was less unambiguous: on the one hand, the communist government fought against the so called "hostile" emigration, which consisted mainly of political émigrés and anti-Yugoslav as well as anti-Communist nationalists. Croat *Ustaše* émigrés were the most prominent among them.[86] Concerns about the "hostile emigration" were expressed, especially after labour migration was legalised in the 1960s and hundreds of thousands of Yugoslavs went abroad. The government feared that anti-communist nationalists would gain influence among its citizens, and accordingly took measures to prevent this from happening, including violent ones.[87]

On the other hand, the new regime also attempted to win sympathies among the 'old' emigrants. It even supported the repatriation of those who were deemed loyal to the new regime, as long as they did not belong to any "national minority"; Germans and Magyars especially were to be excluded.[88] In 1947–48 the Yugoslav steamships *Radnik* and *Partizanka* brought home several thousand Yugoslav emigrants. Their number, though, was lower than had been expected. In the 1950s and 60s, special organisations called the "*Matica* (Queen Bee) of the Emigrants" were established in all republics in Yugoslavia for propaganda among emigrants and the establishment of links with them. These organisations published monthly journals which addressed the emigrants and informed them about the progress and beauties of Yugoslavia. The *Matica* organisations also organised concerts of Yugoslav artists among the emigrants and holiday trips of emigrants to Yugoslavia. The ideas behind these activities were expressed in 1955 by Tito, who in his frequent trips abroad also used to meet with delegations of Yugoslav emigrants:

> *The emigrants must be a force that thoroughly connects us, that contributes to better mutual understanding of our peoples and countries. In order to achieve this, they must be, on the one hand, a model of loyalty and respect for the country in which they live* [...]. *On the other hand, they must be informed accurately and correctly about the life of today in their old home country.*[89]

The major official change to socialist Yugoslavia's emigration came in 1963–64, when the government, after controversial discussions in the communist party, decided to abolish most of the restrictions on labour emigration from the country.[90] This change was motivated on the one hand by the emerging difficulties in the domestic labour market, which could not absorb all the rural work force leaving the villages. These problems were intensified after

86 Cf. Doder, Jugoslovenska neprijateljska emigracija.

87 See Novinšćak in this volume.

88 Letter from the Ministry of Labour, which oversaw repatriation, to the Ministry of Foreign Affairs, 14 November 1946, in: ASCG, f. 25, Ministerstvo rada FNRJ; Odelenje za iseljene, 1946–1947, fasc. 66, a. jed. 189.

89 Quoted in *Susreti*, no. 1, 1980, 1.

90 Haberl, Die Abwanderung von Arbeitskräften, 65–74; Novinšćak in this volume.

introducing market oriented economic reforms in 1965, which made many industrial workers redundant and led to growing unemployment. On the other hand, the liberalisation of the exit regime was also an acceptance of the obvious, because even before the legalisation of labour emigration an increasing number of Yugoslav citizens had gone abroad in search of work, many of them clandestinely. According to information by the Central Committee of the League of Communists of Croatia from March 1963, an estimated 8,000 to 9,000 workers from Croatia had taken work abroad illegally in 1962 and 10,754 with approval by the authorities.[91] The party preferred to authorise labour migration and to control it rather than to accept spontaneous emigration; a crackdown on emigration was increasingly unviable given the general liberalisation of the travel regime, the intensifying integration of the country into the global economy, and its dependence on Western loans.

The party, which was less than enthusiastic in its approval of labour migration, aimed at subjecting employment abroad to its wider political agenda. Emigration, thus, was thought to be temporary – as manifested in the official designation of the labour migrants: "workers temporarily employed abroad" (*radnici na privremenom radu u inozemstvu*) – and selective. Already the first party documents on the regulation of labour migration demanded that qualified workers and the *inteligencija* should be excluded from migration, while the exit of unemployed and unqualified workers who did not find a job in the country would be tolerated, if it took place in an "organised manner".[92] The party-state's need to control the migration process resulted in a number of bilateral recruitment treaties with Western European countries (the first one concluded with France in 1965, the most important one with the Federal Republic of Germany in 1968), which regulated in detail the conditions of selection and employment of Yugoslav citizens abroad. The actual recruitment should have passed through the Yugoslav labour service, which, however, only happened in half of the cases until 1975.[93]

The Yugoslav communists had particular concerns about the political consequences of labour migration. First of all, it posed an ideological problem: workers left the 'socialist paradise' to work in capitalist economies where, according to the communist view, they were exploited. This was a continuous point of critique by communists and left-wing groups in Yugoslavia, such as the students' movement in 1968.[94] Yugoslavia's response was, aside from stressing the temporary character of migration, the establishment of a network of social and legal advisers for the workers abroad, which symbolised the continuous care of the party for its working class, of which the migrants remained an integral part. Yugoslavia thus attempted to also extend its sovereignty over the citizens living abroad.[95] The other political problem was related to anti-communist emigration, which was feared to gain influence

91 HDA, f. 1220, CK SKH, D–1774 (1963).

92 Conclusions of the Executive Committee of the League of Communists of Croatia Central Committee, 6 May 1963, HDA, f. 1220, CK SKH, D–676 (1963).

93 Petković, Osnovni faktori odlaska, 32.

94 Mesić, External Migration, 179.

95 See Ragazzi in this volume.

among the Yugoslav workers. Documents from the party archive show persistent fears of "ideological contamination" and attempts to devise strategies to struggle against the "hostile emigration". This was a challenge mainly in the Federal Republic of Germany, which was not only where most Yugoslav migrants went but which also hosted vocal, mainly Croat, anti-Yugoslav émigré organisations.[96] To counter their influence, Yugoslavia supported the establishment of labour migrants' clubs and associations, which organised political, educational and recreational activities that sought to prevent the "assimilation" of the migrants and maintain their "socialist consciousness" and loyalty to Yugoslavia. The largest mass organisation in socialist Yugoslavia, the Socialist Union of the Working People of Yugoslavia (SSRNJ), was charged with overseeing these activities. Their popularity among labour migrants was, however, limited, according to the organisation's internal reports.[97] Providing the *Gastarbeiter* abroad with Yugoslav media was more successful; public radio in Germany and other countries, for example, included special programmes in Serbo-Croatian for the labour migrants, and Yugoslav newspapers, some of them with special sections for migrants, were widely distributed abroad. The major newspapers in Yugoslavia had also regular columns about the plight of the labour migrants and often reported about their problems.

Apart from political concerns, economic interests impacted emigration policies as well. As already mentioned, labour migration was thought to export unemployment; this would not be realised, however, because many of the emigrants were qualified and had held a job in Yugoslavia. Actually, compared to workers from other southern European countries, Yugoslav ones on average were better qualified, which explains their popularity among employers in the West, especially in Germany. The Yugoslav government also hoped that the workers would return with additional qualifications and useful professional experience; the government was interested also in their savings: remittances and repatriated savings from migrants became one of the main sources of hard currency in Yugoslavia. According to estimates, the net-inflow from migrants since the mid-1970s reached more than 1.5 billion US-$ annually; even according to official data they constituted between six and eight percent of the total national income in the 1970s until the mid-1980s.[98] The government attempted to persuade migrants and their families to invest their savings in the economy, and not to use them only for consumption. Yugoslav banks, for example, offered special interest rates on bank accounts for migrants. Local communities put pressure on their migrants to give for the improvement of the communal infrastructure. However, despite these efforts, the overwhelming share of the savings was used for private consumption.[99] The establishment of so-called *Gastarbeiter* factories, such as the emblematic *Pionirka* textile mill in the town of Aržano (1969), remained the exception.[100]

[96] See Novinšćak in this volume.
[97] See for example reports in ASCG, f. 476, Socijalistički savez radnog naroda Jugoslavije, fasc. 476, Koordinacioni odbor za pitanja naših radnika u inostranstvu (1971).
[98] Baučić, Gross, Rückkehr und Reintegration, 12.
[99] Nikolić, Neke karakteristike jugoslovenske migracije, 5.
[100] Baučić, Gross, Rückkehr und Reintegration, 98.

The return of the labour migrants was of particular concern to the Yugoslav government – and also to the governments of the destination countries, which did not envisage the *Gastarbeiter* turning into immigrants. In comparison to other Mediterranean sending states, Yugoslavia made a real effort to encourage and facilitate return for ideological as well as economic reasons. Pertinent policies were developed especially in the 1970s and 80s, after it had become obvious that most Yugoslav labour migrants did not return. In the early 1970s, Yugoslav migration specialists asserted the negative effects of labour migration for the Yugoslav economy. Yugoslavia would train workers who then went abroad, while many of the returnees were worn out or unqualified and had therefore become unemployed in their destination country. The economist Ivo Vinski, for example, concluded that Yugoslav labour migrants contributed much more to the prosperity of the destination countries, i.e. capitalist economies, than of Yugoslavia.[101] A new law on labour migration in 1973 aimed at restricting the emigration of qualified workers (though with little success) and at regulating the conditions of return and the integration of the returnees into the domestic economy.[102] The tenth party congress in 1974 demanded immediate measures be taken to eliminate the reasons for emigration and to facilitate return.[103] The new legislation, which was amended and extended over the next decade, was also a reaction to the expected mass return of migrants because of the stop on recruitment in 1973–74 and the growing unemployment in Western Europe. The Yugoslav government declared that returnees would be treated equal to domestic job seekers; they also enjoyed exemptions from import duties upon return (especially for machinery) as well as tax breaks, and had the opportunity to buy a job for themselves in a Yugoslav public enterprise, if they invested in such a company.[104]

However, as with so many other policies in socialist Yugoslavia, the effects of these measures were modest. Local practices by municipalities often differed from federal regulations; the individual republics also had quite different interests, and potential returnees were reluctant to invest in Yugoslavia given the persistent economic crisis and the difficult conditions for private enterprise. The high number of returns in the 1970s – estimates range between under 200,000 to over half a million – was conditioned less by the lure of the communist government than by the original intention of many a *Gastarbeiter* and the economic difficulties they faced in Western Europe at that time. Once at home, most of them found it very difficult to find a job because local enterprises and municipalities were less than enthusiastic about additional competitors for the scarce resource of employment and disregarded the government regulations regarding equal treatment of returnees. Many re-emigrated as a result, now often taking their family with them. Hence, despite the sincere efforts of both Yugoslavia and the destination countries to prevent *Gastarbeiter* migration becoming permanent, it eventually did. The migrants' own interests as well as the dysfunctional political system of Yugoslavia prevented the convergence of emigration policies and practices.

[101] Vinski, Ljudski capital.
[102] Mesić, External Migration, 193.
[103] Leković, Ugroženi identitet, 56.
[104] Baučić, Gross, Rückkehr und Reintegration, 94–97.

Summary and Conclusion

Labour migration has in many ways shaped the societies in the territory of the former Yugoslavia. Emigration provided a lifeline for families and individuals who faced economic difficulties and it became a major way to find access to incomes not available at home. In the emigration regions, migration eventually became part of the typical life trajectory, deeply ingrained in individual life cycles and expectations. Hence, we can speak of "cultures of emigration",[105] which became generators of new migration. These also built on the long tradition of (seasonal) migration and geographic mobility, which goes beyond the wave of overseas emigration that started in the late nineteenth century. The Yugoslav region has been characterised by a high degree of spatial mobility in the past as well as in the present. Considering also the extent of forced emigration and political exile, the importance of migration can hardly be exaggerated. The significance of emigration is not only judged by the migrants' experiences themselves but also by the omnipresent nature of emigration in public discourse. Politicians in this area repeatedly turned their eye on migration; newspapers and other media regularly reported about "our emigrants" and thus popularised the notion that (co-ethnic/national) emigrants continued to be part of the nation. Domestic emigrant organisations also contributed to the creation of imagined diasporas.

These diasporas would play a significant role during the dissolution of the former Yugoslavia, especially in Macedonia and Croatia, where the nationalist movements sought the support of their 'diaspora' and returned émigrés gained influence in the 1990s.[106] 'Long-distance' nationalism was not only a sentiment nourished by emigrants and their descendents but also a goal of state policies. Governments in this area from the early twentieth century onward continued to address emigrants with identity policies so that they would retain their loyalty for their home country. First of all, emigrants were supposed to return, so their 'assimilation' had to be prevented by reminding them of their roots and strengthening their supposed or real ethnic identities. Governments also saw the emigrants as a source of financial support – thus urging them to remit savings – and of political lobbying for their 'home country' in the country of destination. The examples from the area of the former Yugoslavia show that polities which experienced significant emigration felt the need to extend the limits of their sovereignty over the state borders; emigrants, thus, were considered to be transterritorial subjects, even if they had forgone their former citizenship. Emigration policies also sought to regulate population movements and to bring them into accordance with the development goals of government. Hence, emigration provided an important stimulus for societal policies, which aimed not only to alleviate concrete social problems but also to reconfigure the structures of social reproduction; politics provided one of the links between emigration and domestic development.

105 Cf. Brettell, Anthropology and Migration.
106 Hockenos, Homeland Calling.

The development of the Yugoslav societies was indeed affected by emigration. The architecture of migrants' houses, for example, is an obvious symbol of the repercussions of emigration. Emigration provided substantial financial benefit for many families; returnees introduced new cultural patterns and values; links between local communities and the world were established, and migrant networks were of tremendous help for the many refugees of the Yugoslav succession wars.

The consequences of emigration on the macro-economic level, however, seem to be less positive. Remittances and repatriated savings were evidently an important source of hard currency and also resulted in some productive investment. The opportunity to go abroad also eased the pressure on the domestic labour market (and the need for structural reforms as well). But as Yugoslav migration experts claimed already in the 1970s, labour migration did not transform the peripheral position of the region in the global division of labour.[107] The Yugoslav lands, and the Balkans in total, exported labour to the metropolitan regions of the world economy, while capital remained scarce. Emigration, therefore, created new dependencies because the local economies would be affected severely by crises in the business cycle of far-away countries. The labour migrants experienced these dependencies in the form of poorly paid jobs under harsh working conditions, which characterised the typical occupation of both the overseas migrant before World War One and the *Gastarbeiter*. From the economic point of view, the contemporaneous assertion of economists in the socialist Yugoslavia that labour migration contributed to modernisation – in the sense of introducing modern consumer goods – but not to development, does seem to provide a good summary of more than a century of external labour migration.

Acknowledgment

Research for this article was made possible by grants from the German Research Foundation (Deutsche Forschungsgemeinschaft, DFG).

Newspapers and Journals

Susreti (Podgorica)
Matica (Zagreb)
(Novi) Iseljenik (Zagreb)
Makedonija (Skopje)
Jutarnji list (Zagreb)
Službene novine (Belgrade)
Politika (Belgrade)
Narodna obrana (Osijek)
Službeni list (Belgrade)

[107] See MESIĆ, External Migration.

Marjan Drnovšek

Fragments from Slovenian Migration History, 19th and 20th Centuries

1. Introduction

The Slovenian territory is a geographical meeting point, and at the same time an intersection between the Mediterranean and Pannonian worlds on the one hand and the Alpine and Dinaric worlds on the other. Hence the lively course of migration, which has been going on for centuries, does not come as a surprise. Throughout history, this was a place where various civilisations, ideas and cultures from all parts of Europe and beyond intertwined.[1] There have always been considerable numbers of immigrants and emigrants (Slovenians and others) who arrived here or left this place. The historical record confirms the thesis of geographers that the continuity of migration activities among the inhabitants of this territory is centuries old.[2] As regards the nineteenth and twentieth centuries, until the 1960s emigration dominated, but after 1960 immigration also became a trend; today, Slovenia is mainly a transitory area for migrants on their way to the wealthy parts of Europe.

Throughout the period of emigration during the last two centuries, public opinion in Slovenia viewed this phenomenon more with hostility than with understanding. Why? Many have pointed out the small number of Slovenians and the demographic decrease of the population in comparison to other comparable European nations. The Catholic Church feared the loss of Slovenian identity abroad; it called attention to the potential moral decline due to the separation of families and warned against the loss of religious faith, the dangers of foreign ideas, etc. Its influence on forming the attitudes of the people towards emigration was strong in the nineteenth as well as the twentieth centuries. Foreign countries were always pictured as something dark, cold and hostile in relation to the homeland. It is therefore no surprise to come across the opinion, which was persistent during the time of the Habsburg monarchy and the First Yugoslavia, that emigration was a "cancerous sore on the body of the Slovenian nation".[3] However, emigration continued despite all warnings. Even more, migration currents were, on the whole, only interrupted or diminished because

1 Šumrada, La Slovénie, 26–7.
2 Gosar, Obseg, vzročnost in karakteristika, 149.
3 Quoted in Drnovšek, Izseljevanje je rak rana, 9.

of curbs on immigration by the countries of destination and not because of the perception of emigration as something "harmful" to the Slovenian nation.

The second Yugoslavia did open its borders for emigration, but at the same time it feared that migrant workers would be alienated from Yugoslavia's political order and fall under the influence of the political emigration from that country.[4] The argument about the threat to the nation was replaced by an ideological and political argument. In other words, while communist Yugoslavia never reconciled itself with the capitalist system, it nevertheless tolerated capitalism in the area of migration because of the increasingly difficult economic and social situation in the country. It did, however, invent a special label for labour migrants: "workers temporarily working abroad", who were considered part of the Yugoslav working class, although they were employed in foreign countries.

In terms of typology, Slovenian emigration, immigration and return migration in the nineteenth and twentieth century consist of internal and external, voluntary and forced, economic and political, permanent and temporary, continental and intercontinental, male and female, blue-collar and white-collar, etc. migrations. Usually, the typologies were interrelated.[5] In this essay I only focus on several aspects of the topic of emigration, and I do so with the eyes of an historian. For the sake of clarity, I therefore use only the spatial and temporal approach, although this somewhat narrows the scope of migration problems addressed. Although the Slovenian territory is small, we can observe big differences on the regional level with respect to migration. Above all, the constantly changing borders – state borders, less important administrative borders and imagined regional ones, but also ideological, religious, political, personal, gender-related, educational, and other borders – played a very important role in the migration processes of Slovenians and other ethnic groups. I want to emphasise two problems. First, it was the state borders that played a major role in the phenomenon that Klaus J. Bade named "people crossing borders and borders crossing people".[6] Second, for the Slovenians, the twentieth century was marked by the intertwining of voluntary and forced migrations; the latter led to some serious reflection about the fate of Slovenian existence, such as the case of the inhabitants of the Primorska region (*Primorci*)[7] under the Fascist Italian regime in the interwar period. And finally, Slovenian historiography is more and more interested in the destinies of "individuals and families [...], female emigrants in relation to males [...], individual stories in relation to the grand migration phenomena".[8]

In this article, emphasis is placed on quantitative dimensions of migration; I will refer to official and non-official numeric data concerning the migration processes of Slovenes, often in comparison with other ethnic groups, for example in the first and second Yugo-

4 Drnovšek, Pot slovenskih izseljencev, 21–36.

5 Cf. Lucassen, Lucassen, Migration, Migration History, 9–38.

6 Bade, Migration in European History, x.

7 In the interwar period, *Primorci* was the name for the Slovenians who lived on the territory that was part of Italy.

8 Kalc et al, Poti in usode.

slavia. Some basic demographic data on the Slovenian population are, therefore, in place. In 1869, 1,447,241 Slovenians lived in the Austrian part of the Habsburg monarchy[9] and 64,795 in the region of Prekmurje, which then belonged to the Hungarian half of the dual monarchy, i.e. 1,512,036 people altogether. In the census of 1910, 1,886,046 inhabitants of the monarchy chose Slovenian as their language of intercourse.[10] In the first census of the Kingdom of Serbs, Croats and Slovenes (Yugoslavia) in 1921, the province of Slovenia was inhabited by 1,054,919 people, and the next census in 1931 counted 1,144,298 inhabitants on this territory. After World War One, a third of Slovenians went to live outside Yugoslavia: 378,234 in the Kingdom of Italy (1920), some 100,000 in the Republic of Austria, and 6,087 in the Kingdom of Hungary (1920). According to estimates by demographers, approximately 373,000 Slovenian emigrants lived abroad.[11] After World War Two, the population of Slovenia developed as follows: 1,439,800 inhabitants in 1948, 1,591,523 in 1961, and 1,965,986 in 1991.[12]

2. Internal migrations inside three countries: the Habsburg monarchy, the first and the second Yugoslavia

Internal migrations are usually defined as migrations within a country. The multi-ethnic structure of the Habsburg monarchy and of both Yugoslav states was the base for experiences of difference by the temporary or permanent Slovenian migrants to the non-Slovenian territories of the same country. The destinations of Slovenian migrations within the borders of the same country were foreign from the linguistic point of view, and different in terms of way of life, technology, economic and social situation, culture and even religion. The two most distinctive marks of Slovenians in other environments were language and culture. From the economic point of view, the most visible difference was in the level of development in comparison to other nations within the same country. If Slovenians were considered among the least developed people in the Habsburg monarchy, they ranked among the most developed in both the first and second Yugoslavia. During the Habsburg monarchy the professional structure of Slovenian migrants in Austria and Hungary[13] ranged from

[9] In the Habsburg monarchy, no separate Slovenian administrative unity existed. Slovenes constituted the majority, or sizable proportions of the population in the crown lands of Carnolia (*Krain*), Carinthia (*Kärnten*), Gorica-Gradisca, Styria (*Steiermark*), Istria, and the free port of Trieste. In Carnolia, they formed the majority.

[10] Kresal, Perovšek, Slovensko narodno ozemlje, 18–19.

[11] Perovšek, Razvoj prebivalstva, 177–178.

[12] Čepič, Razvoj prebivalstva, 817.

[13] In 1867, the Habsburg Empire was divided into an Austrian and a Hungarian "half", acquiring the name Austro-Hungarian monarchy in 1868. The two parts of the Empire had a common ruler and common ministries for foreign affairs, war, and finance. Other policies were autonomously decided by the two parts. In terms of migration, a new internal border between Austria

university professors to sellers of roasted chestnuts in Vienna. Among the larger groups in the migrant population were miners and factory workers in the industrially developed and German speaking parts of the country, particularly in Central and Upper Styria and Lower Austria. A strong Slovenian presence was also felt in bigger cities, such as Vienna and Graz, which at the same time were the two most important university centres for Slovenian students (Slovenians did not get their own university until 1919 in Ljubljana).

It is incorrect to consider these currents of internal migration to consist exclusively of unskilled and manual workers. From the first half of the nineteenth century onwards, we also witness the seasonal migration of reasonably skilled foresters and a slightly less skilled agricultural workforce to Croatia and Slavonia and later Bosnia, which in 1878 was occupied by Austro-Hungary. Since the middle of the nineteenth century, Slovenian migrants have lived in Croatian urban centres along the border, such as Varaždin or Rijeka, working mostly as professionals in the trades, crafts and white-collar professions (e.g. as teachers, doctors, clerks etc.). In the 1880 census of the Kingdom of Croatia and Slavonia, 20,102 persons chose Slovenian as their mother tongue in 1880 and 15,686 in 1900.[14] Across the border, the government of the Serbian principality made some propaganda in the 1860s for permanent settlement in Serbia, but Slovenians did not respond to it.

Migration from the countryside to the city is also an important part of internal migration. Take for example Trieste, the main import and export port in Austria until 1918. From the beginnings of the eighteenth century onwards it attracted the Friulan, Slovenian and Croatian population from its hinterland. It also became one of the important European emigration ports in the beginning of the twentieth century.[15] The gradual industrialisation and the establishment of mining and industrial centres in the Slovenian territory contributed to urbanisation and movements from village to town as well. These centres were essential for educating people, many of whom later emigrated as miners to Germany and the United States of America. The rate of illiteracy among Slovenians dropped from more than ninety percent at the end of the eighteenth century to approximately twenty percent at the end of the nineteenth century as a result of a successful Austrian educational system.[16]

The First World War and the time which followed triggered two internal migration processes. The first consisted of the 1915 refugees from the Soča (Isonzo) front area,[17] who had to leave to central Austria (around 80,000 Slovenians from Goriška and Posočje), while the second was made up of the departing German and Hungarian populations (e.g. clerical force) after the war had ended; they left for Austria and Hungary even before the final borders between the first Yugoslavia and its neighbours were determined.

and Hungary emerged. The citizens from either side of the border had a separate passport to travel abroad, and migration policies differed in the two parts.

14 Szabo, Socijalna struktura Slovenaca, 87.

15 Kalc, Prekooceansko izseljevanje, 23–60.

16 Vodopivec, Temno in svetlo ogledalo zgodovine, 61.

17 Svoljšak, Soča, sveta reka.

Table 1: Immigration to Slovenia: year of immigration, country of first residence and gender

Year of immigration		**Before 1940**	**1941–1947**	**1948–1952**	**1953–1960**	**1961–1970**	**1971–1975**	**1976–1980**	**1981–1985**	**1986–1990**	**1991–1993**	**1994–1996**	**1997–1999**	**2000–2001**
Total	169,605	3,939	6,514	4,477	12,877	26,121	24,083	29,570	18,961	14,495	10,076	5,602	8,672	4,218
Countries of former Yugoslavia	150,763	1,928	3,898	3,959	12,496	24,992	22,278	27,047	17,391	13,529	9,359	4,530	6,783	2,573
Bosnia and Herzegovina	67,670	138	530	528	2,227	7,842	10,675	15,552	10,426	7,091	6,465	2,062	3,001	1,133
Croatia	49,418	1,304	2,067	2,389	7,839	12,059	6,464	5,943	3,633	3,169	1,744	1,134	1,076	597
Serbia and Montenegro	6,437	62	89	100	274	671	744	824	722	818	264	540	973	356
Macedonia	27,238	424	1,212	942	2,156	4,420	4,395	4,728	2,610	2,451	886	794	1,733	487
EU member states	14,000	1,675	2,426	451	286	806	1,453	2,005	1,244	650	384	552	990	1,078
Austria	2,798	432	527	82	52	164	293	334	182	98	57	90	133	354
Germany	6,128	127	651	62	36	426	925	1,370	866	360	180	205	510	410
Italy	2,655	720	732	227	153	92	56	84	61	83	77	114	107	149
France	1,114	236	283	54	14	61	63	80	44	43	15	28	63	30
Other EU countries	1,305	160	133	26	31	63	116	137	91	66	55	115	177	135
Other European countries	2,908	130	162	43	60	124	188	328	195	185	209	337	559	388
EU candidate countries	868	87	124	34	35	76	66	91	55	51	30	52	75	92
Other European countries	2,040	43	38	9	25	48	122	237	140	134	179	285	484	295
Non-European countries	1,934	206	28	24	35	199	164	190	131	131	124	183	340	179
Males	**90,675**	**1,392**	**3,088**	**2,336**	**7,521**	**15,021**	**13,793**	**15,123**	**8,992**	**6,974**	**4,759**	**3,515**	**5,553**	**2,608**
Females	**78,930**	**2,547**	**3,426**	**2,141**	**5,356**	**11,100**	**10,290**	**14,447**	**9,969**	**7,521**	**5,317**	**2,087**	**3,119**	**1,610**

Source: Statistični urad Republike Slovenije (Statistical Office of the Republic of Slovenia), Statistične informacije / Rapid Reports No 92/2003, 14. See: <http://www.stat.si/Popis2002/gradivo/si–92.pdf>.

With the establishment of the first Yugoslavia in 1918, the emigration of Slovenians to the Republic of Austria ceased. The largest source of agrarian migrants was the Prekmurje region, today the north-eastern part of Slovenia. Statistical data from the Job Exchange Office in the town of Murska Sobota (Prekmurje) shows the number of seasonal workers: in 1929, there were 4,264; then the numbers keep decreasing until 1937, when 1,839 left.[18]

Both during the Habsburg monarchy and the first Yugoslavia, individuals and smaller groups from other parts of the country migrated into Slovenian territory, but their numbers were limited. In the Austro-Hungarian monarchy, there was a "brain gain", e.g. of German and Czech engineers, to the Slovenian lands. On the other hand, there was the reverse "brain drain" of Slovenian professionals and members of the intelligentsia leaving for other parts of the monarchy, including Croatia.[19] There was more seasonal migration to Slovenia among the Friulan and Macedonian workers in construction and railway building. In the time of the first Yugoslavia, the migration of Serbian military personnel (soldiers and officers) started; this can be considered as the modest beginning of migration from other parts of Yugoslavia, which grew stronger in the second Yugoslavia. Migration from other Yugoslav republics increased significantly only after 1961, when Slovenia became a distinctive immigration territory. Slovenia used spontaneous and organised ways of attracting a workforce from the less developed parts of Yugoslavia: at first from the neighbouring regions of Croatia and Bosnian Krajina, and later from the entire country (see Table 1).

Taking into account all three countries that are the focus of this article, to which present-day Slovenia has belonged during the last two centuries, we can follow the continuity of internal migration eastwards. In the times of the Habsburg monarchy and the first Yugoslavia, seasonal migration of foresters and agricultural workers seems prominent, but this process ceases in the second Yugoslavia. After the Second World War, there are attempts to colonise Slovenians into the Banat and Vojvodina, but without success (only about 2,500 persons went from Slovenia).[20] The biggest change as far as internal migration is concerned, was the establishment of the border between Austria and the first Yugoslavia (1920), which put an end to centuries old free mobility.

3. Slovenian migration and Western Europe

Slovenian emigration to the economically developed parts of Europe can be traced back for centuries: the mediaeval migration to the Italian littoral town on the western Adriatic coast,[21] and the migration of peddlers from the Kočevje region to Germanic lands from the 15th century onwards, can be mentioned as instances of early migration from Slov-

[18] Škafar, Prekmurski sezonski delavci, 36.
[19] Gantar Godina, Slovenski izobraženci.
[20] Čepič, Razvoj prebivalstva, 887–888.
[21] Gestrin, Slovanske migracije v Italijo.

enian lands.[22] The end of World War One was a turning point for Slovenian emigration to Western Europe because the 'golden gate' of the USA was no longer wide open, but barely ajar. The current of migration turned towards European countries. However, the economically prosperous 1920s, which were favourable years for migrants, were followed by the Great Depression and consequently restrictions and stricter immigration control by the host countries.

Among European countries, Germany was the oldest and at the same time, the most consistent emigration destination for Slovenian migrants during the past two centuries. Hence we can speak of a *longue durée* migration trajectory, which can be divided into three phases: the first between 1880 and 1914, the second in the inter-war period, and the third, the so-called "*Gastarbeiter*" era in the 1960s and 1970s.

The first period from 1880 onwards, in the shadow of mass emigration to the USA, saw Slovenians from coal-mining areas (Zasavje, Carniola) move to the coal-mining and industrial regions of north-western Germany (*Ruhrgebiet*). The Catholic priest Janez Evangelist Krek (1865–1917) informed the public of this Slovenian wave of migration into Germany with his "*Westphalian letters*".[23] In the 1900 German census, 9,193 persons (6,453 men and 2,740 women) stated Slovenian as their mother tongue.[24] As a consequence of the post-World War One political and economic crisis in Germany, a portion of the so-called Westphalian Slovenians moved westwards (to the Netherlands, Belgium and France) and only a small part of them remained in Germany. Since German statistics after World War One only recorded Yugoslav citizens, estimates of the number of Slovenians are rather contradictory. According to Berislav Deželić, the emigrant emissary of the Kingdom of Yugoslavia in Düsseldorf, about 70,000 Yugoslavs were living in Germany on the verge of World War One, the majority of them Slovenians.[25] But these data hardly represent the genuine situation.

In 1925 official German statistics by the *Statistisches Reichsamt* listed 14,067 Yugoslav citizens residing in Germany, and in 1933 the number was 17,258.[26] The Yugoslav authorities estimated that around 25,000 Yugoslav citizens lived in Germany at that time. The large discrepancy between the German 1933 census and the Yugoslav estimation was attributed to dual citizenship (of at least 8,000 persons, who took German citizenship without renouncing their Yugoslavian one). Many researchers also point out the trend for quick assimilation and naturalisation in the time of Hitler's Germany.[27] At the end of the 1930s,

[22] Bade, Migration in European History, 21; Drnovšek, Izseljevanje Kočevarjev.

[23] Dolenec, Izbrani spisi, 125–178.

[24] Valenčič, Izseljevanje Slovencev v tujino, 64; for more about the Westphalian Slovenians see Wörsdörfer, Südosteuropa an Rhein und Ruhr.

[25] Deželić, Naša emigracija, 8.

[26] Croatian National Archives, Emigration Commission (Hrvatski državni arhiv, Iseljenički komisarijat), Zagreb, k. 562.

[27] Valenčič, Izseljevanje Slovencev v tujino, 64; Lipoglavšek-Rakovec, Slovenski izseljenci, 38.

Table 2: Emigration from the Dravska banovina to European countries, 1927–1939*

Year **Country**	**1927/28**	**1929**	**1930**	**1931**	**1932**	**1933**	**1934**	**1935**	**1936**	**1937**	**1938**	**1939**
France	259	1,722	3,634	2,453	1,506	1,898	2,203	2,013	3,027	4,249	2,566	25,530
Germany	345	345	1,921	1,088	457	2	262	442	228	2,238	4,773	13,310
Belgium	255	1,158	146	6	13	12	13	4	5	52	222	
Netherlands	448	279	271	23	16	124	6	6	1	4	4	
Luxembourg	107	8	27	1					1	1		
Switzerland	30	17	20	3	3	2	2	13	2	13	7	
Austria	436	1,242	484	383	213	70	344	357	284	258		
Italy	52	163	11	21	4		8	21	5	4	18	
Total from Dravska banovina	3,737	5,075	6,585	4,032	2,227	2,129	2,935	2,920	3,590	6,865	7,636	15,345
from Yugoslavia	19,098	19,425	25,409	10,560	6,642	7,508	11,004	10,120	8,625	14,287	14,376	23,613

* The Dravska banovina encompassed Slovenia after 1929, when the administrative division of Yugoslavia was reorganised (note by the editor).
Source: Hrvatski državni arhiv (Croatian State Archive), Iseljenički komisarijat, k. 600 (597).

after bilateral agreements between Germany and Yugoslavia had been signed, the emigration of seasonal agricultural workers from the Prekmurje region increased.[28]

Table 2 clearly shows that France was the main destination of Slovenian migrants in the interwar period.[29] In the 1920s, they were leaving for the mines in the northern and north-eastern part of France; after the Great Depression there was an increase in the number of female seasonal agricultural workers and foresters migrating there. Some of the migrants were also leaving for Belgium, the Netherlands and Austria and in smaller numbers to other European countries, for example Switzerland and England.[30] Many Yugoslav communists, including some Slovenians, found political asylum in the above-mentioned countries, except Germany and Austria.[31]

Labour migration to industrialised European countries after World War Two can be divided into four periods. Until 1964, emigration was illegal and spontaneous; (legal) labour migration abroad peaks between 1964 and 1973, which was a real emigration boom; between 1974 and 1979 migration stagnates; between 1980 and 1990 we can observe return migration, which was slowed down by the deep economic, social and political crisis in Yugoslavia.[32] The most important destination for post-war labour migrants from Slovenia was the Federal Republic of Germany, followed by Austria, Switzerland, and Sweden.[33] In the second Yugoslavia, emigration first affected the north-western parts of the country and only later the south-eastern regions. The Federal Republic of Germany was the most popular destination not only for migrants from Slovenia, but from the whole country (see Table 3).

Table 3: Number of Yugoslav workers living in Western Europe, 1971 and 1981

Country	1971	in %	1981	in %
FRG	411,503	69.7	324,324	58.6
Austria	82,957	14.1	97,618	17.6
France	36,982	6.3	32,903	5.9
Switzerland	21,201	3.6	59,624	10.8
Sweden	16,359	2.8	16,829	3.0
Benelux	7,358	1.2	7,913	1.4
Italy	n.a.	n.a.	5,956	1.1
Europe (total)	590,428	100	553,656	100

Source: Malačič, Labor Migration from Former Yugoslavia, 217.

How many emigrants came from Slovenia? In the ten years between 1963 and 1972, an estimate claims that the number of emigrants from Slovenia rose steadily from 29,400 per-

28 Drnovšek, Jugoslovansko-nemška sporazuma.
29 Pislar, Slovenci v železni Loreni; Drnovšek, Jugoslovansko-nemška sporazuma, 137–151.
30 Drnovšek, Slovene Immigrants in Belgium, 357–389.
31 Kolar-Dimitrijević, Djelovanje jugoslovenskih komunista, 5–12.
32 Malačič, Labor Migration from Former Yugoslavia, 207–220.
33 Lukšič-Hacin, Mass Emigration, 325–348.

sons in 1962 to 73,200 in 1972.[34] Official statistical data differ from this estimate: in 1971, 48,086 inhabitants of Slovenia were registered as temporarily working abroad. In 1981 the number of registered migrant workers who had left Slovenia for various western European countries was 41,826 (24,553 men and 17,273 women), while as many as 26,190 had returned.[35] In 1981, Slovenia had 1,891,864 inhabitants. It is estimated that in the 1960s and 1970s between 80,000 and 100,000 Slovenians were part of the Yugoslav labour migration to European countries. In 1991, 40,427 Slovenian workers were temporarily employed abroad, of which as many as 12,445 were working in the other republics of former Yugoslavia. Together with family members, 116,984 Slovenian citizens resided outside Slovenia in 1991.[36]

During this century or so of labour migration to European countries the professional structure of Slovenian migrants changed: until World War One most of the migrants were miners; in the interwar period most of them worked as seasonal agricultural workers, and in the 1960s and 1970s as factory workers. However, migrants were also employed in other sectors of the economy, such as the service sector and in white-collar jobs. The educational achievements of the emigrants were not as low as is usually thought. Let us take the example of 1971 and compare the educational structure of workers in Slovenia and Slovenian workers abroad. The most important difference concerns skilled workers: among those temporarily employed abroad, the percentage of skilled workers is very high (42.9 percent), much higher than in Slovenia.

Table 4: Comparison of education and qualification of workers in Slovenia and Slovenian workers abroad, 1971

	Slovenia	Abroad
	in % of all workers	
University	4.2	1.8
High school	3.0	0.9
Secondary school	13.1	5.9
Elementary school	7.9	6.2
Highly skilled	4.4	1.9
Skilled	27.5	42.9
Semi-skilled	12.6	11.1
Unskilled	27.3	29.3

Source: Družbeni razvoj SR Slovenije 1947–1972, 48.

Migration to the developed European countries in the nineteenth and twentieth centuries was primarily economically and to a lesser extent politically motivated. The reasons for labour migration were similar in all periods: a desire for better payment and/or better work-

34 Družbeni razvoj SR Slovenije, 47.

35 Statistični popis 1987, 74, 618.

36 Drnovšek, Izseljenec: življenjske zgodbe,13.

ing conditions on the one hand and the demand for (migrant) labour on the other. General political and economic conditions on both sides influenced the intensity of these factors. After 1918, migration became better organised, as bilateral agreements about workforce recruitment were signed. The recipient countries began resorting to a selective approach and introduced restrictive immigration policies in times of crises.

4. Slovenians attracted by overseas countries

The fatal attraction of America

The United States of America was the principal destination of Slovenian emigrants in the three decades before the breakout of World War One and in the immediate post-war years until 1924. These emigrants were part of the mass migration wave from Central and Eastern Europe and the Mediterranean to the Americas.[37] The reasons for emigration varied, from the desire for better payment to deserting from the Austrian military service or avoiding other duties to the state. Thus we are not surprised by this joke from 1902: "A: Did the Doctor suggest to your husband a trip to America? B: No, it was his lawyer." On no account should we neglect personal or family reasons for the decision to go to America. The decision was personal and wilful although taken under the influence of the then "American fever".

The image of America at this time was nevertheless not a mythical one because those leaving knew what to expect.[38] Among the Slovenians, a common saying went: "In America the work is hard, but the pay is good." The majority of migrants to America came from the countryside, with basic literacy skills; many were skilled, e.g. miners, foresters, cooks, etc. The leading Slovenian Catholic politician Anton Korošec (1872–1940) said at that time (1906):

> *In the heart of every man there is an instinct of prosperity and greater happiness. Our Slovenian emigrants, who are leaving for larger cities, either in Germany or in America, are not pale, draining, hungry and desperate, but are strong, blooming, young men who are full of life and strength; and there are the most vigorous women. On the sad road out of their homeland they are not accompanied so much by despair but rather by expectations and the awareness of their own forces and strength. Our people are particularly alert. They are aware of their spiritual and physical strength and that they could prosper with it. At home they see with sadness that all their intelligence and diligence are in vain, that it is impossible to develop one's powers as they should be developed and, therefore, they hurry abroad, where they intend to attain happiness and wealth more easily.*[39]

Slovenian demographers and historians pay a lot of attention to the number of emigrants in this period of mass emigration. Despite that, many questions remain unanswered. Between

37 Drnovšek, Mass Emigration and Slovenes, 19–36.
38 Klemenčič, Images of America, 199–221.
39 Lampe, III. Slovenski katoliški shod, 20; cf. Drnovšek, The Attitude of the Slovene Catholic Church, 169–184.

1876 and 1910, 3,547,630 persons emigrated from Austria-Hungary; 1,845,382 from the Austrian half.[40] In 1910, 1,353,148 persons who lived in the Austrian half of the monarchy stated Slovenian as their first language. In the crown lands of Kranjska (Carniola), Koroška (Carinthia), Štajerska (Styria) and Primorska s Trstom (Littoral with Trieste), 76.9 percent of the inhabitants are said to use Slovenian as their first language, 12.1 percent German and 11 percent Italian. The crown land of Carniola was the most homogenous Slovenian part of Austria: 490,978 (94.36 percent) persons declared Slovenian their first language, 27,915 (5.36 percent) chose German and 1,434 (0.28 percent) chose "other".[41] It was also the region of the strongest emigration of both Slovenians and Germans (from the Gottschee region). Incomplete records about emigration from the region for the years 1882–1913 mention 76,195 persons; among them as many as 17,566 (23.05 percent) were from the Kočevje (in German Gottschee) district, which was mainly inhabited by Germans (the so-called *Gottscheer Deutsche*) – in 1910, for example, 91.59 percent of the population of this area was German speaking.[42] On the basis of demographic analyses, various authors estimate that from the middle of the nineteenth century until World War One almost 310,000 people emigrated from Slovenia, which represented almost half of the natural population growth.[43]

After 1898, US immigration records were organised on the basis of the so-called "races and people" criterion, which grouped together Slovenians and Croats, although the American authorities knew the distinction between their territories very well.[44] Annual Reports from the Commissioner General of Immigration state that 458,580 Croatians and Slovenians entered through the gates of Ellis Island between 1889 and 1914.[45] The US census of 1910 showed 183,431 persons in the United States who chose Slovenian as their mother tongue, of which 123,631 were first generation immigrants and 59,800 second generation. For comparison: that same year 92,234 persons in the US stated Croatian as their mother tongue, of which 64,295 were born abroad.[46]

What were the fortunes of Slovene immigrants in the United States? These were as diverse and specific as the people, their characters and decisions. Among the early Slovenian immigrants to the USA were peddlers and packmen that came from Bela krajina (part of the Austrian province of Carniola, mainly populated by Slovenians). They emigrated in large numbers in the 1840s and above all the 1850s. They continued to be peddlers in the USA, and later became established as merchants in major towns, especially in Chicago. The first famous peddlers in America from the Slovenian side were Matija Premuta and Janez Gorše, who travelled to New York in 1839. Premuta's letter in German about the journey

40 Chmelar, Höhepunkte der österreichischen Auswanderung, 24.
41 Zwitter, Nacionalni problemi, 221.
42 Ferenc, Kočevska, 28.
43 Fischer, Migracije, 125; ibid, Prebivalstvo, 252.
44 Dillingham, Dictionary of Races.
45 Klemenčič, Slovenci v ameriški statistiki, 27.
46 Ibid., 28; Daniels, Coming to America, 217–218.

across the Atlantic and the first steps in America has been preserved and was published in the journal *Carniolia. Zeitschrift für Kunst, Wissenschaft und geselliges Leben* in Ljubljana in 1841. A letter from him in Slovenian from 1845 was published in the same year in the periodical *Novice* in Ljubljana. Both letters were addressed to his father. In the first letter, Premuta describes his journey from New York to Cincinnati in the state of Ohio, which he and his companion Gorše carried out on foot and with the aid of river transport. America enthralled them because of its freedom, free trade, equality among people, etc. By the mid-1840s, Matija Premuta had become a substantial merchant and hotel keeper in St. Louis. He lived there with his family, built a house in the very centre of the town, and bought a further 225 acres of land by the river Mississippi. Numerous other prominent merchants and businessmen came from the ranks of the Slovenian peddlers. They did not find it difficult to fit into American society, since they were already accustomed to working in foreign lands from peddling throughout Europe, and foreign languages presented them with no problems. Since many of them moved among German settlers in America, they could use German, which for the most part they mastered well.[47]

"In America, we are welcomed to the land of the free!" wrote Matija Šavs in a description of his journey across the Atlantic, which was published in the magazine *Dom in Svet* ("Home and World") in Ljubljana in 1897. He arrived in New York in September 1891 and the sight of the Statue of Liberty in front of the port gave birth to the above thought. For many Slovenians, America also meant a land of greater freedom, which was reflected in the greater equality of people, in the free choice of religion, in American individualism, etc. For the intellectually enlightened, especially, American freedom was a blessing, and some wrote about Europe and their homeland as a dusty, closed and boring environment. Even for a simple man, America was kindlier than home: the patriarchal, tight, interwoven environment, in which everyone knew everyone else and life ran along well established trajectories and under the powerful control of the local priest. Those who were enthusiastic about American freedom even included the priest Alojz Kastigar, who arrived in America in the same year as the above mentioned Šavs (1897) and who wrote in one of his letters to his friend Matija Hiti:

> *Everything is going well for me in America and I am content in all things. It is different here from Carniola, since in this land of golden freedom we are all of one thought and one heart, and there is no distinction among people. The different strata of people don't quarrel among themselves, and even members of different religions live together in tolerance!*[48]

However, critical ideas about America also appear in the migrants' letters, especially in times of economic or political crisis. The letters of 'simple' people also reveal terrible stories, for example those of women emigrants. At the time of mass emigration to America between 1898 and 1914, Slovenian women between the ages of fourteen and forty-five represented

[47] Kodrič, Slovene Emigration to the United States, 149–169; Drnovšek, Pot slovenskih izseljencev, 81–3.
[48] Quoted in Drnovšek, Usodna privlačnost Amerike, 257.

little more than eighteen percent of all emigrants of Slovenian and Croatian nationality. They worked as housekeepers, waitresses, servants, cooks and factory workers or as teachers in the Slovenian schools. Liza, born in 1871 in Ljubno in Štajerska (Styria), went to America with her sister around 1896, where their cousin already lived. She served as housekeeper's assistant and as cook in rich families in New York, in 1915 obtaining work with a German apothecary and during that time saving a significant amount of money. During these years, she had no complaints about her earnings. She saved and also sent money home. She was very modest in her own needs and lived poorly. She was beset by homesickness although she was content in the USA. However, she was also often without work, and could then not afford normal food, which damaged her health. Immediately prior to her death in February 1919, the doctor found that she was undernourished. So ended the life of a woman who had presented her American life in a bright light in letters to her mother, all the while her path was thorny and full of disappointments. She was one of many Slovenian immigrants to the new world for whom fate had a different plan than they wished for themselves.[49]

The United States limited immigration by introducing a restrictive quota system in 1921 and further restrictions in 1924. A smaller wave of migrants would follow after 1947, when many displaced persons from Slovenia found asylum in the United States and Canada – among them also wartime collaborators and opponents of the communist regime in the new Yugoslavia, as well as a number of intellectuals.

Aleksandrinke: Les Goriciennes / les Slaves / les Slovènes

From the time when the Suez Canal opened (1869), women from the Slovenian Karst, the Lower Vipava valley and the hinterland of Trieste were employed as cooks, nurses, wet nurses, servants and governesses in Egypt, mainly in Alexandria. As a rule, this was temporary labour migration. Many young girls left to earn money for their wedding or to pay for the trousseaux. In Slovenian they were usually called *Goričanke* (from the district of Goriška / Gorizia) or *Aleksandrinke* (from the name of Alexandria in Egypt where they lived), and from the side of the employers *Les Goriciennes, les Slaves* or *les Slovènes*.[50] A particularity of this wave of migration is the relatively small geographical area from where these women came, for which the vicinity of the port of Trieste undoubtedly played a large role. The study of emigration from the area of Gorizia during the years 1907–1913, published in 1914, showed that of a total of 1,793 people who went abroad, over 48 percent were women.[51] Slovenian women were also leaving for cities and larger towns such as Trieste, Gorizia, Milan, Rijeka and elsewhere. To give a typical example: from the district of Postojna women

49 Drnovšek, Kuharica Liza v New York, 43–6.
50 Makuc, Aleksandrinke.
51 Kalc et al, Poti in usode, 20.

went to work ('to serve') in Rijeka and Trieste during winter until spring when they returned home to help work in the field.[52]

Their number in Egypt varied, according to estimates. For example in 1897, around 7,700 women and only 300 men were said to live in Egypt; the Austrian statistical sources for 1900 gave a lower number and established 2,434 persons with official residence ('*Heimatrecht*') in Carniola and Primorska to be in Egypt.[53] The emigration of women from Primorje did not find unanimous approval. For example, in 1897 the unnamed correspondent of the *Soča* newspaper commented critically about female emigration to Egypt, which had become:

> *A bad habit that all people who wear a woman's skirt try to arrive in the land of the Nile, and they actually do; but it is not of such importance because they all at least after some years return.*[54]

The emigration of *Aleksandrinke* actually lasted until the outbreak of World War Two. Even nowadays, the memory of these women's emigration is firmly grounded among the people of Primorska in their perception of their life fortunes, of which we learn from modern literature[55], theatre[56] and film. Of all migration groups from the territory of present-day Slovenia, the *Aleksandrinke* have most strongly impressed themselves in the historical memory as a special group of emigrants who not only suffered abroad but were an important and reputable part of the families of wealthy businesspersons in Alexandria and Cairo.[57] This was the sole female *longue durée* migration pattern among Slovenians, which was only interrupted by crises in Egypt and the two world wars. The last *Aleksandrinke* returned from Egypt to Yugoslavia in the 1960s and 1970s but their memory lives on due to rich literary representations.

Others transoceanic destinations

Brazil and to a lesser extent Argentina were also important emigration destinations in the period before the First World War, particularly for migrants from the Primorska region. Brazil was the country of choice for the most impoverished of the population and it figures in the Slovenian memory as the country with the most tragic human fates. "Not to Brazil!" was the cry of the church and the state in the Austrian period. In the twentieth century, Argentina became a destination for many Slovenians.[58] Due to ethnic, civil and legal discrimination

[52] Valenčič, Izseljevanje Slovencev v druge dežele, 54.

[53] Drnovšek, Pot slovenskih izseljencev, 73; Valenčič, Izseljevanje Slovencev v tujino, 64.

[54] *Soča*, XXVII, no. 15, 1897 (local newspaper).

[55] Among recently published is a novel by Marjan Tomšič, Grenko morje (Bitter Sea). Ljubljana: Kmečki glas 2004.

[56] "Trieste-Alessandria Embarked – štorja od lešadrink", Slovensko narodno gledališče Nova Gorica (2005).

[57] Barbič, Miklavčič-Brezigar, Domestic Work Abroad.

[58] Brecelj, Nekaj podatkov o izseljevanju, 215–236.

and economic problems in the Primorska region, (which was part of Italy between 1918 and 1945), a veritable exodus of Slovenians to Argentina followed. When Italy restricted the emigration of its citizens in 1927, Venezia-Julia (Julijska krajina), where the majority of Slovenians lived in Italy, was exempted from this, primarily due to the large percentage of the Slovenian population. Slovenian emigrants had no problems obtaining emigration permits to leave Italy. In this period, we can talk about the intertwining of ideological, political, and economic pressure on the Slovenians in Italy, which led to such a massive emigration.[59]

After the Second World War we can observe overseas migration processes in two directions. Post-war refugees from Slovenia (12,617 persons) were dispersed all over the world after 1947. Peron's government in Argentina was willing to accept 10,000 Slovenian refugees regardless of sex and age and by 1951, 5,282 had arrived. At the same time, pre-war emigrants returned from Argentina, mostly people from the Primorska region. Upon Slovenian independence (1991), only a small part of the so-called political emigrants and their descendants returned, the majority of them from Argentina.

Australia was the last destination in the post-war Slovenian migration overseas. Three different groups of emigrants to Australia can be identified. The first consisted of post-war refugees or DPs (displaced persons), who left refugee camps in Italy and Austria via Germany. The second was made up of the mid-1950s wave of Italians and Slovenians from Trieste and its hinterlands. Many also crossed the border from Slovenia illegally to join this 'Triestine-Australian wave' in Trieste. And the third was created when the Yugoslav authorities began permitting emigration, with Australia being one of the destinations.

5. Borders, migrations and Slovenians on the other side

Slovenians, who remained outside Habsburg Austria, the first and the second Yugoslavia, and after 1991 the Republic of Slovenia, are called Slovenian (ethnic) minorities. When the Kingdom of Italy annexed regions inhabited by Slovenians in 1866, we encounter the migration of Slovenians from this area to the other side of the border. With the Treaty of Rapallo on November 12, 1920, a quarter of the Slovenian population (327,230) was finally annexed by Italy.[60] This situation changed after World War Two; however, a part of the Slovenian population still remained in Italy. After World War One, part of the Slovenian population remained in the Austrian region of Styria as a result of the Treaty of Saint Germain from September 10, 1919; a small Slovenian minority came to live in Hungary (the so-called Raba Slovenians) as a result of the Treaty of Trianon from June 4, 1920; and the Carinthian plebiscite of October 10, 1920, resulted in a number of Slovenians remaining in Austria (the so-called Carinthian Slovenians). After World War Two, the border between Yugoslavia and Italy was finalised with the London Memorandum on October 5, 1954,

59 Kalc et al, Poti in usode.

60 Wohinz-Kresal, Troha, Slovensko-italijanski odnosi, 34.

which made part of the Slovenian population an ethnic minority in Italy. Finally, the 2006 "Law on the Relations between the Republic of Slovenia and Slovenians Abroad" (*Zakon o odnosih Republike Slovenije s Slovenci zunaj njenih meja*)[61] granted the status of Slovenian (ethnic) minority to part of the Slovenian population living in Croatia.

The migration of Slovenians from Italy, Austria and Hungary is undoubtedly a special phenomenon, for they were required to conform to the legislation of their country of residence, and that also included migration legislation. Their legal and social status in their countries of destination was, thus, determined by the bilateral agreements between their country of residence and the country of immigration. As Italian, Austrian or Hungarian citizens, they were treated in the same way as other emigrants from these countries. If we focus on Italy, for example: between the two wars, Slovenians in Italy were part of the general Italian migration waves, which were directed primarily towards more developed European countries (France, Belgium, and Switzerland). At the same time, the pressure of Fascism and the economic situation forced them to emigrate to Argentina and Yugoslavia. This emigration can be called a real exodus of Slovenians, and Croats (from Istria) as well. It is estimated that around 70,000 persons emigrated from Italy to Yugoslavia, around 30,000 to South America (of which 20,000 to Argentina) and around 5,000 to other European countries. Among them an estimated 53,000 persons were Slovenians who lived in Venezia-Julia.[62] The Italian state even supported the emigration of people who were of Slovenian or Croatian origin, because it facilitated the Italianisation of the annexed territories with predominantly Slavic populations.

The end of the Second World War caused a new exodus, this time of mostly Italian inhabitants of Istria: in 1947, and during the time preceding and following the London Memorandum (1954). This emigration wave also included Slovenians and Croats; for example: from the relatively small Koper district, 10,156 persons emigrated legally. 7,926 of them were Italians, 2,992 Slovenians (about a third of whom were Italian-speaking) and 138 Croats.[63] These migrations were both forced and voluntary; the motives for emigration were extremely varied, from political pressure to economic reasons.

In the mid-1950s emigration from Trieste to Australia began. It was typical for the urban population, who had professional skills, as Australia was in need of a skilled workforce. Slovenians and Italians were both leaving. Official figures show that the emigration wave included about 19,000 persons, of which as many as 15,000 went to Australia; about one third of them were Slovenians.[64] However, this was also the time when many individuals fled across the Yugoslav border to Austria and Italy, mainly for economic reasons. As asylum seekers, they were placed in refugee camps and directed to different countries as part of the workforce. Thus state and ideological borders had a significant impact on the migration

61 Published in Slovenian in *Uradni list RS*, no. 43, 2006, 4605 (*Official Gazette RS*).
62 Pirjevec, Slovenci v Italiji, 265.
63 Gombač, Jure, Esuli ali optanti?, 126.
64 Kalc et al, Poti in usode, 121.

movements of Slovenians, and also other inhabitants of the territories on either side of the border.

6. Slovenian political migrants after 1945

The post-1945 Slovenian political emigration was part of the Yugoslav emigration.[65] Despite the different political and social developments in Yugoslavia compared to other states on the eastern side of the iron curtain and despite, from the 1960s, Yugoslavia's greater openness to the world, the policy of the Communist Party and the state were nevertheless firmly grounded in communist ideology. The Yugoslav political system rejected the world of capitalism and was hostile towards people of different opinion, including emigrants. The citizens, for example, were not allowed to have contact with political emigrants. Such contacts were liable to legal punishment. This negative standpoint towards political emigration was reflected by the terminology used as well. Until the disintegration of Yugoslavia, Slovenian political emigration was labelled in official documents and various publications as the "White Guard" (a right-wing political movement in Slovenia during World War Two), "fascist" or, in the mildest form, "hostile emigration". All the time the state accused the emigrants of "logically promoting anti-communist and contra-revolutionary activity, clericalism, nationalism and separatism". The state knew about the ideological and programme differentiations within the emigrants, yet on the principal level it considered them as a whole. Continual pressure from the post-war refugees (among whom were also people who had collaborated with the enemy during World War Two) to create a Slovenian political emigration, exacerbated the hatred felt among Slovenians towards the political emigrants, even though many of the politically active emigrants had been under-aged when leaving their country or were even born abroad. Their cardinal 'fault' was the rejection of communism as the leading ideological-political orientation. The Yugoslav state also classified as post-war Yugoslav political emigrants all individuals who found themselves outside the borders of Yugoslavia at the time of its re-establishment and who did not return because of their refusal of the communist system and the new state.

An important turning point in official relations towards political emigration was the amnesty law of 1962. Before that time the official policy had not even acknowledged emigration for economic reasons, which to the ruling communists was a phenomenon only possible in the capitalist world. All who left the country and did not return were automatically defined as political emigrants. However, at the beginning of the 1960s Yugoslavia began a more open policy towards the rest of the world. This was also the time of the beginnings of the non-aligned movement, in which Yugoslavia played one of the leading roles. As a con-

65 Archival material about the Slovenian political emigration is stored in the Archive of the Republic of Slovenia (AS), Department for Dislocated Archival Matter I (Section I.), fund of the Central Committee of The League of Communists of Slovenia, No. 1589.

Table 5: Quantitative differentiation of Slovenians outside Yugoslavia in 1968

Slovenians* living abroad	
Economic emigrants	388,500
Minority members	180,000
Political emigrants	20,261
Total	**588,761**

* The author of the study took the Slovenian language or the mother tongue as defining criteria. *Source:* Arhiv Republike Slovenije (The Archive of the Republic of Slovenia) (AS), Section I, fund 1589, part 507.

Table 6: Directions of political emigration from Slovenia (as of 1968)

State	**Number of emigrants**
Austria	3,519
Belgium	287
France	1,015
Italy	1,221
FR Germany	3,972
Sweden	270
Great Britain	408
European countries, total	9,692 (10,692*)
Argentina	1,979
Australia	1,464
Canada	2,927
USA	1,931
Overseas, total	8,301
Other countries	2,268
Total	**20,261**

* The sub-total for European countries was recalculated by the author of this article because the total given in the study is obviously miscalculated by 1,000. *Source:* see Table 5.

sequence the state had to find a new policy towards all the people who had left Yugoslavia after 1941. In July 1961, the vice-president of the Federal Executive Council, and Minister of Interior, Aleksander Ranković (1909–1983), announced the new policy towards "hostile emigrants". He mentioned that an estimated 200,000 people had left the territory of Yugoslavia during and after World War Two. Many of them wanted to regulate their civic relations with the state and to obtain Yugoslavian citizenship. Ranković attributed that fact to the great reputation of Yugoslavia in the world and to its domestic as well as economic successes. The 1962 amnesty enabled the civic status of many migrants to be regulated but excluded all "who stained themselves with heavy war crimes or were actively involved in hostile activities abroad against the FNRJ [Federal People's Republic of Yugoslavia]", as pointed out by Ranković in a speech published in 1962 in *Slovenski izseljenski koledar* ("Slovenian Emigrant Almanac").[66]

A point in case is an unpublished policy analysis on Slovenian political emigration from 1968.[67] The analysis was prepared by the Secretariat of Internal Affairs of the Republic of Slovenia in Ljubljana. The object of the analysis was to "highlight the hostile activity of Slovenian emigration". The methods used were the identification and evaluation of past activities and attitudes of individual emigrants, based on the records held on emigrants and other "unquestionable documentation" (see Tables 5 and 6).

How much was the Slovenian public informed about the life and activities of the Slovenian emigrants? It knew more about the pre-war and the new post-war economic emigration in the 1960s and 1970s and less or next to nothing about all the rest, particularly the political emigrants. Although the Yugoslav and Slovenian constitutions from 1974 granted all "members of the community the right to be informed about events at home and abroad that are significant for their life and work, and on issues important for the community"[68], there was a considerate discrepancy between this constitutional right of being informed and its practical realisation.[69]

An interesting question in this respect is the way in which publications printed abroad were brought to and distributed in Yugoslavia, especially regarding political emigration prints. Legislation was precise concerning this issue.[70] It was forbidden to bring into the country and to distribute printed matter that undermined the foundations of the political system and the security of the state, offended the reputation and good name of the nations and nationalities of Yugoslavia and its leadership, brought untruthful and stirring news that threatened order and peace and upset the public, etc. The state borders were closed to emigrant publications containing different views from the tolerated ones, and access to those materials was hindered. The republic Law on Public Information[71] experienced some modifications concerning the definition of bringing into the country and spreading "untruthful and annoying" news, while the definition in the Federal Law on this subject remained unchanged until the fall of Yugoslavia. The regime for Slovenian print in the neighbouring states was rigorous in the sense that all magazines printed in Slovenian had to wait for permission from the Federal Secretariat for Internal Affairs before they could

66 Ranković, Domovina je odprla vrata, 46–7.

67 AS, Section I, fund 1589, part 507: Commission for ideological political problems of the Central Committee of the League of Slovenian Communists / Slovenian political emigration, Secretariat of Internal Affairs of the Republic of Slovenia, 10 January 1968.

68 Ustava SFRJ, člen 168, Ustava SRS, člen 290/4–6, *Uradni list SFRJ,* no. 4, 1974.

69 Kristan, Ustavni okviri javne besede, 60.

70 Zakon o vnašanju in razširjanju tujih sredstev množičnega komuniciranja in o tuji informacijski dejavnosti v Jugoslaviji, *Uradni list SFRJ,* no. 39, 1974, and no. 74, 1987, particularly article no. 13.

71 Zakon o javnem obveščanju (Law on Public Information), *Official Gazette of the Socialist Republic of Slovenia,* no. 2, 1986.

be imported.[72] More obstacles preventing access to emigrant print in Yugoslavia could be enumerated. When the political emigrants increased their propaganda activities, the press was their most frequently used means. It was estimated that the Yugoslav political emigrants issued approximately two hundred periodicals with an annual circulation of about two million copies in the mid-1980s. According to these estimates, an average of 100,000 copies reached Yugoslavia every year.[73]

More attention from political structures and the state was devoted to informing economic emigrants about the achievements of Yugoslavia and Slovenia than to informing the domestic public. In 1950 the Society of Journalists of Slovenia began publishing *Glas domovine* ("Voice of the Homeland"), which was intended for Slovenian emigrants. The Slovenian Emigrant Society (*Slovenska izseljenska matica*) was founded in 1951 for establishing and maintaining contacts to emigrants sympathetic to the new Yugoslavia. This society started to publish the *Slovenski izseljenski koledar* ("Slovenian Emigrant Almanac") in 1953 and a year later the monthly magazine *Rodna gruda* ("Native Soil"), and in 1987 the quarterly *Slovenija*. In 1978 the Slovenian newspapers started to publish the joint journal *Naš delavec* ("Our Worker") intended exclusively to inform Slovenian workers on temporary work abroad. After a two-year break the magazine was replaced by *Naša Slovenija* ("Our Slovenia") in 1989.

7. The fate of the Gottscheer Germans

The fate of this German linguistic island in the south-eastern part of present-day Slovenia is tragic: its population co-existed with the Slovenian inhabitants for centuries, but today have disappeared from this territory almost completely. Only a handful of people declare themselves *Gottscher Deutsche*, i.e. Germans in the Kočevsko region today.

Their roots go back to the mediaeval past, when Otto V (d. 1343) and Otto VI (d. 1374) from the House of Ortenburg moved some of their subjects from eastern Tyrol and western Carinthia to the Kočevsko (Gottscher) region, which was part of Carniola (the south-eastern part of present-day Slovenia) in the first half of the fourteenth century. It was a premeditated agrarian colonisation. The settlers and their descendants became known as the *Gottscheers* or the Gottscheer Germans, who spoke their own local German dialect, followed their own traditions and more or less lived in their own way. They were known as peddlers who sold tropical fruits, mostly in German-speaking countries. Already in 1492 the Habsburg emperor Friedrich III (1415–1493) granted them the right to engage in the travelling trade – which they in fact continued to practise until World War Two.

Their migration history is divided into four broad processes: first, the time of their arrival and settlement in the fourteenth century; second, their participation in the mass emigra-

72 Deisinger, Prepoved razširjanja, 117.
73 Dolanc, Vejnović, Snage, sredstva i metodi, 67.

tion to the USA at the turn of the twentieth century; third, their removal from the Italian to the German occupation zones in 1941 and 1942; finally, their expulsion after 1945 by the new Yugoslav government. They have been dispersed all over the world: Austria, Germany, Switzerland, the United States, Canada, Australia and elsewhere. Except for emigration to the United States during the time of the mass emigration, all other forms of migration for the Gottscher Germans were thus forced migrations.[74]

8. Conclusions

This brief outline of the continuous migrating movements in Slovenia focused on different processes and events, which shaped the migration history of these territories in the nineteenth and twentieth centuries. A particular emphasis was placed on the question to which states the territory of present-day Slovenia belonged in the past, because political order is essential for understanding the changes of migration processes: each new state brought a new social and political system which in turn influenced migration. Slovenian historiography lacks detailed research on migration, which would enable us to move from the particular to the general. This is also the result of the exclusion of migration history from the general history of both Slovenia and the Slovenians, although some progress has been made recently. Dispersed, incomplete and unorganised archive materials present an additional difficulty. From the historian's point of view, a return to the facts is very often essential. Comparison is a rare component in Slovenian research, and even rarer are joint projects, which would cover wider areas and longer periods. There are very few studies that would cover all three phases of the migration process, i.e. emigration, settlement, and return migration. Here, the Slovenian-German research project "Slovenians in Germany 1880–1973" ought to be mentioned, which researches the three above-mentioned stages with equal intensity and places special emphasis on contemporary theoretical and methodological approaches.

The Institute for Slovenian Emigration Studies at the Scientific Research Centre of the Slovenian Academy of Sciences and Arts in Ljubljana veers towards inter-disciplinary research; it emphasises social and cultural history and the history of particular migrant groups (e. g. female migrants), but it is more concerned with the present than the past. Since 1990, the Institute publishes its own journal *Dve domovini/Two Homelands*, which mirrors the shifts in the research of Slovenian emigration. Although few in number in terms of both the population and researchers, we aim to add our piece to the mosaic of the European and world migrations.

[74] Ferenc, Kočevska; Drnovšek, Izseljevanje Kočevarjev.

Edvin Pezo

'Re-Conquering' Space. Yugoslav Migration Policies and the Emigration of Non-Slavic Muslims to Turkey (1918–1941)

Introductory remarks

It was perhaps characteristic of the idea of population exchange in the interwar period that the start of the final negotiations concerning the Convention signed in 1938 between Yugoslavia and Turkey about the resettlement of 200,000 "Turks" from Yugoslavia to the Republic of Turkey occurred in the presence of a Romanian representative and a Greek observer. Romania (Bucharest Convention of 1936) and Greece (Lausanne Convention of 1923) had concluded their own agreements with Turkey regarding the exchange of populations. These three Balkan countries were hoping to solve their 'minority problems' with such conventions. During the Balkan Pact council meeting in Ankara from 25 to 27 February 1938, the Turkish Minister of Foreign Affairs, Tevfik Rüştü Aras, even proposed the appointment of a commission for discussing the resettlement of Turks from the Balkans.[1] These talks began in Istanbul on 9 June and ended after eight rounds of negotiations on 11 July 1938 with the adoption of the "Convention réglementant l'émigration de la population turque de la région de la Serbie du Sud en Yougoslavie" signed by the Republic of Turkey and the Kingdom of Yugoslavia.[2]

Even at that time, the controversial idea of population exchange met with wide acceptance, not only among the political elites of the 'nationalizing' Balkan states but also outside Southeastern Europe. Various treaties were aimed at helping those 'un-mixing' regions where a high share of their population were considered by the majority population or government as not able to assimilate and who were seen as a 'security problem' to sensitive border regions. The above-mentioned Convention between Turkey and Yugoslavia, which was never implemented, was the final act of the Yugoslav emigration policy towards its

1 Archive of Yugoslavia, Belgrade (*Arhiv Jugoslavije*, further abbreviated as AJ), Poslanstvo Kraljevine Jugoslavije u Turskoj – Carigrad, Ankara (370), fasc. 9, jedinica br. 42, list br. 894–897 [AJ 370/9/42, 894–897]: Iseljavanje muslimanskog stanovništva iz Južne Srbije (opšti referat), Beograd 06.04.1939.

2 AJ 370/9/42, 898–909; PROCES-VERBAUX. Des réunions de la Commission pour l'Emigration, Istamboul, 09.06.1938–11.07.1938. For a summary of these transcripts see Avdić, A., Jugoslovensko-turski pregovori.

non-Slavic Muslim citizens in the southern parts of the country. This policy was inherently connected to the nation-building and state-building processes in Yugoslavia.

Nation-building and migration policies

These measures were aimed at the political and economic integration of those parts of the former Ottoman Empire that were acquired by Serbia and Montenegro in the Balkan Wars of 1912 and 1913 and were populated by large and compact ethnic minorities. After the creation of the Kingdom of Serbs, Croats and Slovenes in 1918, Yugoslav politicians envisioned building a state for and mainly of South Slavs – "the state of and for a particular nation".[3] The policies for integrating the nation were implemented by various strategies under the primacy of a vague concept of Yugoslavism, which ranged from the idea of a South-Slavic "cultural nation" (*Kulturnation*) to one of a politically defined "nation-state" (*Staatsnation*).[4] Since Southern Serbia[5] was part of the Serbian sphere of political influence, its 'nationalisation' and incorporation into the power structures of the state were mainly linked to the Serbian national question, respectively to Serbian nationalism, which meant to consolidate the region under Serbian auspices. In peace time, the government refrained from 'ethnic cleansing' as a means to achieve a homogenous nation-state,[6] but resorted to other means which were closely linked to the capabilities of the modern state and its institutions. One of the instruments the government used to achieve its national goals and security interests was a deliberate migration policy aimed at changing the ethnic composition of the population in the southern areas of the countries in favour of the Slavic-speaking population. This was especially the case in the regions of present-day Kosovo and Macedonia with their high percentages of Albanian and Turkish speaking people. Like other Balkan countries, Yugoslavia practised a two-fold migration policy: one of an open door for presumed co-nationals from neighbouring countries, and a liberal emigration regime for members of ethnic minorities. This implied as a final consequence that the latter could be subjected to forced emigration by means of 'political pressure'.

This article does not aim to recall the Serbian-Albanian conflict history in interwar Yugoslavia, which in some accounts is presented in very static terms. Instead of repeating

3 Brubaker, Nationalism Reframed, 63.

4 Jakir, Dalmatien zwischen den Weltkriegen, 57–8.

5 Southern Serbia was the contemporary expression, though with partly different associations, for the former territories of the Ottoman Empire which had been occupied by Serbia and Montenegro in the Balkan Wars: the Sandžak of Novi Pazar (today the border region between Serbia and Montenegro), Kosovo and the so-called Vardar-Macedonia (the territory of the present day Republic of Macedonia).

6 Examples of 'ethnic cleansing' by Serbia include the expulsion of Muslims (mainly Albanians) from the Sandjak of Niš in the aftermath of the Serbian-Ottoman War of 1876–77 (Müller, Das "lange 20. Jahrhundert", 38 passim) and forced expulsions during the Balkan Wars 1912–1913 (Boeckh, Von den Balkankriegen).

these well-known narratives which concentrate on the history of conflict in Kosovo, it is the purpose of this paper to identify and analyse the instruments and strategies of Yugoslavia's migration policy towards its non-Slavic minorities in the southern parts of the country during peace time. For this purpose, the driving forces of migration policy have to be examined against the backdrop of the state-building and nation-building effort in Yugoslavia as well as the different circumstances under which the various instruments of the migration policy were designed. The application, radicalisation, and also failure of these measures will be analysed, taking into consideration also Turkish immigration policies. Such an analysis of policy will help to identify the different dimensions and motives of the emigration movement of Muslims to Turkey, which affected the attitude of the non-Slavic Muslim population to the state.

In geographic terms, my research concerns Southern Serbia, which was an administrative unit after these former parts of the Ottoman Empire had been acquired by Serbia and Montenegro in the Balkan Wars. The region encompasses the Sandžak of Novi Pazar, Kosovo and Vardar-Macedonia.[7] This area was governed by special legislation, related to agrarian and colonisation policies as well as to the possibility of emigrating to Turkey in accordance with Article 55 of the Citizenship Law, 1928. Most emigrants who left for Turkey came from this area. A smaller part of the Muslim[8] emigrants went to Albania, but the political instability of Albania, the sentiments towards the former Ottoman Empire, respectively to Turkey, as the cultural and political centre of the Balkan Muslims, and family relations to Turkey made the latter the most important destination country.

With regard to Southern Serbia we can define a set of migration policies by the Yugoslav Regime including: legal regulations on emigration and repatriation, and international treaties (e.g. Treaty of Neuilly, 1919; internal instructions regarding the return migration of Muslims from Turkey; Emigration Law, 1922; official and unofficial regulations concerning the distribution of passports; Citizenship Law, 1928); the bilateral convention between Yugoslavia and Turkey regarding the resettlement of "Turks"; repressive political measures by the police or other state organs stimulating the emigration of Muslims; agricultural and colonisation policies.

The analysis of these polices must also take into account the gradual radicalisation of attitudes towards the 'integration' of Muslims in the southern parts of Yugoslavia in the interwar period. At the time, they were faced with the choice between assimilation and dissimilation. Initially after World War One, the integration of minority groups in Southern Serbia, who were deprived of all the minority rights that Yugoslavia had agreed upon in

7 Jovanović, Jugoslovenska država, 9.

8 The term "Muslim" subsumes Muslims from all ethnic groups who emigrated from interwar Yugoslavia to Turkey or to Albania, such as Albanians, Slavic Muslims from Bosnia and the Sandžak of Novi Pazar, Gorani, Turks, Pomaks, Torbeši and Muslim Roma. Unfortunately, the Yugoslav documents concerning this question are very imprecise and only use the terms Muslims (for those of Slavic origin as well as for all ethnic groups migrating to Turkey), Albanians or Turks, though it should be noted that the latter was also used (pejoratively) for all Muslims.

Saint-Germain-en-Laye (1919), was understood as assimilation and cultural homogenisation. During the 1920s the prevailing intention of the government was to assimilate the non-Slavs although their emigration was also approved and welcomed. Initial steps towards economic dissimilation were already intended at this time.[9] However, after assimilation apparently failed, the government of Milan Stojadinović (1935–1939) tried to expel a large number of non-Slavic Muslims from the country in order to reduce their demographic strength. The main target of this policy was the Albanians in Kosovo, who could also not count on support from their 'kin national state', Albania, which was politically unstable and not powerful enough to intervene in their favour. In contrast (to the Albanian and Turkish population), the emigration of Slavic Muslims, who both the Serbian as well as the Croatian side considered to be an integral part of their nation, was officially unwanted, albeit tolerated in reality.

My hypothesis is that the Yugoslav, respectively Serbian, emigration policy towards the Muslims in the southern parts of the country symbolised not only endeavours to 're-conquer' the space of Southern Serbia in the narrow sense of national and security concerns, but also illustrates the gradual radicalisation of a dissimilation strategy by the state. This was also related to the changing cycles of the various concepts of Yugoslavism and their enforcement, as well as to the bilateral relationship to Albania and Italy, which affected the Albanians in Yugoslavia insofar as they stood under suspicion of being 'instruments' of Albanian irredentism, which in turn was supported by the expansionist Italian foreign policy in the Balkans. In the second half of the 1930s, when the overall state concept of Yugoslavism had obviously failed, the policy changed radically and it was now the primary intention, carried out by state organs, to push non-Slavs, especially Albanians, out of the country. Assimilation was not a desirable aim anymore and pressure generated by the state prevailed in the area of emigration policy.

However, the emigration of Muslims was not only a result of state policies. There was also labour and seasonal migration, which could lead to permanent settlement in Turkey. Generally, people emigrated to places where they expected a better life. Hence it can be argued with Anthony Richmond that "the distinction between 'free' and 'forced' or 'voluntary' and 'involuntary' is a misleading one. All human behaviour is constrained".[10] Nevertheless, the constraints generated by the different means of migration policy and especially its gradual radicalisation were crucial for the emigration process of Muslims from Yugoslavia.

[9] Müller, Staatsbürger auf Widerruf, 435.
[10] Richmond, Sociological Theories, 17.

Waves of emigration to Turkey and their numbers

It is difficult to establish even approximate numbers for emigration from Yugoslavia to Turkey because the available Yugoslav and Turkish statistical materials are often incomplete or incorrect. Establishing an ethnic breakdown is even more difficult because the nationality of emigrants was not noted. The return migration of Muslims was also often not registered. The number of emigrants, nevertheless, will be discussed in detail, firstly because they are still unclear and disputed, and secondly because the estimates can at least give an idea about the highs and lows of emigration to Turkey.

Table 1: Population of Southern Serbia according to religion, 1921 and 1931

	Total	**Orthodox**	**Muslim**	**Other**
1921*	1,476,747	739,278	711,481	25,988
In percent	100 %	50.06 %	48.8 %	1.76 %
1931**	1,782,511	958,223	783,700	40,588
In percent	100 %	53.76 %	43.97 %	2.27 %
Change 1921–1931	305,764	218,945	72,219	14,600
In percent	20.71 %	29.62 %	10.15 %	56.18 %

* The 1921 figures refer to the administrative districts (*srezovi*) of Berane, Bijelo Polje, Bitolj, Bregalnica, Zvečane, Kosovo, Kumanovo, Metohija, Ohrid, Plevlje, Prizren, Prijepolje, Raška, Skoplje, Tetovo and Tikveš.
** The 1931 figures include the Vardar banovina without the districts of Bosiljgrad, Jablanica, Leskovac, Masurica, Pčinja, Poljanica, Vlasotinci, but with the districts of Lab and Vučitrn of the Morava banovina and the districts of Berane, Bijelo Polje, Deževa, Drenica, Đakovica, Istok, Kosovska Mitrovica, Mileševo, Nova Varoš, Peć, Plevlje, Podrima, Priboj, Sjenica, and Štavica of the Zeta banovina.
Source: Definitivni rezultati popisa; Gliederung der Bevölkerung.

It was difficult to obtain exact numbers for the religious and ethnic composition of Southern Serbia. Nevertheless, the census dates from 1921 and 1931 suggest a decrease in the share of the Muslim population from 48 to 44 percent (Table 1). The increase in the Orthodox population and "others" was primarily due to their being settled in Southern Serbia as part of the government's colonisation policy. However, these numbers have to be taken with a grain of salt. In 1921, for example, many Albanian residents, who had fled their homes as a consequence of Belgrade's struggle against the Albanian *Kaçak* guerrilla operating in Southern Serbia, were still in Albania. They probably numbered up to several tens of thousands. Furthermore, politically motivated irregularities in the census can be assumed.[11] The (probably small) number of return migrants who had emigrated between 1912 and 1921, and had come home after 1921, was also left out of the count; the assessment of the

[11] Clewing, Mythen und Fakten, 50.

ethnic affiliation of Muslims in Southern Serbia is equally problematic (Table 2). The Albanian population apparently increased by eleven percent between 1921 and 1931, which was well below the Orthodox population increase in the region. The Turkish population even decreased by twelve percent. Both the relatively small increase in the number of the Albanian and the decrease in the Turkish population resulted from emigration to Turkey and, to a lesser extent, Albania. The strong increase in Muslim Slavs and Muslim Roma (by thirty percent) has probably to be seen in the context of fluid ethnic identities and also mimicry vis-à-vis a 'nationalising' state which defined itself as Slavic, thus applying pressure to non-Slavs.

Table 2: Ethnic division of the Muslim inhabitants of Southern Serbia, 1921 and 1931

	Total	**Muslim Albanians**	**Muslim Turks**	**Slavs and Roma of Muslim Faith**
1921	711,481	416,977*	148,019	146,485
In percent	100 %	58.61 %	20.80 %	20.59 %
1931	783,700	463,131	130,008	190,561
In percent	100 %	59.09 %	16.59 %	24.32 %
Change 1921–1931	72,219	46,154	- 18,011	44,076
In percent	10.15 %	11.07 %	- 12.17 %	30.09 %

* The 1921 figure contains Albanians of both Muslim and Christian faith. However, the number of Christian Albanians was very small (approx. two percent of the Albanians in the Vardar banovina were Christians). *Source:* as Table 1.

Regarding the quantitative dimensions of emigration, the numbers published in the Statistical Yearbooks of Yugoslavia should only be taken with reservation because they also contain a considerable number of seasonal migrants.[12] However, they reveal a contrasting trend of emigration to Turkey and Albania compared with emigration to other European and overseas countries. At the same time that emigration to the West decreased and many migrants actually came back to Yugoslavia, emigration to Turkey and Albania increased significantly (Table 3 and Figure 1). We can assume that the overwhelming majority of these people were Muslims from Southern Serbia, who only participated in the emigration to overseas or Western Europe in negligible numbers (see Table 4). The notable increase of emigration to Turkey and Albania between 1932 and 1935 was related to the economic depression as well as to new regulations concerning the agrarian and colonisation policies that were introduced in 1931 with amendments in 1933, and which served as 'push-factors' for the Muslim population of Southern Serbia.

12 See the annual emigration reports of the Emigration Commissariat (Iseljenički komisarijat) in Zagreb. AJ 14 [Ministarstvo unutrašnjih poslova]/36/112,262–268; Naša migraciona statistika za godinu 1928. Godišnji izvještaj.

Table 3: Emigration from Yugoslavia to European countries, 1928–1937

	Total	**Turkey**	**In %**	**Albania**	**In %**	**Other countries**	**In %**
1928	12,538	1,369	10.92	-	-	11,169	89.08
1929	19,425	618	3.18	-	-	18,807	96.82
1930	25,409	1,911	7.52	594	2.34	22,904	90.14
1931	10,560	877	8.30	210	1.99	9,473	89.71
1932	6,642	1,433	21.57	289	4.35	4,920	74.07
1933	7,508	1,931	25.72	880	11.72	4,697	62.56
1934	11,004	4,123	37.47	653	5.93	6,228	56.60
1935	10,120	3,305	32.66	363	3.59	6,452	63.75
1936	8,625	969	11.23	573	6.64	7,083	82.12
1937	14,287	1,106	7.74	340	2.38	12,841	89.88
Total	**126,118**	**17,642**	**13.99**	**3,902**	**3.09**	**104,574**	**82.92**

Source: Statistički godišnjak 1938–1939, 154.

Table 4: Migrant destinations from the southern parts of Yugoslavia, 1934

Banovina	**Total**	**Europe**	**Overseas**	**Turkey**	**In %**	**Albania**	**In %**	**Other coun-tries***	**In %**
Morava	76	65	11	0	0	2	2.63	74	97.37
Vardar	5,171	5,001	170	3,639	70.37	75	1.45	1,457	28.18
Zeta	1,017	916	101	348	34.22	561	55.16	108	10.62
From the rest of the country	7,647	5,022	2,625	136	1.78	15	0.20	7,496	98.03
Total	13,911	11,004	2,907	4,123	29.64	653	4.69	9,135	65.67

* Mainly to Bulgaria, Greece and Romania. *Source:* Statistički godišnjak 1934–1935, 66.

The data obtained from the Statistical Yearbooks, available for Turkey from 1928, are insufficient for establishing realistic numbers of Muslim emigrants to Turkey. Firstly, most Muslim emigrants apparently left Yugoslavia for Turkey and Albania between 1923 and 1925, i.e. before these countries were included in the official data on emigration. During the immediate years after World War One and the period of the Greek-Turkish War of 1920–1922, little emigration to Turkey can be assumed.[13] In 1923, however, emigration

13 The lack of any significant migration to Turkey until 1923 is indicated also by a letter from the political department of the Foreign Ministry to the legation in Istanbul, which says that in the second half of 1922 in the district of Kumanovo five passports were issued for migrants to Turkey. AJ 370/9/42, 496; Pov.Br. 1.303, Beograd 14.02.1923. See for the difficult post-war situation in Turkey Zürcher, Turkey. A Modern History, 138–172.

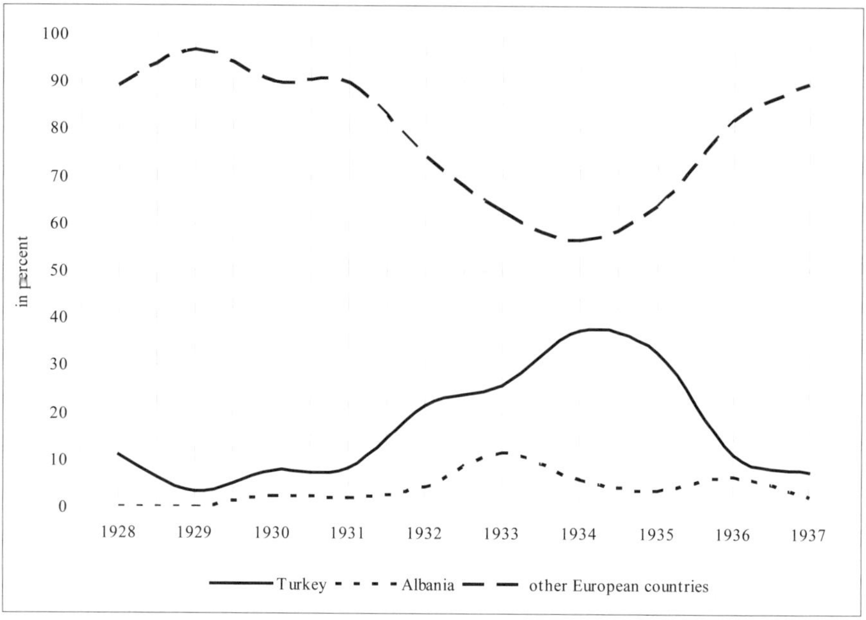

Figure 1: Share of emigration from Yugoslavia to Albania, Turkey and other European countries, 1928–1937.

from Yugoslavia to Turkey increased noticeably, which even provoked the Turkish government to implement restrictions on the immigration of Muslims from Yugoslavia because Turkey was fully occupied organising the population exchange with Greece and settling approximately four hundred thousand 'Turks' from Greece in Turkey.[14] The emigration flow, thus, grew weaker in 1924, but resumed in 1925. Bogumil Hrabak mentioned that one thousand families emigrated during two and a half months in 1925.[15] Muhamet Pirraku quotes a report from the former Chairman of the district of Zvečan, saying that 32,000 people emigrated to Turkey in 1925 and 1926.[16] This emigration wave forced the Turkish government to react, and in 1925 they ordered a stop on immigration from Yugoslavia in view of this new wave of emigrants who had moved to Turkey. The 1925 annual report of the British legation to Yugoslavia described these events:

> *During the first six months of 1925 the Moslem emigration to Anatolia was very considerable, and with the encouragement of the Serbs, except in the Bregalnica district, some 4,000 to 5,000 emi-*

[14] [No Name] 1923: Muhadžirima na znanje!, *Hak*, 21 November 1923, 1.

[15] Hrabak, Džemijet, 274.

[16] Pirraku, Kulturno-prosvetni pokret, 363, Footnote 46.

grants left each month. This continued till the Angora Government put an embargo on emigrants from Southern Serbia.[17]

After this decree, and also due to the Turkish Settlement Law of May 1926 (see below), it became more difficult, but not impossible, to immigrate into Turkey.

It is not easy to assess the numbers of emigrants involved because of the non-availability or unreliability of official data. Zoran Janjetović, in his book on national minorities in interwar Yugoslavia, presents various estimates from the Serbian and Albanian literature about the number of Muslim emigrants: they range from a few tens of thousands to 260,000 Albanian emigrants.[18] Noel Malcolm estimated that from 1918 to 1941 between 90,000 and 150,000 Albanians and Muslims left Kosovo,[19] whereas Michel Roux arrives at an estimate maximum of 77,000 emigrants from Kosovo during the interwar period, calculated on the basis of demographic data.[20] But these estimations regarding Kosovo are problematic insofar as contemporary sources always cover Southern Serbia and not just Kosovo, which at that time did not exist as an administrate unit as we know it today. Even sources from the Albanian Foreign Ministry speaking about "Kosovars" meant the Albanian-speaking population in the whole of Southern Serbia – the former Ottoman Vilayet Kosovo – and not only in "Kosovo". Furthermore, and this is also relevant, we do not know much about the regional distribution and strongholds of emigration in the different parts of Southern Serbia.

More precise estimates regarding gross emigration can be made if unpublished information from archival sources is used. Ilija Pržić, civil servant at the Yugoslav Ministry of the Interior and expert in minority law, for example, estimated in 1930 that from 1919 to 1929, "according to known information, about 37,000 Muslims emigrated to Turkey".[21] A Foreign Ministry report in 1939 gave the number of 40,000 to 50,000 "Turks" who had emigrated "in the course of the first years" after 1918.[22] For the period after 1928, Foreign Minister Milan Stojadinović mentioned to the Yugoslav legation in Ankara in 1935 that 21,500 persons (4,940 families) had emigrated to Turkey after opting for release from citizenship under Article 55 of the Citizenship Law of 1928, and 1,350 persons (338 families) had left for Albania.[23]

The Turkish data complete the Yugoslav ones, but need to be scrutinised equally carefully. According to Cevat Geray's calculations, 108,179 immigrants came from Yugoslavia to Turkey between 1923 and 1933.[24] This number – an estimation – seems problematic because the Statistical Yearbook of Turkey does not offer country-specific data for this period,

17 Jarman, Yugoslavia, 709.
18 Janjetović, Deca careva, 69–72.
19 Malcolm, Kosovo, 286.
20 Roux, Les Albanais en Yougoslavie, 222.
21 AJ, Zbirka Ilije A. Pržića (398), fasc. 1: Položaj Turaka u Jugoslaviji.
22 AJ, Zbirka Aleksandra Cincar-Markovića, fasc. 3: Referat IV političkog otseka, [Beograd] 12.02.1939.
23 AJ 370/9/42; Str.pov.br. 1.426, Beograd 18.10.1935.
24 Geray, Türkiye'den ve Türkiye'ye, 11.

as they do for the years from 1934 until 1941, when 8,825 immigrants from Yugoslavia were registered.[25] Furthermore, it is not very realistic that in view of the above-mentioned restrictions, such a great number of people would have emigrated from Yugoslavia to Turkey, especially in the years between 1923 and 1925. Summarising these various data and considering the conditions of emigration and immigration, I suggest the following estimates for emigration from the southern parts of Yugoslavia (Sandžak of Novi Pazar, Kosovo and Vardar-Macedonia) to Turkey in the interwar period (Table 5):

Table 5: Approximate number of emigrants from Southern Serbia to Turkey, 1919–1941

1919–1922	no considerable emigration
1923–1926	40,000 – 50,000
1927–1935	22,000 – 25,000
1936–1941	2,000 – 3,000
Total (1919–1941)	64,000 – 78,000

Debates in Yugoslavia about emigration and return migration to/from Turkey

The 1920s public debate about the emigration of Muslims reached a peak in the second half of 1923 and again in 1925, when the emigration movement suddenly increased. At both times the political atmosphere in the southern regions of the country was tense. In 1923 and 1925, fierce election campaigns resulted in bloody clashes between Muslims and Serbs in Southern Serbia.[26] In the Sandžak of Novi Pazar violence escalated when Montenegrins committed a pogrom against their Muslim neighbours in the towns of Šahovići and Pavino Polje in November 1924.[27] Muslims emigrated in huge numbers while others, who had left before or after 1918, came back. These movements provoked public debates which not only reflected the migration process and the mood of the majority population relating to it, but also revealed a lot about the Belgrade political leadership's perception of Albanians and Turks and their opinion regarding the 'integration capacity' of these minority groups. Milosav Jelić, one of the leading journalists at the daily newspaper *Politika*, for example, wrote on the front page of his paper in connection with the emigration of "Turks" in the August of 1923:

25 Most of them came in 1934 and 1935: 6,708. For 1934–1940 see: Istatistik yıllığı 12 (1940–1941), 88; for 1941 see: Türkiye istatistik yıllığı 18 (1950), 67.

26 For the 1923 municipal elections see: Krvavi izbori u Mitrovici. Kako je sam događaj počeo i kako se svršio, *Pravda* (Beograd), 26 August 1923, 1; Opet strašan pokolj muslimana na Kosovu, *Pravda* (Sarajevo), 11 September 1923, 1. For the 1925 elections in Southern Serbia see the report of the opposition introduced in parliament: Stenografske beleške Narodne skupštine Kraljevine Srba, Hrvata i Slovenaca, 3. prethodni sast. (22.03.1925), 41–51.

27 Avdić, H., Položaj Muslimana, 124–138.

> *Nowhere coincides our interests as much with the Turkish ones as in this question.* [...] *On the other hand, our national interest is to Serbify and Slavify Kosovo and the valley of the Vardar.* [...] *These people cannot be assimilated and no reasonable person thinks about such an idea.* [...] *All that can be demanded from them in our interest is that they do not stay here.*[28]

He goes on to describe the historic causes of the emigration and condemns members of parliament, such as Božin Simić, who supported their return. Three days later Dragiša Lapčević, a social democrat and one of the few who raised his voice against the emigration of Muslims, replied to Jelić, also on the front page of the same newspaper:

> *I cannot agree with many people not only in this question, that Christians and Muslims cannot stay together, one beside the other.* [...] *It is not as the whole world thinks it is: the religious moment was not the only and main reason that caused our Muslims to emigrate to Asia. They are leaving first of all because of the social situation.*[29]

He additionally explained that Muslims had been the ruling class for hundreds of years but now, after this was no longer the case, were not prepared to make the necessary adjustment to the rules of the market economy. Besides, he correctly pointed to other 'push-factors' such as the agrarian reform with its land redistribution and the – as he calls it – "new social order".

Between the Democratic Party (DP) and the Radical Party (RP), a controversy about the question of Muslim emigration broke out on the pages of its newspapers, Democratic *Pravda* and Radical *Samouprava*. The DP was the Yugoslav party most attached to the idea of *Yugoslovenstvo*, i.e. the existence of a Yugoslav nation, and was mostly in the opposition between 1923 and 1925. It criticised the RP harshly because of their laissez-faire attitude towards the return migration of Muslims to Southern Serbia. Jovan Magovčević (DP), a member of parliament from Kosovo, attacked the Muslim *Džemijet* party,[30] calling it an anti-state party. The latter was one of the partners in the coalition government led by the Radical Party and gathered most of the Muslim politicians from the southern parts of the country. With regard to the return migration of Muslims he said in parliament:

> *But when order and peace came back to our country, here they* [Muslims who served in the Bulgarian or Ottoman Army during WWI] *are like rats which slip through cracks in the walls. Thanks to the help of individual political figures of a certain political party, they are coming back again into our country through these gates. One returned from Asia, the second from Stambul, the third from Vienna.*[31]

28 Jelić, Iseljavanje Turaka.

29 Lapčević, Iseljavanje muslimana.

30 *Džemijet* (Alb.: *Xhemijet*, Turk.: *Cemiyet*), the "Islamic Organisation for Defending Justice", was the political representation of all Muslims in the southern parts of the country. Until 1923 Džemijet leaned towards the Radical Party and was its coalition partner in government, before becoming part of the opposition. After the arrest of their Albanian leader Ferhadbeg Draga in 1925 the party disappeared from the political scene and the Muslims of Southern Serbia lost their only genuine political representation (Hrabak, Džemijet).

31 Stenografske beleške Narodne skupštine Kraljevine Srba, Hrvata i Slovenaca, 64. red. sast. (20.03.1924), 416 passim.

Some months earlier *Pravda* had published an article about an alleged agreement of *Džemijet* with the Bulgarian government to close the Bulgarian borders for Muslim emigrants from Yugoslavia and had commented that "the policy of our state must be the homogeneity of our national elements and if the Turks want to emigrate from our country already, nobody is permitted to stay in their way."[32]

The policy of *Džemijet* was to influence the Radical Party and the government with respect to the question of return migration and especially of agrarian policy. However, it is doubtful whether they exerted great influence with regard to the returnees. The government was not interested in stopping emigration to Turkey and kept to a restrictive policy as regards repatriation, refusing Muslims wanting to return from Turkey to the Kingdom.[33] It is obvious that the Radical Party stayed in the background during this debate probably because they faced a dilemma between not scaring their Serbian voters and also their coalition partner *Džemijet*. Characteristic for their balancing attitude is the article "About the emigration of the Muslims", published in the party newspaper *Samouprava* in November 1923:

> *Almost no newspaper differentiated between Slavic Muslims, Turks and Albanian Muslims* [...] *In Bosnia, the Sandžak and in the small oases of Macedonia live Muslims of pure Slavic descent. This is our autochthonous element.* [...] *With the depopulation of Turks and Albanians our southern regions will weaken economically because in most cases the life of trade and industry depends on them. From our point of view, national as well as economic reasons matter."*[34]

However, reflections like these on the economic consequences of the mass emigration of Muslims from this region were very rare in the political debate.

The remarks quoted reveal some aspects of the state-minority relationship concerning the 'integration' of Muslims living in Southern Serbia into the state during the period of the parliamentary system (1918–1929). This relation ranged from indifference to open rejection but was consistent in supporting the emigration of non-Slavic Muslims to Turkey who were finally seen as not to be assimilated. Against the background of the ongoing state and nation-building processes the enduring emigration of Muslims was considered as a way to get rid of remnants of the Ottoman Empire and thus became part of a policy of "accelerated de-Osmanisation and re-Occidentalisation", i.e. a modernisation policy rhetorically orientated towards the West.[35]

32 Akcija Bugara i džemijeta. Protiv ugleda i interesa naše države, *Pravda* (Beograd), 23 December 1923, 2.

33 In one of the orders about the returnee question, the Ministry of the Interior explained: "All persons, who at the time of the annexation in 1913 were found at their homes, became our subjects. Those persons, who had themselves removed at that time and did not come back until August 18, 1920, are not our subjects" (AJ 14/32/98–541; Beograd, 04.06.1925).

34 O.K.: O iseljavanju muslimana, *Samouprava*, 8 November 1923, 2.

35 Höpken, Flucht vor dem Kreuz, 11–2.

Agrarian reform and colonisation in Southern Serbia

'Reconquering' the area of Southern Serbia in the sense of its nationalisation meant first of all to changing the population composition in favour of the South Slavs. This was to be achieved, on the one hand, by the emigration of a high number of non-Slavic Muslims, on the other, by state-sponsored settlement policies supported by land redistribution. Đorđo Krstić, director of the agricultural department in Skopje in 1927 and 1928, summarised the aims of colonisation in his well-known study about colonisation policy in Southern Serbia:

> *From our point of view the colonisation in the south is a matter of utmost importance for the state. It contributes to solving the economical and social problem and carries out our nationalising and assimilation agenda in these regions. It is the moving force of free ideas and economic-cultural progress: a guarantee of public security and a better pledge for the stability of our state borders.*[36]

Accordingly, extensive colonisation activities were mainly carried out in regions that had a concentrated population of non-Slavs, such as in the region bordering Albania, where a huge percentage of the population spoke Albanian. The colonies of the settlers, therefore, did not only mark the outpost of the nationalising state in order to integrate these regions into Southern Serbia but also had military functions vis-à-vis Albania and the Yugoslav Albanians. These strategic considerations must be read against the accusation of "disloyalty" against the Albanians, especially in the first years after the proclamation of the Kingdom of Serbs Croats and Slovenes, when the *Kaçak* movement fought Serbian rule, and in the second half of the 1930s, when the government re-adjusted the country's domestic and foreign policies. The ideological basis of the colonisation policy had been created and propagated in particular by Serbian geographers and ethnographers who 'surveyed' the southern regions before and after the First World War. Their mental mapping of Southern Serbia and their explanation of the ethnic distribution of settlements and of Islamisation formed the ideological framework, upon which Serbian claims on this area were predicated. The most notable exponent of the 'scientific' buttressing of territorial claims by Serbia in the first two decades of the twentieth century was Jovan Cvijić, the leading Serbian geographer and ethnographer at that time.[37] This endeavour was also thought to win foreign acceptance for Serbia's aspirations.

The Kingdom undertook several attempts to regulate colonisation on the basis of legal regulations from 1914, implemented by the then independent states of Serbia and Montenegro after their acquisition of former Ottoman territory. Land redistribution was not only motivated by national concerns but was also a social and economic necessity. However, it proved a rather unwieldy political instrument in the hands of the numerous Yugoslav governments (between 1919 and 1928, ten different ministers in 24 governments were responsible for the agrarian reform). In the whole country, non-Slavic minority groups suffered from the agrarian reform and the colonisation policy, which were used to marginalise

36 Krstić, Kolonizacija, 1.
37 Clewing, Pezo, Jovan Cvijić.

them.[38] These policies after World War One were intended to change the ethnic composition of regions with a high percentage of minority members in favour of the South Slavic element.

However, the attempt to realise the reform got stuck after the first regulations were made between 1919 and 1922. Another push was made after the establishment of the king's dictatorship in 1929, when the idea of "integral Yugoslavism" was promoted.[39] In the flood of new laws declared by the king and his government, two new laws concerning agrarian reform and colonisation were introduced: the "Law on the Regulation of Agrarian Affairs in the Former Provinces of Southern Serbia and Montenegro" and the "Law on the Settlement of the Southern Regions". Both laws were stipulated in 1931 and amended in 1933. Their effects can be seen in the immediate increase of the number of emigrants from Southern Serbia to Turkey and Albania, especially in the years from 1932 to 1935 (see Table 3) – a process described as "economical dissimilation" by historian Dietmar Müller.[40] However, Serbian politicians were not satisfied with the results and the participants of the first interministerial meeting convened by the Ministry of Agriculture emphasised in late September 1935:

> *The compact masses of Turks and Albanians along the Albanian border present, from the national and military points of view, a considerable problem.* [...] *Why did the nationalisation of the non-Slavic elements fail? The reason is that the number of the Orthodox population in the southern regions is small* [...]*, and our element was not sufficiently prepared to carry out the nationalisation. Hence, we need to resort to resettling the non-Slavic element from the country.*[41]

The then-formed committee thus concluded amongst other things to "strictly apply all instructions concerning the settlement of the southern regions in the sense of demarcating necessary complexes for the settlement, first of all in frontier districts."[42]

Agrarian policies were purposefully used to aggravate the problems of the Albanian minority. In this process, the state-minority relationship gained a new 'quality'. One of its features was the intensification of the colonisation policy in Southern Serbia. Supposedly 5,000 families were settled in Southern Serbia in 1936 on land primarily gained by taking state owned land (so-called *mirijsko zemljište*) and by buying land from emigrating Turks and Albanians.[43] Later, the Agrarian Department in Southern Serbia granted Albanians only 0.40 hectares of land per family member. This unlawful act happened very probably in

[38] Janjetović, Deca careva, 328.

[39] Müller, Staatsbürger auf Widerruf, 437–444.

[40] Ibid., 433.

[41] AJ 370/9/42, 637–643: Zapisnik interministerijalne konferencije, održane u Ministarstvu inostranih poslova, po pitanju iseljenja neslovenskog stanovništva iz Južne Srbije (20.09.1935) i projekt plana o iseljenju užeg komiteta interministerijalne konferencije, koji je donet na sednici od 24. septembra 1935 god.

[42] Ibid. For a recent discussion of this first conference see Jovanović, Interministerijalna konferencija.

[43] AJ 370/9/42, 894–897: Iseljavanje muslimanskog stanovništva iz Južne Srbije (opšti referat), Beograd 06.04.1939.

the shadow of talks between Yugoslavia and Turkey in 1938 about the agreement to "prepare the ground" for an "effective" resettlement of the Albanians and Turks to Turkey.[44]

It is difficult to confirm the exact results of the colonisation policy because the statistic data are partially contradictory. They did not take into account the considerable number of colonists who left the allocated land and went back to their home villages because of the difficult living conditions in Southern Serbia. Nikola Gačeša estimates that there were 14,772 colonist families (approx. 75,000 persons) settled in Southern Serbia in the interwar period, most of them (10,714 families) in Kosovo.[45]

The Citizenship Law

The Yugoslav bureaucracy categorised citizens as "wanted" and "unwanted". The return of Muslims from Turkey was unwanted, while their emigration, much like the emigration of members of other minority groups, was wanted. Political pressure against the Muslims in the first years of the Kingdom, though, did not have the same meaning as in the 1930s. It was not yet as purposeful as it would be under the government of prime minister Milan Stojadinović (1935–39). In the first years after the foundation of the state, these policies existed in a fragmentised form, as the Kingdom was still finding its position towards national, social and minority questions and towards neighbouring countries. Official interventions in the matters of minority members were characterised by uncertainty when dealing with persons whose status was unclear, as was the case with returnees. One logical consequence that came out of this ambivalent situation was to sharpen citizenship legislation after at least two fruitless attempts to pass a law on citizenship had been made in 1919 and 1922.[46]

In 1928, therefore, the parliament in Belgrade passed the first Citizenship Law of the country, based on the principle of *ius sanguinis* but including some elements of *ius solis* as well. The new law was also necessary because the peace treaties signed by the Kingdom in St. Germain, Neuilly and Trianon had not clarified all citizenship issues. Regarding emigration

44 In fact very little is known about the often quoted instruction to grant only 0.40 hectares of land per household member. Neither Pirraku (Pirraku, Kulturno-prosvetni pokret, 366, fn. 63) nor Obradović quote from the original document (Obradović, Agrarna reforma, 186). Additional information provides a letter from Senator Andra Kujundžić to Milan Stojadinović in which he spoke of the "definitive implementation" of the measures announced by the Ministry of Agriculture and mentioned the "legal norm for the southern regions" to grant 0.40 hectares of land per family member. This "should be put into effect as soon as possible" (AJ 37/53/332, 54–55; Beograd 19.02.1938). The expropriation of Albanians by the state ended presumably in 1939, when "rumours" about the Convention subsided in the population (Avramovski, Prilog pitanju, 129).

45 Gačeša, Radovi iz agrarne istorije, 249; Obradović, Agrarna reforma, 211.

46 Stenografske beleške Privremenog narodnog predstavništva Kraljevstva SHS, 19. red. sast. (13.05.1919), 393–403; Stenografske beleške Narodne skupštine Kraljevine Srba, Hrvata i Slovenaca, 69. red. sast. (23.05.1922), 96–97.

to Turkey, the law's importance lay in the fact that it was the regulation of the permanent emigration of Muslims. Article 55 of the new law declared the right for non-Slavic citizens who had been citizens of the Ottoman Empire until 1913 to opt for release from Yugoslav citizenship within a period of five years. If they chose to opt for release, they had to leave the country within one year.[47] In 1933, after the initial five-year period had expired, the time for opting out of Yugoslav citizenship was extended at the request of the Foreign Ministry until November 1, 1938. Its intention to exclude non-Slavic Muslims was clearly stated: the aim was to facilitate their emigration to Turkey under the assumption that persons opting for release from citizenship would feel stronger attachment to the Turkish state than to their birthplace or place of residence.[48] Legally, only non-Slavic inhabitants of the southern parts of Yugoslavia could use this option but in practice, Slavic Muslims made use of it as well.[49]

This section of the Citizenship Law, however, was not passed without opposition. The leaders of the Peasants Democratic Coalition in the parliament, Stjepan Radić and Svetozar Pribičević, harshly attacked the bill of the legislative committee of the parliament. They declared the formal act of giving non-Slavic people the right to opt for release from Yugoslavian citizenship an illegal measure against citizens of the state and incompatible with minority rights. Vladko Maček, another prominent member of this faction, expressed his opposition in a session of the legislative committee:

> *He* [Svetozar Pribičević] *said it well. Such a right could be carried out if we had a European administration. But we don't have such a European administration. And we know very well what this means. He* [a citizen of Albanian or Turkish extraction] *will be ordered and said: Listen, either you sign the application that you will get this privilege to emigrate and you obey, or you just see* [what will happen].[50]

The opposition by some members of parliament was ignored. The adoption of the Citizenship Law with discussed provisions for non-Slavic Muslims made finally clear that the ruling regime did not consider the inclusion of Turks and Albanians as citizens of the Kingdom to be a realistic option. Ideas of dissimilation and exclusion got the upper hand over forms of integration, even in the face of assimilation. The self-perception of the state as a Slavic one was too strong to make room for more inclusive policies. Thus it did not come as a surprise when the most prominent Slovenian politician in Yugoslavia, Anton Korošec, Minister of

47 *Službene novine Kraljevine Srba, Hrvata i Slovenaca*, no. 254, 1 November 1928.

48 Similar measures had been taken by Greece after her independence in the first half of the 19th century, as a means to exclude Muslims from citizenship of the new nation-state (Sundhaussen, Unerwünschte Staatsbürger, 199–200).

49 During the first Inter-Ministerial Conference in 1935, one participant declared that a lot of "our Muslims from the Sandžak, who are in fact our people" used Article 55. The Ministry of the Interior would not accept such applications in future (AJ 370/9/42, 637–641).

50 Stenografske beleške zakonodavnog odbora Narodne skupštine Kraljevine SHS, 14. red. sast. (29.05.1928), 300.

the Interior and head of this legislative committee, dubbed the possibility to opt for release from citizenship a "privilege" for the non-Slavic citizens.[51]

Turkey and the immigration of Muslims from Yugoslavia

Apart from the political and legislative efforts of the Yugoslav government regarding the emigration of Muslims to Turkey, the significance of the nationalising Turkish state in this process must not be underestimated. Turkey regulated the immigration of Muslims from Balkan states in a way similar to how other Balkan and Central European states regulated the immigration of 'co-nationals': through specific migration and settlement policies as well as a Citizenship Law. These instruments served the new republic by shaping a modern nation-state which would be based on the principles of the inclusion and exclusion of specific religious and ethnic groups.[52]

After the end of World War One, the war with Greece (1920–22) and the compulsory population exchange between Greece and Turkey as sanctioned by the Peace Treaty of Lausanne in 1923, Turkey was faced with the problem of settling and integrating hundreds of thousands of Muslim refugees from Greece. One consequence of this mass movement of people in a relatively short period of time was the attempt to reduce the number of immigrants from other Balkan states, such as the Muslims from the South-Slavic Kingdom. Given the dramatic conditions of the first years after the wars, the Republic of Turkey's Ministry of the Interior and Ministry of Foreign Affairs employed various ways to reduce the number of immigrants to the country. It is apparent from the files of the Yugoslav legation to Turkey that especially in 1923 and 1925, the Turkish Foreign Ministry appealed to the government of the Kingdom to reduce the emigration of Muslims, referring to the difficulties of supplying the refugees coming from Greece. However, these efforts did not bear a significant success: the Yugoslav legate to Ankara pointed out that Muslims who fulfil the legal requirements requested by the Yugoslav Law on Emigration are eligible to emigrate.[53] In fact, the influx of migrants from Yugoslavia was particularly high in 1923 and 1925, whereupon the Turkish government made fresh efforts to restrict them. More stringent regulations for the allocation of entry permits and, eventually, the stop on the immigration of Muslims from Yugoslavia in 1925, succeeded.[54] These efforts led to the Turkish Law No. 885 from May 31, 1926, which defined categories of wanted and unwanted people. Article 2 classified as unwanted those who were not of "Turkish race", and placed war and political

[51] Ibid., 299.

[52] Çağaptay, Citizenship Policies; Soyarik-Şentürk, Legal and Constitutional Foundations.

[53] AJ 370/9/42, 522: Pov. No. 760, [Istanbul] 07.11.1923.

[54] AJ 370/9/42, 570: K.T.Br. 5.046, Beograd 22.07.1925.

criminals, anarchists, spies and "Gypsies" together as another unwanted group.[55] Thus, Turkey formalised its practice to prevent "unpleasant" ethnic groups from immigrating there.[56]

Another important law in this respect, serving as a "major development in the process of Turkification" under the "motto of the republic: 'one language, one culture, one ideal'" was Law No. 2510 (Settlement Law) enacted on June 14, 1934.[57] This law intended to assist the assimilation of those who regarded themselves as non-Turkish or who allegedly had lost their Turkish identity. For that purpose Article 1 of the law stated that the dispersion and settlement of the population would be regulated according to the degree of their adherence to Turkish culture. People of Turkish descent or "close to Turkish culture" (Article 3) would be accepted on the decision of the Ministry of the Interior, whereas those who did not adhere to Turkish culture as identified also by the above-quoted Law No. 885 – anarchists, spies and Gypsies – would not be admitted as immigrants according to Article 4.[58] These Turkish policies indeed seemed to have restricted the immigration of Muslims from Yugoslavia after 1925/1926 and 1934 (see Table 3). It is difficult to evaluate all the reasons for this decline but the nationalising Turkish state certainly played an important role, by influencing the stream of emigrants from the Kingdom according to its own interests.

The radicalisation of the emigration question

Under the rule of Milan Stojadinović, Prime Minister and Minister of Foreign Affairs between 1935 and 1939, who brought the country close to the Axis Powers Germany and Italy,[59] the question of the non-Slavic Muslims in the southern parts of the country took on a new dimension. Problems related to foreign and domestic policy intensified the processes of national inclusion and exclusion. Stojadinović's policies were also a result of the obvious failure of "integral Yugoslavism", which had been imposed by the dictatorship of King Aleksandar I after 1929, but had resulted in stronger and radicalised particular nationalisms within Yugoslavia. These nationalisms also reoriented themselves towards foreign powers and domestic 'enemies'.

The measures described above, in particular colonisation and the Citizenship Law of 1928, had not achieved their national-political intentions, i.e. to fundamentally change the ethnic composition of Southern Serbia, especially in the border regions to Albania, in favour of the "Slavic element". Against the background of a new "Serbian question" within

55 La Législation Turque, 510.

56 In 1923 the Turkish Ministry of Foreign Affairs informed the legate of the Kingdom "que tous les sujets étrangers, à l'exception des sujets russes, bulgares, hellènes, albanais, géorgiens et transcocasiens, voulant entrer à Constantinople, seront admis" (AJ 370/53/136, 74; [No.] 2958–82, Constantinople 08.07.1923).

57 Soyarik-Şentürk, Legal and Constitutional Foundations, 130.

58 Ibid.,129.

59 Gašić, Beogradska politička i vojna elita, 68–71.

the context of changing domestic and foreign policy orientation – the Serbs in Yugoslavia, especially those in Serbia, positioned themselves in a new manner towards the state, the "Croatian question" and towards the minorities living in their sphere of influence – the emigration of Muslims appeared again on the agenda of the Serbian political and intellectual circles in Belgrade. Stojadinović occupied an outstanding position in this process. His government planned an unprecedented attempt to resettle Albanians and Turks employing the various horizontal and vertical structures of the state machinery for that purpose.

The plan for the resettlement of Albanians and Turks was drafted by the previously mentioned Inter-Ministerial Conference on September 20, 1935; this meeting included representatives from the Foreign Ministry, the Ministry of Agriculture, the Ministry of the Interior, the Ministry of Finance, the Ministry of Transport, and also a colonel from the general staff of the Yugoslav Army.[60] Its decisions were confirmed, with slight changes, in a second meeting on October 1, 1935, and included four major points:

to regulate the resettlement as soon as possible with a special convention between Yugoslavia and Turkey and Albania;
in case an agreement with Albania cannot be reached or the Albanians will not emigrate to Turkey, they should be resettled from the border region into the interior of the country;
to waive all pertinent costs of emigration for people who opt for the release from Yugoslav citizenship under Article 55 of the Citizenship Law and to exempt them from recruitment into the Army;
to introduce mechanisms for the successful and quick handling of the emigration process.

These policies were to be applied first at the Yugoslav-Albanian border and to be reached by specific measures: to suppress Albanian counter-propaganda against emigration from Yugoslavia; to put pressure on the non-Slavs by the strict application of existing laws and rigorous control of specific regulations, such as the observance of compulsory schooling and tax regulations; the admission of potential emigrants to the civil service was to be refused; acting Muslim civil servants were to be moved to places where the "national element" prevailed; toponyms and surnames were to be nationalised, i.e. Slavicised.[61] At approximately the same time Stojadinović requested the Yugoslav legation to Ankara to approach the Turkish foreign ministry in relation to talks about a convention similar to those between Romania and Turkey and with regard to the Turkish Law on Settlement from 1934. This law opened, as Stojadinović explained, "unexpected possibilities as regards the emigration of Turks from Balkan states to Turkey. [...] We should take advantage of the favourable opportunity which is presented to us."[62]

[60] The extent to which Anton Korošec, Minister of the Interior and a Slovene, and Mehmed Spaho, Minister of Transport and a Muslim from Bosnia, were involved in or informed about these plans, is an open question.

[61] AJ 370/9/42, 649–650: Zaključak interministerijalne konferencije o iseljenju neslovenskog elementa iz južnih krajeva, održane 1 oktobra 1935 god. u Ministarstvu inostranih poslova, Beograd 01.10.1935.

[62] AJ 370/9/42, 630–631; Strogo Pov.Br. 1.426, Beograd 18.10.1935.

Even before formal negotiations about a convention between Yugoslavia and Turkey could begin, the pressure had increased against the Albanians, which led to the radicalisation of the situation in Southern Serbia. The decisions described above went down the vertical axis of state power, to the middle and lower levels of the state machine such as the administration of the Vardar banovina and its district captains. The banovina directed the district captains to take steps to push the Albanians to emigrate from the country to Turkey "by propaganda as well as by taking extraordinary measures."[63] Since neither "propaganda" nor "extraordinary measures" were exactly defined, the order opened the way to arbitrary acts by local officials, which were accepted and eventually welcomed. The situation for the Muslims/Albanians got increasingly worse, especially in 1938. Violent encroachments by the police against them significantly increased as the government of Stojadinović made use of the repressive instruments of the bureaucracy to an unknown degree in Southern Serbia.[64]

The Yugoslav-Turkish Convention was initialled in July 1938 and regulated the resettlement of 40,000 "Turkish" families (200,000 persons) from Yugoslavia and utterly terrified the Muslim population. The Yugoslav and Turkish governments saw the Convention as a legitimate instrument for creating a homogenous nation-state. Both states regarded minorities as something 'abnormal': a 'disturbing' element preventing the development of the nation-state, which was either to be assimilated or removed by the state. This attitude becomes explicit in the preamble of the Convention, which says about the Turkish Muslim population in Southern Serbia: "... est uniquement déterminée à quitter le territoire du Royaume par le légitime désir de se rattacher à son tronc ethnique naturel." Article 1 defined the concerned group of people:

> *Seront admis à bénéficier de la présente Convention, les sujets yougoslaves musulmans d'origine et de langue turque et ceux ayant la culture turque. Ne seront pas admis aux bénéfices de la présente Convention, les personnes dont l'entrée en Turquie est interdite selon les lois et les règlements turcs actuellement en vigueur, la population nomade et les Tziganes.*[65]

[63] AJ 37/51/315, 40–41; Str. Pov. II Br. 6, Skoplje 29.04.1936.

[64] It is difficult to evaluate the exact extent of police violence in Southern Serbia between 1936 and 1938, which also depended on the local relations between the Christians and Muslims, which were not always bad, and on the attitudes of district captains towards the Muslims. As numerous political leaflets indicate, 1938 was something of an *annus horribiles* for the Albanians in Southern Serbia. A "Muslim student youth from Kosovo, Metohija and Macedonia" wrote in a pamphlet, obviously completed after the signing of the Yugoslav-Turkish Convention: "Recently in our regions intensive violence by the rulers against the Muslim people has started once again. The pain, which our Muslim brothers, particularly Albanians, are exposed to recently has become unbearable" (Arkivi Qendror i Shtetit – AQSH, 251 [Ministria e Punëve të Jashtme], viti 1938, dosja 107, fleta 206 [AQSH 251/1938/107, 206]. According to the Albanian legate to Skopje, encroachments by state organs also occurred in connection with the search for weapons (AQSH 251/1938/107/2, 591; Nr. 21/VIII. Rez., Shkup 17.05.1938).

[65] Forty-five districts were affected by the resettlement (Article 2): 37 from Vardar banovina, five from Zeta banovina and three from Morava banovina (AJ 370/9/42, 910–920: Convention réglementant l'émigration de la population turque de la région de la Serbie du Sud en Yougo-

Nevertheless the aim of the Yugoslav side was primarily to resettle the Albanian population and we can assume that the Turkish side knew very well that the majority of the new settlers would be Albanian speaking Muslims and not ethnic Turks.[66]

However, the Convention did not go unopposed in Yugoslavia. It provoked political resistance against Stojadinović from the Muslim population but also from delegates of his own party, the Yugoslav Radical Community (JRZ). Twenty-two sitting and former senators and members of parliament mainly from Macedonia and Kosovo (ten Muslims and twelve Orthodox Christians) turned against the Convention in their Memorandum to Milan Stojadinović from July 3, 1938 in an act of solidarity, documenting the difficult situation of the Muslims in 1938. The Memorandum described the Muslims of the southern regions as respectable people, who are loyal to state and society and recently worried by rumours about their alleged resettlement:

> *Unfortunately these rumours become credible through the actions taken by many organs of the state, which expose the peaceful Muslim people to harassment and ill-treatment.* [...] *This all means for the Muslims a great disappointment and has caused a feeling of humiliation and slight.* [...] *To oppose this evil and to re-establish peace and confidence among the Muslim masses* [...] [the following measures are suggested]*: 1) to officially deny the rumours regarding an alleged resettlement of Muslims from our native land to Turkey; 2) to end the expropriation of land from Muslim farmers;* [...] *3) to end the ill-treatment and beating of Muslims, which were practised by local constabularies under the pretext of searching for supposedly hidden weapons.*[67]

Eventually, the Convention was never implemented because of differences among the involved parties about the financial side of the agreement. The idea for the Convention had emerged in a European atmosphere where the resettlement of peoples was seen by the core of society as an effective and legitimate method to solve minority problems. Vasa Čubrilović, historian at the University of Belgrade, whose ideas to push out the Albanians from the country coincided with the measures of the state as described above, frankly made this point clear. In a popular lecture about "The emigration of the Albanians (*Iseljavanje Arnauta*)" delivered in the Serbian Cultural Club on March 7, 1937 he claimed:

> *When Germany can expel tens of thousands of Jews and Russia can shift millions of people from one part of the continent to another, the resettlement of a few hundred thousand Albanians will not set off a world war.*[68]

slavie). For the published text of the Convention see Bajrami, H., Konventa jugoslavo-turke e vitit.

66 A summary about the Convention noted that "the resettlement of the Albanian population is their real secret purpose" (AJ 370/9/42, 921–922; Beograd 05.04.1939).

67 AQSH 251/1938/107/2, 853–856; Skoplje 03.07.1938.

68 Quoted in Čović, Izvori velikosrpske agresije, 112.

Conclusion

The Yugoslav migration policy towards Muslims in Southern Serbia and their geopolitical implications highlight the political concepts and designs for the Serbian nation-space. However, the radical measures drafted by the Stojadinović government were also a proof of political failure and an indicator of state crisis. They had resulted from an atmosphere of increasing political crisis in the country and disappointment by the leading Serbian politicians about the results of the previous attempts to assimilate and exclude minority groups. In this situation the government took to extraordinary measures.

These policies also remained relevant for later periods because the migration of Muslims from Yugoslavia to Turkey in the interwar period was an important element during the last decades of various debates about the 'Kosovo problem'. Opinions on the migration issue therein were strongly influenced by the individual position towards the Kosovo question. The emigration of Muslims has been presented in an almost simplistic way in almost every representation of the history of Kosovo, by making an argument for one or the other side without taking into account chronological sequences, Turkish immigration policy and questions relating to foreign affairs and domestic policies in the process of Yugoslav nation-building and state-building. This article does not claim to discuss all these topics to the same extent. But what should have become clear is that the Yugoslav migration policy towards Muslims in the southern part of the country, which is discussed here, consisted of complex and multi-layered fields of influence and was very context-sensitive. Further research is necessary to illuminate important questions related to this problem, such as the role of violence and political repression, the radicalisation of the Yugoslav and Serbian society in the second half of the 1930s, the impact of migrants' networks, the influence of the 'patron countries' Albania and Turkey on the Muslims who wanted to leave the country, and the economic and cultural consequences of the emigration of Muslims on the micro- and meso-levels of society in the region concerned.

Aleksandar R. Miletić

(Extra-)Institutional Practices, Restrictions, and Corruption. Emigration Policy in the Kingdom of Serbs, Croats, and Slovenes (1918–1928)

This paper elaborates on the general features of emigration policy conducted by the Kingdom of Serbs, Croats, and Slovenes (Kingdom of SCS) in the first decade after World War One. It explores different aspects of the phenomenon, ranging from general legal provisions to the particular features of state policy and the technical details of the emigration procedure. The paper asks whether the emigration policy of the newly created Kingdom of SCS followed the essential changes in emigration policies that occurred on a global level in the aftermath of World War One. It sheds light on the local particularities of Yugoslavia within the global phenomenon of emigration by covering a significant period in the administrative development of Yugoslav emigration authorities and offices. To date, this issue has remained largely under-researched.

Former Yugoslav and modern national historiographies (such as the Serbian, Croatian, or Slovenian ones) examined only particular aspects of emigration, but there is neither a monograph nor a study on the general phenomena of Yugoslav emigration policy in any given period of the state's history. The following paper is based mostly on previously unexplored archival sources on Yugoslav emigration kept in archives in Belgrade and Zagreb. The most important documents were issued by the Belgrade and Zagreb based emigration offices and institutions, which were subordinated to the Ministry of the Interior and the Ministry of Social Policy of the Kingdom of SCS. They represent various materials ranging from official correspondence, expertise or legislation drafts, to the dramatic and picturesque reports on the living conditions of Yugoslav emigrants in the countries of immigration. In the private archive of Ninko Perić in Belgrade, I found several important documents on the particular phenomenon of corruption in the administration of emigration affairs. The most precious archival source for this paper proved to be the Artur Benko Grado Bojnički Collection (*Ostavština Artura Benka Grada Bojničkog*) in the Croatian State Archive in Zagreb. It contains various material issued by the Yugoslav Emigration Commissariat based in Zagreb, a key institution in the administration of the emigration policy of the Kingdom. Bojnički was one of the best, if not the best interwar Yugoslav expert on emigration affairs. The archival material left by him, therefore, is of great relevance since he was holding important positions in the Commissariat in Zagreb throughout the period under research.

A particular problem encountered in the Archive of Yugoslavia (*Arhiv Jugoslavije*)[1] in Belgrade was a shortage of essential archival material originating from the Ministry of Social Policy of interwar Yugoslavia. This came as the consequence of neglect and deliberate mistreatment of archival sources by the Yugoslav communist authorities after World War II.[2] Almost the entire archival content of the aforementioned ministry was simply recycled, as the newly established regime needed paper for its publications. Since the general policy and administration of emigration affairs in the Kingdom of SCS was concentrated at the Ministry of Social Policy, the deficiencies of its archival remains represent a huge problem for establishing the full picture of emigration policy in the interwar period. For this reason, the examination presented in this paper was not able to discuss all relevant dimensions of this issue.

The first section of this paper sheds light on some remarkable changes and disturbances that occurred on a global level in emigration in the period under review, the complexity of which can only be alluded to due to limited space. The second section introduces the Yugoslav story by elaborating on pre-1914 practices and experiences of emigration policies conducted in different territories, which would become part of Yugoslavia in 1918. Implications of the first Yugoslav regulations on emigration and its administration are analyzed in the third and fourth section of the study. A specific feature of the Yugoslav emigration procedure was its exploitation by the hidden national minority policy of the state. This aspect of the emigration policy is explained in the fifth section. The sixth section is devoted to the problem of misuse and corruption that occurred among state personnel in charge of the administration of emigration affairs. Yugoslav state policies towards emigrants' remittances and their importance to the monetary balance and stability of the country are examined in the seventh section.

World War One and the global migration system

Global migration movements made a significant contribution to the convergence of labor markets in Europe and the New World throughout the 19th century and especially in its second half.[3] The mass supply of newly arrived labor from Europe was constantly decreasing the average wage differences between the sending countries and the countries of

1 The official name of this archive, which stores the archival documents from central state authorities and other institutions and organizations from interwar and socialist Yugoslavia, the Federal Republic of Yugoslavia and the state of Serbia and Montenegro, has been changed into *Arhiv Srbije i Crne Gore* (Archive of Serbia and Montenegro). Since the dissolution of the state of Serbia and Montenegro, a new name for the archive is under discussion.

2 Stanković, Dimić, Istoriografija pod nadzorom, 176–7.

3 Hatton, Williamson, Global Migration, 110–25. The authors limit the effects of the mechanism of convergence only to the so-called Atlantic economy, which excluded the economic periphery of Europe, such as Southern and Eastern Europe.

immigration. Hatton and Williamson describe, quite convincingly, how this convergence mechanism functioned and what brought it to an end. The very basis of their explanation is the economic calculation of changes in labor supply and demand; owing to the mass-emigration, average salaries in Europe went up, while on the other side of the Atlantic they were declining. In this way, international migration fuelled the ongoing processes of globalization and contributed to equalizing labor market conditions throughout the globe. In the decades preceding the First World War, the system of the global market economy was inclined towards a state of equilibrium. However, after July and August 1914, this subtle mechanism suffered a set of serious disturbances.

Almost every war in the history of mankind has been followed by restrictions on the freedom of movement of the warring sides' citizens. When most parts of the globe became engaged in warfare during the late summer of 1914, these disturbances developed into a worldwide system. Even after the global conflict was over, the system continued its existence through inertia. The control over and restrictions on the freedom of movement of citizens that the states applied during the interwar period, appeared to be the continuation of the general state of emergency created by the first case of truly worldwide warfare.[4]

The US quota system and restrictions in European countries decisively contributed to weak international migration on a global level in the interwar period. Emigration from European countries came under the control of their governments. No matter whether they restricted or supported it, national governments gained decisive control over emigration. For many European countries there was no return to the pre-war laissez-faire regime in this domain.[5]

The introduction of US immigration quotas in the 1920s has found ample discussion by academic scholarship. Authors tried to establish the major cause for the harshening of US immigration policy during the 1920s. Was it increasing xenophobia and racialist attitudes towards immigrants from Southern and Eastern European countries, newly developed eugenic reasoning, or the short-lasting economic crisis between 1920 and 1921? Was it the result of the sudden change that occurred in the economy and public opinion after the war, or of the long lasting structural transformation that developed behind the scenes?

Economic historians Hatton and Williamson have a complex, analytical approach and offer interesting findings regarding this question.[6] According to their analysis, mass-migrations would contribute to the convergence of the global labor market only while limited to the countries of the so-called Atlantic economy. The convergence mechanism, namely,

4 Bade, Migration in European History, 169, 188–93; Castles, Miller, The Age of Migration, 63; Bessel, Mobilizing German Society, 442–5; Harvey, Effects of the War, 667–71; Fridenson, The Impact of the First World War, 235–48; Becket, The Great War, 263; Strachan, The First World War, 169–70.

5 Ipsen, The Organization of Demographic Totalitarianism; Cannistraro, Rosoli, Fascist Emigration Policy; Bade, Migration in European History, 187–8, 191–3; Felshtinsky, The Legal Foundations.

6 Hatton, Williamson, The Age of Mass Migration, 236–52.

functioned only within a range of comparatively small wage differences that existed inside the system and could become balanced. The arrival of the new kinds of immigrants after 1890 disturbed the mechanism. It was very difficult to integrate the labor force of underdeveloped, poor ('low-wage') countries of South and Eastern Europe into the global labor market system; or at least it was not possible without a number of unwanted consequences in the countries of immigration.

Timmer and Williamson particularly stress the negative impact that the mass arrival of immigrants from 'low-wage' countries had on the stability of US society.[7] The intensified decrease in the wages of unskilled workers augmented the inequalities between them and the rest of American society. This was evident even before World War One, for instance, when a state-appointed commission, which investigated immigration issues in 1907–1910, came to similar conclusions. Timmer and Williamson and Hatton and Williamson, therefore, claim that labor market related issues were the principal causes for the restrictive US immigration policy of the 1920s.[8] War, xenophobia, and eugenics played only a secondary role in this theory. So, while emigration might have decreased the general level of social tensions and inequalities in the 'low-wage' European countries, it was raising them in the New World; the Atlantic system was not able to integrate these latecomers into the global economy. A new global system developed during the 1920s: one of tariffs, control, prohibitions, and restrictions imposed on international trade and emigration affairs. The particular Yugoslav emigration processes and policies must therefore be seen in this context within the global system.

Emigration affairs in the Yugoslav territories before 1921

The first Yugoslav state was proclaimed as the Kingdom of Serbs, Croats and Slovenes on December 1, 1918. Some of its provinces (Croatia-Slavonia, Dalmatia, Montenegro, Slovenia) had notable traditions of mass emigration in the period before World War One. Although the streams of overseas emigration revived after the war, the central authorities of the newly created Kingdom of SCS were not preoccupied with the issue immediately. It was only in the third year of its existence as a state that the Yugoslav government issued the "Decree on Emigration", on May 21, 1921. Previously, emigration affairs were treated differently under the jurisdiction of the different Provincial Governments.[9] Among them, only the "Emigration Department of the Commissariat for the Social Care of the Provincial Government of Croatia-Slavonia" (*Povjereništvo za socijalnu skrb Pokrajinske uprave za*

7 Timmer, Williamson, Racism, Xenophobia or Markets?

8 Ibid.; Hatton, Williamson, The Age of Mass Migration.

9 The provincial governments for Bosnia-Herzegovina, Croatia-Slavonia, Dalmatia and Slovenia, which were leftovers from Habsburg rule, continued functioning even after the new Yugoslav state was created. Some of these governments or their departments survived until 1924.

Hrvatsku i Slavoniju) had practice and experience in dealing with mass emigration and the administration of emigration affairs.

Some of the high officials at the Zagreb-based Emigration Department had an excellent education and maintained what might be called the good tradition of Austro-Hungarian bureaucracy. Between 1920 and 1922, the institution was under the guidance of the outstanding expert and able administrator Artur Benko Grado Bojnički. A Croat, born in Ogulin and educated in Zagreb, Vienna, and Paris, Bojnički became one of the most eminent specialists on matters of emigration in the newly created Yugoslav state. His detailed *exposé* on the "History of our state emigration service from its foundation in 1901 until the formation of the Emigration Commissariat in 1923" provides us with a good insight into the early history of the codifications and regulations of emigrational matters in one of the Yugoslav territories, i.e. Croatia and Slavonia.[10]

According to this source, prior to 1918, only the Hungarian part of the Dual Monarchy had systematic emigration regulations stemming from legislation passed in 1909. In Austria there was no such body of law even up until the end of the Empire. Due to its large number of emigrants, the Kingdom of Croatia and Slavonia, which was part of Hungary but enjoyed certain rights of autonomy within Hungary and had its own diet, the *Sabor*, stipulated its own regulation in the domain of emigration policy. Another territory of what was to become Yugoslavia, the Vojvodina (Banat, Bačka and Baranja), was an integral part of the lands of the Hungarian Crown and, therefore, in terms of emigration policy under the authority of Budapest-based institutions that conducted emigration affairs. The entire administrative procedure for emigration in the Hungarian Kingdom was concentrated in Budapest, whereas Fiume-Rijeka served as the emigration seaport. It seems that the Hungarian authorities did not care too much for the high rate of ethnic non-Hungarian emigration from the country. About 74 percent of emigrants from Hungary were ethnic non-Hungarians during the period 1899–1913.[11] No matter whether it came as a consequence of deliberate state policy or not, one can accept that during the last decades of the Monarchy, there was an almost complete freedom of emigration from Croatia-Slavonia and Dalmatia, which was part of Austria, where emigration was hardly regulated at all. According to Yugoslav sources from the 1920s, prior to 1914, there were no procedural requirements imposed by central authorities to be fulfilled; no papers, no requests, no administration, allegedly not even passports were required for overseas emigration.[12] Practically, a steamship ticket was the only paper one was supposed to have for this journey.

Contrary to this almost ideal picture of a *laissez-faire* regime in the domain of emigration, in Serbia one would find quite a different situation. In this country, as well as in neigh-

10 Historijat naše državne iseljeničke službe od njezina osnutka 1901 do obrazovanja Iseljeničkog komesarijata 1923. In: Hrvatski državni arhiv (Croatian State Archive, Zagreb), HDA, OABG, k. 7, f. 4.

11 Puskás, From Hungary to the United States, 28.

12 Izveštaj o radu Iseljeničkog komesarijata u Zagrebu za razdoblje od 1. januara 1925 do 30. januara 1926. In: Arhiv Jugoslavije (AJ), 39–9–26.

boring Bulgaria, control over emigration was imposed even before 1914.[13] The requirement of high dues to be paid or deposited for travelling papers was the main tool of state control in these countries. An emigrant from pre-war Serbia was supposed to pay 250 Dinars, the equivalent of about US $ 50, only to be provided with a valid passport.[14] Taking into account additional travelling costs and the average daily salary of about three Dinars, one can easily understand why it was so difficult for an ordinary Serbian citizen to travel overseas (see Table 1). In Bulgaria the procedural requirements were even harsher. According to the 1907 Law on Emigration, a Bulgarian citizen of military age was only allowed to travel as an exception and after paying a large deposit as a security to ensure that he would come back. The sum, between 1,000 and 5,000 Leva (US $ 200 to US $ 1,000), was arbitrarily determined by the local authorities for each individual case. On the other hand, prior to 1914, in many countries of Europe and for America, people could travel with no traveling papers, and no border control or surveillance at all.[15] From this point of view, the backward Balkan countries seem to be a vanguard of the policy of restriction and control over emigration, which was later imposed on a global level.

In his summary of the information on the pre-1918 human and administrative resources and experiences with emigration affairs, Bojnički underlined that Serbia, Montenegro, Bosnia-Herzegovina as well as Slovenia[16] and Dalmatia – as Austrian provinces – had neither separate regulations nor administrative experiences on the issue except for police regulations on the procedures and requirements for issuing passports.[17] Furthermore, these provinces lacked administrative personnel experienced in such matters. For this reason, the Zagreb-based emigration offices and personnel were to have a principal role in creating Yugoslav emigration policy.

Table 1: Emigration and repatriation from the USA, 1911

	Serbs and Montenegrins	**Croats and Slovenians**	**Dalmatians, Bosnians and Herzegovinians**	**Total**
Emigration	1,363	42,499	4,520	48,382
Repatriation	2,028	10,209	849	13,836

Source: US official numbers, quoted in: Izvještaj. In: HDA, OABG, k. 3, f. 10.

13 Zakon o taksama 1911, 59; Dăržaven vestnik, Zakon za emigracijata.
14 Purić, Naši iseljenici, 69.
15 Torpey, The Invention of the Passport.
16 Slovenia had not been an administrative unit in the Habsburg Empire but for the sake of simplicity the name is used for these former territories of Austria, which were populated by Slovenes and were put together to form 'Slovenia' in the Kingdom of SCS.
17 Historijat naše državne iseljeničke službe (footnote 10).

The Decree and the Law on Emigration of 1921

There is much archival material on the inter-ministerial commission that concluded the work on the draft of the first Yugoslav decree on emigration in 1921.[18] The Zagreb-based Emigration Department contributed with precious expertise, instructions, and proposals to the process. The draft was prepared in consultation and collaboration with the central government's Ministries of Social Policy, Foreign Affairs, and the Interior. Yugoslav experts were provided with the corresponding Italian, Austrian, Greek, German, and French legislation. These materials were obtained through diplomatic channels from the embassies of the Kingdom of SCS in those countries. After a scrupulous comparison and analysis, the Italian legislation of 1918 in particular was taken as a model for Yugoslav lawmakers.

Italian authorities had great experience on the issue of regulating emigration since a large number of Italian citizens emigrated to overseas countries every year.[19] The inter-ministerial commission decided to acquire Italian regulations, which strictly prescribed sanitary and technical requirements for the steamships engaged in the transportation of emigrants. Yugoslav experts emphasized the fact that the entire Italian emigration was directed to domestic seaports, which made it possible for the whole business of emigration to become 'nationalized', i.e. organized within the framework of national regulations, companies, and infrastructure. That way the state would gain full control over emigration affairs and privilege domestic steamship companies. Even without large-scale state intervention, emigrants would benefit from the fact that they could buy tickets with cheap, domestic currency. In addition, the Italian state enforced efficient controls over the activities of steamship agents since it was proved that they would otherwise exploit the emigrants' lack of information to impose high commissions for their services.

The Yugoslav "Decree on Emigration" of 1921 and later the "Law on Emigration" of the same year followed the Italian model in all points of the prescribed 'nationalization' of the emigration procedure. However, there were some rather technical problems in carrying it out in practice. First, the Kingdom of SCS lacked appropriate transport and boarding facilities on its seaports. At that time, only Dubrovnik's seaport Gruž had a railway connection to the interior of the country. It was a narrow gauge railroad and quite uncomfortable and inadequate as it passed through the isolated territories of Bosnia and Herzegovina. The ports of Split (up to 1925) and Šibenik had no railway connection to the rest of the country whereas the Sušak seaport, with a normal gauge connection to the rest of the country, was under Italian occupation until February 1924.[20]

In spite of these facts, the 1921 decree (Article 8) prescribed that all emigrants had to leave the country only through domestic ports. It was only five days after the publication of the decree that a subsequent order was issued to revoke this provision.[21] The same happened

[18] Priprema projekta Uredbe o emigraciji, 9.V.1921. In: AJ, 14–34–104.
[19] Bade, Migration in European History, 112–5.
[20] Miletić, Unutrašnja trgovina; Kos, Rijeka kao slobodna luka, 349–51.
[21] Naredba o stupanju, *Službene novine,* 21 May 1921.

when the provision reappeared in the Law on Emigration (Article 10) from December 30, 1921,[22] soon annulled by a regulation decreed by the government.[23] There are many reasons why emigration procedures could not be carried out through domestic harbors. Apart from inadequate or nonexistent railway connections, Yugoslav seaports had no technical infrastructure to accept and facilitate great steamships for transoceanic navigation. There were neither adequate boarding facilities, nor clinics for the necessary medical examinations of the emigrants. Due to these facts only a small minority of the Yugoslav emigrants left the country from domestic ports. In 1922, only 257 out of 6,086, or 4.22 per cent of all Yugoslav overseas emigrants left the country from domestic seaports (234 passengers from Dubrovnik's harbor Gruž, eighteen from Bakar, and only five from Split). Most emigrants traveled by train to European harbors, Cherbourg (1,573 Yugoslav emigrants), Hamburg (1,250), and Le Havre (1,050), where they embarked for their overseas journey.[24] Once more, an attempt to 'nationalize' domestic emigration was taken after certain improvements in railroad communication to the Adriatic seaports were carried out in 1924 and 1925. The withdrawal of Italian forces from Northern Dalmatia made possible normal gauge railway transport between Zagreb and the seaport of Sušak (on the southern outskirts of Fiume-Rijeka).

Soon after the Italians left and the city was put under the control of the authorities of the Kingdom of SCS, the first Yugoslav steamship company for the transportation of emigrants, *Vesna*, was established there. The owners of the company tried to obtain an exclusive state concession justified by the need to 'nationalize' the entire emigration process. In this way, the basic stipulations of the Law on Emigration (Article 10) would have been ultimately fulfilled. However, according to the documentation gathered by the officials of the Emigration Commissariat, the company did not have enough capital assets for ensuring the steamship voyage standards required by US immigration regulations. Moreover, the seaport Sušak did not have the technical infrastructure required for the docking of large transoceanic ships. For these reasons, the expert of the Emigration Commissariat, Artur Benko Bojnički, was decisively against granting a monopoly to the *Vesna* steamship company. He was convinced that under the then current conditions of the Yugoslav seaport infrastructure, the 'nationalization objective' might have been fulfilled only within the following ten years.[25] A similar conclusion was reached at the Conference on Emigration organized in Zagreb, November 16–18, 1924: given the existing conditions of Yugoslav seaport infrastructure and the decreasing number of emigrants (due to the US immigration quota) there was no hope for the nationalization of the domestic emigration procedure.[26]

Yugoslav law (in Articles 10–13) followed strict Italian regulations in the domain of requirements imposed on the steamship companies. According to the Italian legislation,

22 Zakon o iseljavanju, *Službene novine*, 30 December 1921

23 Pravilnik o izvršenju, *Službene novine,* 1 September 1922.

24 Statistika iseljavanja. In: AJ, 14–36–112.

25 HDA, OABG, k. 10, f. 24.

26 Stenogram Ankete o iseljavanju, održane 16–18 septembra 1924. In: HDA, OABG, k. 7, f. 4.

representatives of these companies were allowed to perform agent activities only if they had special approval from state authorities. The same rule existed for steamship companies, which could not transport emigrants or sell tickets without state approval, which also entailed the payment of a certain sum of money for the concession. The prices of tickets were to be approved by state authorities. Steamship companies were obliged to pay different taxes and they had to deposit a certain amount of money as security for the good conduct of the company. Italian legislation also prescribed mandatory and free of charge repatriation for all emigrants who would not be accepted by the country of immigration. Technically, this meant that the steamship company had the obligation to return the emigrants at its own expense. Yugoslav law incorporated this regulation (Article 19), which proved to be one of the key provisions for the protection of the emigrants.

Administration of emigration affairs

According to Yugoslav regulations, the Ministry of the Interior with its local branches was partly in charge of the administration of emigration affairs. They were administrating the technical service, such as the verification of identity and personal characteristics of emigrants, and issuing passports. However, the general emigrational policy and the most important tasks in the administration of emigration affairs were in command of the Ministry of Social Policy. On the other hand, the Zagreb-based Emigration Department played a key role in performing the policy and technical conduct of the Yugoslav emigration from the very beginning of the newly created Kingdom as well. What place was occupied by this institution and what role did it play in the unified emigration policy of the Kingdom?

The Emigration Department remained under the jurisdiction of the provincial government up to November 1922, when reorganization of the administration occurred. The department's prerogatives were transferred to the General Emigrational Commissariat (*Generalni iseljenički komisarijat*, GEC), which was to have the same personnel as the previous institution and to be situated in Zagreb. The GEC was placed under the jurisdiction of the central government's Ministry of Social Policy, since the provincial government for Croatia-Slavonia was to be terminated after the new Yugoslav constitution was enacted in 1921.[27] Apparently, the central government only renamed the institution and placed it under its direct control. Fedor Aranicki became head of the newly created GEC, replacing Bojnički in this position. The latter was appointed head of the Information Section of the Commissariat. Later he served as expert-consultant on emigrational matters to the Commissariat.

Zagreb was chosen to be the centre of the state emigration office not only because of its experienced personnel and the fact that the greatest number of emigrants had come from Croatia and Slavonia in the previous period (Table 1), but also for reasons of communication. As the great majority of Yugoslav emigrants used German and French ports for emigra-

[27] Historijat naše državne iseljeničke službe (footnote 10).

tion, they travelled through Zagreb, which became a suitable place for issuing all the papers and conducting final administrative procedures for the emigrants. In addition, there was a state boarding house in Zagreb with a clinic for the emigrants and branches of all steamship companies had offices there.

The last reorganization of the emigration administration for the period under review occurred in March 1923. It seems that the Radical Party, which dominated the central government of Nikola Pašić, wanted to gain even more control over emigrational affairs. It transferred some important powers (such as decisions on issuing passports to the emigrants) from the Commissariat in Zagreb to the newly created Emigration Department of the Ministry of Social Policy in Belgrade. From that time, the Zagreb-based General Emigration Commissariat continued to exist as the Emigration Commissariat under the authority of the Emigration Department in Belgrade.

One of the tasks of the Commissariat in Zagreb was to defend the interests of emigrants. Some of these cases dated from the period of the former Austro-Hungarian Empire. The case for the compensation of the families of 26 citizens of Austria-Hungary who perished on the Titanic in 1913 was probably one of the most interesting. These persons had been living on territories which would be included in the Kingdom of SCS in 1918. As the legal representative of their families' interests, the Zagreb-based Emigration Commissariat insisted on compensation payments which had been sent by US insurance companies during the war but had been withheld by Austro-Hungarian authorities. The Austrian authorities, however, did not permit the transfer of money as long as there were any unsettled issues in the legal succession between Austria-Hungary and the Kingdom of SCS. The case was still not concluded in 1925, twelve years after the tragedy of the Titanic.[28]

Statistics of Yugoslav emigration in the interwar period

The introduction of the emigration quota in the USA and unfavorable living conditions in South American countries significantly decreased Yugoslav emigration after World War One. In connection with the establishment of the US quota system, the Yugoslav authorities were obliged to control the fulfillment of this quota. According to data cited by Artur Benko Bojnički at the Conference on Emigration in 1924, a total of 34,700 emigrants had left the Kingdom between 1918 and 1923, while at the same time 43,048 persons came back from overseas countries: "Before the war, it was a different situation. [...] We had in only one year from Croatia and Slavonia more emigrants who left for the USA than today for five years from the whole Kingdom into the whole world."[29] The great number of repatriated emigrants proved to be a kind of Yugoslav or Eastern European peculiarity, as compared to

28 Izveštaj o radu Iseljeničkog komesarijata u Zagrebu za razdoblje od 1. januara 1925 do 30. januara 1926. In: AJ, 39–9–26.

29 Stenogram Ankete o iseljavanju, održane 16–18 septembra 1924. In: HDA, OABG, k. 7, f. 4.

migration in other European countries. Since the number of repatriated persons in the period 1918–1923 was greater than the number of those who moved abroad, Benko Bojnički concluded in the above quoted document, that emigration ceased to be a problem of state policy.

The number of emigrants from the Kingdom of SCS to the USA followed the general trend of Eastern and Southern European countries in the period under review (Figure 1). After the introduction of the first quota regulation in 1921, the contingent of Yugoslav emigrants was reduced by more than fifty percent. While in 1921 there were 12,461 immigrants from the Kingdom of SCS to the US, in 1922 there were only 5,436 (of the annual national quota of 5,600). According to the official Yugoslav statistics, the establishment of an even more restrictive quota in 1924 did not affect the national emigration contingent, which remained steadily at about ten percent of the pre-war level. The annual quota was reduced to 671 immigrants from the Kingdom of SCS to the US but the Yugoslav statistics also counted US citizens of Yugoslav origin who were exempted from the US quota.

Yugoslav emigration to South American countries, quite weak before the introduction of the quota system in the US, became unexpectedly the most important direction throughout the 1920s (Figure 2). In spite of the continuous warnings and appeals against emigration for these countries, quite a significant number of Yugoslav emigrants found themselves there during the period under research. From the point of both the Yugoslav authorities and emigrants, economic conditions in South American countries, if compared with the US or with the British dominions, were much less favorable. Emigrants had many problems due to the unstable political and economic situation there and the weak currencies of these countries. Thus even the financial account of the Kingdom would not gain any benefit from emigration. Therefore, Yugoslav emigration authorities tried to prevent people from going to South America.[30]

The rise of Split as an emigration port was connected with this particular emigration stream. According to official Yugoslav statistics, 1,797 emigrants left the country from the port of Split in 1925, the year when the town received railway access to Zagreb. That year, Split was the third most important seaport for Yugoslav emigrants after Cherbourg in France and Hamburg in Germany (Figure 3). The successful performance of Split harbor can be explained by the fact that all emigrants who transited from there left for countries in Central and South America for which authorities did not request any special conditions regarding the hygiene and technical facilities of the ships or ports of departure. This policy explains why so many emigrants left the country from Split.[31] Due to the important role that Split played in Yugoslav emigration affairs, a new building of the Emigration Boarding House was inaugurated in 1925. Full comfort was thus provided to emigrants waiting

[30] Iseljenički komesarijat, Zagreb, 2. mart 1925: Južna Amerika, nepovoljne prilike naših iseljenika. In: AJ, 14–35–109.

[31] Izveštaj o radu Iseljeničkog komesarijata u Zagrebu (footnote 28).

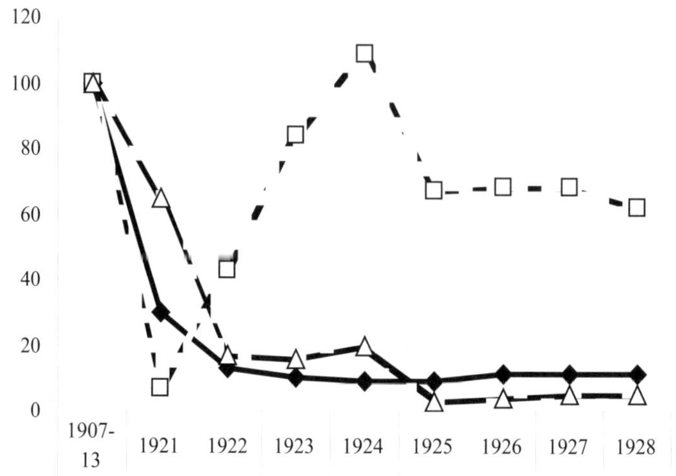

	1907-13	1921	1922	1923	1924	1925	1926	1927	1928
Kingdom SCS	100	30	13	10	9	9	11	11	11
NWE countries	100	7	43	84	109	67	68	68	62
ESE countries	100	65	17	16	20	3	4	5	5

Figure 1: Annual number of immigrants coming to the US from the Kingdom of SCS, North/West European and East/Southeast/South European countries, 1907–1928 (1907–13 = 100).[32] *Sources:* Historical Statistics: 105; HDA, OABG, k. 3, f. 10.

for their departure from Split, similarly to that offered by the boarding facilities in major European harbors.

Unfortunately, I could find neither exact statistics nor a reasonable estimation of the total overseas emigration from the Yugoslav provinces before World War One. Taking into account only available data on emigration for the USA, the decrease after the war, in any case, seems considerable. For instance, in 1922 the total Yugoslav emigration (for all overseas countries) was only fifteen per cent of the average annual contingent of Yugoslav immigrants to the US in the period 1907–1913. This reduction might have been not only the consequence of the US quota but also of restrictions in issuing passports imposed by the Yugoslav authorities. But was there a legal basis for the imposition of restrictions on emigration from the country? In the first place one has to point out that the newly established Kingdom of SCS did not continue the previous Serbian policy of high fees demanded for issuing passports. Actually, the nominal amount in Dinars remained the same but its real

32 North and Western European countries are: Great Britain, Ireland, Scandinavia, Netherlands, Belgium, Luxembourg, Switzerland, France, and Germany; Eastern, Southeastern and South European countries are: Russia, Baltic States, Italy, Spain, Portugal, Greece, Yugoslavia, Romania, Bulgaria, and Poland.

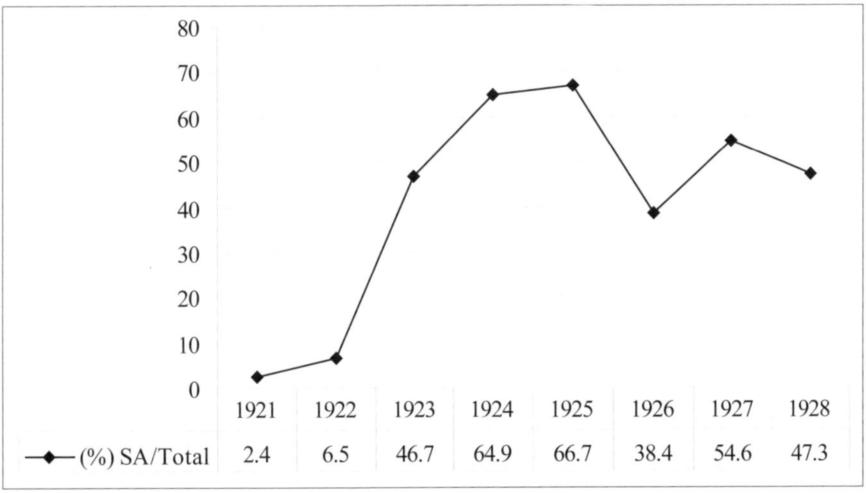

Figure 2: Share of South American countries in the total of Yugoslav emigration, 1921–1928. *Source:* Various statistical materials on Yugoslav Emigration kept in the Archive of Yugoslavia. In: AJ, 14–36–112.

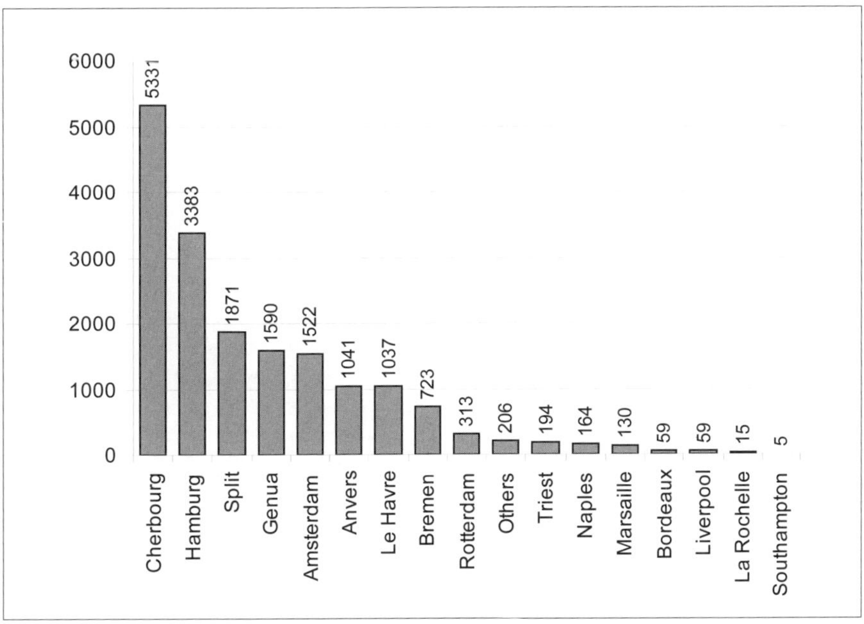

Figure 3: Number of Yugoslav emigrants according to ports of departure, 1925. *Source:* AJ, 14–36–112.

value was immensely reduced by huge post war inflation. In this respect, one rather sees a certain liberalization of emigration policy compared to the situation in Serbia before the war. This was also manifest in Article 6 of the Yugoslav Law on Emigration, which guaranteed the freedom of movement and emigration of Yugoslav citizens. However, it also authorized the Minister of Social Policy "to impose limitations on emigration or to stop it completely". In the period under review, this provision had never been exercised within the given legal framework. It was carried out unofficially, though, through confidential instructions sent to the administrative personnel. The mechanism of these unofficial restrictions will be discussed in the next section.

Emigration affairs and minority policy of the Kingdom of SCS

The Kingdom of SCS encompassed a great share of ethnic minorities. According to data from the 1921 census, the constituent nationalities of the Serbs, Croats, and Slovenians made up 82 percent of the population, while the most numerous national minority groups were Germans (4.22 percent), Hungarians (3.90 percent) and Albanians (3.67 percent).[33] According to Ivo Banac,[34] the proportion of the constituent nationalities in 1918 should be consequently reduced for the number of Macedonians (4.87 percent) and Slavic Muslims (6.05 percent). The Yugoslav emigration policy towards the members of the German, Hungarian, Macedonian (*Bugarophil*), and Muslim minorities possessed revealing particularities.

The minority issue became a matter of international concern after the enactment of the 1919 Versailles and Saint Germain Peace Treaties, which obliged the signature states to also protect minorities. Since the Yugoslav authorities wanted to liberate themselves of this burden, emigration policy appeared as an ideal opportunity to decrease the share of ethnic minorities. From the point of view of the Yugoslav emigration policy, the issue is of great interest especially regarding the large percentage that minority groups comprised among the emigrants from Yugoslavia. According to official Yugoslav statistical data (Table 2), members of the Hungarian and German national minorities made up a large proportion of all emigrants who left the Kingdom of SCS during the 1920s. Archival materials reveal that there was a hidden political agenda and planned minority policy carried out in state emigration affairs. As a result, national minorities that made up only seven to eight percent of the total population would annually provide up to fifty percent of all "Yugoslav" emigrants. Let us first elaborate on the issue of the German national minority.

In an article written by Bojnički on the general points of the emigration policy of the Kingdom of SCS in 1924, only praises and compliments can be found for the members of the German national minority.[35] The article was published in the official periodical of

33 Crampton, Atlas of Eastern Europe, 124.
34 Banac, The National Question, 58.
35 Bojnički, Koje bi smjernice, 215.

the Ministry of Social Policy (*Socijalni preporođaj*) and had a strongly negative undertone towards those who were encouraging the emigration of Germans from the country. Bojnički praised Germans as a "hard-working people", who represented "by its industrial property, [...] advanced production technique, discipline, and obedience, an element of the order in the country, whose emigration should not be favored." Apart from these favorable words, it is apparent from the text that actually there were people in the Yugoslav administration who did not share Bojnički's attitude and who thought that the emigration of the Germans should be favored. To what extent this attitude was institutionalized or imposed from above upon the subordinate personnel, one can assess only through insight into confidential materials that circulated in the Yugoslav administration. The subject was too sensitive to be announced publicly or to be included in the provisions of official orders or regulations. The document quoted below is a confidential order that circulated between the Ministries of the Interior, Social Policy, and Foreign Affairs during the preparation of the Decree on Emigration of 1921:

> *A principle which will be accepted in carrying out the police measures is as follows: to make difficult the procedure of issuing passports in a material and formal way. This is the command of our state's military, economic, and political conditions. The emigrants' own interests concerning the present situation in America also demand it.*[36] [...] *By the provision of the Order and the Decree of Emigration, we want to make procedural difficulties in obtaining passports. Namely, we will deprive of power authorities that are regularly authorized for issuing the passports* [i.e. the local authorities] *and we will reserve this authority to the provincial governments in the cases of the families of overseas emigrants and non-Slavic emigrants; for all other* [citizens] *this right will be reserved for the central government.*[37]

In other words, within the new system of imposed limitations no one could get a passport regularly from the local authorities. Only "non-Slavic emigrants" and the family members of overseas emigrants would be issued passports on first demand by the provincial governments. For all other citizens, passports were to be issued by central authorities. This institutional mechanism was covered by an instruction of the Ministry for Social Policy from July 19, 1921, which had prescribed that the decision on issuing passports could be decided at two levels, either by provincial governments or the Ministry of the Interior.[38] When the provincial governments were terminated under the provisions of the new Yugoslav constitution, its prerogatives in the domain were taken by the district authorities. In view of the quoted confidential document and its consequences it seems that applications for passports submitted by Germans and Hungarians were solved immediately in the first administrative instance, while the applications from other citizens were delayed by transferring them to the uncertainty of decisions made by central authorities.

36 The document refers to the short-lasting economic crisis, which occurred in the US at the beginning of the 1920s. The crisis led to rising unemployment: from 1.4% in 1919 to 5.2% in 1920 and 11.7% in 1921 (Mitchell, International Historical Statistics).

37 Policijski propisi iseljavanja. In: AJ, 14–34–104.

38 Naredba o stupanju, *Službene Novine*, 21 May 1921.

These double standards in emigration policy could not have been kept secret for long among the citizens of the Kingdom of SCS. In 1925, the Croatian newspaper *Hrvatski list* reported on the situation in Slavonia:

> *Previously, some agents appeared who tried to convince people to leave for Brazil* [...] *One hundred families are preparing themselves for emigration. It is interesting that these agents address only the Germans and Hungarians. We hear but we still do not believe that those emigrants, who report themselves to these agents, get their passports in Belgrade with no subsequent delay or investigation* [...].[39]

Let us now examine the different strategies of emigration policy recommended for the different national minorities. Information is provided by a document written in 1925 by Bojnički while he was working as an expert for the Emigration Commissariat. Bojnički wrote a report on how to treat the representatives of the different national minorities such as Germans, Hungarians, and the so-called *Bugaraši* ("Bugarophiles") from Macedonia throughout the emigration procedure. In this document, written for the internal use of the administration, he reiterated his attitude towards the Germans. His praise for German virtues and their loyalty to the Yugoslav state was even more pronounced than in his above-mentioned article. Bojnički stated that their emigration should not be encouraged, but in case they really wanted to leave the country, there should be no obstacles from the part of the authorities. Policy concerning German emigration should be "one of a *laissez passer* kind" as he summarized at the end of the report. As far as the *Bugaraši* (pro-Bulgarian Slavs) from Macedonia were concerned, he suggested that local authorities should decide on every individual application: "If the Bulgarophiles' organization is more vigorous in America than here, it is better to keep them at home and vice versa."[40] The only negative attitude in Bojnički's report was that displayed towards the Hungarians, whose emigration should be supported and favored. Interestingly, he did not even try to explain or argue this firmly negative opinion. One can speculate that there was a kind of consensus among Yugoslav policymakers concerning this minority group so that any further explication was needless.

The discussion of the emigration policy towards members of the German and Hungarian national minority so far leaves some doubt of whether it can be safely portrayed as a case of state repression against them. Taking into account the generally bad prospects for the economy and for employment in the overpopulated rural areas of the Kingdom of SCS, one could claim that these populations were, in fact, privileged over the members of the state's constitutive nations who also wanted to emigrate. This would be true, of course, if the nationally biased project of the Yugoslav land reform, which made them ready to leave the country, were not taken into consideration. Taking this additional dimension into account, the two policies of land reform and emigration appear causally connected.

[39] *Hrvatski list*, 23 October 1925.

[40] Mišljenje eksperta Iseljeničkog Komesarijata Artura B. Bojničkog – Predmet: Emigraciona politika prema narodnosnim manjinama, Zagreb, 7.IV.1925. In: HDA, OABG, k. 9, f. 24.

The emigration of the Muslim population from the provinces of Macedonia, Kosovo-Metohija, Sandžak, and Bosnia-Herzegovina to Turkey is still one of the great controversies of Yugoslav interwar emigration.[41] This emigration pattern was a continuation of the migration process that had started during and after the Balkan Wars of 1912–1913. There are some serious obstacles to the exploration of these phenomena, at least when it concerns Yugoslav statistical data. Namely, in spite of the large-scale nature of emigration among the Muslim population of the Kingdom of SCS, it had never been listed in the official state emigration statistics. Benko Bojnički, as an expert at the Emigration Commissariat, raised this question in 1925 in his official correspondence with Fedor Aranicki, the director of the institution. He warned Aranicki that the neglect of the issue of Muslim emigrants in official documents had been in serious violation of the existing regulations on the matter.[42]

Table 2: National structure of emigrants from the Kingdom of SCS, 1921–1928

	1921	1922	1923	1924	1925	1926	1927	1928
Germans and Hungarians	3,294 (25.40 %)	1,019 (16.91 %)	3,491 (37.25 %)	8,457 (49.06 %)	6,774 (45.14 %)	4,234 (26.92 %)	5,318 (24.20 %)	4,077 (18.71 %)
Serbs, Croats and Slovenes	9,516 (73.40 %)	4,880 (80.98 %)	5,698 (60.81 %)	8,525 (49.45 %)	7,824 (52.14 %)	11,044 (70.23 %)	13,775 (62.68 %)	14,939 (68.56 %)
Total number of emigrants	12,965	6,026	9,370	17,238	15,005	15,726	21,976	21,789

Source: AJ, 14–36–112.

Perhaps as a consequence of this exchange of opinions and Bojnički's warnings, the special issue of Muslim emigration was briefly mentioned in the Report of the Emigration Commissariat to the parliament from 1925, signed by Fedor Aranicki: "I underline that about 4,000 Turks have left our country (Kosovo and Kumanovo region) and emigrated for Turkey."[43] However, this figure did not enter the official statistics, although there was a rubric for the religious denomination of the emigrants. In the official statistics, one can find only eleven emigrants of Islamic faith in 1925. For the whole period 1921–1928, there were only 166 Muslim emigrants on the official Yugoslav record.

One can presume that the Yugoslav authorities were quite content with this particular emigration stream. It corresponded with the state project of national colonization of so-called South Serbia. In an article written by Đorđe Krstić, the chief state Commissionaire for Agrarian Affairs, published in the review *Izseljeniški magazin* ("Emigrant Magazine") in 1927, one can find exact data on the financial aid provided for the purpose of purchasing Muslim property in the "South Serbian" provinces of Kosovo-Metohija and Macedonia.[44] It is rather surprising that Krstić wrote openly in a periodical on such sensitive matters which

41 See Pezo in this volume.

42 Memorandum eksperta iseljeničkog komesarijata Artura Benka Bojničkog – Predmet: Iseljavanje Muslimana, 15.III.1925. In: HDA, OABG, k. 10, f. 24.

43 Izveštaj o radu Iseljeničkog komesarijata u Zagrebu (footnote 28).

44 Krstić, Južna Srbija.

one would suspect to be kept in high secrecy as a hidden policy agenda. With full patriotic vigor and enthusiasm, Krstić wrote on the state-designed program of colonization. According to this source, the market price of the "Turkish immovable property" was between 1,200 and 1,500 Dinars per hectare. Krstić claimed that the state-supported bank *Hipotekarna banka* was ready to provide colonizers with an immediate loan of 2,000 Dinars per hectare for the Muslim estates they were purchasing.

Let us go back to the statistical data on the proportion of members of national minorities in the "Yugoslav" emigration. If one adds the actual number of at least 4,000 Muslim emigrants (as estimated by Aranicki) to the number of German and Hungarian emigrants in 1925, the total comes to 10,774 'minority emigrants', or 58 percent of the total, against 7,824 (42 percent) ethnic Serb, Croat, and Slovenian emigrants. Although the economic reasons for leaving Yugoslavia were obvious, this high number in 1925 of 58 percent of emigrants belonging to national minorities was also connected to political reasons.

Misconduct and corruption of state personnel

The study of the legal framework on emigration would be incomplete without insights into the mechanisms and techniques used to implement or even 'abuse' its spirit in practice. In the following section, the overall system of misconduct and corruption that occurred in the administration of emigration affairs in the Kingdom of SCS is explored. The central government's policy of issuing emigration passports only to a limited number of ethnic Serb, Croat, and Slovenian citizens proved to be a window of opportunity for large-scale corruption and mistreatment of the applicants by the administration.

Low-style corruption and misuse appeared as state officials gained the right to make arbitrary decisions on each individual application. More to the point, one should take into account the fact that the purchasing power of Serbian state employees in the newly created state was less than half of the pre-war level.[45] A similar phenomenon was recorded in other European countries but in the Kingdom of SCS it had some additional political implications and consequences. In the emigrants' case, the majority of the maltreated applicants were from Croatia, the region with the largest number of 'national emigrants'. Since the personnel engaged in such misconduct were usually Serbs working in the Belgrade-based institution after March 1923, when the procedure of issuing passports was relocated to Belgrade, the whole case acquired broader ethnic/national connotations, being linked to nationalist tensions.

Let us begin with a document found in the Private Archive of Ninko Perić,[46] representing an original note sent to Perić, Minister of Social Policy, from the Presidency of the Provincial Government for Croatia-Slavonia on July 28, 1923. The note commented on

[45] Mirković, Ekonomska struktura Jugoslavije, 25.
[46] Miletić, Iz Memoara dr. Ninka Perića.

the mistreatment and exploitation of the applicants from this province. The Presidency sent Perić a certified copy of a letter mailed from Belgrade lawyer Dragiša Leovac to Ivan Lovrenić, an applicant interested in emigrating to Canada, who lived in Crikvenica on the Croatian coastline. Lovrenić referred to the newly created Emigration Department in the Ministry of Social Policy situated in Belgrade. As already shown, this institution was established in March that year, when it took over the competencies of the Zagreb-based General Emigration Commissariat. Interestingly, Perić's decision to move the institution to Belgrade was motivated by the eagerness of the central authorities to prevent cases of misconduct and bribery that had occurred in the General Emigration Commissariat. Apart from the Emigration Department, a Counseling Board was also established, which was presided over by the Deputy Minister of Social Policy, Petar Protić. The Board was asked to give its opinion on the general policy concerning emigration as well as on each individual application for passports. There is reasonable evidence of direct involvement of this institution in the above-mentioned abuses. Let us turn now to Dragiša Leovac's incriminating letter, dated July 10, 1923, sent to Lovrenić and many other applicants. Leovac was so confident in his position that he displayed the precise contact information of his Belgrade attorney bureau in the city centre:

> *Very respected Mr Lovrenić,*
>
> *I found out that you intend to travel for Canada this very month in order to make use of the prospect for good earnings during this year's harvest. As you probably know, the procedure for issuing passports lasts for several months, so you would miss the term for travel to Canada. I can help you to get your passports by the 23rd of this month by a special organization I have inside the Ministry, if you send me the following information:*
> *1) First name and family name*
> *2) Home village, community, district, province* [...]
> *5) Send for my expenses and labor to my address: 1000 Din.*
> *If you fulfill the above-mentioned requirements, you will be informed of the place where you can collect your passport by the 23rd of this month.*
>
> *With best regards,*
>
> *Dragiša Leovac,*
> *Lawyer, Belgrade, 32 Kralja Milana Street*

The chief of the Department of the Interior of the Provincial Government of Croatia and Slavonia warned of negative, anti-state and anti-Serb feelings that might have been provoked by this affair, especially as Lovrenić's application was not the only such case under investigation. According to sources from the Croatian Department of the Interior, similar offers were sent to many other applicants who were waiting to be issued a passport by the Ministry. Minister Perić reacted by delivering a press declaration concerning the issue. Applicants were warned "not to fall into the pitfall of criminals" who were trying hard to exploit them. There was also information on the criminal investigation of certain perpetrators, but it did not mention any names. As far as could be confirmed from the Belgrade newspapers of that time, Leovac's name was not mentioned in connection with the case.

He later appeared as a member of parliament for the ruling People's Radical Party, in fact as one of the distinguished representatives of the so-called *Pašićevci* (pro-Pašić) faction of the Party.[47] He was even a member of the Parliamentary Commission, which was established to investigate the responsibility of Minister Edo Lukinić in the famous Thurn-Taxis affair.[48]

An even better source that provides insights into the anatomy of corruption among the state personnel of the Kingdom of SCS is a report written by Milan Kuzmanić, secretary of the Emigration Department of the Ministry of Social Policy. The report was typed on three pages and was submitted to the Minister in August 1923.[49] Kuzmanić warned the Minister of the privileged status of the Hamburger Line Company in transporting Yugoslav emigrants, and informed him of the system of misconduct and extortion of the applicants for emigration passports. In the official Yugoslav regulations, the system of concessions for steamship companies for the transportation of emigrants was designed to be the key mechanism for protecting emigrants from high commissions on steamship tickets. The only intermediary between the passenger and the company was to be the state, which provided legal protection, regulated the price and conditions of travelling and all other important issues concerning the relations between emigrant and steamship company. State authorities were obliged to make sure that in the end, emigrants would get all necessary papers and pay the lowest possible price for their tickets. In theory, this is how the system was supposed to function. The reality was different, though, as made clear by Kuzmanić's Report. Kuzmanić pointed out the unacceptable "familiarity" that existed between the chief of the branch agency of the Hamburger Line, a certain Mr. Petrović, and the head of the Emigration Department of the Ministry of Social Policy, Dr. Nestorović. Nestorović was allowing the former unrestricted entrance into departmental offices. Moreover, Petrović had access to the lists and files of the applicants, making it possible for extra-institutional arrangements and financial extortion to be prepared. In this way, the state's painstaking legislation efforts to protect emigrants were ruined in practice by the irresponsibility of one official.

Emigration affairs in the Belgrade-based Ministry of Social Policy were in such a mess that even lower clerks came into possession of individual applicant's cases. They were taking home these files and then exploiting the applicants by promising intervention with the authorities. As a consequence of bureaucratic misconduct and irresponsibility, complete administrative chaos emerged. The embittered Kuzmanić wrote a detailed description of these anomalies:

> *There is no evidence, either on the applications sent by the district authorities, or on the approved applications, so that one cannot check either how many or even which passports were sent to the district authorities in order to be issued to the emigrants. Even in the subsequent procedure of expedition, traveling papers, which have already been approved, are still kept back* [in the Department], *in order to exploit their holders in the nearby streets.* [...] *Of course, there are cases in which the reports on the issued traveling papers do not match the approvals of the Counseling*

[47] Jovanović, Politički sukobi, 145.

[48] Miletić, Iz Memoara dr. Ninka Perića; ibid., Afera Turn-Taxis.

[49] Izveštaj Milana Kuzmanića sekretara. In: AJ, 14–34–105.

Board. Moreover, within all this mess, how can anyone guarantee that passports have not been issued without any consideration from the Board?

The large advertising sign of the *Medijator* Agency might be taken as a metaphor and one of the most striking symbols of the corruption of the Yugoslav state personnel. The Agency Headquarters was on Kraljice Natalije Street, just next to the Ministry of Social Policy building. The sign offered "mediation" for almost all sorts of businesses that one might have with state authorities, from employment in state administration and compensation for war damages, to prolongation of the validity of visas and issuing passports. Once again, the direct connection between 'mediators' and applicants was facilitated by corrupt bureaucrats who neglected the basic principal of the secrecy of the applicants' personal data. The archive in the Ministry was in practice open to the entire personnel at all levels. Any clerk could gain possession of individual cases and then contact the applicant promising conditional help.[50] Instead of serving and protecting the interests of the citizens, low-paid administrative personnel in Belgrade tried to improve their material wealth by abusing their position. State competencies were not only violated but they also ended up serving the private interests of individuals employed by the state.

Remittances from the US and the Yugoslav economy

In spite of the fact that they did not do much to help emigrants in their enterprise, from the very beginning, the authorities of the newly formed Yugoslav state had an eye on the economic importance of remittances sent from the US by emigrants and the savings brought back to the country by returnees. Bojnički estimated the total amount of remittances sent from US immigrants to be US $ 26–27 million between 1919 and 1923 only. Calculated in domestic currency, it amounted to 10.2 billion Yugoslav Dinars, an enormous sum compared to the country's fiscal performance at the time. It almost equaled the total amount of revenue projected for the Yugoslav state budget for 1924–1925, which was 10.4 billion Dinars.[51] The influx of this amount of hard currency unquestionably helped to alleviate Yugoslavia's monetary situation.

Later, when the Dinar was stabilized, the influx of emigration dollars played an important role in maintaining the trade balance (see Figure 4). Dr. Ivo Bilin, a collaborator on the journal *Revue économique de Belgrad*, ascertained that in 1927, the amount of emigration savings and remittances sent to the country of 800 million Dinars was equivalent to the foreign trade deficit of the country that year.[52] The author emphasized the importance this money played in assuring the bare survival of the poor regions of Lika, Dalmatia, Herzegovina, and Montenegro.

50 AJ, 14–37–114.
51 Bojnički, Smjernice emigracione politike, 35–6.
52 AJ, 81–1–3.

During the second half of the 1920s it was often commented that the Yugoslav national currency had a "wooden standard", referring to the great proportionate share that the lumber industry had in the export earnings of Yugoslavia. Taking into consideration the previous figures, one could argue that the Yugoslav Dinar also had a solid basis in the economic performance of Yugoslav emigrants abroad. Yugoslav authorities were very much aware of this fact. Benko Bojnički wrote in an *exposé* in 1920 that the only dilemma faced by authorities was whether to press emigrants to return home and bring all their savings with them, or to stay in America and continuously send smaller amounts of remittances to their family members.[53] In order to point out the dilemma, Bojnički used the English saying: "You can't have your cake and eat it [too]."

In order to secure a continuous and uninterrupted influx of US hard currency, Yugoslav authorities provided help in negotiating between the postal authorities of the US and Canada and the Belgrade-based Yugoslav *Poštanska štedionica* (Post bank). Milorad Nedeljković, head director of the *Poštanska štedionica*, explained in a newspaper article how the system of money transfer worked.[54] According to him, the contract concluded between the two national postal companies enabled Yugoslav emigrants to send their remittances from any post office in these two North American countries. The procedure was quite simple as the emigrant only had to write down the exact address of the postal destination in Yugoslavia.

Much has been written on the ambiguous economic outcomes and effects of the influx of remittances in developing countries. In a very useful article W. R. Böhning summarized both the positive and negative implications associated with this phenomenon.[55] The author pointed out the fact that most of the money sent from abroad usually ended up being extensively consumed by the individuals who received it. Hardly ever has it been employed for capital investments on the level of individual or family enterprises. From the point of view of the state, the influx of a considerable amount of hard currency might have ambiguous results. It can "enable the nation's economic agents to import capital goods and raw materials to strengthen the productive capacity, as well as to import basic consumer goods". On the other hand it might provoke some problems. The great problem with remittances, as argued by Böhning, is that they "symbolize dependence", especially in the case of the economic performance of underdeveloped or so-called developing countries. These countries can easily become dependant on the continuous influx of the remittances, which for many unpredicted reasons can be interrupted. Böhning is resolute in claiming that sending people abroad for the reason of improving the trade balance or the monetary situation of the state through remittances is completely improper as a state developing strategy. This is especially true in the case of the so-called 'brain drain' emigration of educated or qualified specialists.

The case of interwar Yugoslavia almost entirely fits into Böhning's model of dependency. However, the question remains of what might have been better for Yugoslav society if there

53 Organizacija iseljenčke službe u Kraljevini SHS, Zagreb, 15.VIII.1920. In: HDA, OABG, k. 3, f. 10.

54 Nedeljković, Iseljeničke uštede, 19–20.

55 Böhning, Elements of a Theory, 39–42.

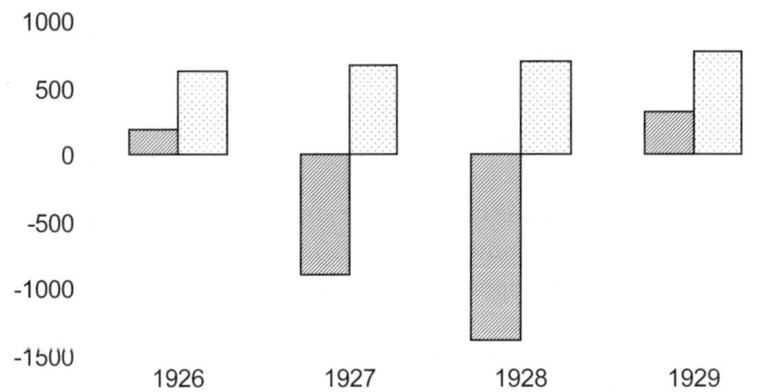

	1926	1927	1928	1929
trade balance	186	-886	-1390	327
remittances	631	662	695	766

Figure 4: Trade balance and remittances of the Kingdom of SCS (in million dinars), 1926–1929. *Source:* Nikolić, Kurs dinara, 153–5.

had not been any emigration and remittances from abroad. Given the fact that the Yugoslav economy did not possess the capacity to absorb the superfluous labor supply of the country, one cannot see an alternative way out. For Yugoslav state officials involved in the matter, the only important question was how to employ the remittances in a more useful way. Yugoslav emigration representatives and policymakers discussed, for example, apart from other topics, some of the undesirable effects related to remittances at their 1924 Zagreb Conference.[56] They were unanimous in pointing out that almost all of the money that came from this source had been invested either in consumption or in the improvement of private housing. A few participants suggested measures which would facilitate a more active role for the National Bank of the Kingdom of SCS (*Narodna Banka Kraljevine SHS*) in the management of the financial aspect of emigration affairs. They argued that the central bank should not be limited entirely to the conversion of emigrants' remittances, as any other financial institution could do this. Moreover, the National Bank should be engaged in a much more ambitious project of building up a US filial, which was to collect all emigrants' savings and remittances in one place. Only in this way, the huge potential of emigrants' money could be used for large-scale investment projects in Yugoslavia. However, nothing of this initiative came into practice during the period under review.

[56] Stenogram Ankete o iseljavanju (footnote 29).

Conclusions

The violence of the First World War and subsequent government restrictions in the domain of international migrations had a considerable impact on global migration. The almost complete and uncontrolled freedom of movement and travel between Europe and the overseas countries of immigration, which had existed until 1914, would never come again. A new age emerged in which countries of immigration and emigration began to establish restrictions and quotas for migrants. Since these international limitations on migration have survived in a different form and extent until today, the First World War and the 1920s, in particular, appear to be significant turning points in the European and global history of migration. Yugoslav emigration policy followed the global changes, both on the legal level and, even more so, in administrative practice.

After 1921, the emigration procedure in Yugoslavia was integrated into a unified system based in the emigration offices in Zagreb and later also in Belgrade. In connection with the establishment of the US quota system, the Yugoslav authorities were obliged to control the fulfillment of the quota for the Kingdom of SCS. Apart from this limitation, no formal restrictions existed on emigration in the Kingdom. The decrees, laws, and regulations by the state guaranteed citizens an unrestricted freedom of movement. Due to the legal limitations and discriminative policy against national minorities in the Kingdom of Serbs, Croats and Slovenes, these restrictions could not be officially spelled out. They were nevertheless carried out through confidential and extra-institutional orders that circulated among state personnel.

Under the new policy, the procedure of issuing passports became utterly complicated. The discretionary rights given to officials opened the door for corruption and the financial exploitation of applicants. This misuse of power and low-style corruption damaged the reputation of the state, particularly the Belgrade administration, and discredited the noble cause of a great legislative and administrative effort in the domain of emigration, which had aimed at protecting emigrants from exploitation. The complete administrative chaos, misconduct, and extortion from applicants reached such a level that one might have wondered whether it would not have been better if the state had not intervened in emigration matters at all.

Only members of the German and Hungarian national minorities had the 'privilege' of receiving all the necessary papers in the shortest possible time within the new restrictive guiding principles. This policy accounts for the poor performance regarding the emigration of 'Yugoslavs' and the large proportion of 'non-Slavic' minorities in the annual contingents of emigrants from the Kingdom of SCS. This was probably the only point of 'successfully' conducted state intervention in emigration affairs, namely, to prevent the emigration of 'nationals' and to favor the emigration of the 'non-national' element. As a result, compared to pre-war levels, emigration from the Kingdom of SCS was almost negligible. The state authorities' concern for these emigrants did not go further than providing channels for the efficient transfer of their remittances back home. In return, the steady influx of hard currency essentially contributed to the monetary stability of the first Yugoslav state.

It is apparent that the emigration flows of the backward Southeast European countries did not fit into the patterns of the global labor movements during the period of the first globalization (1846–1914): the numerically significant Croatian emigration was part of the 'low-wage' emigration streem eventually incompatible with the Atlantic labour market system;[57] Serbia and Bulgaria even created big obstacles to the transoceanic emigration of their citizens. Ironically, the only global system that these countries would have been fully integrated into was that one of trade tariffs and restrictions on the freedom of transport and movement of people imposed in the rest of the world during and after World War One.

Acknowledgements

This study developed from my MA thesis at the Central European University in Budapest. My debt to Professor Constantin Iordachi is especially deep since he did the lion's share of supervising and assistance on my work in progress. The research project and the paper would not have been possible without institutional help and funding received from the Institute for the Recent History of Serbia (*Institut za noviju istoriju Srbije*) in Belgrade and the Central European University in Budapest. Particularly, I wish to thank Momčilo Mitrović, the Institute's Director, who supported my project and took care of my well being throughout my studies and research. I wish to thank also my dear friend and colleague, Thomas Szerecz, of the Central European University, for his assistance in the editing of this manuscript. In the final phase, the text was significantly improved thanks to numerous suggestions and advice given by Ulf Brunnbauer.

57 See footnotes 7 and 8.

Karolina Novinšćak

The Recruiting and Sending of Yugoslav *'Gastarbeiter'* to Germany: Between Socialist Demands and Economic Needs

"The Federal Republic of Germany, our country, is very satisfied with them. These are workers of high quality, able to adjust quickly to a new environment. That is why our main effort for the selection of workers is at the moment in Yugoslavia." – These words were spoken by the head of the German medical delegation, which was carrying out medical examinations for recruited labour migrants from the Socialist Federal Republic of Yugoslavia (SFR Yugoslavia) in a Yugoslav employment office.[1] The medical examination was mandatory for all people applying for a job in the Federal Republic of Germany (FR Germany) through the Yugoslav employment offices, and the ones regarded as healthy and fit for work were allowed to board the "special trains" for *Gastarbeiter*[2] via Munich.

This article looks beyond the working qualities of the Yugoslav labour migrants and asks for additional reasons for the recruitment of workers from the Yugoslav socialist state to the FR Germany, just as it examines the sending policy of the Yugoslav authorities. The migration of Yugoslav *Gastarbeiter* to the FR Germany will be examined in its political and economic context on the eve of the German-Yugoslav recruitment agreement, which was negotiated by the delegations of both governments and signed on October 12, 1968, in

1 The recruitment procedure in the SFR Yugoslavia is documented by filmmaker Krsto Papić in the documentary film *Special Trains* (Zagreb Film, 1971). Papić filmed the medical examination in the employment centre of Zagreb, accompanied the recruited labour migrants on their train journey to the FR Germany and followed the migrants down to a bunker on their arrival in Munich.

2 Here, the term "*Gastarbeiter*" (guest worker) is used as a historical expression for workers who migrated to the FR Germany during the European labour migration process of the 1950s–1970s. Politically, the term is no longer accurate, as many former "Gastarbeiter" have become permanent residents of the FR Germany. But the term is still used to denote foreign workers in some contemporary English (gastarbeiter), Greek (gastarbáiter/γκασταρμπάιτερ), and Russian (gastarbajter/гастарбайтер) texts. It is preserved also in the languages of the republics of the former Yugoslavia, where it is spelled "gastarbajteri" or "gastoši" and mostly refers to labour migrants and their descendents.

Belgrade. The bilateral agreement on the recruitment of Yugoslav workers from the SFR Yugoslavia to the FR Germany was determined firstly by the economic needs of the labour markets in both countries and their bilateral economic relations, and secondly, by the political rapprochement between the FR Germany and Yugoslavia.

Bilateral relations and the recruitment agreement

When Tito's partisans gained power, the German atrocities in occupied Yugoslavia during World War II on the one hand, and the forced displacement of Germans by Yugoslav partisans on the other hand, weighed heavily on the relations between the two states in the first years after the war. However, Tito's break with Stalin and the East Bloc in 1948 put Yugoslav-German animosities gradually in the background. Since then, political and economic considerations in the new international context led to the gradual improvement of bilateral relations between the SFR Yugoslavia and the FR Germany.[3]

German-Yugoslav cooperation was firstly achieved on the economic level. In 1956, an agreement was signed on economic cooperation between the two states, and the FR Germany granted an interest-free loan to Yugoslavia of 240 Million DM, repayable for 99 years. At the same time, Tito looked for a rapprochement with the Soviet Union and subscribed to the Soviet view that the FR Germany and the German Democratic Republic (GDR) were two separate states. Eventually, in 1957 the SFR Yugoslavia established diplomatic relations with the GDR. In reaction to this, the FR Germany applied for the first time the so-called "Hallstein Doctrine", meaning to cut diplomatic relations with countries that recognised the GDR. Thus relations with the SFR Yugoslavia were severed for the next eleven years. On January 31, 1968, German-Yugoslav diplomatic relations were restored and nine months later, the Yugoslav transfer of workers to the FR Germany was agreed.

The "Hallstein Doctrine" and the Yugoslav demands for German reparation payments were two central issues that complicated the first phase of the German-Yugoslav rapprochement and also the negotiations for a bilateral recruitment treaty. Historian Zoran Janjetović pointed out in a well researched book the dynamics of the debate on German reparation payments and their relation to the improvement of German-Yugoslav bilateral relations.[4] When the restoration of German-Yugoslav diplomatic relations was negotiated in 1967 and again in 1968, Yugoslav demands for reparation payments slipped down the agenda because Yugoslav policy makers gave priority to the resolution of trade issues and the *Gastarbeiter* status.[5] Historian Vladimir Ivanović stresses that during the preliminary negotiations about the resumption of diplomatic relations between the FR Germany and Yugoslavia, the question of the recruitment of Yugoslav workers was of great importance.[6] Furthermore, Karen

3 Sundhaussen, Jugoslawisch-deutsche Beziehungen, 134.
4 Janjetović, Od Auschwitza do Brijuna.
5 Ibid., 73.
6 Ivanović, Obnavljanje diplomatskih odonosa, 136, fn. 22.

Schönwälder, Monika Mattes and Senad Hadžič point out that the resumption of negotiations about the recruitment of Yugoslav workers to the FR Germany became a significant part of Willy Brandt's *Ostpolitik*.[7] These studies, based on files from German ministries, prove the primacy of German foreign policy concerns determined by the Ostpolitik in the preliminary recruitment negotiations with Yugoslavia.

In this text, I will concentrate on the development of the state-organised recruitment and sending policies respectively of the FR Germany and the SFR Yugoslavia, addressing the perspective of both states. Labour migration policies will be analysed in the context of German-Yugoslav bilateral relations and their economic and political interdependencies. Hence, the recruitment of Yugoslav workers to West Germany was a result of both Brandt's Ostpolitik and Tito's Western orientation. My research is based on files of the German Federal Archive in Koblenz and of the Archive of Yugoslavia (now called Archive of Serbia and Montenegro) in Belgrade.

Basically, the German government preferred recruitment agreements with befriended states. Signing a bilateral recruitment agreement and institutionalising people transfer from a socialist country was quite a remarkable overture, yet from the economic point of view a further consequence of increasing economic cooperation between the two states. Even though political relations had been frozen since 1957, the FR Germany upheld economic relations with Yugoslavia. German external trade with Yugoslavia developed favourably and German imports were of high significance for the Yugoslav industry. On the other hand, Yugoslav natural resources such as bauxite and wood were highly requested in the FR Germany: in 1956, 40 percent of the bauxite used by German industry for the production of aluminium came from Yugoslav mines.[8]

In addition, the number of Yugoslav workers in German companies grew constantly: in 1954, 1,801 Yugoslavs were registered at the German Federal Labour Office and by 1962 their number had increased up to 23,608.[9] Since the German labour market had not been able to satisfy the huge demand for labour force by the end of the 1950s, the German employers' recruitment strategy for low-paid employees constantly reached beyond the state border. The first state-organised recruitment of foreign workers was from Italy in 1955, then from Spain, Turkey, Portugal, Greece, Morocco and Tunisia. The last recruitment agreement was signed by the German government with Yugoslavia, ensuring that cheap labour from this socialist country would enter the FR Germany in huge numbers. Yugoslav workers enjoyed a regulated legal status on a temporary, non-immigrant basis and social insurance. By 1968, when the German-Yugoslav recruitment agreement was signed, 148,400 Yugoslav citizens had already moved to the FR Germany.[10] The following year their number increased up to 297,000 and reached its climax in 1973, when 535,000 Yugoslavs lived in

[7] Schönwälder, Einwanderung und ethnische Pluralität, 343–4, 365; Mattes, „Gastarbeiterinnen" in der Bundesrepublik, 53; Hadžič, Titos „Gastarbeiter", 109.

[8] Anić de Osona, Die erste Anerkennung der DDR, 304.

[9] Baučić, Socialno-ekonomske posljedice, 27, Tab. II.

[10] Haberl, Die Abwanderung von Arbeitskräften, 276, Tab. 17.

Germany. Yugoslavia was the only socialist country to join the organised transfer of workers from Southern to Western Europe and the Yugoslav labour force was highly requested in the West, especially by German employers until the 1973 recruitment ban.

In economic terms, pull factors in the highly developed industrial economy of the FR Germany during the 1960s as well as push factors in Yugoslavia, e. g. the weak economy and the preponderance of its agrarian population, shaped the Yugoslav labour migration process, which was thus in line with other economically motivated migrations from the southern periphery to the industrial centres of Western Europe. The particularities of the Yugoslav labour migration process lie in its political implications. The 'transfer' of over one million Yugoslav citizens from a socialist into a democratic-capitalist system, in accordance with the governments' plans, differentiates the Yugoslav labour migration to the FR Germany from labour migration from democratic-capitalist countries within the European Economic Community. In the Yugoslav socialist 'workers' state', the idea of a state-organised labour transfer and the ensuing sending policy of the League of the Communists of Yugoslavia had to pass several ideological, political and institutional barriers.

Firstly, sending abroad the unemployed challenged the basic legitimacy of Tito's imagined workers' state. Sine qua non of the state-organised labour transfer in the 1960s and 1970s was, therefore, the new ideological interpretation of Yugoslav socialism. Yugoslavia's 'third way' started with Tito's break with Stalin and the founding of the Non-Aligned Movement. Gradually it experienced further modifications through the economic system of self-management, which was accompanied by the open border policy for tourists and jobseekers. The Yugoslav labour migration policy was embedded in the dynamic of rewording socialism that was affected by economic and political needs. Correspondingly, the ruling party transformed the restrictive migration policy of the post-war era into a supportive sending policy from the beginning of the 1960s to the middle of the 1970s.

Secondly, in the execution of the latter, the government of the recruiting state became an indispensable partner, as its will to sign a recruitment agreement and to actually recruit Yugoslav workers in cooperation with the state of origin was the precondition for any sending and controlling strategy of the Yugoslav government in the period of labour migration. Thirdly, the institutions that would organise, send and control the labour force transfer had to be built up, based on the principle of Yugoslav federalism and partly in collaboration with the recruiting state on a bilateral basis. After the signing of the recruitment agreement a mixed German-Yugoslav commission, based in Belgrade, regulated and carried out the decentralised recruitment procedure in the employment centres of the individual republics.[11] As Yugoslav labour migration policy reached beyond the Yugoslav state borders, it had to be brought in line with the law and migration policy of the recruiting state. The establishment of Yugoslav institutions for labour migrants abroad and the political conception of national assistance for the citizens abroad required further adjustments, also to German migration policy.

[11] Manfrass, Die Beziehungen, 270–276.

The Yugoslav 'gastarbeiter export' between socialism and capitalism

After the Yugoslav communists broke with the Soviet Union and were thrown out of the Cominform in 1948, they gradually adopted a new, more independent course towards socialism, which would be known as 'Titoism'. Regarding foreign affairs, Yugoslavia became one of the leading powers of the Non-Aligned-Movement, which sought a balance between the Western and Eastern blocs. As the only non-aligned socialist country in Europe, Yugoslavia enjoyed good relations with the West, which also financially supported the country in order to preserve its military and economic independence from the Eastern bloc. Internally, the Yugoslav communists embarked on an ambitious decentralisation programme, which gave increasing powers to the republics (and autonomous provinces within Serbia) and lessened central control over the economy. So-called 'workers' self-management' in public enterprises, and later also state institutions, became the embodiment of the Yugoslav 'third way'. Closer economic and political but also social relations with Western countries were one of the results of these policies. The turn towards a liberal labour migration policy by opening the borders for citizens to migrate to Western industrial countries has to be seen also in this context.

This shift meant a radical break with the initially restrictive migration policies. In the first seventeen years after coming to power, the Yugoslav communists treated people who left the SFR Yugoslavia for economic reasons as enemies of the state. Departure would not be accepted or justified because it contradicted socio-political norms.[12] For the Yugoslav policymakers, it was a point of honour to provide work for everyone in a society self-managed by the workers.[13] Such as in other socialist societies, work was seen as a moral duty and being unemployed – from a socialist point of view – not only was a "moral scandal and personal shame"[14] but also a criminal act.

The party's ideological disaffirmation of labour migration was soon challenged by economic needs. The Yugoslav labour market suffered heavily after the economic reforms of the 1960s. With the introduction of the self-management system and the abandonment of the full employment policy, the transfer of labour from the agricultural to the industrial sector almost stopped at once. At the same time, the baby-boomers from the countryside were entering the labour market. The industrialisation process, the most prestigious economic and social achievement of the communist government, was faltering and seemed to be in jeopardy. For many unemployed young people, accepting work abroad was the only way to meet the basic needs of everyday life. According to official statistics, between 1953 and 1963 277,675 people had already gone abroad; estimations claimed that half a million ille-

12 Baučić, Stanje vanjskih migracija, 7.
13 Marković, Verloren in der Transmigration?, 239.
14 Niedermüller, Arbeit, Identität, Klasse, 25.

gal emigrants had left the country during this period.[15] For many illegal labour migrants the economic pressure or incentive to migrate was higher than the fear of being expelled from Yugoslav society. These economic difficulties forced the communist party to face the reality of labour migration. Although labour migration officially remained illegal, it was tacitly accepted as a necessity and the Yugoslav authorities even issued exit visas.[16]

The shift in Yugoslav emigration policy became visible in 1962, when the Vice President of the Federal Executive Council (the federal government), Aleksandar Ranković, suggested a decree for the amnesty of emigrants.[17] The aim of the decree was to allow all Yugoslav emigrants to return to their homeland, apart from war criminals, collaborators, spies and persons who had been involved in actions and campaigns against the Yugoslav state. Since amnesty had been granted to all economic refugees, labour migration was no longer condemned as illegal.

In economic discussions, some voices demanded the dogma be dropped that the labour force was not an economic good.[18] Yugoslav politicians and economists, who called for an extended, state controlled labour migration, argued that the Yugoslav economy would benefit from the regulated and monitored transfer of unemployed abroad and from the expected remittances. The new interpretation of socialism in Yugoslavia also allowed for a new approach toward labour migration, viewing it as a consequence of internationalism and of Yugoslavia's political and economic cooperation with other nations. Economists argued that the successful integration of the Yugoslav economy into the world market had to include the free circulation of goods and capital as well as the circulation of workers. "The debate whether it is good or bad that more and more Yugoslav workers get employed abroad is not yet finished", says an article in *Ekonomska Politika* on July 4, 1964, pointing to the discrepancy between the theory and reality of employment abroad. The author argues that wishful thinking concerning the full employment of workers in the domestic economy does not help the Yugoslav economy. Labour migration should rather be considered as a fact of life that is grounded in economic developments and regularities. Tito himself showed the party's new pragmatism in a speech in 1965, in which he stressed that it did not make sense to hold someone back by force, preventing him from searching for work somewhere else, "if he cannot immediately be employed in our own country anyway".[19]

The restrictive labour migration policy did not fit any more into the new self-conception of Yugoslav society and state in terms of 'humane socialism', which also included the right for individuals to look for and accept employment abroad. The new ideological definition of labour migration resulted also in a new definition of the role of the state in the labour migration process. On the one hand the socialist state renounced responsibility for the outflow of people, as the main reason for labour migration was located in the international labour

15 Mesić, Vanjske migracije, 13.

16 Baučić, Die Auswirkungen der Arbeitskräftewanderung, 195.

17 Archiv der Gegenwart (AdG), 9738/C, 14.03.1962.

18 Haberl, Die Abwanderung von Arbeitskräften, 70.

19 Quoted in ibid., 73.

market; Yugoslavia was seen as joining the international labour market and the migration processes from Southern to Western Europe. On the other hand, the reinterpretation and liberalisation of labour migration enabled the Yugoslav government to organise and control the complete act of labour migration and to establish legal protection over the migrants. By stressing the Yugoslav worker's freedom of individual choice to go abroad for work, it consequently became a duty for the Yugoslav worker's state to care for its citizens abroad. Henceforth, the state's labour migration policy was communicated as a supporting measure for the development of the self-management economy and – quite optimistically – the labour migrants were supposed to return when the Yugoslav economy was consolidated. Therefore, the vision of a final return of the labour migrants was a constitutive element of the liberalised Yugoslav labour migration policy, which was strongly connected with the expectation of successful economic development in Yugoslavia. In fact, departure and return were not merely individual decisions, but viewed as a necessity in a developing socialist society.

This explains the specific expression used to officially denominate Yugoslav labour migrants, "*Radnik na privremenom radu u inozemstvu*": worker temporarily employed abroad. The stress on the "temporary" character of Yugoslav labour migration was of ideological and political importance. The creation of a collective name for the labour migrants made clear that they continued to belong to the society of socialist Yugoslavia; in the official view, they had gone abroad to work for a limited period only. The expression "worker temporarily employed abroad" was mostly used together with the possessive pronoun "our", suggesting that the Yugoslav worker abroad was still an 'organic part' of the working class of Yugoslavia. Political scientist William Zimmerman describes the concern of the Yugoslav authorities for their labour migrants in terms of an imagined "seventh Yugoslav republic" beyond the state borders: "[...] the Yugoslav decision makers acted increasingly as though they had to treat the workers, while abroad, as nearly as possible as a matter of domestic politics".[20] By giving the emigrated population a collective name, the government pressed its claim on the citizens abroad, emphasising that their labour migration was temporary and that the party attached great importance to their return. The ideological legitimisation in stressing that labour migrants belong to Yugoslav society implied that their status in the Western countries and their final return was not a private matter but one concerning the whole socialist society.[21] It also distinguished labour migrants semantically from political exiles, the so-called "*politička emigracija*", who were treated like enemies of the state and who were forbidden to return to their home country. In the Yugoslav public and political discourse the word "emigrant" was commonly used for hostile political exiles and due to its negative and political connotation, labour migrants were never called nor perceived as 'emigrants' by the government.

The expression "worker temporarily employed abroad" also correlated with the recruitment strategy of the Western states and employers, who issued fixed-term labour permits to foreign workers. In the FR Germany, Yugoslav workers were usually called *Gastarbeiter*,

20 Zimmermann, Open Borders, 112.
21 Mesić, Vanjske migracije, 20.

a label they shared with Italian, Spanish, Portuguese, Greek, Turkish and other foreign labour migrants who had come earlier in the 1950s and 1960s. The term "Gastarbeiter" emphasised the labour migrants' status as welcome guests who were expected to work hard and leave when their work was no longer needed. In 1973 the German Federal Minister of Labour, Walter Arendt of the Social Democratic Party (SPD), still pointed out:

> *The FRG does not envision itself as a classical immigrant country. We principally proceed on the assumption that the people who come to our country will return to their homeland after a certain time voluntarily and will contribute to the further development of their country.*[22]

The Yugoslav assumption of the temporary nature of labour migration was paralleled by decades of the German policy of refusing the deeper integration of labour migrants, which would otherwise have meant that the FR Germany, for all intents and purposes, would be turning into a country of immigration.The ideological reinterpretation of labour migration led to the gradual expansion of Yugoslav institutions that would channel the labour migration flow. In 1963, the Yugoslav government drew up guidelines for regulating the employment of Yugoslav workers abroad.[23] According to these, the coordination and regulation of the employment of Yugoslav workers abroad was in the hands of a special commission at the Yugoslav Federal Office for Employment. Special commissions for coordinating the labour migration process were also established on the republican level, whereas the labour permits for employment abroad were issued by the municipal employment offices. The first law that delineated functions and responsibilities between the Federal Office for Employment and the republican and local employment centres came into force on April 6, 1965.[24] The Federal Office for Employment was authorised to monitor labour migration out of Yugoslavia, to establish agreements with foreign employers and to coordinate the work of all administrative bodies that were engaged in the employment of workers abroad. In 1966, the employment offices of the communes were also authorised to sign agreements with foreign employers on the employment of Yugoslav workers. The foreign employers had to pay a fee to the Yugoslav employment officials for every successful contract. Haberl points out that these financial incentives fostered the further maximisation of labour migration out of Yugoslavia.[25]

After labour migration was made ideologically compatible with Yugoslav socialism, the government supported it by signing bilateral recruitment agreements, first with France (1965), then Austria and Sweden (1966), the FR Germany (1968), and finally Belgium, Luxembourg, The Netherlands, and Australia (1970). In political and public discourse, these agreements and the organisation of the departure of workers through Yugoslav employment agencies were presented as a caring measure of the government, which sought to protect Yugoslav workers abroad as far as possible.

22 Quoted in Lohrmann, Politische Auswirkungen, 119, fn. 53.
23 Uputstvo o postupanju, *Službeni list,* 23 October 1963.
24 Haberl, Die Abwanderung von Arbeitskräften, 74.
25 Ibid., 77–8.

Negotiations between the SFR Yugoslavia and the FR Germany towards the recruitment agreement of October 12, 1968

As a result of the deteriorating economic situation in the country, the Yugoslav government had to acknowledge the fact that by the end of 1963, about 140,000 Yugoslavs already worked and lived in Western Europe, 80,000 of whom were in the FR Germany. They came mainly from the Republics of Croatia and Bosnia and Herzegovina.[26]

High-level talks about the regulation of Yugoslav labour migration to the FR Germany had already started in 1963 in the context of trade negotiations in Munich, when the Yugoslav desire was met to talk about the situation of Yugoslav workers and a social insurance agreement.[27] The consultations were concluded with the statement that both sides were interested in regulating the entry of Yugoslav workers into the German labour market, but the Yugoslav side asked for more time to lay the foundations in organisational terms for the regulation of interstate labour transfer. In April 1964, in a meeting in Genoa, the representatives of the German Foreign Ministry and the Yugoslav Office for Foreign Affairs agreed that negotiations about the employment of Yugoslav workers and social insurance should precede other economic and financial negotiations.[28] The Yugoslav Deputy Secretary of State for Foreign Affairs, Marko Nikezić, explained to the Yugoslav Federal Executive Council that a social insurance agreement would help the Yugoslav workers to assume their rights in the FR Germany. Yugoslavia would also gain benefits from a social insurance agreement as Yugoslav citizens would spend their old-age pensions in their homeland and the foreign currency inflow would increase. Nikezić deplored that the flow of labour migration from Yugoslavia to the FR Germany took place without government oversight. He underlined further that the Yugoslav workers in the FR Germany were at the mercy of illegal employment agencies, which were often run by "unfriendly emigrants". To avoid the further political mobilisation and material exploitation of Yugoslav workers, Nikezić recommended a German-Yugoslav recruitment agreement that would regulate not merely the status of Yugoslav citizens already living in the FR Germany, but also future Yugoslav labour migration to that country.[29] Finally, on June 29, 1964, the Yugoslav Federal Executive Council agreed to enter into negotiations with the FR Germany about the employment of Yugoslav citizens.

[26] Archive of Yugoslavia, Belgrade (*Arhiv Jugoslavije*, further abbreviated as AJ), Savezno Izvršno Veće (SIV), fond 130, fasc. 780 (AJ 130/780): Informacija o problemima u vezi sa zapošljavanjem naših gradjana u inostranstvu, Beograd, 30 May 1964.

[27] Bundesarchiv Koblenz (further abbreviated as BA Ko), B 149/6241: Bericht des Referenten RD Dr. Dahnen, Abt. II, IIa 4 – 2430.6: Beschäftigung jugoslawischer Arbeitnehmer in der Bundesrepublik; hier: Sachverständigengespräche in Belgrad vom 21.–24.7.1964, Bonn, 5 August 1964.

[28] AJ 130/626/1034: Državni sekretariat za inostrane poslove Saveznom Izvršnom Veću, br. 423534, Beograd, 4 June 1964.

[29] Ibid.

After the FR Germany and the SFR Yugoslavia finalised a trade agreement in 1964, the Yugoslav government initiated special expert talks from July 21–24 of that year, to re-examine whether the establishment of a recruitment and social insurance agreement was possible.[30] The Yugoslav delegation presented a proposal for a recruitment and social insurance agreement which included child benefits and four particular points, different from other recruitment agreements that the FR Germany had signed with other countries: firstly, the Yugoslav government pointed out that a German commission that would decide whom to recruit was not conformable with the self-confidence of Yugoslav citizens, who would run the risk of being denied recruitment by the commission. From the Yugoslav point of view, a German commission for recruitment that would recruit and select the workers in Yugoslavia, such as the FR Germany practised in other countries of recruitment, would be an unjustifiable limitation of Yugoslav sovereignty and was therefore rejected. The recruitment procedure should be in the hands of Yugoslav administrative bodies only. Secondly, the Yugoslav delegation demanded the right to recall their employed workers from Germany, which in turn the German delegation could not accept. Thirdly, the Yugoslav delegates asked for approval to send representatives of the Yugoslav trade unions and cultural organisations to Germany in order to facilitate the accommodation of Yugoslav workers in the FR Germany and to meet their cultural needs.[31] But the mere idea of communist institutions working in the FR Germany generated rejection on the German side. The attending Officer of the Ministry of Labour, Dr. Dahnen, reported that the German side had reservations about the presence of Yugoslav government authorities in Germany with regard to conflicts with exile organisations, "which, in general, in a fully satisfactory manner take care of employed Yugoslavs here – mainly Croats".[32] Fourthly, the Yugoslav proposal lacked the usual 'Berlin Clause', which regulated the application of international contracts for West Berlin.

The delegations pledged to continue their negotiations after the German side had come up with a proposal. They met again in March 1965 without finding an agreement about the recruitment of Yugoslav workers, and the negotiations on this topic were postponed again. Although the Yugoslav side had already dropped their refusal of a German recruiting commission based on Yugoslav soil, the German side showed no real interest in the conclusion of an agreement partly due to the lack of economic interest and partly due to their irritation about Tito's visit to the German Democratic Republic in the same year.[33] In the meantime, economic relations between Yugoslavia and the FR Germany remained vital through loan

[30] BA Ko, B 149/6241: Bericht des Referenten RD Dr. Dahnen, Abt. II, IIa 4 – 2430.6: Beschäftigung jugoslawischer Arbeitnehmer in der Bundesrepublik; hier: Sachverständigengespräche in Belgrad vom 21.–24.7.1964, Bonn, 5 August 1964.

[31] Ibid.

[32] Ibid.

[33] Hadžić, Titos "Gastarbeiter", 109.

and trade agreements. From 1964 to 1966, the bilateral trade volume rose by nearly 35 percent and the German trade surplus with Yugoslavia reached 470 Million DM.[34]

The political relations, however, were put on hold and can be characterised by distrust on both sides. The Yugoslav government registered that the "unfriendly" political situation between the two states had negative consequences on the control and regulation of the labour migration process in the FR Germany. The isolated political exiles, whose number is not recorded, came into contact in the FR Germany with a larger number of Yugoslav people during the labour migration period. The latter represented a part of the Yugoslav population that the political emigrants considered valuable for political mobilisation as the labour migrants were allowed and supposed to return to Yugoslavia. Henceforth, the political exiles took the opportunity to spread their political agendas in the labour migrants' communities. The fear of political mobilisation and radicalisation by anti-Yugoslav political organisations in the FR Germany, especially the Croat labour migrants, constantly worried the Yugoslav authorities. Due to the frozen political relations to the FR Germany, the Yugoslav state was pushed to the rear of the labour migrants' communities, as no Yugoslav embassies even existed and the Yugoslav diplomats had to work under the diplomatic protection of Sweden. However, the Yugoslav state could easily put pressure upon the labour migrants through the revalidation of visas. Many labour migrants, who had houses and family in Yugoslavia, feared repressions against them, e. g. having their passport seized, so they mainly avoided political gatherings during their stay abroad. The Yugoslav passport was thus an effective means of exerting pressure upon the Yugoslav labour migrants, who reacted with high adaptability to the demands of the Yugoslav state.[35]

Nevertheless, the toleration of mainly Croat exile groups in the FR Germany, as well as the unsolved problem of reparation payments for the victims of World War II, strained the German-Yugoslav relations. As early as November 1961, the German government received a note in which the Yugoslavs complained about the anti-Yugoslav operations of Croat political exiles in the FR Germany.[36] The Yugoslav government demanded that the German side laid the foundations for 'normal' working conditions for Yugoslav Consulates and normal living conditions for Yugoslav citizens in the FR Germany. In its answering note the German government refused to accept any responsibility for anti-Yugoslav campaigns in the FR Germany and, in turn, accused the Yugoslav politicians and press of uncritically adopting the anti-FRG agitation of the Soviet bloc. Putting the internal affair into the context of the tensions of the Cold War, by implication, the German policy makers made it quite clear to the Yugoslav government that no German-Yugoslav cooperation concerning political emigrants could be expected if the Yugoslav agitation against the FR Germany were continued.

[34] Akten zur Auswärtigen Politik der Bundesrepublik Deutschland (AAPBRD), 1967, Band II, Dok. 156: Aufzeichnung des Botschafters Emmel, Bericht über die deutsch-jugoslawischen Wirtschaftsverhandlungen vom 24. bis 29. April 1967 in Belgrad, 3 May 1967, 699.

[35] Goeke, Jugoslawische Arbeitswanderer, 733.

[36] AdG, 1962, 9.621 B.

On November 29, 1962, a bomb attack was carried out on the Yugoslav mission in Mehlem, Bad Godesberg, whereupon the Yugoslav foreign ministry declared that this attack was one of the most brutal anti-Yugoslav provocations committed in the FR Germany ever.[37] In reaction to this, the FR Germany outlawed the right-wing extremist Croat exile-group "*Hrvatsko križarsko bratstvo*" in 1963.[38] These measures would not really satisfy the Yugoslav policymakers, as the political activism of the political exiles continued. In 1964, the Yugoslav Federal Office for Employment presented a report on "the problems connected with the employment of our citizens abroad" to the Yugoslav Federal Executive Council.[39] The report stated that due to the lack of language ability, the insecure housing and working situation, and the financial difficulties of a considerable number of labour migrants, the political 'emigrants' seized the opportunity and offered them help:

> *In this manner the emigrants practise upon our workers political-propagandistic activities against the SFRY, in order to spread and revolve their organisations, in which they are relatively successful. This is especially characteristic for the FRG and France* [...].[40]

The report warns that some citizens already spoke out that they would never come back to Yugoslavia as long as "the communists rule". The emigrants' work in the labour migrants' communities was defined as a long-term effort aiming for political action, intelligence and sabotage against Yugoslavia. By the mid-1960s, the situation in West Germany had escalated. In 1965, the Yugoslav Vice-Consul Andrija Klarić survived a murder attempt in Munich and only one year later Consul Savo Milanović was murdered in Stuttgart by a Croat. The German weekly newspaper "*Die Zeit*" described the shooting in Stuttgart as a violent conflict between brothers, Croats and Serbs:

> *With over 30,000 Yugoslavs, the Gastarbeiter-stronghold of Baden-Wuerttemberg (Stuttgart) became the Texas of Croats and Serbs.* [...] *In the Federal Republic of Germany some Yugoslavs live, who have severed ties with their communist government. Then again, the Yugoslav Gastarbeiter are allowed to come together in internal communist meetings.*[41]

In 1966, the Yugoslav State Office of Foreign Affairs informed the Yugoslav Federal Executive Council about the acute worsening of the German-Yugoslav relations.[42] The FR Germany had still not answered the pending economic questions and not yet reacted to the Yugoslav proposal for a recruitment agreement. Furthermore, the Yugoslav foreign ministry noticed that the FR Germany had abstained from voting for the admittance of Yugoslavia to the General Agreement on Tariffs and Trade (GATT). The West German press was charged

37 AdG, 1962, 10.271 B.
38 AdG, 1963, 10.469 H.
39 AJ 130/780: Savezni sekretarijat za rad Sekretaru Saveznog izvršnog Veća; Informacija o problemima u vezi sa zaposljavanjem naših gradjana u inostranstvu, Beograd, 30 May 1964.
40 Ibid., 5.
41 NL, Schüsse in Stuttgart.
42 AJ 130/626/1034: Državni sekretarijat za inostrane poslove, II uprava, broj 432162; Informacija o najnovijem pogoršanju u odnosima SRN-SFRJ, Beograd, 12 September 1966.

for colouring the terrorist acts of political emigrants by giving them a political character and the German government was accused of using the anti-Yugoslav activities of political exile groups as a method of exerting pressure as part of its policy towards Yugoslavia:

> *Such a policy of the FRG government towards the SFRY carries the momentous features of heavy interventionism in the internal affairs of a sovereign state and constitutes pressure on the sovereignty and integrity of the SFRY.*[43]

The Yugoslav State Office for Foreign Affairs saw a strong link between political relations with the FR Germany and the activities of their political opponents in exile: the worse the bilateral relations, the more intense were the anti-Yugoslav actions of exiles among the labour migrants in the FR Germany.[44] The Yugoslav government, therefore, deeply desired to radically and permanently eliminate the political and anti-Yugoslav actions among its labour migrants abroad, which was possible only in cooperation with the host country. Signing a recruitment agreement would not only help reduce unemployment in Yugoslavia and increase the amount of remittances sent to the country, but the Yugoslav state would also return, both in public and in the labour migrants' perception, to being a regulative and protecting force among the migrants' communities in the FR Germany.

However, during the Cold War the German government's policy towards foreigners was determined by their 'panic-fear' of communists.[45] In the 1960s, the administrative bodies of the FR Germany had exceptional concerns about the "import of communism in the shape of communist Gastarbeiter".[46] In 1966, the journal of the German employers association "*Der Arbeitgeber*" ("The Employer") noticed that the Yugoslav workers were preferred by employers but seen with mixed feelings by government officials, the police and the *Verfassungsschutz* (the domestic intelligence service): "What is sure is that apparently political functionaries from the Yugoslav side are smuggled in an organised way as workers into the FR Germany in order to come to grips with the Yugoslavs employed here."[47] On August 30, 1966, the German Federal Labour Office edited a regulation for the employment of Yugoslav workers in German factories in which it was determined that in general, employers should give priority to foreign workers from the European Economic Community countries.[48] Yugoslav male labourers would be given a work permit only if they were skilled, whereas the employment of Yugoslav female labourers was not restricted.

From the early 1960s until 1966, German recruitment and the Yugoslav sending policy were trapped between economic and political demands: on the one hand, German employers asked for Yugoslav workers who had a good reputation; on the other hand, German

43 Ibid.
44 AJ 130/626: Državni sekretarijat za inostrane poslove, II uprava, broj 418385; Informacija o poseti Jugoslaviji vice-kancelera i ministra spoljnih poslova SR Nemačke Willy Brandta, od 12. do 14. VI 1968, Beograd, 29 May 1968, 9.
45 Schönwälder, Einwanderung und ethnische Pluralität, 281.
46 Herbert, Geschichte der Ausländerpolitik, 214.
47 Weber, Problematische Jugoslawen, 652.
48 Ibid.

officials and politicians feared communist infiltration. By the same token, the Yugoslav government maximised labour migration to the FR Germany due to economic needs but at the same time, Yugoslav politicians and journalists condemned the developments of German foreign and domestic politics as a grave danger to peace in general.[49] Nevertheless, in Yugoslavia the pressure of unemployment prevailed over the political concerns and the Yugoslav policy makers fostered further labour migration. In 1966, the number of employed Yugoslavs in the FR Germany was 51 percent higher than in 1965.[50] However, despite massive labour migration to the FR Germany, France, Austria and other Western countries, unemployment in Yugoslavia kept on rising: from 212,400 job seekers in 1964 to 258,000 in 1966.[51]

For the deteriorating Yugoslav economy, labour migration was a compensation valve, as thousands of young job seekers were shown the way out of the country by Yugoslav employment centre officials. By 1966, 74,460 Yugoslavs were already registered in Yugoslav employment centres, ready to take a job abroad.[52] Meanwhile, remittances from labour migrants more than doubled, from 30.5 million US dollars in 1964 to 64 million in 1966.[53] Due to the negative balance of trade and the permanent shortage of foreign currency, the Yugoslav state desperately needed the remittances to pay for imports from Western European countries, mainly from the FR Germany. After 1963, the amount of foreign currency that was sent to Yugoslavia was monitored and registered with great attention by Yugoslav policy makers.[54]

In 1966 and 1967, at the beginning of the Great Coalition (consisting of the Christian Democratic Union, CDU, the Christian Social Union, CSU, and the Social Democratic Party of Germany, SPD), the German economy was hit by a recession. For the first time after the post-war economic 'miracle', the FR Germany was confronted with increasing unemployment. In 1966, over 300,000 people were jobless and their number grew to 460,000 in 1967. Ulrich Herbert stresses that this period was also characterised by negative sentiments of the German population towards recruited foreign workers; according to a survey of 1965, 51 percent of the polled had objections against the recruitment of foreigners as 'Gastarbeiter'.[55] Nevertheless, in November 1967 the Yugoslav government was informed that the FR Germany was willing to resume negotiations for an agreement on employment, social security and unemployment insurance for Yugoslav workers in December that year.[56] It was the first time that the German side offered and initiated negotiations about all the

[49] Reuter-Hendrichs, Jugoslawische Außenpolitik, 234.
[50] Weber, Problematische Jugoslawen, 651.
[51] Vinski, Wirtschaftliche Schwierigkeiten, 349.
[52] Ibid.
[53] Baučić, Die Auswanderung der Arbeitskräftebewegung, 189, Tab. 11.
[54] Ibid., 196.
[55] Herbert, Geschichte der Ausländerpolitik, 221.
[56] AJ 130/626: Savezni savet za rad Saveznom Izvršnom Veću, Predlog SR Nemačke za zaključenje sporazuma o zapošljavanju i konvencije o socijalnom osiguranju, Novi Beograd, 24 November 1967.

three topics – something which the Yugoslav policy makers had long been yearning for. This was a result of the entry of the Social Democrats in the government and their new foreign policy towards the communist countries.

Willy Brandt, the Great Coalition's foreign minister and vice chancellor, provided the initial spark for the preliminary talks on the German-Yugoslav recruitment agreement in 1967. His Ostpolitik, which was based on the principle of "change through rapprochement" towards the East, first and foremost required an improvement of German-Yugoslav relations by taking up diplomatic relations with this socialist but non-aligned state. On March 6, 1967, Brandt informed the Federal Chancellor Kiesinger that Belgrade was willing to resume diplomatic relations without preconditions.[57] In order to prevent setting a precedent, i.e. that other states of the Third World would wish to take up diplomatic relations with East-Berlin, guarantees from the Yugoslav state as one of the leaders of the Non-Aligned Movement during the German rapprochement period were needed. To improve the German-Yugoslav relations immediately, Brandt suggested to the Chancellor – apart from other measures – to take up negotiations about a Gastarbeiter and social insurance agreement.[58]

Although the Yugoslav government did not attach any conditions to the resumption of diplomatic relations, the Yugoslav side required the satisfaction of reparation demands, the prohibition of 'terrorist' exile groups and a contractual regulation of the Yugoslav Gastarbeiter status.[59] German ambassador Emmel remarked in his report about the German-Yugoslav trade negotiations that took place in April 1967 that in fact, the Yugoslavs attached great importance to the recruitment agreement and the fact that the German side had not yet put forward the date for these negotiations "overshadowed the negotiations completely and nearly led to the failure of the negotiations".[60] Further, he stated that the development of relations with the SFR Yugoslavia would crucially depend on the recruitment negotiations:

> *If this does not happen, the present Yugoslav attitude towards us could abruptly and considerably lead towards a new low point, a condition that cannot be brought back to the present status by granting all remaining concessions, even through future trade negotiations.*[61]

Although the German government refused any reparation payments, the German Foreign Ministry tried to reach normalisation by signalling its readiness for negotiating a recruitment agreement in small steps. On June 5, 1967, the German Ministry for Foreign Affairs

[57] AAPBRD, 1967, Bd. I, Dok. 88: Bundesminister Brandt an Bundeskanzler Kiesinger, 6 March 1967, 412–415.

[58] Ibid., 413.

[59] AAPBRD, 1967, Bd. I, Dok. 15: Gespräch zwischen Brandt und Couve de Murville, 13 January 1967, 85, fn. 33.

[60] AAPBRD, 1967, Bd. II, Dok. 156: Aufzeichnung des Botschafters Emmel, Bericht über die deutsch-jugoslawischen Wirtschaftsverhandlungen vom 24. bis 29. April 1967 in Belgrad, 3 May 1967, 702–3.

[61] Ibid., 703.

requested the German Federal Cabinet decide whether the negotiations about a recruitment and social insurance agreement should be resumed.[62] The Foreign Minister stated that there was little scope for improving the relations with Yugoslavia in the context of the 'Ostpolitik'. As reparation payments could not be accepted due to political and financial reasons, the continuation of recruitment negotiations was an opportunity to come closer to improving German-Yugoslav relations. Furthermore, the Foreign Minister argued that nearly 100,000 Yugoslavs were already working in the FR Germany and that German employers appreciated Yugoslav workers. The Foreign Ministry warned that foreign economic relations would suffer if the employment of Yugoslav labourers were not solved satisfactorily. If Germany wanted to keep on exporting to the SFR Yugoslavia, Yugoslavia in turn should be given the chance to pay for the imports. Concerning foreign economic relations, the Yugoslavs should be given the possibility "of matching up to us in economic transactions with their means at hand; that means to deliver, next to the export of goods, manpower to us."[63] The Foreign Minister stressed that since 1965 the Yugoslavs had been waiting for a continuation of the recruitment negotiations and warned of a refusal: "Such an affront should be avoided at a time when it is the Federal government's stated aim to improve relations also to Yugoslavia within the scope of its Ostpolitik."[64] By the middle of 1967, it was of great importance for the German Ministry for Foreign Affairs to leave the doors open for further negotiations concerning the recruitment of Yugoslav Gastarbeiter. To bridge the divide between East and West it was necessary to find areas of cooperation without discriminating Yugoslavia as an East European state.

Nevertheless, in times of recession, the Ministry of Labour had strong reservations against a German-Yugoslav recruitment agreement. Hans Katzer, Minister for Labour, pointed out to the Office of the Federal Chancellor that the German public might criticise another agreement for the recruitment of foreign workers, as 460,000 people in Germany were unemployed as of May 1967. Furthermore, he stated, "It is known that the vast majority of the German population – rather for emotional than for rational reasons – is against the employment of foreigners."[65] Moreover, an agreement would raise the number of Yugoslavs in Germany, and paying child benefit to the Yugoslavs would encourage them not to return but to stay in Germany, Katzer warned. He recommended not to negotiate the signing of a recruitment agreement until there was a different economic and employment situation.

[62] BA Ko, B 149/6241: Der Bundesminister des Auswärtigen Amtes an den Herrn Chef des Bundeskanzleramtes, Anlage zur Kabinettsache des Auswärtigen Amtes vom 5. Juni 1967, Betr.: Fortsetzung der Verhandlungen über eine Anwerbevereinbarung und ein Sozialversicherungsabkommen mit Jugoslawien, Bonn, 5 June 1967, 3.

[63] Ibid.

[64] Ibid.

[65] BA Ko, B 149/6241: Der Bundesminister für Arbeit und Sozialordnung an den Chef des Bundeskanzleramtes, Bonn, 9 June 1967.

The Ministry of Labour's objections were not shared by Foreign Minister Brandt. Continuing the recruitment negotiations with the SFR Yugoslavia was of high significance for the Foreign Ministry's preliminary talks about the resumption of diplomatic relations, even if, from the domestic and economic point of view, a reasonable case for new Gastarbeiter was missing. Already in April 1967, Foreign Minister Brandt made clear his opposing position to the Ministry of Labour:

> *I am not unaware of the fact that – in view of the present market situation and also with regard to other countries with which recruitment agreements have already been completed – certain reservations exist as to whether this is the right time to resume the German-Yugoslav negotiations. Nevertheless, I think the foreign policy reasons, which speak in favour for the continuation of the negotiations, should be given priority. It could be doubted that the Federal Government genuinely wishes to improve relations also with Yugoslavia, if we keep on refusing to discuss all questions related to the employment and occupation of Yugoslav workers in Germany and the possibility of their regulation.*[66]

Due to the differing positions expressed by the Foreign Ministry and Labour Ministry in 1967, the rapprochement through recruitment negotiations with the Yugoslavs were, in the end, based on a compromise. The German proposal, which was sent to the Yugoslav negotiators in November, suggested starting with talks in December but negotiating the recruitment of skilled workers and women only. In reaction to this the Yugoslav Federal Executive Council decided to continue the negotiations under the premise that they should accord with the same principles and conditions that were applied in recruitment agreements which Yugoslavia had already signed with other states (France, Austria and Sweden) as well as with the principles the FR Germany usually applied.[67] The Yugoslav government could not accept that the unskilled male population was excluded and that the Yugoslav workers were deprived of the child benefits that were given to other foreign workers in the FR Germany.

On December 13, 1967, the German Federal Cabinet authorised Minister Brandt to take up negotiations with the Yugoslav government about diplomatic relations, but was not willing to accept any reparation claims. Nonetheless, both states established diplomatic relations on January 31, 1968. The Yugoslav policy makers continued to negotiate with the FR Germany about the further liberalisation of trade and asked for the opening-up of the German market for Yugoslav goods. Finally, the German-Yugoslav negotiations about a recruitment agreement were resumed in March 1968. On March 14, 1968, Willy Brandt stressed in an interview with "*Politika*" that Yugoslav workers in the FR Germany should be given the same rights as German workers and that any discrimination of the Yugoslavs should be avoided. Furthermore, Brandt stressed the readiness of the FR Germany to negotiate a social and unemployment insurance agreement. The Foreign Minister pointed out that the recent German proposal for the recruitment of skilled workers only should be seen as a temporary

66 BA Ko, B 149/6241: Der Bundesminister des Auswärtigen Amtes an den Bundesminister für Arbeit und Sozialordnung Herrn Hans Katzer, Bonn, 21 April 1967.

67 AJ 130/626: Savezno Izvršno Veče Saveznom Savetu za rad, br. 39/67, Beograd, 2 December 1967.

measure dictated by the current conditions of the German labour market and he asked the Yugoslav government for understanding. Brandt stressed that the German-Yugoslav relations offered the chance for both societies to come closer together:

> *The German-Yugoslav relations offer many opportunities for a get together of people resulting in the growth of understanding. The Yugoslav workers in the FRG get to know the country and the people the way they really are; and we have learnt to appreciate the Yugoslav workers because of their professional abilities.*[68]

Apart from the controversial subjects – the selection of skilled workers only and the payment of child benefit – the question of how to deal with Yugoslav political opponents in the FR Germany was again an important issue in the German-Yugoslav preliminary talks in 1967 and 1968. This German-Yugoslav controversy about political emigrants has to be seen before the background of two political systems, as the way to treat political opponents within the one-party system of Yugoslavia collided with the pluralistic democracy of the FR Germany. With regard to political emigrants, the Yugoslav side urged the German one to "eliminate this disturbing factor" of bilateral relations.[69] The Yugoslav concept of the elimination of active political exiles went contrary to the instructions given to the German delegation. These underlined that the legal system of the FR Germany sets limits on preventive and repressive sanctions against political emigrants and that

> [...] *the German government doesn't support any efforts against the integrity of the Yugoslav state but cannot cut down the right to free expression, which is guaranteed in the constitution for foreigners as well.*[70]

Nevertheless, on several occasions the German negotiators stressed that some measures had been taken to tackle the problem of political emigrants. Even on the highest level, when Minister Brandt visited Yugoslavia from June 12–14, 1968, the matter was raised. At Brandt's meeting with Tito on the island of Brioni, the "Gastarbeiter agreement" and the "emigrant terror" were specifically discussed alongside economic, political and military issues.[71] Brandt expressed his hope that after the resumption of negotiations a successful conclusion of the recruitment agreement would be achieved.[72] In this context, Tito deplored that Yugoslav "fascist elements" in Germany were causing trouble with terrorist actions, which in turn were affecting the domestic atmosphere. Brandt pointed out that in this field, cooperation between the German and Yugoslav authorities had improved and he declared the desire "to keep this problem under control".[73]

68 Quoted in Dikić, Intervju Vili Branta, 3.

69 AAPBRD, 1968, Bd. I, Dok. 30: Ministerialdirektor Ruete, z.Z. Paris, an Bundesminister Brandt, 25 January 1968, 93.

70 Ibid., 93, fn. 12.

71 AAPBRD, 1968, Bd. I, Dok. 194: Ministerialdirektor Ruete, z.Z. Belgrad, an das Auswärtige Amt, Betr.: Jugoslawien-Besuch des Bundesaußenministers, 15 June 1968, 734.

72 Ibid.

73 Ibid.

In 1968, the short recession in Germany was overcome and annual economic growth rose to 7.3 percent.[74] The more advantageous economic conditions and the good reputation of Yugoslav workers, especially in the building industry, aided the further recruitment of Yugoslav workers to the FR Germany. In July 1968, the German Federal Cabinet even decided to allow the recruitment of unskilled male Yugoslavs and to pay Yugoslav workers child benefit to the amount of the usual Yugoslav child benefit.[75] But the Yugoslav government still insisted on equal treatment and demanded that regular German child benefit also be paid to the Yugoslav workers.

Finally, from October 7 to 12, 1968, negotiations for the conclusion of a German-Yugoslav recruitment agreement were held in Belgrade. Once the German Federal Cabinet eventually decided to pay Yugoslav workers the full amount of child benefit on October 9, the recruitment negotiations could enter their ultimate phase. The talks finished on October 12, 1968 with the signing of agreements on recruitment, social insurance including child benefit, and public unemployment insurance. A permanent mixed committee, based in Belgrade, was established to organise and accomplish the recruitment procedure in which the Yugoslav Federal Office for Employment and the German Federal Labour Office would send three representatives each.

The German-Yugoslav recruitment agreement differed in several aspects from previous proposals. Firstly, unskilled male workers were eventually included, which met the Yugoslav demands because unemployment was especially high among the unskilled agrarian population. State-organised recruitment also served the German interests, as resumed economic growth demanded more foreign workers to keep labour costs low. Secondly, the Yugoslav delegation renounced the establishment of Yugoslav institutions for the support and supervision of their labour migrants in the FR Germany, but the Yugoslav state was allowed to send commissioners in accordance with the German Federal Labour Office from time to time.[76] Article 13 of the German-Yugoslav recruitment agreement determined that Yugoslav employees enjoy the same working and wage conditions as domestic workers; further, they enjoyed the same treatment and protection as German workers. Moreover, it was guaranteed that German authorities would work towards the creation of adequate conditions for a social and cultural life for Yugoslav employees (Art. 13.3). Article 17 ensured Yugoslav employees could transfer their savings to Yugoslavia according to German foreign currency regulations. The Yugoslav government also accepted the obligation of taking back those Yugoslav workers who had no permission to stay in the FR Germany (Art. 20). Another innovation was that the FR Germany was obliged to bear all the costs, including the transpor-

74 Herbert, Geschichte der Ausländerpolitik, 223.

75 BA Ko, B 149/22399: Abteilung II, IIa5 – 2430.6 – 208/68, Deutsch-jugoslawische Verhandlungen über den Abschluß einer Anwerbevereinbarung, eines Abkommens über soziale Sicherheit einschließlich des Kindergeldes und eines Abkommens über Arbeitslosenversicherung, Bonn, 18 October 1968.

76 Ibid.

tation of recruited workers, as well as the rent and furnishings of the offices of the German delegation in Belgrade.

In contrast to other German recruitment procedures, the FR Germany was not allowed to open its own office for recruitment with its own status in the SFR Yugoslavia. Instead, the German delegation was integrated into the Yugoslav Federal Office for Employment in Belgrade.[77] The German delegation carried out the recruiting and sending of workers in cooperation with the authorities in Yugoslavia under a decentralised procedure, as the competencies of the labour employment service were in the hands of the employment offices of the republics or municipalities. The German recruiting commission had to travel all around Yugoslavia to carry out the medical examinations of labour migrants and to decide whom to recruit or reject. Nevertheless, in 1972-3, 48.2 percent of all Yugoslav workers going to the FR Germany had still been directly recruited by German employers, who sent working contracts with the names of individual workers to the Yugoslav employment offices.[78] Direct recruitment had already started before the recruitment agreement was in existence; some companies continued with this practice because they had had a good experience with workers from a particular region, e.g. Siemens and Audi preferred to recruit from Croatia, Continental from the Vojvodina and AEG-Telefunken and Trumpf from the coastal region of Dalmatia.[79]

West Germany had the highest demand for Yugoslav workers of all the West European economies recruiting workers from Yugoslavia. In 1971, 66.1 percent of all labour migrants from Yugoslavia came to the FR Germany due to its much higher wages and geographical proximity.[80] In 1969, the average monthly wage in Yugoslavia was about 80 US dollars, whereas 255 US dollars could be earned working in German industry.[81] The peak of recruitment of Yugoslav workers to the FR Germany was achieved in 1973. Their number fell slightly on account of the stop on recruitment in the same year, although family members continued to follow them there.

Summary

The signing of the recruitment agreement served the economic interests of both states. Labour migration immensely relieved pressures on the reform-shaken Yugoslav labour market. Moreover, between 1968 and 1976, the labour migrants' remittances increased by about 36 percent annually; in 1976 they even surpassed the revenues from tourism.[82] Remittances

77 Manfrass, Die Beziehungen, 270.
78 Ibid., 274, Tab. I.
79 Ibid., 272, fn. 51.
80 The percentages for other Western European countries as destinations for Yugoslav workers as of 1971 were: Austria (13.6 %), France (8.6 %), Switzerland (4.1 %), Sweden (3.3 %), Italy (1.0 %), The Netherlands (1.0 %). See Baučić, The Effects of Emigration, 1, Table 1.
81 Baučić, Socialno-ekonomske posljedice, 31.
82 Künne, Die Außenwanderung, 183–5.

played an important part in the balance of payments for Yugoslavia, whose trade balance with the FR Germany remained negative. The economic significance of remittances which helped to alleviate poverty and to pay for imports from the FR Germany was an incentive for both the Yugoslav and German policymakers to foster temporary emigration and to promote the attachment of labour migrants to their home country. In this respect, the Yugoslav transfer of workers not only affected the German and Yugoslav domestic economy, but also improved external trade between the two states.

By the same token, the state-organised recruitment of Yugoslav Gastarbeiter served the political interests of both the FR Germany and Yugoslavia. With regard to Willy Brandt's Ostpolitik, the FR Germany made the first approaches to Yugoslavia by signalling interest in the resumption of negotiations about the recruitment of Yugoslav workers, which was desperately desired by the Yugoslav government.[83] The German willingness to ease tensions between East and West was exemplified by the invitation of labourers from a socialist country and the readiness to cooperate with a socialist state. The German fear of communism seemed to belong to the past and the negotiations about a recruitment agreement ushered in a new era of rapprochement as the FR Germany and the SFR Yugoslavia not only negotiated about the exchange of goods but also of people. Regardless of the fact that the initial promotion of internationalism and cultural exchange by officials at the start of German-Yugoslav labour migration soon fell into oblivion, the open border policy between these two countries, as manifested by the intense labour migration of Yugoslav citizens to the FR Germany and the visit of many German tourists to Yugoslavia, had a lasting effect on both societies, whose members came together on a personal level despite the curtain of the Cold War.

Moreover, the German recruitment of Yugoslavs helped to guarantee Yugoslavia's independence from the Soviet Union, but also created increased dependencies between the FR Germany and Yugoslavia. Next to goods, people were transferred, who were supposed to maintain relations to the Yugoslav state by sending remittances and by avoiding political and oppositional actions against the socialist state. By taking up diplomatic relations and signing the recruitment agreement with the FR Germany, a signal to political opponents was given that the Yugoslav government returned as a respected partner of the German authorities. Last but not least, the open borders served political stabilisation within Yugoslavia, as opponents of the regime were shown the way out of the country, as Ludwig Steindorff asserts.[84]

[83] In his memoirs "Encounters and Insights 1960–1975" Willy Brandt recalls the talks with Tito about the recruitment of Yugoslav workers, without broaching the subject of his mediating role during the German-Yugoslav recruitment negotiations. Instead, Brandt criticises in retrospect the recruitment of the Gastarbeiter: "Indeed, beyond a given case, the easy way out was taken, as plenty of foreign labourers were brought to capital haphazardly instead of giving more thought to the question of how capital and technology could be brought to the people" (BRANDT, Begegnungen und Einsichten, 233).

[84] STEINDORFF, Kroatien, 199.

Anxious to avoid the cultural and personal alienation of Yugoslav workers, a labour migration policy was adopted in cooperation with the host state, which would tie the labour migrants to Yugoslavia. The political refusal of the FR Germany to accept being an immigration country and to integrate the foreign workers on a long-term basis, worked in favour of the Yugoslav government's aim to keep the labour migrants loyal. Thus, the FR Germany as the recruiting and Yugoslavia as the sending state shared the common assumption of the 'temporary nature' of labour migration, which justified their workers' transfer in public but lacked a sustainable economic foundation. The short-sighted economic interests that foster labour migration on a temporary basis are obvious: the recruiting country counts on low integration costs and the sending country benefits from remittances as the materialised form of connections maintained with the homeland. Indeed, the German and Yugoslav policy of temporariness seemed to work: in 1985, more than 86 percent of interviewed Yugoslav labour migrants from Germany still had definite plans to return to their country of origin.[85]

The documentary "Special Trains", which shows the Yugoslav labour migrants travelling on 'special' trains to West Germany, records the ambiguity that the Yugoslav labour migrants perceived in relation to the migration policy of their government. They expressed happiness about the new freedom of travel and the opportunity to work abroad, but also great disappointment that could not be concealed from the camera about having nothing to live on in their home country:

> *I feel like I've been thrown out of society* [...] *I don't have enough to live on! Look at my hands!* [...] *I'm going to be a slave abroad* [...] *I can't speak German. I'm going dumb as a calf – unable to speak a word. I don't know why it's like this. I was an excellent soldier, even escorted Marshal Tito abroad. I was excellent at political lessons; I know the history of my fatherland. Well, if I could do all that, I was probably competent enough to get a job – but I didn't get one.*

Migration changes life significantly. The labour migrants' faces, thoughts, and talk in the documentary "Special Trains" reveal the immense stress these people were exposed to during their departure to a new, unknown life. They took a deep sense of loss of family, friends, language, and homeland with them to the FR Germany. Unable to speak the German language, which neither the German government nor most of the employers required, many migrants stuck together with their co-nationals during their spare time. Without denying that Gastarbeiter were exploited in the economies of the FR Germany and in other Western countries, the chance to leave Yugoslavia through migration was a key way for many Yugoslav labour migrants to improve their material status immensely. In 1985, 67,6 percent of the interviewed Yugoslav labour migrants in the FR Germany had invested their earnings in a house or in renovation or enlargement of an already existing house in Yugoslavia, "evidence of an existing affinity with Yugoslavia and a perspective for a future that is called return".[86]

85 Baučić, Gross, Rückkehr und Reintegration, 158.
86 Ibid., 75.

However, the premise of temporary migration turned out to be an illusion. The Yugoslav economy would never recover from the Yugoslav 'third way'. The debt crisis kept on worsening and led to economic collapse in the late 1980s. For most of the former Yugoslav labour migrants, their migration to the FR Germany turned out to be permanent. In 2005, people from the former Yugoslavia formed the second largest foreign population in the FR Germany, with 963,000 persons; most of them are former labour migrants, who came between the 1950s and 1970s, and their descendents.[87] In the 1990s, refugees from the wars in the former Yugoslavia sought refuge mainly in the FR Germany for the reason that many of them had relatives – former labour migrants – in Germany who offered them help. Yugoslav labour migration thus had a lasting effect on the multiculturalism of German society; the history of the Yugoslav labour migration is inevitably a part of Germany's history, too.

This article showed the interrelation between the Yugoslav sending and German recruitment policies, which were determined not only by labour policy concerns but also by international relations. The case of the Yugoslav labour migration to the FR Germany shows that the "politics of exit"[88] and the state as a major actor in the labour migration process played a decisive role in migration from Yugoslavia. The historical process of the Yugoslav labour migration is a movement across nation-state borders and between places but for all that, the Yugoslav labour migration did not take place in a political or national vacuum. The national belonging of the Yugoslav labour migrants was an important element in this bilateral labour migration policy, which was built on the myth of "temporariness".

87 The average length of stay for migrants in Germany in 2005 was, by country of origin (in years): Slovenia 27.7, Croatia 24.7, Bosnia and Herzegovina 17.1, Serbia and Montenegro 14.4, Macedonia 17.2. See Bundesamt für Migration und Flüchtlinge, Migration, Asyl und Integration, 83, Table 29.

88 Green, The Politics of Exit.

Francesco Ragazzi

The Croatian 'Diaspora Politics' of the 1990s: Nationalism Unbound?

Introduction

The waters have calmed considerably in Croatia. Dubrovnik, it seems, has definitively lost its image of a city under siege and is now again, as a symbol of the whole country, the holiday destination it had been in the 1970s and 1980s. Yet nothing is the same as before. From a planned socialist system, the country is now a (post)transitional market economy. From a state within a wider communist federation, it is now an independent republic. Although it is today a parliamentary democracy in the full sense of the term, the country is still scarred by the remnants of the nationalist wave of the 1990s, slowly dealing with the consequences of ten years of semi-dictatorial rule.

The sea change of the 1990s has radically modified the nature of what belonging to a nation, a community or a territory means. It has also brought into focus a new, until then unknown, historical subject: the 'diaspora'. This statement from President Franjo Tuđman was published in a handbook for returning Croatian migrants by the Croatian Ministry for Return and Immigration in 1997:

> *Dear Croats. When in 1990 we started to create the independent state of Croatia, the main thought and moving force was the union between the Homeland and Emigré Croatia.* [...] *In the past seven years, Croatia has followed a path which has taken other countries decades – from the hardest days of the Yugo-communist and Greater-Serbian aggression – when the world even questioned our survival, to today, when Croatia is a key factor in the peace and stability of this region, respected by the most important international actors. All of this would have been impossible, if from the very beginning the historical moment had not been grasped, both within Croats in the Homeland and within the Croatian Emigration, which can be counted in million.*[1]

This short passage, as a manifestation of the political project of Franjo Tuđman's *Hrvatska Demokratska Zajednica* (Croatian Democratic Union, HDZ), but also as an indication of the political atmosphere and distribution of merits in post-conflict Croatia, raises a number of questions. How can a nation be conceptualised in terms of an 'internal' Croatia and an 'external' Croatia? What does it mean for a head of state like Franjo Tuđman, a leading figure in the war in the former Yugoslavia, one of the most horrifying conflicts of the end of

1 TUĐMAN, Poruka Predsjednika Republike.

the past century, to insist that the "*thought and moving force*" had precisely been "*the union between the Homeland and Emigré Croatia*"? What does it mean for a statesman to claim that part of his constituency actually lives outside the internationally recognised territorial borders of his state, and that it has been a leading force in national history?

The aim of this chapter is to understand the way contemporary nationalism operates in relation to the management and government of the migratory phenomenon. A lot has been said about the dynamics of the conflict, the aspects of Tito's rule, the emergence of nationalist parties, the ethnic cleansing, and the horrendous consequences of a war which has been labelled, probably too quickly, as 'ethnic'.[2] However, by looking at the question of migration and how it evolved throughout the twentieth century, both during and after the war, it seems that important, but overlooked aspects of the new modalities of this contemporary nationalism – an exile nationalism that has adapted to the transnational condition of globalisation, as will be developed in this chapter – can be traced. In many ways, Croatia's 1990s brand of nationalism is, in its origins and policies, a *diasporic* or *transnational nationalism*: coming from exile and addressing the diaspora as a central piece of its political cosmology.[3]

But this is only part of the answer. In order to fully understand how the diaspora came to play such an important role in the 1990s – years in which a Ministry for the Diaspora, then a Ministry for Return and Integration were created in Croatia, in which ten percent of the seats in parliament were reserved for a specific diasporic electoral unit from 1995 onwards, and in which between fourteen and sixteen percent of neighbouring Bosnia's population was considered as part of the national 'corpus' of Croatia – one has to look at deeper 'path dependencies', i.e. at the practices of the Yugoslav state before the fall of the regime. It is clear in this history that we find the progressive acceptance and legitimisation of long-distance practices of 'inner' politics, namely the progressive institutionalisation of the principle that it is acceptable to 'govern' groups living outside the territorial borders of the state, as if they were population within the territorial borders.

These two paths of analysis seem to neatly converge in the 'diaspora policies' of the 1990s, yet the Croatian case presents an apparent paradox. Before the 1990s, the question of the importance and the role of the diaspora had never gained such public attention. Never had the external populations been as included in the political and social system of Croatian society as they were during those years. However, the 1990s are probably the years in which the flows of remittances, the travels back home, and state policies in emigration are the rarest of all. By the 1990s, remittances represented a marginal and dying phenomenon. Apart from refugees who escaped during the war, emigration almost stopped, and Croatia became a country of immigration. Nevertheless, despite the progressive 'normalisation' of the relationship with the diaspora, and the gradual severing of ties that was carried out by

2 See Gagnon, The Myth of Ethnic War.

3 This argument echoes the analyses of Nina Glick-Schiller, Terrains of Blood, and Riva Kastoryano, Vers un nationalisme, on respectively 'unbounded' and 'transnational' nationalism.

each new government, Croatian voters were reminded that there was an important political actor, the 'diaspora', which could have a formidable impact on their everyday lives. The most recent example of such an influence is the outcome of the parliamentary election of 2007, in which the 'diaspora' vote (only five seats in parliament) was enough to shift the balance of power from a potential Social Democratic Party (SDP) based coalition to a coalition formed around the HDZ. So, if the 'real' political and material importance of the diaspora is so disproportionately small in comparison to the political weight and attention that is devoted to it, then what purpose do the diaspora policies serve?

My main argument regarding the Croatian case – but the case of the former Yugoslavia is only one among many others (suffice to think about larger countries and diasporas, such as India or China, to name only two) – is that the discourse of diaspora is one of the possible rhetorical tools available to governments to redefine the borders of the nation and the borders of sovereignty in an increasingly transnational world. If one considers sovereignty most of all as a principle of division of the state's legitimate spheres of actions between an 'inside' and an 'outside', my argument is that the transnational discourses and practices taken in the name of the 'diaspora' are a means to legitimise the renegotiation of this very limit, in the relationship between power and populations on the one hand, and between power and territory on the other. This is why the promotion of 'diaspora policies', if initially intended to address the concerns of a population abroad, can exist without a real link with those populations: the discourse of diaspora has become an institutionalised discourse which permits governments to carry out policies which redefine the 'borders' of a nation.

Methodological notes

But what exactly is a 'diaspora'? Social scientists are divided when it comes to the definition of the term. Some sociologists and political scientists, such as Safran,[4] Cohen and Sheffer,[5] have formulated a definition of the term based on a certain number of criteria, in order to distinguish diasporas from other migratory phenomena.[6] The problem is, as for all 'essen-

4 Safran, Diasporas in Modern Societies.

5 Cohen, Global Diasporas; Sheffer, Modern Diasporas; ibid, Diaspora Politics

6 According to Robin Cohen, Global Diasporas, 29, the defining features of diasporas are the following:
"1. dispersal from an original homeland, often traumatically, to two or more foreign regions; 2. alternatively, the expansion from a homeland in search of work, in pursuit of trade or to further colonial ambitions; 3. a collective memory and myth about the homeland, including its location, history and achievements; 4. an idealization of the putative ancestral home and a collective commitment to its maintenance, restoration, safety and prosperity, even to its creation; 5. the development of a return movement that gains collective approbation; 6. a strong ethnic group consciousness sustained over a long time and based on a sense of distinctiveness, a common history and the belief in a common fate; 7. a troubled relationship with host societies, suggesting a lack of acceptance at least or the possibility that another calamity might befall

tially contested concepts',[7] that the very definition of the object of study, 'diasporas', has with the passing of time charged itself with such a wealth of meanings and connotations that other authors have come to question the criteria that are used. On the other hand, authors such as Clifford and Gilroy have proposed to use the term as a signifier, a marker of hybridity and the '*changing same*'.[8] The problem with this approach is that it comes to encapsulate various heterogeneous processes, losing its usefulness as a concept. In an article on the notion of 'diaspora', French sociologist Stéphane Dufoix proposed in 2002 an original way to approach the problem: if the term is changing so much through the uses that are made of it, then the attention of the scholar should go to the political processes that take place under this particular term.[9] A quite similar view, equally inspired by Pierre Bourdieu's reflexive sociological approach,[10] was again proposed by sociologist Rogers Brubaker in 2005.[11]

The hypothesis suggests that, if the definition of the word 'diaspora' is so hard to seize, it is because the word has become a word of politics. A precise definition is difficult to nail down because each political actor, by using the word and the discourse of diaspora, engages in a double process. Firstly, he or she mobilises all the connotations and meanings that the history of dispersion, struggle and mobilisation has given to the term. But secondly, political actors recuperate, enlarge and bend the definition of the term in order to fit it to their particular political objectives. The scholar is forced to take these modifications into account. It therefore follows that a study of diasporas cannot but start from the *practices* of diaspora, namely the social practices that occur 'in the name of' diasporas. Very much like the case of signifiers such as 'race', 'ethnicity', 'nation' or 'class', 'diaspora' is one of those words which is used by political actors to 'frame' their political action.[12] Therefore, what is needed is an analysis of what these words 'do'; language is in fact always performative.[13]

Once we set aside these few methodological preoccupations, an important set of questions emerges. How does the word 'diaspora' appear in political discourse? What are the policies that are undertaken under the word 'diaspora'? Why 'diaspora' and not another word? What sort of mobilisations is at stake? In the first section of this chapter, I briefly out-

the group; 8. a sense of empathy and solidarity with co-ethnic members in other countries of settlement; and 9. the possibility of a distinctive creative, enriching life in host countries with a tolerance for pluralism."

7 Connolly, Essentially Contested Concepts.

8 Clifford, Diasporas; Gilroy, Diaspora.

9 Anteby-Yemini, Berthomiére et al., Les diasporas; Dufoix, Notion, concept ou slogan.

10 For Dufoix, the concept of *exopolitie* is directly built upon Bourdieu's theory of fields. See Dufoix, Notion, concept ou slogan; ibid, Les Diasporas. Rogers Brubaker, along with Craig Calhoun and some others, is considered to be one of the 'introducers' of Bourdieu's sociology in the United States.

11 Brubaker, Nationalism Reframed.

12 Regarding the classical notion of framing see Goffmann, Frame Analysis.

13 See Austin, How to do Things; Searle, The Construction of Social Reality; Bourdieu, Language and Symbolic Power.

line the history of governmental practices towards their populations abroad, showing how the division between the legitimate 'inside' and 'outside' practices is progressively blurred. In the second part, I then look more in detail at the practices of diaspora that came after the breakup of Yugoslavia. I show how these practices were much less oriented towards populations abroad than they were set up to carry out a political programme of redefinition of the borders of the 'national population', independently from the territorial borders. In this part, I analyse the birth of a bureaucratic category and the long-distance mobilisation during the war. I then move to the relationship between the category of 'diaspora' and the policies of ethnic cleansing, before finally considering the policies of diaspora and the legitimation of the 'non-territorial' annexation of Herzegovina.

1. A genealogy of the transnational control of populations

In order to understand the 'diaspora' policies of independent Croatia, both for the 1991–1995 period and the post-conflict era, it is crucial to understand the genealogy of state practices until the fall of communism. In fact, tracing back the relationship between the homeland and 'its' (the definition of which is always at the centre of political struggle) population abroad helps us unveil a distinctive set of state practices related to different claims. These practices have resulted in three distinctive relationships, producing three types of knowledge for three different bureaucracies, implying three different types of relations of power. My account will mainly focus on the relationship between the Croatian government and its 'diaspora' in the United States.

1.1 From losing to managing populations

1.1.1 From 1870 to 1914: the fear of depopulation

It is estimated that 350,000 migrants of Croatian 'nationality' arrived in the United States between 1880 and 1910.[14] Overall, approximately 600,000 Croats are estimated to have left the Habsburg Empire by the eve of World War One.[15] The first years of emigration were, however, mainly characterised by apathy from the side of the Austro-Hungarian authorities. Their acknowledgement of the phenomenon did not start before the first statistical data were collected in 1880, making the phenomenon 'visible'[16] to the central pow-

[14] U.S. Immigration Commission 1911, 371.

[15] Prpic, The Croatian Immigrants, 91.

[16] The American Anthropologist James Scott, as well as many other scholars inspired by the work of Michel Foucault, shows how the emergence of statistical tools are the necessary precondition for the appearance of "populations" as an object of government, as opposed to "territories" or simply "subjects". For more on this question see Scott, Seeing Like a State. For Michel Foucault's work on populations, see Foucault, Naissance de la biopolitique; ibid, Sécurité,

ers.[17] The first bureaucratic bodies within the Interior Ministry destined to deal with the question of emigration were set up on a very limited scale, and the official knowledge was built upon pre-existing sources and books, mainly coming from harbour registers and the steamship companies. In 1883, the first decree regulating emigration was passed in Croatia-Slavonia,[18] charging the enforcement of this policy to police forces. Another tool of control had been introduced in 1881 – by then in fact, a passport became required to emigrate. As the document was often refused, the phenomenon of illegal emigration became widespread.[19] Abroad, consulates were considered not only the expression of the Austro-Hungarian oppressor, but largely inefficient and oblivious to the fate of Croats.[20] The relationship between the homeland and 'its' population abroad was therefore essentially non-existent: the authorities' rationality during these years was in fact based on a territorial understanding of the question. When emigrants crossed the border, they were 'lost'. The large exodus of 'nationalities' probably did not raise particular concern as it was most likely viewed as a solution to both the national homogenisation of the empire and the problem of the management of the paupers.[21]

Among the Croatian intellectual and political elite, the vast phenomenon of emigration, which translated into the fear of depopulation, was understood in the framework of two rising political ideologies of the social sphere: nationalism and socialism.[22] Fear of the biological death of Croatian-ness (*hrvatstvo*) by the physical extinction of the nation on the one side, and fear of the dissolution of productive forces on the other side, dominated political speeches and newspaper articles.[23] On many occasions, political movements and associations tried to gain the attention of the authorities. Under the pressure of association figures such as Juraj Biankini and Fran Lupis-Vukić, a department for emigration was created within the Interior Ministry of Croatia-Slavonia in 1893. From 1899, the government of Croatia and Slavonia collected statistical information on emigrants which was published in the statistical yearbooks. Several governmental instructions prohibited the activities of emigration agents and the agitation for emigration. The administrative concern over the phenomenon increased in 1905 with the creation of the Emigrant Fund, destined to provide welfare to future emigrants. In 1910, the first "Basic Law on Emigration" was proposed to the Croatian parliament, the *Sabor*. The real awakening of the Austro-Hungarian monarchy, however, did not take place before 1913, when the possibility of armed conflict became imminent. Military circles in fact became very worried about emigration as a means

territoire, population. For an interesting intellectual history of the "invention" of populations, see Le Bras, L'invention des populations.

17 Holjevac, Hrvati izvan domovine, 37.

18 Ibid., 21.

19 Macartney, The Habsburg Empire, 755.

20 Antić, Arhiv Jugoslavenske Narodne Obrane, 250.

21 Banović, Emigracijska Politika.

22 Šidak, Gross et al., Povijest hrvatskog naroda.

23 Čizmić, Emigration from Yugoslavia.

of escape for future soldiers, and the Austro-Hungarian 1913 law was thus the harshest and best-enforced law to prevent the emigration of draftees.[24] However, by 1918, the 'rotating' nature of migration, the importance of Croats abroad during World War One, and the inclusion of Croatia in the Kingdom of Serbs, Croats and Slovenes following the dissolution of the dual Monarchy, changed the nature of the relationship between the home government and the population abroad.

1.1.2 From 1918 to 1941: from loss to management

The period running from 1918 to 1941 is characterised by the passage from a framing of the question in terms of territorial sovereignty (prohibition of emigration and fear of depopulation) to an understanding in terms of deterritorialised management of the migrants abroad. Correlated with this process is the passage from a police-enforced regulation to the conceptualisation of the question in socio-economic terms.

In 1918, Croatia joined the Kingdom of Slovenes, Croats and Serbs, to become Yugoslavia in 1929. As the emigrant population – mostly from Croatia – was reaching approximately ten percent of the total population, the royal authorities switched from attempts to prevent the phenomenon to attempts to regulate it.[25] The government's concern switched from policing migration to incorporating emigration into the national political economy: ensuring the emigrants' economic success and the preservation of their national identity therefore became primary concerns. It is in this context that the main law on emigration was passed in 1921; its application decree followed in 1922.[26] Within the Ministry of Social Affairs, the Emigration Commissioner was designated to carry out a certain number of long-view welfare tasks such as the care for deceased emigrants, the protection of migrants from abuse by industrial or steamship companies, and the statistical registration of vital records, emigrant properties and remittances.[27] However, changes in the structure and flow of migration provoked a change in state policies. US policy on quotas in 1924, as well as the dire situation of Canada and Latin America rendered emigration less desirable.[28] In addition to this, the 'rotating' character of migration slowly faded and migrants started to settle and assimilate in their respective countries of residence. The question of return hit the top of the agenda.[29]

Likewise, non-governmental organisations grew and became active in shaping governmental policies. They became organised in 1928 under the Union of Emigrant Organisations (*Savez Organizacija Iseljenika*, SORIS) and were particularly important in shaping the debate on emigration, notably through regular publications such as the newspaper *Novi Iseljenik* ("The New Emigrant"). The need to take care of the emigrant and his connec-

24 Antić, Prilog istraživanju, 245.
25 Ibid., 229.
26 Ibid., 230.
27 Ibid., 231.
28 Hranilović, Iseljenička politika i služba, 326.
29 Antić, Iseljenićka politika; Bartulica, Iseljenička konferencija.

tion to the homeland became embodied in the idea of the "*deseta banovina*" (the "tenth banovina" – administrative region of Yugoslavia). The "tenth banovina", it was stated, "is somehow our colony"; there "not only lives a part of our nation ethnically, but part of our kin socially and economically, and therefore politically".[30]

From the beginning of the first departures up until World War Two, the governments' reasoning and policies towards emigration and the migrants abroad therefore considerably shifted, affecting a move from a territorial conception and modality of government to a deterritorialised practice, now essentially concerned with populations.[31] The deterritorialised conception of the management of a population arose from a fear of losing the national body, and entailed a practice whereby the link with the 'centre' was not determined by territoriality, but by something else: kinship, ethnicity, Croatian-ness (*hrvatstvo*). Therefore, the emigrant body of population is conceived as a full member of the nation, which was to be thanked and rewarded for its help, and taken care of in times of difficulties. The 1930s were therefore probably the first years when, in Yugoslavia, and Croatia as part of it, the idea of deterritorialised practices of 'inner' sovereignty seem to be formulated, even if still attached to blurred conceptions of migration, sovereignty and colonialism.

1.2 Long-distance policing

The first years of communist Yugoslavia (from 1945 to the late 1950s) were very close, in many aspects, to the totalitarian systems of most of the eastern bloc. Freedom of movement became very limited, and police ruled the everyday dominant praxis of power. 'Sovereignty' as the binary practice of enforcing the permitted and the prohibited, combined with heavy disciplining technologies, became (again) the predominant modality of government. The surveillance capabilities of the state dramatically increased and penetrated society like never before; the new state's authority was built on suspicion, and on the struggle against two types of enemies: the 'internal' and the 'external'. An important bureaucratic dichotomy emerged at that time in regard to emigration.

Inside the territory, Yugoslavia's policies were characterised by a limited freedom of movement – any form of emigration became illegal again. Outside, a sharp distinction was made between the "old Yugoslav emigration" (*staro jugoslovensko iseljeništvo*) and the "fascist and extremist" emigration. As can be read from a manual on "national security" printed in 1985:

[30] Ibid., 233; Bartulica, Iseljenički kongres. This is a very common pattern in many emigration countries. In Haiti, for example, the government often refers to the Haitians abroad as the "*Diziem Department*": the tenth department. The island is divided into nine departments – territorial administrative units. See Ratia, Le dixiéme département.

[31] I draw here on Michel Foucault's insights on the passage from *sovereignty* to *governmentality* as the contemporary modality of power (Foucault, Naissance de la biopolitique).

> *The largest parts of our old emigrants (iseljenici) are loyal citizens where they live, and have a positive attitude towards the SFRY (Socialist Federal Republic of Yugoslavia).* [...] *Our state offers support to the activities of old emigrant associations and encourages an intense communication with the old country. This activity is* [however] *under heavy pressure from fascist and extremist organisations, who oppose it'.* [...] *Enemy activity by fascist and extremist emigrant organisations has taken place continuously since the end of World War II until now. The main goal of all forms of enemy activity is to overthrow or subvert the socio-economic and political system in the SFRY, as well as to oppose the non-aligned orientation of Yugoslavia.*[32]

This clear distinction between the "old emigrants" (*iseljenici*) and the "Yugoslav enemy emigration" (*jugoslavenska neprijateljska emigracija*) translated into bureaucratic practices. In order to deal with the 'enemy emigration', a traditional feature of sovereignty, the ban was coupled with modern techniques of surveillance. Moreover, the traditional sovereign 'right to kill' was extended beyond the territory. The moment of the 'ban' took place mainly in 1945, when around 300,000 former Ustaša officers, along with anti-communists of all sorts, fled the country and found refuge in Argentina, Chile, the United States, Canada and Australia.[33] However, throughout the first years of the regime, expulsion from the territory (direct or induced) was used as a common way of handling political dissidents. Once banned, these individuals and organisations were still to be controlled, in order to prevent 'enemy activity'. The function of the surveillance of emigrants depended mainly on two organs: the Military Intelligence Agency (*Vojna obavještajna služba*, VOS), part of the Secretariat (Ministry) for National Defence; and the Agency for Intelligence and Documentation (*Služba za istraživanje i dokumentacija*, SID), part of the Secretariat for Internal Affairs.[34] A third civil organisation on the level of the Republic, which took more importance later, was the Directorate for State Security (*Uprava državne bezbednosti*, UDBa). Interestingly, all organisations, including the SID and UDBa, had undercover agents in 'outside bureaucracies' such as Yugoslav embassies and consulates. It is considered that a great number of the emigrant political organisations were either infiltrated or even controlled by the secret services. Apart from accumulating large amounts of police knowledge on individuals and organisations, the secret services proceeded with extrajudicial executions whenever Yugoslav authorities gave the orders. Between 1946 and 1969, approximately twenty-two executions took place, including a failed attempt to kill former Ustaša leader Ante Pavelić in his exile in Buenos Aires.

On the other hand, the 'old emigrants' were granted particular attention. The Yugoslav government created in 1951 the Emigrant Foundation of Croatia (*Matica iseljenika Hrvatske*) – an organ directly dependent on the political authorities. The goal of the agency was to create a respectable image of communist Yugoslavia among the 'old emigration' and, indirectly, in the countries where they lived. It was also a way of fighting the political migrants' activities, and, finally, possibly generating income in foreign currency through visits.

32 Đorđević, Osnovi državne bezbednosti, 152–3, 183; my translation.
33 Bilandžić, Historija Socijalističke Federativne Republike, 99.
34 Žunec, Domišljanović, Obavještajno-sigurnosne službe, 33–6.

Organised visits to the "old country" were encouraged to disrupt the "fascist propaganda".[35] Moreover, a depoliticised folkloristic culture was promoted in various forms, through competitions for traditional music orchestras (*tamburice*) and through publications such as the journal *Matica*. *Matica iseljenika Hrvatske* was not directly represented in consulates and embassies, but its activities among the 'old emigration' were relayed though a network of immigrant organisations that had chosen to cooperate with Yugoslavia, such as the Croatian Fraternal Union in the USA.

In this first period of SFRY history, we therefore see the enactment of a dual policy towards emigration. Two traditional claims of state monopoly were formulated and pursued outside the territory towards the 'national' population: the claim to the legitimate long-distance monopoly of internal violence through the activity of VOS, SID and UDBa on the one side, and the long-distance monopoly of symbolic violence and culture, through the *Matica iseljenika Hrvatske*, the organ for the preservation of the 'official' Croatian identity abroad. Two sets of practices, two sets of bureaucracies and agencies, as well as two sets of knowledge were established: police knowledge on the one side, and an almost non-existent, folkloric and historic knowledge of the 'old emigration' on the other. This was, however, going to change with the opening of the Yugoslav borders.

1.3 The return to management

Until the mid-sixties, the quasi-Stalinist planned economy of Yugoslavia provided employment for the large numbers of rural population who migrated to the cities: more than 160,000 are estimated to have migrated internally from 1945 to 1961.[36] However, the break with Stalin in 1948 and the promotion of self-management, the international non-aligned position of Yugoslavia, as well as the decrease to direct 'threats' to the state, pushed for a liberalisation of public and economic life. With the socio-economic reforms of 1965, economic growth slowed, many workers became redundant, and for the young it became increasingly difficult to find a job. From then on, growing unemployment haunted the Yugoslav economy. The opening of the border in 1964, which was pushed by the liberal trends of the Communist Party, was effective, though not without great debate.[37]

The period from 1962/1963 until the fall of Yugoslavia is characterised by a return to the long-distance 'management' of populations practiced by the Kingdom of Yugoslavia in the 1930s. This time, however, the emigration was state-driven and encouraged, in obvious contrast with the previous disciplinary practice. Even if long-distance surveillance and the use of force continued and was even reinforced, these practices concerned a small parcel of the emigrant population – the 'enemy emigration'. The overall form of control was closely associated with the socio-economic policy: much more subtle and indirect, nonetheless

[35] Matica iseljenika Hrvatske, Izvještaj o Radu, 52.

[36] Heršak, Mesić, L'espace migratoire, 45.

[37] Zimmerman, Open Borders.

efficient. Power was no longer exercised principally through disciplining and punishing techniques, but through the management of what were considered 'natural flows'. The logic of control was in fact understood in an overall mercantilist logic of long-distance monopolisation of the allocation of resources. Much as in the economically liberal approach of the Austro-Hungarian Empire, emigration became conceived to be a natural way to solve the imbalances of the Yugoslav economy. The goal of the 'workers temporarily employed abroad' programmes was in fact double: to alleviate unemployment at home, and to produce foreign currency abroad.

The 1960s therefore saw the appearance of a third bureaucratic category for the 'nationals' abroad. Not the 'old emigration', which was lost and to be 'seduced', not the 'enemy emigration', which was to be fought, but the 'labour emigration', which was to be managed. The year 1963 marked a new form of transnational governmental practice, which could be defined as the claim to long-distance monopoly over the allocation and redistribution of resources. In the "Instruction on the Procedure of Work Abroad",[38] work abroad was in fact encouraged by a series of measures through employment offices and different agencies.[39] Consular powers were augmented, and the number of consulates multiplied. The number of migrants increased progressively and is estimated to have reached about one million in 1971. Care for the workers abroad was mainly the responsibility of the Secretariat for Labour.

The forms of control of this large population were subtler than the police control targeted at the limited number of emigrant political organisations. The Yugoslav League of Communists (SKJ) monitored the migrants' actions through an independent specialised authority, the *Opunomoćstvo za jugoslovenske radnike na privremenom radu u inozemstvu*,[40] yet the most efficient form of control was the fear of unemployment, the loss of personal resources and exit from a wide system of social and health insurance. This was carried out by a certain number of controlling techniques. The most obvious one was the issuing (or not) of a passport. This document guaranteed in fact the possibility of coming and going between Yugoslavia and the work place abroad. Any suspicion by the police, when returning to Yugoslavia, could have led to confiscation of the travel document, and loss of the position abroad. Moreover, Yugoslavia had negotiated a great number of bilateral agreements regarding different types of insurance,[41] particularly health insurance and social security (regarding unemployment). Any 'wrong move' would have meant the loss of these benefits. This was the best way for the Yugoslav government to prevent workers from being lured by the 'enemy' political emigration. Moreover, the consulates, in the 'self-management tradition', promoted the creation of workers' clubs and associations, which were another strong means of social and political control.

38 Uputstvo o postupanju pri zapošlavanju u inozemstvu, *Službeni list SFRJ*, no. 42, 15 October 1963.
39 Baskin, Political Innovation, 50.
40 Žunec, Domišljanović, Obavještajno-sigurnosne službe, 36.
41 Heršak, Mesić, L'espace migratoire, 46.

A monopoly of long-distance symbolic power was claimed in many instances; the most powerful, however, was school programmes. Yugoslavia signed bilateral agreements to set up courses in language and culture for the children of migrants. The identity to preserve, in contrast to the one of the 'old emigration', was not a national one, but the 'self-management' (communist) identity.[42] This new category gave birth to a third form of governmental knowledge: not a vague, folkloristic knowledge, not police knowledge, but a socio-demographic and economic knowledge. As regular citizens, 'workers temporarily abroad' formed part of the 1971 and 1981 federal censuses: a clear extension of internal knowledge prerogatives to 'outside' populations. Economic flows and remittances were carefully documented through the work of various offices and agencies in the Secretariat for Labour. The workers abroad programmes also gave birth to an emerging sociological literature created within the Institute for Migration and Nationalities in Zagreb (*Zavod* – later *Institut – za migracije i narodnosti*)[43].

The state policies, however, encountered a considerable amount of resistance. Inside the country, the dire economic situation became a source of social unrest, lead by student and nationalist movements. Student organisations accused the authorities of selling the Yugoslav labour force to 'global capitalism'. Nationalist movements re-enacted the fear of 'depopulation', claiming among other things, that the migration policies were a Yugo-Serb complot to extinguish the Croatian nation. Outside the country, the state's claims had to face the fierce competition of rivals, not so much the political emigration, as the Croatian Catholic Missions. Parallel to the establishment of migrants in Germany, Austria, Sweden or Belgium and the opening of consulates, Franciscan-led Croatian Catholic Missions started activities in the same locations as the Yugoslav consulates. The missions gathered statistical information, offered welfare and provided a powerful nationalist narrative on Croatian national identity as well as direct competition with the long-distance sovereign prerogatives of the Yugoslav state.[44]

After the Croatian Spring of 1971,[45] any kind of émigré population became suspicious among the communist elites. Moreover, after the crisis of 1973 and the stop in the recruitment of workers from Yugoslavia by France and Germany in 1974, the question of return became, as in the 1930s, one of priority. The state policies were, however, inefficient; the successful 'temporary workers' stayed where they lived and only the unsuccessful returned.[46] At the same time, surveillance and killings by the UDBa and other secret agencies increased.

[42] Baskin, Political Innovation, 73.

[43] See <http://www.imin.hr/>.

[44] Vijeće BK za hrvatsku emigraciju, Crkva i hrvatsko iseljeništvo.

[45] In 1971, the 'Croatian Spring' echoed the social movements in Europe and in the Communist bloc. A heterogeneous movement of reform-minded communists, nationally oriented organisations, student movements, and the Catholic Church pushed for economic reforms, civil liberties and national autonomy. Tito crushed the movement, but its claims were taken into account. See Tanner, Croatia, and for an actor's perspective; Tripalo, Hrvatsko proljeće.

[46] Heršak, Mesić, L'espace migratoire, 47–49.

The Croatian Spring in fact produced a new wave of emigration, which came to reinvigorate the activities of the post-WWII emigration. Radical Croatian organisations were responsible for a large number of spectacular actions, such as the hijacking of a TWA aircraft or the assassination of the Yugoslav ambassador to Sweden. The intra-emigration fight became just as fierce, and organisations considered too close to the SFRY, such as the Croatian Fraternal Union (CFU), were targeted. It is considered that between 1971 and 1989 approximately 46 state assassinations organised by Yugoslav special agents took place.

The last period of Yugoslav claims to 'inner' forms of sovereignty outside its borders were therefore characterised by a more subtle mode of control, in phase with the new 'market socialism' promoted by the Yugoslav communist party. If the two previous bureaucratic categories of 'old emigration' and 'enemy emigration' continued to coexist, the new category of 'workers temporarily abroad' formed a new, separate group, which was dealt with by a different rationality, and different bureaucratic entities and practices. It was also the object of a differentiated kind of bureaucratic knowledge. Overall, the relationship between the state and its population abroad can be characterised as a form of long-distance management of populations. Even if a minority continued to be subjected to long-distance policing and punishment, the majority of the population abroad is included in a more subtle modality of power based on a system of insurances, echoing the 'security societies' depicted by Michel Foucault.[47]

As a conclusion to this section, it can therefore be said that three state categorisations, three types of knowledge and three types of bureaucratic agencies defined the legitimate link between social groups in dispersion and the home government. The war in Yugoslavia and the passage from communism to 'democracy' provided the conditions for the reconfiguration of the adequacy between words and things – a *practical epochè*.[48] The arrival of nationalist forces in the government marked the establishment of a new legitimate link between independent Croatia and its populations abroad. 'Diaspora', as both a container of repertoires of enunciation[49] and legitimate action[50], became the political blueprint for the new relationship that had to be established between the government and its nationals abroad – its 'diaspora'. The bureaucratic use of the signifier 'diaspora' mobilised the repertoires of enunciation and action that had been constituted through governmental practices throughout the twentieth century. In a sense, the history of these practices created a stock of myths, taken-for-granted associations of meaning, contradictory and heterogeneous blueprints for the relationship between the state and the 'nationals' abroad. As we have seen, these discourses did not 'float freely'; they were tightly associated with state practices or discourses in the past, which had carved the boundaries of their possible enunciation for the future.

47 Foucault, Sécurité, territoire, population.

48 Bourdieu, Thompson, Language and Symbolic Power.

49 For more on the idea of the repertoire of enunciation, see Voloshinov [Bakhtin], Marxism and the Philosophy.

50 On repertoires of action, or repertoires of contention, see Tilly, Popular Contention.

2. *What the Diaspora* Does: *Practices of the Diaspora*

At the turn of the 1990s, the separated state categories, discourses and practices merge into the discourse of the 'diaspora'. The word, both in English and in Croatian – *dijaspora* – becomes the predominant signifier to define the 'Croatian nation' outside the borders of the homeland. State discourses and practices merge symbolically, but also bureaucratically: on 2 August 1991, a month and a half after the declaration of independence, the Croatian Ministry for the "old emigration" (*Ministarstvo za iseljeništvo*) is born. 'Diaspora' now serves as a powerful signifier to define a homogeneous population with political, economic and cultural links to its homeland which are legitimate and intimate. This allows the legitimisation of national and transnational political practices of associations all around the world in the direction of Croatia. It becomes the banner under which the Croatian state will carry on a certain number of transnational practices towards its population in countries such as the United States, Canada, Australia, and Germany.

Paradoxically, however, if the government's use of diasporic discourse allows for a certain number of outbound policies, in comparison with the years of Yugoslavia, the actual transnational practices of sovereignty towards populations in Europe, Australia or the Americas dramatically diminish. Police control is not on the agenda anymore, the worker population has either come back or is assimilated, and the cultural policy shows mixed results. Why then is this discourse so present? The mobilisation of the Croatian diaspora discourse will serve as the translation, in acceptable terms, of an old idea: the idea of an ethnically clean and territorially expanded 'Great Croatia'.[51] By framing a certain number of practices as such, the Croatian government and HDZ will in fact pursue three main strategic goals: the ethnic reshuffling of the national body, a vote-catching strategy for the HDZ, and a way of putting up with the failed annexation of Herzegovina.

2.1 Diaspora, the speech act: the discourses and practices of a new category

2.1.1 The social construction of the 'Croatian Diaspora'

It is almost impossible to retrace with certainty when this word started being used, both in Croatia or abroad to designate the entire population of Croats abroad. What is certain, however, is that the term starts making sense when what is sought is the national unity of a fragmented population, as well as a normative incentive for economic, political and cultural participation in homeland affairs. It is probably looking into the activities of the so-called

[51] For a detailed study of the development of the nationalist idea of 'Great Croatia' in the emigration, see the works of Marina Glamočak, Koncepcije Velike Hrvatske; ibid., La genèse de l'émigration.

'Yugoslav enemy emigration' that we find the first uses of the word[52] – and the discourse associated with it.

In 1974, the first successful attempt to create a united umbrella organisation of the political emigration takes place under the name of the Croatian National Council (*Hrvatsko narodno vijeće*), based in Toronto, Canada. In a 1984 document by the organisation, we already find the following reference:

> *When it is the question of the fight to establish legal rights for the Croatian nation, then it has to be taken into account that these rights* [...] *have to be enacted by the will of the whole Croatian nation: and the Croatian nation lives not only in the historical and ethnic Croatian countries* [...] *but also in the Emigrant Croatia (Iseljena Hrvatska), this is to say the Croatian Diaspora (Hrvatska Dijaspora).*[53]

Both these terms then start to be commonly used in the émigré circles. In Croatia, for Franjo Tuđman, who throughout his political career gets closer and closer to the émigré political ideas, the concept of a 'Croatian Diaspora' or 'Emigrant Croatia' matches his understanding of the 'Croatian Nation', which explicitly includes not only the Croats in the Yugoslav Socialist Republic of Croatia, but also the Croats from Bosnia and Herzegovina and the Croats abroad.[54] The efficiency of the diasporic discourse lies for Franjo Tuđman in its articulation of a broad, non-territorial and ethnically based conception of the Croatian nation. Not only does it formulate a homogeneous idea of the Croats abroad, but it also draws on pre-existing sedimented repertoires of meaning, attributing to the diaspora the legitimacy of a link with the homeland. This discourse particularly resonates in countries such as the United States, Canada and Australia, where the bulk of Croatian organisations can be found.[55]

2.1.2 Mobilising the 'diaspora' for the elections in Croatia

The discourse proved instrumental on several occasions. The first occasion was mobilisation to finance the HDZ's political campaign. In 1987, his political isolation inside Yugoslavia's Croatia pushes Tuđman, who had been imprisoned for dissident activities in 1981–1983, to reach out for help from outside. During several trips to the United States and to Canada, Tuđman visits both the 'romantic nationalist' political emigration, and the 'radical' political emigration, meeting with various political leaders, businessmen, and intellectuals.[56] In 1989, the evolution of the international situation will encourage these groups of exiles and emigrants to mobilise and finance the political campaign of the party Tuđman had just

52 As well as its close equivalents: Emigrant Croatia: *Iseljena Hrvatska*, 'Emigration': *Iseljeništvo*, 'Croatians outside the homeland': *Hrvati izvan domovine*.

53 Vidović, Što je Hrvatsko, 2.

54 Hudelist, Tuđman, biografija, 455.

55 For more on the institutionalisation of the diaspora discourse, particularly in countries with multicultural policies, see Dufoix, Généalogie d'un lieu commun; Schnapper, De l'Etat-nation; Tölölyan, Rethinking Contention.

56 For more on these two different groups and their links with Franjo Tuđman, see Meštrovic, U vrtlogu hrvatske politike; Kušan, Bitka za Novu Hrvatsku; Hudelist, Tuđman je "norvalcima"; Erceg, Bojim se za Hrvatsku.

created, the HDZ, on 17 June 1989.[57] In Canada, focused around the Franciscan friars' centre at Norval, Tuđman raises more than 500,000 dollars in a single banquet organised by local entrepreneurs from the recent and 'old emigration'.[58] In Germany, former 'workers temporarily abroad' and 'political emigrants' set their differences aside, found HDZ sections and organise themselves for fundraising. It is estimated that all around the world, Franjo Tuđman raised between 1.5 and two million dollars for his political campaign.[59] On 30 May 1990, Tuđman wins the elections and the HDZ obtains 206 of the 351 seats in parliament.

One of the first effects of 'diaspora' as a performative is therefore the attribution of a new name to a 'population abroad', erasing the previous differences between groups, in order to gather financial and political support for a long-distance political endeavour. Of course, this speech act is successful only because the relations of power are changing, and the former divisions do not hold true anymore. However, the instance of the war gives particular strength to the new 'category', disrupting the traditional adequacy between 'words' and 'things'. It creates a feeling of 'community' among the previously compartmentalised Croatian groups abroad, accentuated by the hesitations of Western powers to act.[60] In order to assert its existence as a political actor, the associations have to make the 'diaspora' visible. They have to appear united for the cause of independence, and prove themselves to be an important share of the electorate, in order to make successful claims during political campaigns. Secondly, speaking in the name of the 'diaspora' was aimed at gaining legitimacy to lobby the White House, the State Department and other relevant institutions. Finally, the strategy is to 'Americanize' the issue, to make it a stake for elections and re-elections.

2.1.3 Establishing an efficient lobbying strategy

From 1991 to 1992, the 'diaspora' manifests itself on many occasions. On 26 July 1991, more than 35,000 people demonstrate in Washington, DC, following the call of the Croatian American Association, and the movement proves its unity. All the associations, such as the Croatian American Association, the Croatian Fraternal Union, the Croatian Catholic Union, the Croatian Academy of America, are present. The Croatian government is present through its representative in Washington, Frane Golem.[61] The demonstration serves as a particularly symbolic moment, which makes the community visible. In the words of Pierre Bourdieu,

57 Hudelist, Banket u Hrvatskoj.
58 Hudelist, Tuđman, biografija, 608.
59 Ibid., 586.
60 As Bourdieu puts it "[...] the heretic rupture with the established order and with the dispositions and the representations that it generates among the agents shaped according to these structures, supposes itself the conjunction between the critical discourse and an objective crisis, able to break the immediate concordance between the incorporated structures and the objective structures they are the product of, and to institute a sort of *practical epochè*, a suspension of the primary approval of the established order" (Bourdieu, Ce que parler veut dire, 150).
61 35,000 Join Croatian Peace Rally in Washington, *Zajedničar*, 7 August 1991.

> *The officialisation finds its accomplishment in the demonstration, a typical act of magic (which does not mean it is not deprived of efficiency), by which the practical, virtual, denied, repressed group becomes visible, manifest, for the other groups and for itself, and testifies its existence as a known and recognised group, with pretensions to institutionalisation.*[62]

Lobbying is also tackled through the conventional methods of American politics. Ruder & Finn, a public relations firm, is hired to better 'resonate' the Croatian agenda in Washington.[63] Meetings with congressmen are organised during the "Croatian Days on the Hill"; pressure is put on the legislators for example on the "Nickels Amendment", to prohibit bilateral aid to Yugoslavia, or for the "Direct Aid to Democracies Act" or "Bob Dole Bill" to provide direct assistance to USSR Republics as well as SFRY Republics. Finally, during the 1992 presidential elections, most of the Croatian-American associations actively support Bill Clinton's ticket, hoping for a change in foreign policy.[64] More than the lobbying actions, aimed at direct political efficiency, the demonstrations and gathering of support increase the awareness (or illusion) of community.[65] This proves particularly relevant for the organisation of humanitarian and military support.

Humanitarian aid is mostly organised and coordinated by the Croatian 'diaspora' associations, without much influence from the government. At this point, in fact, state institutions are weak, and the government has to face the uprising of the Serbian provinces. The catastrophe of Vukovar, the destruction of this town in eastern Croatia by Serbian troops in October 1991, is the 'electroshock' which triggers massive humanitarian support and around 300 different organisations are created in the US. In Canada, Australia, Germany, and Austria, the situation is similar. The biggest effort, in the United States, is provided by the Croatian Fraternal Union. It is estimated that the Union raised more than 24 million dollars worth of aid, shipped in more than 141 containers between 1991 and 1999. This is to say, as a comparison, more than ten percent of the EU foreign aid to Croatia through the ECHO programme for the same period.[66]

Similarly, the diaspora associations were crucial in providing military support for the war, be it directly, through arms smuggling, or indirectly, through financial support. It is still very difficult to know exact figures for the importance of the 'diaspora' contribution to the war effort. What is certain, however, is that it was determinant in the first years. The

62 Bourdieu, Ce que parler veut dire, 142.

63 Interview by the author with Jim Harff, former President of Ruder & Finn Global Public Affairs, current President of Global Communicators, Washington, 20 June 2003.

64 Clinton / Gore Listen to Croatians, *Zajedničar*, 6 January 1993, 2.

65 As Sidney Tarrow explains about the barricades: "Like the demonstration and the strike, the barricade had an internal as well as external logic. As they faced off against hostile troops, the defenders came to know each other as comrades, developed a division of labour of fighters, builders and suppliers, forming networks of comrades that would bring them together in future confrontations" (Tarrow, Power in Movement, 41).

66 The overall ECHO humanitarian aid amounted to 293.8 million Euros between 1991 and 1999. See: Facts and Figures, EC Assistance to Western Balkans, *South East Europe Online*, <http://www.southeasteurope.org/documents/facts_figures.pdf>.

funds raised were transferred through two public bank accounts opened by the Republic of Croatia: one in Austria, another one in Switzerland, under the name of 'Croatian National Fund'. Anthony Peraica, active in the Croatian American Association, estimates that seven to ten million dollars were gathered solely from the region of Chicago and 25 to 30 million dollars for the whole of the USA. For Miomir Žužul, the contribution of the diaspora to the war effort was a 'simple figure percentage', whereas for Peraica, the proportion is more around 20–25 per cent. What is certain, however, is that the money was crucial during the first years of the war, up until 1993.[67]

The mobilisation was so successful that once the urgency of the conflict had ended and did not mobilise all the resources of the state, several initiatives came from Zagreb to place its grip on the diaspora. The initiative proved extremely inefficient. In 1993, in the United States, the division of labour between the various associations was relatively clear. The Croatian American Association did the lobbying work, the Croatian Catholic Union and the Croatian Fraternal Union provided for the coordination of humanitarian and economic support through their infrastructure and programmes. The first 'incursion' of the government in the discourse and practices of the diaspora occurs in 1993, when Franjo Tuđman's HDZ attempts to create a world forum for all Croatian organisations in the world through the creation of the *Croatian World Congress*. However, the initiative is cut rather short as it becomes very clear to all participants that the only goal of the Congress is total control by the party. Even if in Canada the operation meets some success, in the United States the organisation does not hold. Rapidly, the main organisation (the Croatian Fraternal Union) and the majority of the other Croatian American associations pull out from the initiative and form a rival association, the National Federation of Croatian Americans. While the Croatian World Congress and the Croatian American Association (CAA) support Croatia's policy in Bosnia and Herzegovina, the National Federation of Croatian Americans is prompt to condemn it. Moreover, as the Croatian American Association continues to support Croatian policies condemned in the White House, it starts losing 'resonance'. HDZ therefore enters into the struggle for the definition of the 'official diaspora organisations', but fails. Croatian-American organisations, entangled in normative webs of their country of residence, the United States, did not become subordinate agents of the aggressive and nationalist homeland.[68]

67 Interviews by the author with: Miomir Žužul, Ambassador of Croatia to the USA (1996–2000), Zagreb, 15 February 2003; Mate Granić, Ministry of Foreign Affairs of Croatia, Zagreb, 19 February 2003; Anthony Peraica, Former President of the Croatian American Association, Chicago, 27 June 2003.

68 This example therefore shows that although governments can be particularly strong in the long-distance shaping of identities and political behaviour, they always face resistance and processes of subjectification. This clearly contradicts the myth of the *Manchurian Candidate* underpinned in the realist literature on the danger of diaspora politics for the national interest. See HUNTINGTON, The Erosion, as well as SMITH, Foreign Attachments. The plot of the *Manchurian Candidate* features a former American soldier who had been brainwashed by Chinese Communists during the Korean War. Upon his return, the soldier unwillingly became an agent

To sum up, 'diaspora' served as a performative framing of the new relationship to be established between the homeland and the Croats abroad. It therefore served to discursively generate a new homogeneous community legitimately linked to its homeland. For the HDZ, this was instrumental in providing financial support for the political campaign and for the military effort. For Croatian associations, it proved politically efficient to place a certain number of claims, and to organise pressure on the national authorities. However, as we have already outlined, paradoxically, the moment of 'diaspora politics' and the progressive constitution of diaspora as a state category, coincides with a retreat of the state from its claims and practices abroad. The claim to the long-distance monopoly of violence is abandoned here with the end of communism: policing the political emigration was no longer needed. Regarding the 'workers abroad', those who had to return did so, the others were already integrated in their countries of residence, and the state did not have any particular policy towards them. Only the claim to the monopoly of 'symbolic' violence abroad was maintained through the use of *Matica Hrvatska Iseljenika* as the agency for the diffusion of the 'official' new Croatian identity, although the school programmes were marginalised. Finally, bureaucratically, the 'Ministry for the Diaspora' was underfunded, and rapidly abandoned. So why is the discourse of diaspora so present? Why is there so much emphasis on the importance of the diaspora and the necessity to include it in the Croatian nation?

2.2 The Croatian diaspora and the politics of an ethnically clean 'Great Croatia'

2.2.1 Bureaucratic diaspora and citizenship: an ethnically clean citizenry

The new Croatian Constitution of 1991 and the new Citizenship Law voted at the same time[69] to give citizenship to all former citizens of the Socialist Republic of Croatia registered before 8 October 1991. It also allowed for the acquisition of citizenship for individuals residing outside of Croatia under 'ethnic' criteria.[70] Article 10 of the Croatian Constitution reads:

> *1. The Republic of Croatia protects the rights and interests of its citizens living or staying abroad, and promotes their links with the homeland. 2. Parts of the Croatian nation in other states are guaranteed special concern and protection by the Republic of Croatia.*[71]

The Criteria for belonging to the Croatian nation for residents abroad are defined by Article 16 of the Citizenship Law:

of the Soviets who could 'activate' him and manipulate him just by a telephone call (see CONDON, The Manchurian Candidate).

69 *Official Gazette of the Republic of Croatia,* no. 53, 1991; modifications and amendments in *Official Gazette of the Republic of Croatia,* no. 28, 1992.

70 For a comprehensive analysis of the citizenship policies of post-1991 Croatia, see RAGAZZI, STIKS, Croatian Citizenship.

71 Republic of Croatia, The Constitution of the Republic of Croatia.

> *A member of the Croatian people who does not have a place of residence in the Republic of Croatia can acquire Croatian citizenship if he or she meets the prerequisites from Article 8, paragraph I, point 5 of this Law and if he or she issues a written statement that he or she considers himself or herself to be a Croatian citizen.*

Article 8.1.5 asks for "a conclusion to be derived from his or her conduct that he or she is attached to the legal system and custom persisting in the Republic of Croatia and that he or she accepts the Croatian culture". This law effectively meant, for all Croatian-Americans, Croatian-Canadians, -Australians, -Argentineans, etc., as well as political exiles and third generation Croats: "You are part of the Croatian nation." The attribution of the passport becomes therefore not only the bureaucratic means of embracing and controlling the nation,[72] but a symbolic document signifying belonging to the nation, and abolishing the previous distinction between political exiles, third generation migrants and workers temporarily abroad.

However, the legislative disposition creates this paradoxical situation: Croatian nationality is given to the 'diaspora' on an 'ethnic' and 'cultural basis' while it has been systematically denied or obstructed for ethnic Serbian populations. The Croatian citizenship and nationality is in fact given to individuals who never had the nationality nor ever lived in Croatia – ten per cent of the 1997 voters, according to an OSCE report – while certain individuals, of Serbian 'nationality' but Croatian 'citizenship', who were forced to flee combat zones during the war found themselves without nationality nor civic rights.[73] They are administratively excluded from the 'diaspora' and from the 'nation' as a whole. As the Human Rights Watch report shows:

> *Human Rights Watch is also concerned with the citizenship law, especially as it makes it difficult for Croatian Serbs outside the country to assert the right to citizenship, leaving some stateless and many unable to return to Croatia or to exercise their rights as citizens to participate in elections.*[74]

According to the OSCE report and the report of the Council of Europe of January 2000, the Law additionally put in place unequal administrative barriers depending on the ethnicity of the applicants to nationality. 'Ethnic Croats' do not have to prove a particular link to the Croatian territory, whereas non-Croats have to prove five years of residency on the Croatian territory immediately before their request.[75] Moreover, the candidates for Croatian citizenship have to declare their "attachment to the legal system and to the customs of the Croatian Republic", accept the Croatian culture and be able to prove fluency in the Latin alphabet (in contrast with Cyrillic). Overall, the administrative and legal obstacles, according to the

72 Torpey, The invention of the Passport.

73 OSCE, Statement, Presidential Election.

74 Human Rights Watch, Croatia's Democracy Deficit.

75 Communist Yugoslavia's, just like the Soviet Union's way of solving the problem of nationality by recognising them and institutionalising them gave paradoxical results in the 1990s. As Rogers Brubaker shows, the inscription of the "ethnic nationality" in all official documents and registers, initially planned to guarantee equal representation, has reified and fixed "ethnic" identities to the point of rendering them "natural" (Brubaker, Nationalism Reframed).

OSCE report, have proven to be an insurmountable barrier for a great number of Croatian citizens of Serbian ethnicity. Through the monopoly of the attribution of citizenship, conferred to Croatia by its sovereign status, the state has been able to define administratively the 'ins' and the 'outs' of its population abroad. More broadly, however, the bureaucratic category of diaspora is used selectively to 'include' a large number of 'ethnic Croats' abroad, and exclude 'Serbs' inside. The 'diaspora' category therefore allows for the reshuffling of the ethnic balance of the nation, an objective which was planned for a long time by the political emigration, Franjo Tuđman, and the leaders of the HDZ. The definition of 'diaspora' as a bureaucratic category therefore accompanies and justifies an overtly nationalist policy of cleansing, which would have been very difficult to otherwise justify.

2.2.2 Electoral tactics

The 'diaspora' politics of the HDZ allow for another practice in obvious contradiction with international norms of sovereignty, violating a certain number of international agreements, including the 1995 Dayton Agreement. The issue at stake here is one fundamental element of representative systems: the right to vote and the right to be elected.

The Constitution of 1990 guaranteed the right to vote to all Croatian citizens, regardless of their residential status. Article 45 of the Constitution therefore reads:

> *All Croatian citizens of the Republic of Croatia who have reached the age of eighteen years shall have universal and equal suffrage. This right shall be exercised through direct elections by secret ballot. In elections for the Croatian Parliament and for the President of the Republic, the Republic of Croatia shall ensure suffrage to its citizens who are abroad at the time of the elections, so that they may vote in the countries in which they are or in any other way specified by law.*[76]

For the elections of 1995, it was decided there would be a fixed number of representatives for the parliament; they would be elected in a separate electoral unit, and on a separate electoral list. The idea proposed by the HDZ government was that the constituency in the diaspora would represent ten percent of the overall electorate in Croatia. Ten percent of the seats (twelve seats) were therefore *a priori* reserved for the diaspora vote. The twelve seats were won by the HDZ.

Rapidly, the diaspora vote was contested on several fronts. The first was that technically, the mandate on the 'diaspora' list represented less people than for the average seat: as only 107,772 voters abroad had participated (27 percent of the 'diaspora' constituency), one 'diaspora' representative stood for 8,981 votes, instead of the 30,217 votes for the other representatives, which is to say three times as many. The effect on the electoral outcome was quite important: as with the diaspora votes the HDZ obtained a large majority (59.1 percent) instead of the 54.8 per cent which they would have gained without it.[77] The legitimacy of the vote was also contested for wider reasons: how can people who do not pay taxes vote? How can people who do not have to live the consequences of their choices vote? As

[76] Republic of Croatia, The Constitution of the Republic of Croatia (Italics added by the author).
[77] Kasapović, Hrvatska politika, 28.

Mirijana Kasapović put it in an opinion paper, the right to vote of the 'diaspora' was posing central questions for the functioning of a democracy:

> *Who has the right to vote and to be elected in this country? All the bearers of a Croatian passport, from Vinjan Donji to Alaska? All ethnic Croats with a passport? Only the real Croatian emigration, i.e. citizens of the Republic of Croatia who emigrated for political or economic reasons and for whom it is easy to prove a former stay in the country? Only the ones who completed military service and pay taxes in Croatia?*[78]

In 1999, after heated debates, the electoral system was changed. From a fixed number of seats, the law passed to proportional representation on the basis of voter turnout. This again guaranteed to the HDZ six seats out of six in the 2000 elections. The political impact was again quite important. Although the HDZ lost overall, the SDP-HSLS coalition (lead by Ivica Račan and Stipe Mesić) obtained 47 percent of the votes instead of the 50.7 percent majority they would have had without the diaspora seats. Moreover, the addition of the extra seats gave the HDZ first position in terms of single party representation in the parliament. Looking at the electoral results, we see that the HDZ constantly obtained between 80 and 90 percent of the diaspora votes in 1995 and 2000 at the parliamentary elections. This confirmed the idea that there was a particular 'pact' between the HDZ and the 'diaspora'. This special pact, however, was obtained through a play on the various meanings of the word and the discourse.

In fact, if we look at the geographical composition of the 'diaspora' constituency, we see that what is in question is not the 'diaspora' in the world, but essentially the Croats from Bosnia and Herzegovina (BiH). In fact, after the new laws on citizenship, 90 percent of those who acquired Croatian nationality outside of the territory were the Croats from BiH. After the right to vote was given to Croats residing outside of national territory in 1995, 80 to 90 percent of the electorate was in fact from a single location, BiH.[79] The overall support for the HDZ in BiH has, however, to be understood in a broader framework, that of the failed annexation of Herzegovina during the war. For Kasapović,

> *The Croatian ethnic community in Bosnia and Herzegovina is a separate vote-catching group which has been during the war, and still is today politically and financially dependent on the government of the Croatian state. The HVO – the so-called 'Croatian component' of the armed forces of Bosnia and Herzegovina, the administrations in the communes and cantons with a Croatian majority, the schooling, pension and health care system, all these services are directly financed by the budget of the Republic of Croatia. This is 'paid back' by the absolute electoral support of the Croats of Bosnia and Herzegovina to the HDZ.*[80]

We can therefore draw a few concluding remarks. Firstly, the question of the right to vote and to be elected of the diaspora not only constitutes the 'diaspora' as an all-encompassing, ethnic bureaucratic and political category, but it also becomes the point of contention for electoral politics. In this sense, the question of diaspora opens a new front in the classic stra-

[78] Kasapović, Znaju li uopće.
[79] Kasapović, Hrvatska politika, 24.
[80] Ibid., 23–4.

tegic struggles between political forces for the definition, enlargement or restriction of the constituency. After distinctions on the basis of income, gender or age, residence and territorial presence can now be a point of contention and a strategic asset for the electoral strategies. Secondly, the particular case of Croatia and its 'diaspora list' shifts our attention, as political sociologists, towards new understandings of the territorial dimension in the practices of the legitimisation of power, breaking along one more line the traditional entanglement of territory, population and power. The 'diaspora' discourse allows for strategies and practices that could not be justified except in the name of a particular legitimate social and political link between a homeland and a population dispersed in the world. Finally, since both internal political opposition and international pressure prevented the HDZ and its leader from territorially annexing Herzegovina, the 'diaspora politics' of Zagreb have comprised a way to *de facto* annex the territory without actually having to change the borders. In this sense, the 'diaspora' speech act would allow for the legitimate extension of the three 'inner' monopolies of the state (violence, allocation of resources and symbolic violence) without legally infringing the internationally accepted rules and norms institutionalised into international public law, agreements and conventions.

Conclusion

In this chapter I have argued that 'diaspora', rather than an *a priori* category, is a word of politics: a linguistic and social construction that serves a particular purpose. By fusing the three previous categories of emigrants (the 'old emigration', the 'political emigration' and the 'workers temporarily abroad') into the category of diaspora, the nationalist regime of Franjo Tuđman created a very useful political actor to deploy various forms of 'deterritorialised nationalism'. But this trend does not go unquestioned. I have not covered here the relations between the government of Croatia and the European Union, particularly in the light of the talks for accession to EU membership, yet it is probably from these discussions that profound changes are to be expected. The Croatian conception of citizenship and political representation, the implications of its government in Bosnia-Herzegovina as well as its problematic treatment of the rights of minorities will in fact very quickly emerge as issues to be dealt with. It will be interesting to see to which extent the European Union's dominant conception of citizenship favouring civic, political and territorial criteria will impose itself over the current transnational conception of nation and citizenship, profoundly rooted in a primacy of blood and culture.

Dubravka Mlinarić

Emigration Research in Croatia: An Overview

Introduction

This paper discusses how Croatian emigration has been studied during the last five decades.[1] As a critical overview of the research on emigration from Croatia, it especially discusses Croatian sociology, historiography and demography, and is based on numerous secondary sources and literature. The discussion, however, limits itself to depicting dominant research tendencies and evaluating the relevance of certain migration issues for everyday life. For that purpose, we will compare some public debates on emigration which reveal the potential of migration becoming a politicised topic.

Emigration processes and emigrant societies, in this case the Croatian one, have always attracted considerable public interest. Emigration has also been a political issue in past and present political systems in Croatia. In this regard, the question comes up of how to define 'Croatian migrants'. In the literature various definitions of this denomination can be found. The situation becomes even more complicated if we ask who was defined as Croat and/or a descendant of Croat emigrants abroad. Official categories based on the country of origin and personal identification of the individual are rather ambiguous, reflecting the fact that Croatia neither comprises all persons who identify themselves as Croats in an ethnic sense nor is it populated only by Croats. In this paper, the term 'Croatian emigration' primarily includes citizens of Croatia or citizens of those political units and states which existed on the territories of present-day Croatia.[2]

1 This article is part of the project "Transnational Migration – Challenges to Croatian Society" by the Institute of Migration and Ethnic Studies, Zagreb, supported by Grant No. 076-0762385-2378 from the Croatian Ministry of Science, Education and Sports (2007–2009).

2 Heršak, Leksikon migracijskog i etničkog nazivlja, 78. Prior to World War I, the territory of the current Republic of Croatia belonged to different administrative units of the Habsburg Empire (since 1867 Austro-Hungarian Monarchy). The Kingdoms of Croatia and Slavonia were part of the Hungarian 'half' of the Dual Monarchy, while Dalmatia and Istria belonged to Austria. Between 1918 and 1941 and again between 1945 and 1991, Croatia was part of Yugoslavia (Kingdom of Serbs, Croats and Slovenes 1918–1929, Kingdom of Yugoslavia 1929–1941, Federal People's Republic of Yugoslavia/Socialist Federal Republic of Yugoslavia 1945–1991). Between 1941 and 1945 most of the Croat lands belonged to the Independent State of Croatia

The discussion of research in Croatia is further complicated by ambiguous definitions of the term 'emigration', which is not always clearly separated from other forms of mobility and studied together with them. Therefore, explorations of certain elements of external, or transnational, migration can be found in very different publications. The material examined here has been defined as 'research on emigration'. This includes published books, articles from migration and social science journals,[3] and materials on projects on migration carried out by specialised institutions. Not all the selected articles, books and research projects have been authored by Croatian scholars or published in Croatia. All together, one hundred and two pieces were selected. Besides the published results, as the most important kind of source material, other relevant information regarding migration research in the last five decades has been considered. This includes Croatian institutions (institutes and faculty departments)[4] that carry out research projects with leading experts, who significantly shape the research paradigm. Furthermore, seminars, round tables, conferences and scientific debates on specific issues of emigration that attract public interest also went into this review.

Until the 1990s, the study of Croatian emigration was strictly divided into two distinct directions. On the one hand, there was a vast number of studies on the Diaspora;[5] on the other hand, external migration was researched within the framework of broader migration studies. During the Yugoslav socialist regime, research on the large Diaspora was not greatly appreciated, both from a political and an academic point of view. This kind of research, from the political point of view, was suspected to be destructive for Yugoslav society, or at least capable of motivating extreme nationalists because of the Diaspora, especially as it was comprised of political exiles from the defeated Croatian and Serbian nationalists of World War II. From the academic point of view, descriptive Diaspora analyses were regarded as being deficient in their methodology, historically and socially anachronous, or even redundant.

That said, researchers of both Diaspora and migration studies tried to follow contemporary tendencies in international migration research using different methodologies and ap-

(NDH), a German and Italian quisling régime. Istria and parts of northern Dalmatia belonged to Italy in the interwar period.

3 Such as *Migracijske i etničke teme, Društvena istraživanja* and *Revija za sociologiju.*

4 The Institute for Migration and Ethnic Studies in Zagreb has a long established tradition of research on issues of ethnicity and migration in Croatia. The Institute of Social Sciences Ivo Pilar in Zagreb has also undertaken a range of migration related projects, from minority issues to demography and historical research on the Croat Diaspora. The Institute for Social Research and the Institute of Ethnology and Folklore Research in Zagreb have been dealing with migration research to a smaller extent as well. Other places of migration research are institutions of higher education, such as the Department of Sociology at the Faculty of Philosophy, University of Zagreb, and the Department of Sociology at the University of Zadar.

5 Presentations of an academic nature, but also popular essays, journalists' reports and public debates on Diaspora issues are published in the publications of the *Hrvatska matica iseljenika* (Croatian Heritage Foundation) in Zagreb, especially its journal *Matica* and annual *Iseljenički zbornik* (Croatian Emigrant Almanac). They pay special attention to culture (especially the native language) and promote the protection and preservation of the cultural heritage.

proaches, but within the specific social and also political framework of the former Yugoslavia and, then, independent Croatia. During the 1990s, forced migration became the most important topic of migration research due to the war experience and increased number of refugees and displaced persons in the region. During the most recent past, Croatia has seen all kinds of migration side-by-side, which confirmed the high degree of mobility of its population. The plurality of migration patterns also indicates a wide range of factors causing migration, which intensified research on migration in sociology, historiography, social geography, demography, economy, ethnology, anthropology, linguistics, theology and other disciplines.

Historical overview of Croatian emigration

Before discussing the main trends in research on emigration from Croatia, I want to give a brief sketch of the history of Croatian emigration as presented in the works of national historians, demographers, economists and sociologists.

The territory of present-day Croatia has a long emigration history which can be traced back to the fifteenth century. The reasons for emigration were complex and multidimensional, linked also to the fact that Croatian lands had always been on the crossroads of various interests and political powers, and therefore experienced turmoil which in turn spurred migratory activities. Having in mind Croatia's specific geographic position between Central Europe, the Mediterranean and the Balkans, and being a border region in multiple ways (cultural, ethnic, confessional, political), this region was included in numerous migration patterns where various factors impacting migration were present. Croatia is, therefore, an interesting object for the study of emigration, but also immigration processes. The intensity of emigration in the past also made Croatian society a transnational one. Mass migration from the territory of Croatia, though, has an even longer history: as a result of the Ottoman conquest and the frequent wars between the Ottomans and the Habsburgs (fifteenth to eighteenth centuries), an estimated 200,000 people left the region permanently. Present-day Croat ethnic minorities in countries such as Austria (*Gradišće/Burgenland*), Romania, Slovakia, Czech Republic, and Italy, originated exactly from these early migration waves. At the same time immigration processes also took place, especially in the so-called military border, established by the Austrians as a line of defence against the Ottomans, and stretching from the Adriatic to the Banat, encompassing large swaths of today's Croatia. There, the deliberate policies of the Emperor settled people from other parts of Austria, such as Germans, but also Serbian refugees from the Ottoman Empire.[6]

The period of Croatia's overseas emigration starts in the 1890s and continues until 1914, when an estimated 350,000 to 450,000 people left Croatian lands to overseas destinations mainly due to economic reasons, especially the crisis of farming and increasing

6 Roksandić, Vojna Hrvstska.

rural over-population.[7] This wave of labour emigration was also a response to the emerging global labour markets and state-building processes in other parts of the world. 'Empty' or under-populated territories, especially in the Americas and Australia, were the most inviting destinations for people from over-populated but under-developed European regions such as the rural areas of Dalmatia. The first labour migrants and adventurers from this region reached the USA and Canada already by the mid-nineteenth century. This process was to a large extent stimulated by the economic crisis of the late nineteenth and early twentieth century, particularly in farming and shipbuilding, and aggravated by the Phylloxera epidemics, which destroyed much of the Dalmatian wine industry. On the other hand, industrial growth in the USA attracted workers from poor European regions such as Croatia, with the aid of emigration agents who recruited cheap workers for US-American mining companies, shipyards and factories.[8] From the point of view of the migrants, important reasons to leave were the expectations of a higher salary, better working opportunities (especially for the better educated), better living conditions and higher overall living standards in the receiving countries. Nevertheless, many emigrants ended up as "socially discriminated and underpaid people".[9] Still, a whole range of reasons reinforced and strengthened emigration until the implementation of the immigration quota in the USA in the early 1920s. During the period of open door policies in America until World War I, there was no significant emigration from Croatia to European countries.

The emigrants were mostly men in the age range between fifteen and fourty years. The profile of the emigrants was also shaped by the immigration policies of the countries of destination, which wanted to prevent the immigration of people considered unfit for labour or politically suspicious. Overseas emigration after the 1880s achieved such a dimension that some Dalmatian islands, mainly Brač and Hvar, where mass emigration had already started in the 1860s, began to face problems of depopulation. The annual average number of emigrants from the present-day territory of Croatia was estimated to be 8,850 people.[10]

The circumstances for emigration also changed significantly after World War I. In the first Yugoslav state, which was established in 1918, the state pursued colonisation and voluntary migration policies directing settlement towards so-called "economically empty areas" or less developed regions as well as regions in which minorities lived. Croatia, on the other hand, continued to experience emigration because of economic difficulties, intensified by the consequences of World War I. 'Austro-Hungarians' (mainly German and Hungarian speakers but also Czechs) who left Croatia for their new nation-states after the dissolution of the Habsburg Monarchy for political reasons presented a particular kind of emigration.

[7] Lakatoš, Narodna statistika, 65; Čizmić, Sopta, Šakić, Iseljena Hrvatska, 12; Nejašmić, Iseljevanje iz Hrvatske u evropske i prekomorske zemlje, 515; ibid, Iseljavanje iz Hrvstske. Brojčani aspekt, 64; Telišman, Statistički pokazatelji, 130–143.

[8] Čizmić, Sopta, Šakić, Iseljena Hrvatska, 14.

[9] Cf. Wimmer, Glick Schiller, Methodological Nationalism, 589.

[10] Nejašmić, Iseljevanje iz Hrvatske u evropske i prekomorske zemlje, 526; ibid, Iseljavanje iz Hrvstske, Brojčani aspekt, 66.

Destinations for labour migrants soon changed after the war. Due to massive unemployment and poverty, the USA as well as other overseas countries introduced restrictive immigration regulations, which limited the number of immigrants, especially for Eastern and Southeastern European ethnic groups. According to the 1924 regulations, the USA accepted only 671 people per year from the territory of the Kingdom of Serbs, Croats and Slovenes.[11] In spite of such restrictions, a considerable number of people emigrated overseas from interwar Yugoslavia: between 1921 and 1939 almost 200,000, with an additional smaller number of unregistered emigrants. However, the USA, as the most popular destination for overseas emigration, was replaced by Southern America, where roughly half of the Yugoslav emigrants arrived, especially Argentina and Chile. Australia, New Zealand and Canada were new popular destinations as well. While emigration from interwar Yugoslavia to overseas destinations was gradually decreasing, an increase of emigration to European countries was recorded. European countries accepted more than 132,000 persons from the Kingdom of Yugoslavia after 1927, when the Yugoslav government began to publish data on emigration to Europe.[12] The biggest number of Croatian emigrants to European destinations settled in Germany, Belgium and France. Work and residence abroad was planned to be a solution for a limited period of time, hence migrants intended to return. In the years before the German attack on Yugoslavia (April 1941), voluntary emigration became even more complicated, due to countries such as Germany restricting the labour influx by the organised recruitment of migrant workers on the basis of labour contracts.

The political and economic consequences of World War II introduced a new type of migration, new destinations and new motives. Europe became a huge arena for the movement of displaced persons and refugees. War-related emigration from Croatia involved approximately 250,000 people; this volume of migration including defeated collaborators, their families as collateral forced migration, and ethnically 'cleansed' minority groups, especially Germans.[13] 'Emigrants' of the former category, war prisoners and refugees, were first settled in foreign refugees' camps. There was also a large number of political migrants and asylum seekers, who fled the new communist regime to overseas destinations, so that emigration to Australia, New Zealand and Canada increased significantly. But there were also economic reasons for emigration in war-wrecked Yugoslavia, such as the deep agricultural crisis, desperate living conditions, the destruction of the shipbuilding industry, etc. Young people from the Karst regions of Croatia were especially tempted to go abroad. Contrary to the pre-World War I emigrants, who had worked mainly in the steel and mining industries, these latecomers found employment mostly in agriculture and trade. These migrations also resulted in further chain-migration from Yugoslavia, which happened in a rather random, unorganised and spontaneous way during the 1950s.

11 Čizmić, Sopta, Šakić, Iselenja Hrvstska, 15.
12 Ibid., 16.
13 Nejašmić, Iseljavanje iz Hrvatske. Brojčani aspekt, 68.

After the end of the immediate post-war migration and refugee waves, the history of emigration from Croatia until the end of socialism can be divided into two distinct periods: the first, characterised by growing illegal emigration until the early 1960s, and the second starting in 1963/4, marked by state tolerated and even facilitated mass migration of workers. The first form, illegal migration, lasted from 1946 until about 1963/4, when travel restrictions on labour migrants were removed. It was predominantly men who for economic and/or political reasons illegally crossed the Yugoslav borders, mostly to Austria and Italy. Some of them joined the established migration routes to Argentina or other overseas countries.

The second wave introduced a new pattern of large numbers of legal labour migrants (so-called *pasošari*, i.e. migrants with a passport). These migrants were officially not considered as nor called "emigrants"[14] because they were expected to return. The official expression to denominate them, which was also used as a census category, was "workers on temporary work abroad" (*radnici na privremenom radu u inozemstvu*), compatible to the West German notion of the *Gastarbeiter*. This expression covered very different migrant categories: seasonal workers and permanent emigrants, who had spent more than a decade in receiving countries. When people were allowed to work abroad in 1964, many of them left the country in search of work and better pay abroad. The Yugoslav government even facilitated this process by concluding bilateral recruitment treaties with foreign governments and considered the temporary work of Yugoslav citizens abroad as a necessary evil to alleviate labour market pressures, after market-oriented reforms had led to a surge in unemployment in the mid-1960s. According to official data, 671,908 Yugoslav citizens worked abroad by 1971 accompanied by "members of their families living with them". The emigration process reached its peak in the early 1970s, when Western European countries introduced restrictions on immigration and recruitment stops after the oil crisis and recession in 1973/4. Thereafter, most migrants from Yugoslavia were family members who joined their migrant workers abroad; but workers also continued to leave though often not registered by the Yugoslav authorities. The 1971 census also specifically counted migrants and revealed the rate of migration from Yugoslavia. The average rate of Yugoslav external migration was 3.9 per 100 inhabitants; Croatia had the highest (6.1) and Montenegro the lowest (2.0) rate of external migration.[15] Croatia, Bosnia and Herzegovina, and Macedonia had the largest share in terms of emigrants per head of total population (Map 1), greater than their respective share in Yugoslavia's total population. While Croatia's population was 22 per cent of the total population of Yugoslavia, migrants from Croatia made up 39 per cent of all Yugoslav migrant workers.

The resulting wave of labour emigration was not only significantly larger in number but also differing in its character, structure and distribution from previous illegal migration. One of the main characteristics of Yugoslav migrant workers was their comparatively

[14] The Yugoslav Emigration Law of 1922 had defined an emigrant as a citizen who moved overseas to "work physically and earn money or to join his relatives who moved earlier under the same condition".

[15] Baučić, Radnici u inozemstvu, 59, 116.

high level of skills.[16] The most common destinations for migrant workers were European countries, especially the FRG, but the highly skilled ones preferred to leave for the USA. Migrants from Croatia accounted for the majority of Yugoslav migrant workers in West Germany, Switzerland and overseas countries (see Table 1).

Table 1: Share of destination countries among migrant workers from Yugoslavia and Croatia, 1971

	Yugoslavia	**Croatia**
	in %	
Austria	11.4	5.1
France	5.0	2.3
FR Germany	55.2	62.3
Switzerland	3.2	3.6
Sweden	2.8	1.7
Benelux countries	1.4	1.1
Other European countries	2.8	2.7
Europe total	**81.8**	**78.8**
USA	4.2	4.2
Australia	7.6	7.9
Canada	5.2	7.5
Other overseas countries	1.2	1.6
Overseas total	**18.2**	**21.2**

Source: Baučić, Radnici u inozemstvu, 94–5 (Table XXXVII).

As already mentioned, the initial idea of the Yugoslav and destination countries' governments as well as most migrants themselves was that they would not permanently settle abroad. This was, for example, evinced by the fact that emigrants usually did not acquire real estates abroad. Already in the 1970s, though, 86 per cent of 'temporary' labour migrants from Yugoslavia were estimated to have become permanent emigrants, delaying their return and adapting to their destination countries through integration, assimilation and finally naturalisation.[17] The effects of migration were interpreted differently in the receiving countries. The *Gastarbeiter* migration can hardly be discussed without referring to the immigration policies of the host countries; however, these issues were under-evaluated in Yugoslavia until the 1990s.

Croatian demographers evaluated emigration after the Second World War as discouraging for the development of Croatia, since it occurred under the circumstances of accelerated demographic ageing and constant decrease of the birth rate.[18] Calculating approximately 366,000 overseas labour migrants and *Gastarbeiter* in European destinations in 1981, re-

16 Ibid., 87, 121.

17 Grečić, Jovanović, Osnovne komponente pretvaranja, 277.

18 Nejašmić, Iseljavanje iz Hrvstske. Brojčani aspekt, 80.

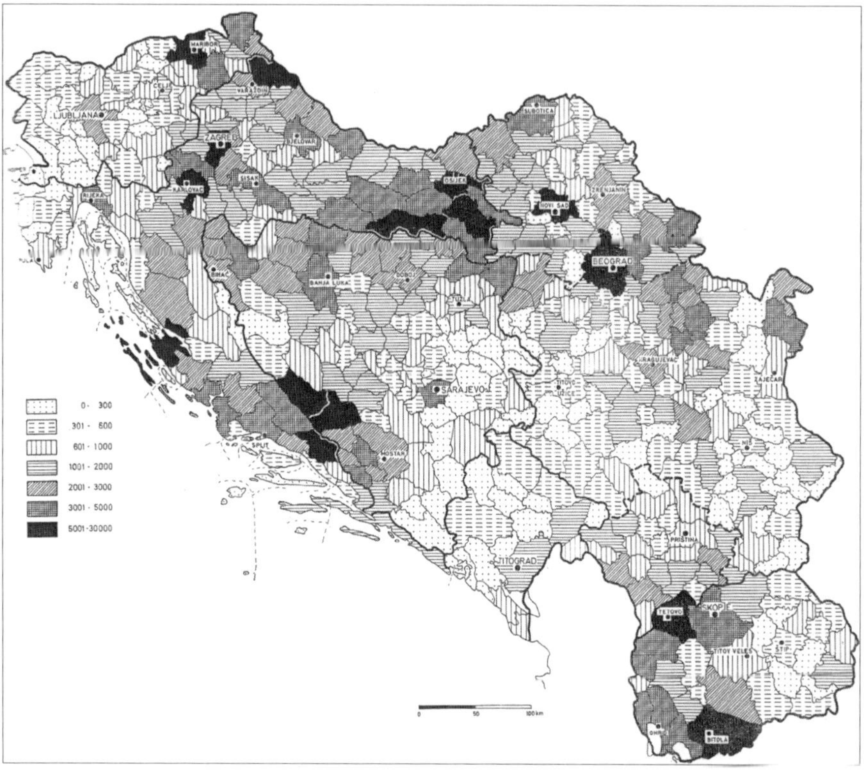

Map: Number of population living abroad by municipalities, 1971. *Source:* Baučić, Radnici u inozemstvu, suppl. 5.

searchers expected retarding effects on the economic and demographic development of Croatia.[19] As the number of returnees was twice as low as those who left, emigration in the 1970s was especially perceived as a negative socio-political and economic phenomenon for the development of Yugoslavia,[20] causing multiple losses of human capital, a drainage of educated people, weakening of the labour force, and demographic losses.[21]

The dissolution of Yugoslavia in 1991 and the war that followed between 1991 and 1995, coupled with the economic crisis after the breakdown of socialism, initiated another wave of mass migration. This wave included victims of forced migration and economic migrants. Various groups of migrants from Croatian territories joined flows of ethnically moti-

[19] Ibid., 73–4.

[20] Baučić, Radnici u inozemstvu, 125.

[21] Grečić, Jovanović, Osnovne komponente pretvaranja, 280–6.

vated migrants, including Croats, Serbs and members of other ethnic groups.[22] The emigration of approximately 456,000 refugees and labour migrants – mainly young people – had a strong impact on the demographic development of Croatia, which, despite simultaneous immigration to the country, ultimately led to a decrease in population growth.[23] Economic security and political stability represented the most common *pull factor* of the last decade. Better professional perspectives and labour market opportunities or relatives who lived in the receiving countries were an attractive enough pull to spark a new wave of emigration, especially of highly educated people. Most recently, more individualised factors, such as career trajectories and quality of life, have prevailed in the decision to leave the country. Young, highly educated, unemployed and unmarried people in Croatia who can utilise their skill potential are more likely to consider emigration. Researchers have estimated that the potential for emigration in Croatia between 1990 and 2005 was constantly about twenty percent of the skilled workforce.[24]

Modern types of migration and spatial mobility can be numerous and diverse even in such a limited area such as Croatia. Some older issues, such as the relatively high emigration potential, the significant number of refugees, the low return rate, problems of repatriation and the relatively high number of irregular migrants are still present. Some emerging migration issues, such as the retention of possible emigrants, regulation of international retirement migration, improvement of labour migrants' status in their host countries, and the social and political integration of labour migrants and other kinds of immigrants to Croatia, require the additional attention not only of researchers but also policymakers.[25]

Academic discourse and scientific research on Croatian emigration

The basic theories of and development in the social sciences concerning the study of migration from Croatia between 1965 and 1990 have already been elaborated by the sociologist Silva Mežnarić.[26] Here, I will summarise and re-evaluate her discussion of Croatian migration research, at the same time trying to fill some of the gaps.

Since Yugoslav sociology did not touch upon the phenomenon of international migration until the early 1970s, migration problems were studied mainly by economists, social geographers and demographers in the 1970s, and also social psychologists and social lin-

22 Zlatković Winter, Imigracijske politike, 65.

23 Lajić, Hrvatske migracije početkom 21. stoljeća, 135–149.

24 Božić, Burić, Migracijski potencijal; Mežnarić, Grdešić, "Odljev mozgova?"; Adamović, Mežnarić, Migration of Young Croatian Scientists.

25 Božić, Strenghtening Cross Border Cooperation, 40.

26 Mežnarić, Jugoslavenska sociologija (vanskih) migracija; ibid, Osvajanje prostora.

guists in the 1980s.[27] In socialist Yugoslavia, the scientific concepts of and practical research on migration were "insufficiently equipped" by academic personnel and knowledge.[28] After a period of surprise regarding the phenomenon of mass migration, Yugoslav sociology turned to empirical research of its own. Research models were taken from contemporary studies on migration and only exceptionally grounded in empirical results.[29]

The turn came with the adoption of international concepts and the application of new empirical models.[30] Widely known schemes of migration analyses (emigration motives, push-pull factors, acculturation-integration, system analysis and cost-benefit approaches) were applied around that time in Yugoslavia also. The most common and broadly used model of explanation was the *push-pull* theory, but this concept failed to explain and predict new migration routes and trends. Motives for migration and cost-benefit analyses were mostly descriptive while empirically collected material was used to predict migration processes. Other significant fields of research were the adaptation, integration and assimilation processes of migrants. Migrants and the labour market was a favoured topic of social geographers and economists,[31] while sociologists turned to the problems of 'commuting' between sending and receiving societies, ideological exchange and class consciousness among Yugoslav workers and their integration into the capitalist system.

The most interesting topics among researchers from other sciences were the practices of the use of the native language or "twofold semilingualism",[32] family disintegration,[33] the psychology disorder of migrants and family anomalies caused by the stress of acculturation,[34] the position of specific groups in migration such as women,[35] problems encountered by the migrants' children, the impact of migration on farming, and finally the reaction of the Yugoslav system to emigration (protection of migrants, distribution of information for migrants, measures to facilitate return). The interest and position of economists in the migration research of the 1960s and 1970s was joined by sociologists in the 1980s. New topics, similar to global trends, gradually appeared in Yugoslav sociological research on migration. Along with the identity problems of the second migrant generation,[36] the 1980s' research included topics like the social perception of *Gastarbeiter*,[37] European migration ties and migration

27 Baučić, Porijeklo i struktura radnika; ibid, Radnici u inozemstvu; Korenčić, Naselja i stanovništvo; Heršak, "Druga generacija migranata".

28 Mežnarić, Osvajanje prostora, 36.

29 Morokvašić, Jugoslaveni u Francuskoj-Istraživanja veze.

30 Toš, Klinar, A System Model.

31 Baletić, Međunarodne migracije.

32 Alund, Teoretski okvir.

33 Katunarić, Vanjske migracije I promjene.

34 Bokun, Faktor migracija.

35 Morokvašić, Žene iz Jugoslavije.

36 Čačić, Francuzi, Jugoslaveni.

37 Jonjić, Identifikacija "gastarbeitera".

networks, the interrelation of migrants and their host societies, practices of inclusion and exclusion,[38] as well as the gendered nature of migration and its increasing feminisation.[39]

Despite the impressive growth in the number of studies on migration issues, many of them were characterised by outdated methodological approaches. Many of these studies only partially processed their empirical data and were burdened with un-reflected stereotypes. The social sciences in Croatia were still unprepared for the study of mass migration as a suddenly growing and widely spreading social phenomenon. For example, the significance of emigration was not sufficiently studied and various aspects of the migrants' everyday life were neglected. The search for new concepts in migration studies, interest in the political economy of Western Europe, research on the Yugoslav labour market,[40] consideration of the integration policies of the receiving countries, and the application of interdisciplinary approaches, were articulated as goals but only partially reached at that time.

Research on the 'Diaspora', i.e. the 'older' emigrants mainly in overseas countries, existed simultaneously from the 1970s as a separate trend of research. It used different methodologies, concepts and sources to migration research and pursued a mainly narrative approach prior to the 1990s. There was an obvious dichotomy between the politically unfavourable, slightly suspicious and academically under-evaluated descriptive Diaspora research and the academically superior and 'politically correct' migration research. Research on the Diaspora focused on the history of Croatian emigration,[41] emigration statistics,[42] the social and political organisation of emigrants,[43] the emigrants' political, cultural and religious development,[44] and finally on their cultural heritage and identity in terms of the preservation of their language and religion. Focusing only on emigration from Croatia was a legitimate choice but at the same time, these researchers neglected the necessary contexts. Therefore these projects mostly failed in putting Croatian emigration, which at times was part of the Austro-Hungarian as well as Yugoslav emigration experiences, into a broader framework of comparative and interdisciplinary research.

Emigration research in Croatia after 1991: New paradigms emerging?

Under the changed political circumstances after 1990–1991, new research priorities emerged. They were initially mainly a direct result of the war of 1991–1995. The previously

38 Milardović, Neokonzervativizam, nove desnice.

39 Švob, Migracije jugoslavenski žena; Oklobdžija, Promjene u obitelji; Morokvašić, Žene iz Jugoslavije; Pavlinić-Wolf, Obrazovanje i zaposlenost.

40 Mežnarić, Osvajanje prostora prekrivanje vremena.

41 Holjevac, Hrvati izvan domovine.

42 Telišman, Statistički pokazatelji.

43 Čizmić, Doseljavanje, struktura i položaj.

44 Antić, Naše iseljeništvo; Čizmić, Jugoslavenski socijalisti.

different strands of research on migration on the one hand and the "Diaspora research" on the other gradually fused in terms of concepts and methodologies. By the inclusion of more profound social analysis into the previously positivistic approaches of the Diaspora research, which was very different from the modern use of the concept of Diaspora, the strict distinction between these two areas of migration research was to a certain extent overcome, though it still remained visible.

A noticeable shortcoming in some works on migration is their politicisation and the reactivation of old fashioned models; they aim to promote the integration of the nation, strengthening national and Croatian ethnic consciousness and providing 'scholarly' support or even arguments for the legal and political battle for Croatian sovereignty. This pertains, for example, to various demographic analyses and attempts at the quantification of the Croatian, or Croat, Diaspora, which omit other ethnic groups from Croatia but include Croats from Bosnia-Herzegovina. The numbers are also often inflated by including all descendents of Croatian migrants, without empirically testing their identification with Croatia.

In the 1990s migration research in Croatia was clearly defined by the dissolution of Yugoslavia and the war. One of the consequences for migration and its research was the fact that forms of migration which previously have been defined as 'internal' (within Yugoslavia, from one republic to another) were now transformed into 'external' migration, thus further complicating its typology. Another consequence of independence and the increased interest in national issues was the strong focus in migration research on the ethnic identity of Croatian emigrants. Processes of identification and the interplay of different layers of identity such as social, ethnic, national, religious, and linguistic were, therefore, widely explored.[45]

Another new trend was forced migration research which already began during the war, in which hundreds of thousands of people were displaced either within Croatia or came as refugees from Bosnia-Herzegovina and Serbia. These studies addressed various problems of the displaced persons and the refugees, tried to assess the quantitative dimensions of the refugee problem, its legal aspects, the problems of refugee housing and psychological consequences of displacement, and finally questions of refugee reintegration.[46] A specific issue was the repatriation of Croatian émigrés and reintegration policies, which in the context of Croatian nation building always received political support from almost all political parties and public opinion. With regard to emigrants and refugees of non-Croat ethnicity, however, the situation was ambiguous. While officially they were welcomed back, the actual process of the return and reintegration of emigrants and refugees from Croatia of non-Croat origin,

45 Čičak-Chand, Kumpes, Etničnost, nacija, identitet; Čičak-Chand, Ethnic and Cultural Identity; Čačić-Kumpes, Nejašmić, Social Changes, Migration; Čapo Žmegač, Constructing Difference.

46 Jonjić, Blažević, Baza podtaka; Anić, Podgorelec, Psihičke tegobe prognane; Mesić, Osjetljivi i ljuti ljudi; ibid, Socijalna obilježja i povratak; Mežnarić, Migracije, prinudne migracije; Čapo Žmegač, Strangers Either Way.

especially Serbs who fled from the Krajina to Serbia in 1995, was fraught with difficulties and obstacles, which can be seen in the results of return. While the number of immigrants from Serbia and Montenegro decreased from 1,854 people in 2002 to 1,508 in 2006, the number of emigrants from Croatia to the same country increased from 401 people in 2002 to 2,907 in 2006.[47]

One of the significant contributions of Croatian migration research in the 1990s was the development of new typologies of migration, based on the specific experiences of war and displacement. The term "forced migration" was deconstructed and a re-categorisation of migration suggested, departing from the notion of the decision making process in all types of migration. According to Mežnarić, the essence of this typology is the questioning of the idea of voluntary migration as a quasi-ontological category. Instead, she suggested the idea of the possibility to choose as the critical variable for the typology of migration.[48] In a similar vein Mesić questioned the role of external push factors in the migration decision of 'voluntary' migrants and explained migration rather through the "theory of turbulence", as a manifestation of the highly conflictual post-modern social processes.[49] In this context Mesić criticises existing migration theories for not being capable of exploring and explaining contemporary migration.

A distinctive field in migration research in Croatia with its own tradition is migration history.[50] Historians are not alone when they try to give overviews on emigration from Croatia and clarify specific migration patterns and processes.[51] However, here we can also find nationalistic tendencies, especially during the times of extreme nationalism and endangered sovereignty in the early 1990s. At that time there was, for example, the reproduction of the essentially political argument that poverty resulting in migration was caused by foreign subjection and exploitation, which led to an increased emigration of Croats.[52] Even demographic interpretations of historical data, correlating poverty, demographic trends and economic misbalance were, in the public sphere, used as arguments for the promotion of Croatian national cohesion and the "strengthening" of ethnic identity.[53] The potential of these topics to be politicised was a big burden for this group of researchers – similarly for geographers and demographers – since they were liable to fall into the traps of methodological nationalism, defined as the naturalisation of the global regime of nation-states by social science,[54] or more generally, of the limitations by the nation-state framework. Concerning this critique, some theoreticians from Croatia expressed doubts as to whether any theoreti-

[47] Statistical Yearbook of the Republic of Croatia 2007,113.
[48] Mežnarić, Migracije, prinudne migracije; ibid, Migracijske aktualnosti, 331.
[49] Mesić, Globalizacija migracije.
[50] See Čizmić, Doseljavanje, struktura i položaj; ibid, Jugoslavenski socijalisti u Sjedinjenim.
[51] Mesić, Međunarodne migracije.
[52] Anić, Tradicija migracija.
[53] Nejašmić, Iseljavanje iz Hrvatske u evropske u prekomorske zemlje.
[54] Wimmer, Glick Schiller, Methodological Nationalism, 576.

cal approach can escape the influences of the social and political forces around us.[55] On the other hand, historical analysis based on archival data can help to understand the origins of migration phenomena that were categorised as 'problematic' by journalists and politicians in the 1990s.[56]

In terms of methodology, an obvious characteristic of research on migration in the 1990s was the preservation of disciplinary fragmentation. In spite of proclaimed trans-disciplinary and inter-disciplinary approaches, or even project teams composed of experts from various disciplines, migration research and accordingly the research methodologies were still clearly defined by disciplinary boundaries. The result is the application of heterogeneous investigative tools and methods, with a consequent lack of trans-disciplinary dialogue. Sociologists still claim priority in the research on theory and methodology of migrations and the production of new concepts and terminology.[57] A particular focus of sociological inquiry is the analysis of social processes generating migration, the social impact of migration, and the integration processes and the social distance between various groups of indigenous and non-indigenous populations.[58] The participation of legal scholars in migration research finally brought in legislative questions concerning migration, minorities and refugee policies and citizenship issues.[59] As concerns the legislation on migration, the Croatian Parliament included Croatian scholars no earlier than 2006 in the creation of migration policies and strategies. In spite of this, the academic community (economists, political scientists, sociologists and demographers) claims that the state is still far from an economically successful management of migration in view of the latest developments in human capital, the labour market, the educational system, and demography.

Economists had also previously studied the significance of migrant remittances, which represented long-distance and cross-border social ties of solidarity, reciprocity and family obligations. The issue of remittances, however, attracted more political and public rather than scientific interest in the early 1990s.[60] Researchers on the economic aspects of migration only rarely considered the wider economic development in the region as a context of migration.[61] They used to mainly point out the costs of migration for Yugoslavia/Croatia and to underestimate its benefits.[62] In the 1990s, the effects of mass labour emigration, including its financial dimensions, were therefore still regarded in public debates as predominantly negative in various fields.

55 Mesić, Metodološki kozmopolitizam.
56 Čoralić, Na drugoj obali Jadrana; Heršak, Etničnost i povijest.
57 Mesić, Međunarodne migracije; Mežnarić, Migracijske aktualnosti.
58 Colic-Peisker, Croatian and Bosnian Migration; Božić, Burić, Migracijski potencijal Hrvatske; Mesić, Osjetljivi i ljuti ljudi; ibid, Globalizacija migracije.
59 Vukas, The Legal Status of National Minorities.
60 Mesić et al., Vanjske migracije i društveni.
61 Mrnjavac, Problem migracija.
62 Mikulić, Vanjske migracije i razvoj, 45.

Recently the most interesting economic consequences of demographic processes and migration and their influence on the labour market,[63] and how they can be addressed by immigration policy have been approached and discussed by business groups (such as the Croatian Chamber of Economy), the government and trade-union representatives as well as scholars (demographers, economists and sociologists). They tried to solve the increasing problem of the shortage of skilled work force in specific economic branches that required highly skilled workers. They also addressed problems of the limited labour mobility as a recently recognised structural problem, the misbalance of employed and inactive (supported) population, the significant share of the grey economy and resulting problems of welfare and pension funds.[64] Obadić, however, argues that while these problems will need to be addressed by the 'import' of specific labour from other countries, immigration will only partially be a redress to the negative demographic trends, the slow growth in the activity rate, and the poor coordination between educational policy and the actual needs of the Croatian labour market.[65] The question of immigration, which is still a rather potential one, prompted sociologists and political scientists in Croatia also to voice concerns about the management of integration processes and the state's role in immigration. They discussed various models of integration (assimilation, rotation, integration and multiculturalism), and their relevance and applicability to the current social reality.[66] Comparisons of recent integration experiences and political models in Croatia's neighbourhood serve as the prerequisite for minimising the social risks of immigration. The risk is embodied in the evident collision of interests: of the long-term functioning of the population system on the one hand and the short-term functioning of the economic system on the other.[67]

The emigration of skilled individuals from Croatia still assumes the form of outflow rather than circulation of labour. It continues to raise considerable concern among Croatian researchers,[68] if not yet among policy makers. This is also a case of the scientific predictions of the early 1990s coming true.[69] Although this kind of migration was negatively assessed by academic and public opinion in the early 1990s, and seen as a socially unfavourable kind of social mobility,[70] the perception has been changing within some academic circles. Contrary to public debates which still treat *brain drain* as the 'impoverishment' of Croatian society, some scholars optimistically predict *brain gain* in the near future due to the further globalisation of migration processes. New migration patterns, new immigration destinations (southern Europe included) and intra-regional migrations have an impact on Croatia as well; with the economic conditions improving, Croatia might become more attractive

63 Obadić, Makroekonomika tranzicijskog tržišta rada; Mežnarić, Migracije u Hrvatskoj.
64 Crnković-Pozaić, Buduće potrebe na tržistu rada.
65 Obadić, Ocejana stanja hrvatskog tržišta rada.
66 Božić, Integration of Migrants; Mežnarić, Migracije u Hrvatskoj; Mesić, Multikulturalizam.
67 Mežnarić, Migracije u Hrvatskoj.
68 Adamović, Mežnarić, Migration of Youth Croatian Scientists.
69 Mežnarić, Grdešić, "Odljev mozgova?".
70 Golub, Neki aspekti potencijalnog odliva.

for immigrants but also returnees.[71] Brain gain and re-migration of the highly educated Croatian emigrants, along with skills transfer and the diffusion of technology, are much appreciated and seen as a crucial topic not only from the public point of view but also from the political and social scientists' perspective.

The rapid growth in and significance of public debates in Croatia on migration is of utmost importance not just for policy makers but for researchers as well, who are responsive to both the migration problems and public debates.[72] Public debates on migration represent a new object of social science research. Some migration issues are of special public importance in contemporary Croatia, while other dimensions of migration tend to be neglected. Following long lasting political debates on the pros and cons of temporary labour migration, sociologists have realised the public and scientific significance of these political evaluations. The re-emigration of Croatian labour emigrants (especially professionals) to Croatia, for example, has always been seen as a desirable social and political goal by the public and in intellectual debates, in contrast to international retirement immigration, which is mainly comprised of Germans and Austrians.[73] Researchers have shown the increasing importance of mass media and public debates for regulating migration because of "their potential to politicize the discourse on migration".[74] In spite of the overall public concern and pressure in Croatia, in recent publications researchers have approached transnational migration processes from sub-and supra-national perspectives, thus abandoning the state-centred approach.[75]

Ethnological research on migration extended significantly over the last decade. Until the 1970s, ethnology in Croatia focused on the diffusion and development of material, social and spiritual aspects of the Croatian traditional culture of the past. Migration was thus implicitly incorporated into the research of traditional culture both in the country as well as in the communities of the Croatian national minorities in the surrounding states, but it did not become a separate field of ethnological inquiry. More recent anthropological and also linguistic studies treated historical migrations in connection with ethno-genesis and the identity formation of ethnic groups.[76] During the last decade, however, the interest in migration has been significantly growing in Croatian ethnology and cultural anthropology. This trend is related to the appeal of contemporary globalisation and transnationalism theories, international migration and Diaspora studies, as well as studies on collective identity. A number of studies based on qualitative methodology have appeared almost simultaneously.

71 Mesić, Globalizacija migracije.
72 Božić, Strenghtening Cross Border Cooperation.
73 The selling of real estates to retired immigrants from Western European countries is publicly perceived as "national deprivation of land and coastline" and publicly debated as "devastation of the coastal region by construction."
74 Božić, Strenghtening Cross Border Cooperation, 13.
75 Mežnarić, Migracijske aktualnosti; Lajić, Hrvatske migracije početkom 21. stoljeća; Mesić, Globalizacija migracije.
76 Černelić, Istraživanje tradicijske baštine; Grbić, Identitet, jezik, razvoj.

Some of them focus on the recent "co-ethnic migrations" of Croats from abroad to Croatia in the 1990s,[77] others on the Croatian *Gastarbeiter* economic migration from the 1960s to Germany and the multigenerational migrant experience.[78]

As one of the specific lines of research in Croatia in the last two decades, psychical or biological anthropology has tried to reveal the prehistoric migrations and the original homeland of the Croats. These studies also asked for the genetic heritage of migrants, using natural sciences such as mitochondrial DNA, Y chromosome variation tests, etc.[79] Prehistoric migrations were discussed within anthropology from various aspects. Heršak focused on early historical and pre-modern migrations on a global scale.[80]

A notable trend during recent years was the increased application of models and the topics of international migration research in Croatia, such as transnationalism, cultural pluralism, multiculturalism, and multiple identities.[81] Transnationalism as a term and concept was thoroughly discussed in Croatia and critically assessed for its applicability.[82] Globalisation emerged as another conceptual frame of migration studies; researchers defined contemporary international migrations as a constitutive part of the process of globalisation, while globalisation showed its existence in the diversification of the forms of migration. These new scholarly trends reflect changes in the dominant patterns of migration in, from and to Croatia and changes in public perception. Some forms of migration which had previously been prevailing, such as economic migration from less developed to more developed areas, seasonal internal migration and rural-urban migrations, have now become phenomena of second-rate importance. Accordingly, research interest has moved to new topics, such as the globalisation of migration processes,[83] calculations of the migration potential based on the Fassmann-Hinterman micro-analytical model,[84] the plurality of transnational migrations,[85] gender issues and the feminisation of migration,[86] international retirement and 'pleasure'

77 Čapo Žmegač, Constructing Difference; ibid, Strangers Either Way.

78 Čapo Žmegač,Transnacionalizam, lokalitet, rod.

79 Peričić et al., Review of Croatian Genetic Heritage.

80 Heršak, Drevne seobe.

81 Mesić, Multikulturalizam; Čačić-Kumpes, Multiculturality in Croatian Education; Čapo Žmegač, Encounters in the Transnational Social Space.

82 Heršak, Leksikon migracijskog i etničkog nazivlja; Mesić, Međunarodne migracije; ibid, Multikulturizam; Božić, Nacionalizam – nacija.

83 Mesić, Globalizacija migracije; Milardović, Demografske dimenzije globalizacije; Skupnjak-Katić, Globalni migracijski trendovi.

84 Božić-Burić, Migracijski potencijal Hrvatske.

85 Colic-Peisker, "Ethnic" and "Cosmopolitan" Transnationalism; Čapo Žmegač, Constructing Difference.

86 Richter-Malabotta, Feminizacija migranskih tokova; Colic-Peisker, Croatian and Bosnian Migration; Čapo Žmegač, Transnacionalizam, lokalitet, rod.

migration,[87] integration polices,[88] as well as undocumented and documented illegal migrations and human trafficking.[89]

Other research interests lie in the social development of migrants in the receiving societies, such as the integration and adoption of, among others, new cultural patterns and processes of acculturation,[90] adjustment strategies,[91] assimilation, xenophobia,[92] and multiculturalism.[93] In the last two decades, following contemporary trends, transnationalism itself has attracted significant attention in Croatia, with various appearances from the 'ethnically defined' to the 'cosmopolitan'.[94] Most recently in Croatia, a retreat from the idea of multiculturalism has been noticeable.[95]

While the receiving state to a certain extent shapes transnational ties, if not by mere regulations then by demands from migrants,[96] the migration policy of sending countries, or its absence, is also an important field of research. However, this topic has not been studied in Croatia and the authors rather focused on immigration policies, status regulations and the citizenship issues of receiving countries.[97] They have compared various legal systems and their implications on different scales of migration, from international migration regulations on the large-scale,[98] through European regulations,[99] to single state regulations.[100] Problems concerning the connections between migration regulations and the social interactions of immigrants in the receiving countries, which have received much attention by international migration research, were rarely studied in Croatia.

The gradual abandonment of old paradigms in migration research in Croatia was closely linked to the adaptation to concepts from contemporary international migration research. Instead of subscribing to the previous systemic and political-economic explanations of migration, new social science research discussed the epistemological foundations of migration theory and concepts.[101] Recent works, therefore, have shown that the traditional paradigms (migration as an unpredictable outbreak or as the predictable resulting long-term develop-

87 Božić, Posljednja avantura.
88 Božić, Integration of Migrants.
89 Mesić, Osjetljivi i ljuti ljudi; Štulhofer et al., Trafficking in Women and Children.
90 Čačić-Kumpes, Kumpes, Etničke manjine.
91 Mežnarić, Europa i Hrvatska u njoj.
92 Milardović, Novi val ksenofobije.
93 Heršak, Čičak-Chand, Kanada: Multikulturalizam; Čičak-Chand, Multikulturne politike; Čačić-Kumpes, Multiculturality in Croatian Education.
94 Colic-Peisker, "Ethnic" and "Cosmopolitan" Transnationalism; Čapo Žmegač, Transnacionalizam, lokalitet, rod; ibid., Encounters in the Transnational Social Space.
95 Mesić, Multikulturalizam.
96 Levitt, DeWind, Vertovec, International Perspectives, 568.
97 Zlatković Winter, Imigracijske politike zemalja; Horvat, Tko nam dolazi u Hrvatsku; Katić, Postojeće zakonske regulative.
98 Mesić, Globalizacija migracije.
99 Mesić, Harmonizacija europske migracijske politike; Mežnarić, Migracije u Hrvatskoj.
100 Milardović, Politika njemačke vlade.
101 Mesić, Međunarodne migracije; Mežnarić, Migracijske aktualnosti.

ments) fail to explain the most recent developments in the international migration arena. They cannot appreciate the complexity and multi-dimensionality of the new migration trends. Therefore, Croatian researchers have been searching for a new theoretical and conceptual apparatus and have lately focussed on the individual migrant as a decision maker.[102]

From this discussion it becomes obvious that Croatian research on migration and the changes of paradigm during the last two decades have followed the general line of public interest and, at the same time, the wider developments in migration studies. Debates on migration and research from other parts of the world are discussed in the recent works by Croatian researchers; books are translated or at least discussed, and methodologies and theoretical approaches developed elsewhere are applied in a critical manner.[103] Surprisingly and quite contrary to this development, there is little debate in Croatia on migration research done in the country among the migration studies community.

However, all these changes in the conceptual framework failed to modify traditional research on the "Croatian Diaspora" by the 'old school' researchers, who preserved their exclusively national focus and failed to relate their research to a broader context and to accept the new plurality of approaches.[104] The critical social analysis and comparison of the ethnic segmentation of the social space of Croatian emigrant communities overseas,[105] and the construction of "Others" within these communities and of political dimensions within the Diaspora, such as the manipulation of political symbols by their leaders,[106] have still been rare topics.[107] The recently created neologism of "Diasporisation" reflects the revival of the term and concept of Diaspora, which is not an exclusive phenomenon to Croatia. The most recent research on transnational migrant processes and Croatian émigrés, including their descendants, has struggled for an unbiased academic approach despite the external pressure, as these topics are attracting huge public interest.

Problems of quantification and demographic concerns

An important question for generations of Croatian migration researchers has been the establishment of the number of emigrants from Croatia. But, such as elsewhere, evidence on migration is one of the most poorly documented demographic phenomena also in Croatia. Here, one of the main methodological problems regarding data on Croatian emigration since the nineteenth century, has been the lack of uniform and systematic official statistical records on emigration for all Croatian territories that were previously under different state jurisdictions; even today, Croatia still does not have a Population Register, which would be

[102] Mežnarić, Migracijske aktualnosti, 341.
[103] Ibid.; Božić, Burić, Migracijski potencijal Hrvatske; Mesić, Metodološki kozmopolitizam.
[104] Laušić, Venezuela i Hrvati; Antić, Hrvati i Amerika; Čižmić, Sopta, Šakić, Iseljena Hrvatska.
[105] Perić Kaselj, Kuti, Croatian Immigrants.
[106] Skrbiš, Long-Distance Nationalism.
[107] Škvorc, Nekoliko napomena.

the most complete data base on migration.[108] However, data on emigration are available. The Kingdoms of Croatia and Slavonia began to make official data on emigration available in 1899;[109] if official data are lacking, there are also substitutes, which were found in various archival sources, such as records of ship companies.

As a result of the uneven empirical base, one can find very different estimations about the number of Croatian emigrants. Furthermore, counting emigrants of Croatian origin was highly speculative since their ethnic identification had changed through processes of integration and assimilation in their new home countries. Due to vague definitions of who the 'Croatian emigrant' is, it is hardly possible to combine or compare the various data. Some records count all people who left Croatia, while others record only ethnic Croats. Even recent demographic analyses vary in their estimated numbers. Nevertheless, these numerical estimations are useful given the statistical problem of methodologically incomparable data and the incompatibility of the twentieth century censuses in Croatia.[110]

The numerical estimates of emigrants of Croat origin are numerous and have been carried out for all large Croat emigrant communities. However, they can extremely differ in numbers. In spite of this, the estimates can generally illustrate the global distribution of Croatian emigrants with at least some sort of salient Croat identity.[111] Their numbers were established or estimated on the basis of varied as well as heterogeneous sorts of census and other types of records, such as church records.[112] Some of these estimations are based on the re-evaluation of miscalculations in official documents,[113] some on secondary publications as an alternative to original statistical data,[114] a widely acceptable practice prior to the 1990s.

Statistical researchers and demographers acknowledged the high political potential of numerical data, especially in public but also academic debates. It was alleged, for example, that inflated numbers were given for overseas emigration before World War I and for emigration from the two Yugoslavias as arguments for the assumption that Croats faced particular push factors and social pressure within the Austro-Hungarian monarchy and Yugoslavia respectively, which made them leave. Politically motivated tendencies in "Diaspora studies" in Croatia to inflate numbers can also not be ignored.[115] Another research tendency with political intentions was to count descendents of emigrants, who were born abroad, within the number of emigrants. This inflated the total size of the Croatian emigration without empirical proof of the role of descendents in the Croatian nation building processes or of practical transnational ties. The pseudo-scientific overestimation of numbers significantly shook the scientific credibility of this sort of research. Critical approximations and the re-

108 Mišetić, Aktualno demografsko stanje, 83.
109 Nejašmić, Iseljavanje iz Hrvatske. Brojčani aspekt, 63.
110 Nejašmić, Hrvatski građani na radu; Lajić, Hrvatske migracije početkom 21. stoljeća, 140–1.
111 Telišman, Statistički pokazatelji.
112 Čižmić, Sopta, Šakić, Iseljena Hrvstska.
113 Nejašmić, Iseljavanje iz Hrvatske. Brojčani aspekt, 63.
114 Such as Lakatoš, Narodna statistika.
115 Škvorc, Australski Hrvati, 26, 181.

evaluation of the numerical dimension of Croatian emigration are therefore perceived as a scientific obligation.[116] However, the problem of the validity and reliability of the existing statistical numbers on migration from Croatia cannot be fully resolved.

The quantitative estimates give numbers for the geographical distribution of emigrants from Croatia and their historical dimensions for the last 150 years (Table 2). Some authors estimate a total number of 1.15 million emigrants from Croatian lands to European and overseas countries;[117] others arrive at a total number of 1.365 million people.[118] These estimates are higher than the official numbers which regularly under-count migrants; however, they are more than simple guesses, being based on empirical sources of different nature.[119]

Table 2: Most recent estimates for emigration from Croatia, 19th–20th Centuries

Period	**Estimated Number of Emigrants**
Mid–19th century–1914; overseas emigration	350,000
Interwar period; overseas emigration	100,000
Mid–19th century–1914; emigration to European countries	16,000
Interwar period; emigration to European countries	9,000
Overseas and European emigration during WWI	100,000
Overseas and European emigration during WWII	250,000
1945–1991; economic and other emigration, all destinations	350,000
1991–2001; economic and other emigration, all destinations	190,000
Total	**1,365,000**

Sources: Čizmić, Sopta, Šakić, Iseljena Hrvatska, 21.

The statistical exploration of the impact of migration is also related to other concerns of demographers, as manifest in concepts such as 'stagnation', 'depopulation', 'negative migration balance' and 'demographic deficit'. On the one hand, these classic discipline terminologies are used by demographers to portray the overall demographic picture of today's Croatia.

In the 1990s demographers stated that the negative demographic trends of the last few decades had resulted in the ageing indigenous population, as the end of demographic transition was reached which contributed to the depopulation of some Croatian regions.[120] This problem became the centre point of public but also academic discussions in Croatia.[121] The overall depopulation due to natural depopulation and the negative migration balance of the Republic of Croatia has resulted in a growing proportion of elderly population, which has significantly shaken the sustainability of Croatia's pension system. This repre-

116 Lajić, Hrvatske migracije početkom, 144.
117 Nejašmić, Iseljavanje iz Hrvatske. Brojčani aspekt, 61.
118 Čizmić, Sopta, Šakić, Iseljena Hrvstska, 21.
119 Nejašmić, Iseljavanje iz Hrvatske. Brojčani aspekt, 74.
120 Wertheimer-Baletić, Stanovništvo i razvoj, 105–93.
121 Nejašmić, Iseljevanje iz Hrvatske u evropske I prekomorske zemlje; ibid, Iseljevanje iz Hrvatske. Brojčani aspekt; ibid., Hrvatski građani na radu; Akrap, Migracije Hrvata.

sents an additional burden on the economically active population and does not provide a solid foundation for regional social and economic development. However traditional or even nationalistic this perspective may appear, it has not been overlooked in public and academic debates due to the high political and public attention it still attracts.[122] According to demographers, the negative effects of emigration on the socio-economic and especially demographic development of Croatia were manifest in the scale of migration, its spatial distribution, its demographic structure and, in particular, the negative migration balance on both the national and regional levels.[123]

On the other hand, it would be fair to say that demographers cannot be optimistic when reflecting on the prospects for successful development, bearing in mind today's demographic situation. Most recently, by correlating the current demographic trends, depopulation and ageing, with the demands of the Croatian economy and labour market, demographers and economists predict the immigration of a labour force will be the solution for labour shortages in the immediate future.[124]

Conclusion

The short overview of the history of Croatian emigration, which represents the first part of this chapter, serves as an example of one aspect of Croatian emigration research and the introduction to a broader re-evaluation of migration studies in Croatia. We were faced by some ambivalent hypotheses, the plurality and heterogeneity of statistical data, unclear explanations, misinterpretations and lots of estimations and historical projections. But the analysis of migration research in Croatia has revealed that this research was strictly separated into two different lines of development from the 1960s until the 1990s.

There were a vast number of Diaspora studies, predominantly of a very general nature without much empirical evidence. Accordingly, these studies could, and occasionally did, offer less than fair approximations, mainly with regard to numerical estimates due to methodological obstacles on the one hand and deliberate political inventions on the other. Diaspora researchers covered many aspects of Croatian communities living abroad mainly in a narrative or folkloristic, but essentially descriptive manner. These researchers had difficulties avoiding a nation-centred focus, ignoring the context of the societies in which the emigrants lived.

Contrary to this line of research, the other group of scholars, predominantly sociologists, studied external migrations from Croatia. They investigated, among other topics, the development of migrant social spaces, of processes of migration within the given socio-economic contexts, and the psychological and linguistic dimensions of migration. In contrast to the

122 Božić, Strenghtening Cross Border Cooperation, 13.
123 Lajić, Hrvatske migracije početkom, 148.
124 Mišetić, Aktualno demografsko stanje; Obadić, Ocjena stanja hrvstskog tržišta rada.

predominantly ethnographic and historic-narrative conceptual frameworks of the Diaspora research, students of internal and external migration in Croatia and the receiving countries were well equipped with contemporary sociological and demographic methods, thus enabling them to communicate their findings within the international scientific community.

However distant these two research trends had been, they started to overlap in the 1990s, preserving their different points of view but sharing the same research object. Under conditions of intense nation-state building in Croatia, these two theoretically and conceptually different levels of migration research showed signs of formal fusion. By including more profound social analysis into Diaspora research, the methodological distinction between these two lines of research became less salient. This fusion in the 1990s resulted in mixed projects, but not quite ignoring the political and social relevance of this problem.

In the 1990s, due to political circumstances and the war in Croatia, new research priorities emerged, notably the study of refugees and displaced persons. A key transformation in Croatian migration studies in the 1990s was also the transformation of a previous domestic migration (within Yugoslavia) into an external one, after the neighbouring former socialist republics became independent states. These sudden and extraordinary circumstances occupied migration scholars in Croatia. Another important characteristic of migration research after 1990 was the increasing fragmentation of interests; however, parallel to this there were also interdisciplinary tendencies, although a genuinely interdisciplinary approach is a goal yet to be reached in Croatian migration research. In any case, external migrations have attracted the attention of scholars from different disciplines (sociologists, historians, social geographers and demographers, economists, linguists, psychologists, ethnologists and others) in the last decade. These phenomena also attracted public or, at least, mass media interest and the attention of the ruling elite, owing to the importance of migration and its impact on the demographic and labour market developments for political decision making.

Since the government underestimates important problems concerning migration that should be addressed by the institutions of the state – such as the transnational ties of migrants, Diaspora identities, long distance nationalism, the legal and social status of labour migrants from South-Eastern Europe in EU countries, and re-emigration of labour migrants and émigrés – scholars should not neglect the public needs. The question of human capital drain from Croatia is still an urgent one, as illustrated by the concerns of the Croatian political elite and public opinion makers. It is therefore unlikely that researchers will lose interest in these issues. As long as the perception of émigrés as members of the 'extended family' of the nation survives in the public sphere, which is the case not only in Croatia but in other parts of Europe as well, the political and social interest in this 'family' will hardly diminish in Croatia.

Mirjam Milharčič Hladnik

From a Dollar Bill in an Envelope to a Petition to the White House: The Significance of Slovenian Migrants for Those Back Home

This text presents two case studies on Slovenian migration, which are based on the personal, intimate accounts of the migration experience and the maintenance of family relationships and bonds of solidarity.

The first case is based on a collection of family letters which in 1930 started to travel between a Slovenian village, a city in the United States, and the capital of Argentina. The correspondence provides an insight into the migration experiences of individuals and their families at home, and at home away from home. It shows that the participants in the migration process were active and dynamic individuals, who made ambitious decisions taking into account the historical circumstances, but also their personal preferences. The analysis of the correspondence is also a *gendered* research in which male and female members of the family provide a comprehensive account of the migration experience of those who left and those who stayed in the complicated social and political context of that time.

The source for the second study is a collection of life narratives of Slovenian women migrants and their descendants in the United States. The main goal of this research was to highlight the women's roles, efforts and achievements in preserving their Slovenian cultural heritage in the family, in the community and at work, from a historical and contemporary perspective. The analysis of the women's narratives has a *gender* research dimension as well, as only women's perspectives are used to provide an insight into migration structures and the processes of socially and culturally constructed subjectivities.

Both case studies challenge the prevailing perceptions of migrants as male and as homogenous groups defined by ethnicity and class. They enable us to re-shape our perception so that migrants appear as individuals with different reactions to a common situation and with uniquely personal and emotional experiences.

Correspondence: The subjective reality of migration processes

The Udovič-Hrvatin-Valenčič family correspondence is an important source for studying migration. It is extensive in its number of items as there are hundreds of letters, greeting cards, postcards, receipts and vast references to parcels, which also became part of the cor-

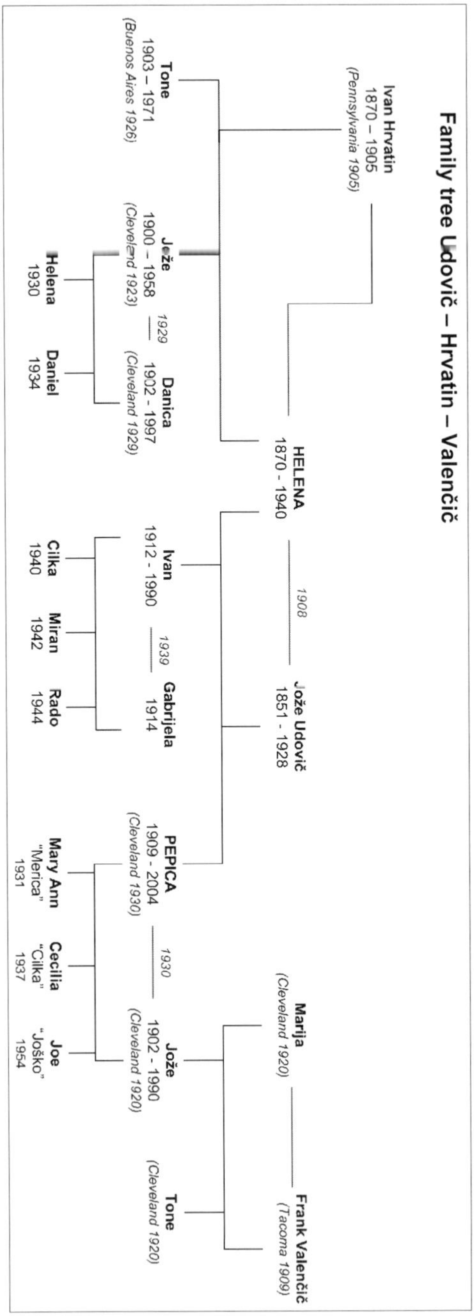

respondence in the decades after 1945. All these were sent to and received from the village of Jelšane in the Primorska region of Slovenia, from Cleveland, the US city with the strongest Slovenian community, and from Buenos Aires in Argentina. The persons taking part in the correspondence at differing periods were mother Helena, her four children, Jože, Tone, Pepica and Ivan, and their spouses and offspring (see Family Tree). The correspondence has been preserved over a relatively long period: Pepica corresponded with her mother Helena from 1930 until her mother's death in 1940, with her brother Tone until his death in 1971, with her brother Ivan until his death in 1990 and with her niece Cilka until her own death in 2004. The correspondence from her brother Jože connects Cleveland, Jelšane and Buenos Aires until his death in 1958. Considering the on-going correspondence among the children of these brothers and sister, the family correspondence has not been interrupted since 1923, when Jože migrated overseas. The more than eight-decade long correspondence has not been fully preserved and not everything is available. This is especially true for the part belonging to the brother in Argentina, as he did not have family to save the letters. However, the majority of the correspondence in Jelšane, as well as most of the letters that Pepica received in Cleveland, have been made available to the author for her research. This means that three parties in the correspondence are covered, which is extremely rare and therefore precious, since in migrant families usually letters from one side only are preserved.

I will present the analysis of the correspondence from two periods: between 1930, when the only daughter left for America, and 1940, when mother Helena died, and between 1945, when the correspondence resumed after the end of World War Two, and 1960, when Pepica visited the old place.

I take the expression "old place" from the migrants' own usage when talking about their home village, region of origin or homeland. Among them, they did not use political-administrative names or official names of the states to define where they came from. The Jelšane area is a good example of how impossible this would have been since the borders around it kept changing. Helena's first husband, Ivan Hrvatin left for the United States in 1905 and died in a mine accident in Pennsylvania the same year. He was a citizen of the Austro-Hungarian Empire. In the reshaping of the European political map after World War One, the western part of the Slovenian territory, where Jelšane is located, was given to Italy in 1920. Helena's two sons from her first marriage thus emigrated as Italian citizens. The eldest son Tone Hrvatin left for Buenos Aires in 1926; the other, Jože Hrvatin, for Cleveland in 1923 and her daughter Pepica joined him after she married Jože Valencich in 1930. Jože Valencich's father had emigrated to the United States in 1909 also as an Austro-Hungarian citizen. He changed his family name to Walencich[1] to sound more German than Polish, which was culturally more acceptable at that time. His wife and two sons joined him in the US in 1920 as Italian citizens. A couple of years later the family took as a boarder in their home another Italian citizen from the same old place, the Slovenian migrant Jože Hrvatin. When Jože Walencich saw the picture of Jože Hrvatin's sister Pepica, he decided to visit Jelšane and meet her. The German sounding family name was changed pragmatically to a more Italian sounding name, Valencich. This was the name Pepica got when she married Jože at the end of the summer of 1930. When she visited the old place thirty years later as the US citizen Josephine Valencich, Jelšane was in Yugoslavia, and when her son visited it another thirty years later, it was in the independent Republic of Slovenia.

The correspondence explored offers an important material for researching the "subjective process of migration", which, as Samuel Baily and Franco Ramella emphasise, was for a long time completely absent from migration studies. The actual people, their decisions and ambitious plans were subsumed to socio-economic and historic forces.[2] Also in Slovenia the established way of studying migration processes talked about emigrants, immigrants and their descendants, the culture and society of emigrants, or the society and culture of immigrants. However, it is obvious that a person moving along the path we call migration is at the same time an emigrant and an immigrant. She or he is leaving behind one society, country and culture at the same time as coming into another. Only the points of view are completely isolated. If we are in the place the persons are leaving, or in the place where per-

1 The original spelling of the family name in Slovenian was Valenčič.
2 Baily, Ramella, One Family, Two Worlds.

sons are arriving, we in fact see emigrants and immigrants, but when we try to understand their migration situation and context, we must take into account that the actual people, so easily blended into a faceless crowd by the researchers, may not share our point of view. They do not stand where we stand, and our standpoint is also completely irrelevant for their experiences, perceptions and emotions. Their experiences are complex and their points of view changing and changeable. In order to present the complex experiences of those who left and those who stayed at home in more detail, I added the oral testimonies of both children of Pepica Valencich from Cleveland and of the daughter of her brother Ivan from Jelšane to the analysis of the family correspondence.

It could be that no other form of communication evokes a stronger perception of the addressees and their expectations – or rather our expectations of what they expect – than letters. Paul Thompson thus says the following about using correspondence as a source of historical inquiry:

> *Certainly letters have the advantage of often being the original communication itself. But this does not free them from the problem of bias, or ensure that what letters say is true, or conveys the real feeling of the writer. They are in fact subject to the kinds of social influence which have been observed in interviews, but in an exaggerated form, because a letter is rarely written to a recipient who is attempting to be neutral like an interviewer.*[3]

Carla Kaplan adds: "We are probably more aware of our audience when we write letters than at any other time. Every letter is a performance."[4] This is why letters can reveal, but also conceal the complexity and the controversy of the constitution of interpersonal relationships and identities of correspondents. Correspondence offers a performance during which the curtain is at the same time up and down. David Gerber even talks about the problem of silences and untruths. He argues that:

> *Immigrant letters are not principally about documenting the world, but instead about reconfiguring a personal relationship rendered vulnerable by long-distance, long-term separation. It is in the service of that goal that the letter develops its content, so that goal, profoundly illusive in its own way because it springs from the most profound recess of human needs and emotions, needs to be understood as the source of the aspirations of the parties involved.*[5]

Due to the lack of space I will only briefly mention the silences and possible untruths in the correspondence. Baily and Ramella present another side of the argument:

> *Letters have unique advantages as sources for studying the process of migration. Private letters – those written for the personal consumption of a specific individual or family – served as a vital link between migrants and families and friends back home. They record the subjective observations of those who participated in the process as it was unfolding, not the reconstruction from memory of past events and feelings nor the observations of simulated or reconstructed behaviour. In addition, private letters permit us to evaluate observations and comments regarding motives, adjustment,*

3 Thompson, The Voice of the Past, 103–104.

4 Kaplan, Zora Neale Hurston, 20.

5 Gerber, Epistolary Masquerades, 143.

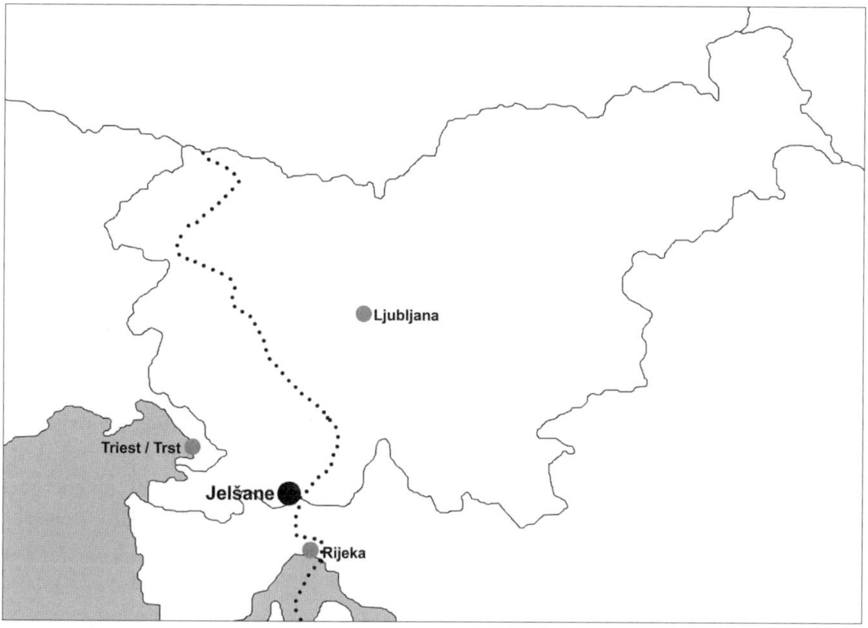

Map: Slovenia. The punctuated line shows the interwar border between Yugoslavia and Italy (according to the Treaty of Rapallo, 1920).

> *and the immigrant experience, especially when we can determine something of the history and the social and economic position of the writer and the family.*[6]

The Udovič-Hrvatin-Valenčič family correspondence discloses various aspects of the subjective migration process set against the historic circumstances and the family's social position. The devastations after World War One and the political discrimination in Italy against Slovenians are of key importance for the Primorska region in the 1920s and 1930s. These historic and social circumstances are meticulously described by Aleksej Kalc:

> *Along with emigration for political and national reasons, economic migration continues throughout the 1920s and partly into the 1930s. At least indirectly, this was still connected to the Italian attitude towards the minority situation: the discriminatory national policy used economic and social levers to achieve its objectives. In addition to the grave situation caused by World War One, the lack of economic development and integration in the Italian economic space, slow industrialisation and agrarian crisis, the 'non-Italian' population of the Venezia-Giulia region suffered the destruction of their own financial and insurance systems in the face of saving and lending societies, which were – together with co-operatives – taken over by managing boards loyal to the regime or were incorporated by Italian institutions. The* [Slovenian] *population was also subjugated to a*

[6] Baily, Ramella, One Family, Two Worlds, 2–3.

> *disproportionately high tax burden and unrelenting treatment at tax exaction. All this caused the weakening and encumbering of small farms, a lot of which were taken over by foreigners.*[7]

In his study of Slovenian migrations, Marjan Drnovšek especially emphasises emigration from Primorska between the two World Wars. He even calls it a

> *veritable exodus of Slovenians from Primorska under the Italian reign over the region, as more than 20,000 emigrated to Argentina* [...] *and by 1931 approximately 22,000 to Yugoslavia.*[8]

In the case of the family under study, of Helena Udovič's four children, only one remained at home and the three who had left sent dollars and liras from abroad so that the fourth could pay off debts and taxes. "There was a time when I could not send you more than a dollar bill for the whole year", wrote Pepica Valencich to her brother and his family.[9] She left behind her widowed mother and youngest brother and landed in the 'Land of Opportunity' at the brink of the decade-long economic crisis in November 1930. The quote above summarises the next decade of her life: one dollar bill per year because her husband was without work for months at a time and often fell sick, she lost her newborn baby and nearly died, gave birth to another one – and the whole time she was thinking about how to help her family in the old place. The letter I quoted was written after World War Two, when she sent hundreds of parcels with food, medicine and clothes to her brother, who had stayed at home, and his family. For the first ten years of her life in the US she had tried to send them money, but money was scarce in 1930s' America. After the war, when life finally got easier, she sent them as much as she could over the fifteen years to come. And in 1960 she visited her homeland for the first and last time.

First, I analysed the correspondence from the period between 1930, when Pepica left home, and 1940, when her mother Helena died. The letters were exchanged between Pepica and Jože in Cleveland, Tone in Buenos Aires and mother Helena and her youngest son Ivan in Jelšane. The correspondence is intimate and emotional on the one hand, and restrained and reserved on the other: emotional where they write about how much they love and miss each other, regardless whether the letter was written by the mother, the son or the daughter, and restrained when they write how difficult and miserable life conditions are, no matter where. They all tried to make the decade of economic depression and political oppression look bearable and manageable.

These ten years of family correspondence can be considered personal. It also needs to be taken into account that mother Helena's letters were read and written by her neighbour Milka, the sister of Jože's wife in Cleveland because she was illiterate. Her illiteracy is understandable considering the historical circumstances: she was born in 1870, when the Austrian Law on Elementary Education had just been passed and its implementation was inconsistent and slow. However, its implementation was thorough enough for all her children and

7 Kalc, Poti in usode, 40.

8 Drnovšek, Izseljenec, 11.

9 All quotes without further reference in this section are from the Udovič-Hrvatin-Valenčič family correspondence.

the majority of the Slovenian migrants in the period of mass migration to be literate. This is clearly seen from their correspondence. However, even if mother Helena had been literate she would not have written letters to her children by her own, or read theirs. We learn from the correspondence that her eyesight was poor, but money was so scarce that neither treatment nor glasses were affordable. We can only guess what the letters would have been like, had there been no intermediary between her and her children. They might have contained more descriptions of problems, difficulties and arguments, but it is difficult to imagine that they could have contained more love. Son Jože wrote the following when Pepica left:

> *Dear Mother! Do not cry too much for Pepica, it might do you harm. I know you feel sad about losing your only daughter, but try to find consolation in the fact that she got a good husband from a good family. I know very well that in her spirit she will always be with you. Maybe she will be able to help you more this way than she could, had she married over there. I beg you one more time, be consoled. Many regards and kisses from your loving son Jože.*

The nature of the Udovič-Hrvatin-Valenčič narratives is complex: on the one hand there is intimacy and emotion, on the other reserve and concealment. One could believe that the reserve was caused by the third party, present as an intermediary during this correspondence. However, it is just as safe to assume that reserve and even concealment stem from the desire to spare the mother unpleasant news, to hide from her how hard life in the promised lands really was. Thus, the intermediary was not really important, but the addressee, their mother, and the relationship of her children towards her were. When mother Helena died in 1940, Tone wrote to his sister Pepica:

> *Dear sister! It will soon be 14 years since I have seen any of my dearest. But it almost seems as if I said goodbye to you all yesterday. Who knows, is it forever? But when I look at the number of things that have happened in the meantime, it seems almost like an eternity. Oh, how many things have changed during this time, how many! Our dear father died, and our Mother. You have all married and some of you already have grown-up children. They make you happy and proud. I am also proud of them and tell people that these are my nephews and nieces. But I have not changed my life at all in this time. I only achieved being 37 years old and still wandering around like a loner.*

In this regard, it is interesting that the correspondence does not include any references to the social context of the United States or Argentina. It looks exceptional since it lacks "the comparative nature of the migration experience" as Nancy Green puts it:

> *The immigrant represents the Other in the nation-state, but the new land is the referential Other for the newly-arrived. The migrant embodies an implicit comparison between past and present, between one world and another, between two languages, and two sets of cultural norms. The immigrant's observations fall somewhere between the tourist's hasty generalizations and the social scientist's constructed comparisons.*[10]

The three migrants of the Udovič-Hrvatin-Valenčič family did not write about everyday life, people, habits, or culture in their new overseas homelands. There are, on the other hand, a lot of descriptions of their encounters with migrants from the same village and the

[10] Green, The Comparative Method, 57.

local area of Jelšane. Sometimes it seems they were leading a life similar to what it might have been back home. In actuality, their lives and personalities changed dramatically. The members of the Udovič-Hrvatin-Valenčič family did not have a choice in the historic set-up of the totalitarian state, but their correspondence shows how they as individuals acted and reacted in this setting. The correspondence introduces us to persons who were active and dynamic in the process in weighing and deciding for or against migration, in the processes of adjustment and learning in their new environment and also in maintaining and nurturing the social networks and family ties in both their old and new environments. These persons live in both worlds, on both sides of the Atlantic, in the old place and the new home. Physically separated, they think of each other, take care of each other, and work keeping in mind their social and family circles here and there. They lived in two worlds simultaneously. Their correspondence shows that their thoughts are intensive, their care genuine and their lives subjected to the actual needs and ambitions in both parts of the world.

When we add oral history and life stories, their migration experience attains an even more complex and sophisticated structure. Pepica from the letters is always thinking about her mother and is interested in every detail of life in her native village. However, when we add the narratives of her children to this image, we see a different kind of person. Pepica from Cleveland did not merely take care of her family, speak Slovenian, receive her acquaintances from the Jelšane area and write letters to the old place. According to her children, she was always stylishly coiffed and dressed, spoke impeccable English and, when necessary, worked full-time. She was adamant in teaching the Slovenian language and songs to her children, sending them to Slovenian choir practice and other Slovenian activities. But on the other hand, she insisted on enrolling them in art courses at the Cleveland Museum of Art every summer, which, on a symbolic level, was just as distant from the Jelšane Slovenian community as it was from the Cleveland one.[11] Pepica lived in a social universe where the distances between Jelšane and Cleveland meant nothing at all, and at the same time she was an active member of American society, thousands of miles away from her native village and its customs. It is precisely this intertwining of tradition and modernity, distance and closeness, maintaining and changing that we can unveil by researching migration processes through oral histories and correspondence analysis. As Paul Thompson emphasises:

> *This ability to make connections between separated spheres of life is an intrinsic strength of oral history in the development of historical interpretation. In studying the transition from one culture to another, in time, or through migration, we can not only look at those cultures separately, but observe the path that individuals took from one culture to another.*[12]

This is the way in which the migration experiences of nameless masses slowly morph into concrete individual and family stories, while the theory and history of migration gain insight into the subjective realities and social organisations of migrants.

[11] Interview with daughter Cecilia (Cilka) Valencic Dolgan, Cleveland, May 2002.

[12] Thompson, The Voice of the Past, 257.

To understand the migrant experience, we must ask also questions regarding the family members who stayed put but are a part of the migrant experience. What does the departure of family members mean for those who stayed behind? How do they organise their lives; what fills the voids left by the people who emigrated; who helps them with their work? What is their status in society when they have "migrants in the house"; what contacts do they have with other villagers? This list is not exhaustive – a series of questions arises, connected to the specific migrant communication between those who left and those who stayed behind.

This dynamic is particularly interesting in the second part of the family correspondence analysis, in letters that cover the period between 1945 and 1960. This period is special because the correspondence did not only include letters but also hundreds of parcels. Two brothers and a sister regularly sent the desperately needed help in food, clothes and other necessities to Jelšane. The reasons for poverty and misery were numerous: the devastation brought to Jelšane by two world wars, a quarter of a century of Fascist Italian rule, post-war Yugoslavian experiments with agrarian reform and industrialisation and the loss of the city of Trst/Trieste, which again became part of Italy and had traditionally been the main place where products were sold by families from Jelšane. In 1946 Pepica wrote:

> *Here we are putting together another parcel for you tonight. If you get it all, it will make you glad. We are sending Ivan material for a suit. I bought all the necessary things to make a suit ... the lining is also for the suit, he can make something for you and maybe something will be left for Marijan ... Some things are for you, Elka ... some small pieces for the children. A cap for Marijan and a chemise for Cilka. 1 pound of coffee, 2 litres of oil, 2 soaps, 6 cans of soup, and those bandies* [band-aids] *for small wounds. And also ointment for cuts and scratches, first you have to wash and then put on the red medicine.*

The letters in this period are full of lists of items sent to relatives, and heartbreaking questions of whether they got the packages. Brother Tone, who lived alone in Argentina, collected clothes, put together food parcels and included careful lists of their contents in his letters. The following example is from 1951:

> *Three pocket pens, 1 for Marijan, 1 for Rado and 1 for Cilka, 1 kilo of coffee, 1 kilo of rice, 1 kilo of sugar, cheese, just over a kilo of soles, 8 boxes of meat, 2 face soaps, 1 soap for clothes, 1 and a half kilos of pasta.* [Some months earlier he had written:] *On 6 December I sent you some clothes (5 kilos), and on 12 December 5 kilos of food. Today, on 24 December, I am sending you the following: 1 kilo of rice and 1 kilo of beans mixed together since it is forbidden to send rice, 1 kilo of dried pancetta, 1 jar of honey, 1 cheese, 4 boxes of canned meat and 2 kilos of white flour.*

Researchers of migration, and especially female migration, suggest that the hearth and the household do not necessarily signify a permanent dwelling – they become "a tight network of exchanges of support".[13] In the correspondence between the Udovič-Hrvatin-Valenčič family this becomes evident. A dense network of support exchange includes innumerable items: before the war, the money to pay the taxes that threatened the existence of the old

[13] Sharpe, Women, Gender and Labour Migration, 3.

home in Jelšane, but also the Jelšane sausages and vegetable seeds that travelled to Cleveland; it means the exchange of food, clothes, shoes, vitamins, medications and tools, coffee, and "bandies" (band-aids) in the times of need after the Second World War. What this exchange meant to the part of the family left on the European side of the Atlantic is – as Ivan's daughter Cilka says – "indescribable".[14]

Love, loyalty, caring and devotion were exchanged. Sometimes they were more important than dollars and flour, for they maintained the density of the family network, even in times of disagreements, grudges, and misunderstandings, further complicated by lost letters, lengthy gaps between receiving a letter and responding to it, and also the personal problems of the correspondents. Just two examples: Jože sent dictionaries to his niece Cilka in Jelšane in 1956 and encouraged his brother to "send her to school to Ljubljana if possible, the child has talent and should study. I will help as much as I can." He also paid his brother's subscription to *Edinost*, a newspaper of Slovenians in Cleveland, so he could have better information. And Pepica sent to her brother Tone a piece of *potica* (traditional walnut cake) carried to Buenos Aires by an acquaintance who was visiting Cleveland.

How the idea of the hearth and the household changes into "a tight network of exchanges of support" is a matter emphasised primarily by (female) researchers of female migrants and their experiences. When reading the Udovič-Hrvatin-Valenčič family correspondence another important detail is revealed: the equal role of the brothers, who took care of the tight network of family ties as seriously as their sister did, and wrote letters equally emotional as hers. All the letters from the period between 1930 and 1960 reveal that for Pepica and her brothers the departure from their native village meant an extension of the hearth to the other side of the ocean. Pepica and her brothers participated and lived in two societies simultaneously. The extensive correspondence over thirty years shows how strong the creation of a transnational family economy was, as it would be called in migration studies today. "The creation of family economies transcending national borders", as Donna Gabaccia calls it, is an old phenomenon.[15] In the past, the migrants simultaneously lived their lives in two societies, though many times not in a physical but in a mental way.

After 1960 the number of parcels crossing the Atlantic gradually decreased, just as the post-war scantiness in Yugoslavia was reduced. For as long as five years after her visit, Pepica sent several parcels a year, and then until the mid-1980s only one every year. Her son Joe Valencic[16] remembers that after 1960 they no longer sent food, only coffee and aspirin; after 1970 they also stopped sending clothes. The parcels were replaced with a visit and an "extra suitcase", in which there were "always many extra things for relatives".[17] This was no longer a sign of need for material things, but rather the need to keep the tightly woven family network of support and solidarity alive – at least for as long as the memories of it were alive.

[14] Interview with Cilka Udovič, Jelšane, March 2006.
[15] Gabaccia, When the Migrants are Men, 196.
[16] The letter 'h' was dropped from the family name sometime after 1945.
[17] Joe Valencic, personal e-mail, March 27, 2006.

Narratives: creative agents of the construction of subjectivities

Picture 1: Memorial to Mary Setina, a Slovenian immigrant in the town of Joliet (Illinois).

At this point it is necessary to add gender as a key tool for the analysis of migration processes to other important aspects, such as class, religion, education and ethnicity. The findings of the research project "The Role and Significance of Women in the Preservation of Cultural Heritage among Slovenian Migrants" will be used for this purpose. The "Slovenian cultural heritage and the woman's role in preserving it" was defined by the women migrants and their female descendants themselves. In the research process they were the main source of information, definitions, interpretations and narratives collected through in-depth listening, conversations, and life story telling. The core presupposition of the study was that the role of women in preserving cultural heritage is specific and special. Demographically and culturally of the same origin, men and women migrants have lived very much the same lives. Nevertheless, women's responsibilities, opportunities, and their roles and experiences at work, at home and in their community are different from that of men. Many studies have shown what Donna Gabaccia sums up as:

> *First as community activists and later as socializers of children and organizers of family and religious rituals, immigrant women reproduced and transformed cultural traditions through their labors. Men at first sought women's help in reproducing ethnicity but then abandoned it, leaving it increasingly to women and their domestic roles. It is scarcely surprising that women, more then*

> *men, continue to view ethnicity and their immigrant 'roots' as an important influence on their lives.*[18]

I have to underline that this study by the Institute for Slovenian Emigration in Ljubljana, starting in 2001, was the first of its kind in Slovenia, and we can only hope that it was not the last. As a sociologist involved in migration and women's studies, I found it challenging to collect the often obscure, undocumented life stories and to analyse and reflect theoretically on the fairly unknown experience of Slovenian immigrant women. At the time I was a migrant myself and having lived in New York for four years, I was reflecting on this research experience also from a personal perspective. I recorded sixty narrations of women from three migration periods: before World War Two, in the immediate post-war years, and from 1960 to the present time.

In terms of methodology, I adopted a pragmatic and eclectic approach to a consistently qualitative manner of research. From different kinds of oral history interviews, I chose the individual life story, recorded mainly in one-to-one encounters and enriched by photos and other kind of memorabilia. However, there were a few times where I interviewed a group: once, there were four sisters sitting in my hotel room, talking about their lives more or less simultaneously and enjoying it tremendously; a few times I had a mother and a daughter sitting together in their living room, the daughter waiting patiently for her turn to speak; and once I listened to two sisters recalling together their childhood in an extended Slovenian family. The choice of women I asked to participate in the study was not restricted by their age, generation, or year of migration, by place of residence, level of education, social status, or their engagement in public life. I call the participants the narrators as I find this description the most accurate in regards to the method of work: instead of asking them a set of predetermined questions and recording their replies I asked them to tell me their life-story which I listened to, recorded and, if necessary, encouraged with an occasional question and/or comment. I found it important to make the participant feel she was a narrator because this turned her into a subject in control of the recollection of her life experience.

However, even though this method results in detailed and personal accounts of life experiences, it also creates a few problems. First, as in any research, it is necessary to understand how our own research interest and approach shape the respondent's narrative, no matter how independent the narrator's position is. In other words, it means that "just as treating women as narrators requires interpreting the telling itself, understanding how the researcher's interest and assumptions shape the narrative requires interpreting the interaction itself".[19] Second, we have to remind ourselves more than once that what we are listening to, recording and going to use as our study material, is not the woman's actual life experience but only her narrative about it. This again makes it more and less interesting and useful at the same time. When an undocumented life experience is recovered by the woman's own recounting, how should I represent it? There are at least three options here:

18 Gabaccia, From the Other Side, 131.
19 Chase, Bell, Interpreting the Complexity, 80.

first, I can publish the life story as it was told (if I get the permission to do so); second, I can interpret the recounted experience and put it in a wider historical and personal context; third, I can only use particular parts of the narrative just to illustrate my own version of the immigrant woman's life as I creatively imagine it, according to my own research interests and assumptions.

Collecting stories was based on the principle of open invitation to the woman I chose to interview. The woman was given all the information about my research, its aims, my track record and an explanation about the method of work in advance. I also made it clear that I was interested exclusively in the woman's perspective on the migrant experience rather than in her political background. Since I openly declared I had no interest in the political aspect of their stories, women generally dropped their concerns and fear in this respect. Even if I rarely experienced rejection and almost never hostility, problems did occur all the time. My incapability of asking potentially embarrassing questions due to my fear of manipulating the narrator into conflicting topics, which were important for the study but might have been a taboo for her, was one of them. Another problem – a more objective one – was inter-subjectivity. It often happens that the narrator does not understand why her life is interesting to the researcher, and it is quite common that the narrator and the researcher only assume that they understand each other's motives and purposes in this complicated communication situation. The most common problem, however, was that women found it hard to believe that somebody might be interested in their lives. Many women feel their everyday life is exactly the thing that is not important and does not call for attention. In their view, there is nothing to tell about the fact they have acted as mothers, wives, employees, activists, volunteers.

In the analysis of their stories, it is necessary to take such an attitude towards the importance of their work and life seriously into account. This modest and humble self-perception seems to be the key element of self-censoring. In other words, this appears to be the main mechanism, which sets limits on the richness of stories and will require serious methodological and conceptual considerations. As I have mentioned before, it is important to reclaim the women's experiences, to record and document them but it is also necessary to understand how complicated the issue of representation and interpretation is. Even if we choose the option of "creative imagining", where many details which are absent from the narrative can be imagined and creatively reconstructed, there are still unbridgeable gaps in the narratives concerning problematic, embarrassing and sad parts of life experiences which can never be fairly and honestly imagined. Not surprisingly, there are also many achievements and public successes that are never mentioned by the women themselves and are

> [...] *muted, particularly in any situation where women's interests and experiences are at variance with those of men. A woman's discussion of her life may combine two separate, often conflicting, perspectives: one framed in concepts and values that reflect men's dominant position in the culture, and one informed by the more immediate realities of a woman's personal experience. Where experience does not 'fit' dominant meanings, alternative concepts may not readily be available. Hence,*

> *inadvertently, women often mute their own thoughts and feelings when they try to describe their lives in the familiar and publicly acceptable terms of prevailing concepts and conventions.*[20]

Although the oral history interview is clearly a valuable method for uncovering women's perspectives and experiences, it is not always easy to reveal them. As Kathryn Anderson and Dana Jack put it:

> *To hear women's perspectives accurately, we have to learn to listen in stereo, receiving both the dominant and muted channels clearly and tuning into them carefully to understand the relationship between them.*[21]

Alessandro Portelli, who claims that oral sources have different credibility and there are no "false" ones, emphasises:

> *Once we have checked their factual credibility with all the established criteria of philological criticism and factual verification which are required by all types of sources anyway, the diversity of oral history consists in the fact that 'wrong' statements are still psychologically 'true', and that this truth may be equally as important as factually reliable accounts.*[22]

Life stories are used and interpreted in two main ways in sociologic and socio-historical approaches: as the material to study narratives in various social contexts or as a text which renders the different ways of constructing personality or personal identity. The definition of a life story stems from these two usages and interpretations, because a life story can be understood as a narrative about events in one's life or defined as a story of a character, as revealed through the narration. When analysing the stories I noticed that, regardless of my analytical and theoretical approach, there is a difference between them, which fits into the categories mentioned above: some narrators mostly spoke of facts and events from their lives, while others dedicated most of their time to describing their emotions and relationships with others. However, the majority of narrators intertwined the two discourses and only their emphasis differed. The division into factual and subjective life-story narration could only be applied to a small number of stories and even there not throughout the narrative, but only to certain parts. It must be taken into account that, because of an inter-subjective situation, a factual narrative may transform into a subjective one after a certain time, and vice versa. My use of life stories has therefore been a combination of both. On the one hand I used narration to describe and illustrate the social and political circumstances in which Slovenian migrants in the United States lived and on the other, their subjective responses to the pressure of assimilation and acculturation.

Pertti Alasuutari suggests an additional approach to the life stories. He places the "discursive approach" between the two already established ones: the socio-structural approach, which views the life story as a picture of life, and the sociolinguistic one, which claims that the life story narration is the picture of a personality. Alasuutari describes the discursive ap-

20 Anderson, Jack, Learning to Listen, 157.
21 Ibid., 157.
22 Portelli, The Death of Luigi Trastulli, 51.

proach as a perspective "where personality is seen as an accounting strategy for maintaining continuity and saving face".[23] He replaces the notion that everyone has an authentic self, which can be captured when this person narrates his or her life story with the important notion that narrating a life story is always situational and always serves a purpose; it depends on inter-personal relationships and expectations. Those who work with the method of listening and recording life stories know that people do not walk around with ready-made narratives – they are constructed during the complex recording process, even though the researcher had arranged to conduct the interview well in advance. The discursive approach draws our attention to the fact that life-story narration may also serve the informant's intimate purpose and that its core is actually the retaining of one's personal dignity and consistency.

What does this mean? As Alasuutari states, and as I experienced myself in the years of recording life stories, narrating or listening to a life story is based on co-operation. In this process, the consistency of the image the narrator creates is as equally important as the consistency of the role the listener has. When a person decides she will share her story, she enters an interactive relationship with the listener, although she understands perfectly well that the target audience is wider and unknown to her. The narrative is a presentation of self, created in – and dependent on – the actual situation of the narrator and the listener.

The stories recorded as a part of this oral history project, confirm that the women's role in preserving the cultural heritage among Slovenian immigrants is extremely important both on the public as well as the private level. Women were and remain activists in the Slovenian community, church and other organisations; they are members of the singing, dancing and theatre groups; they work in countless volunteer projects. But since an important part of the cultural heritage is preserved at home and in the kitchen, i.e. the traditional female domain, their role is wider and its impact on the identity of the family members is crucial. As a home-maker the woman spends more time at home than her husband even if she is employed; she looks after children; she uses the Slovenian language at least when referring to food; she regularly, or at least occasionally, prepares Slovenian dishes; she celebrates Slovenian holidays and adds something Slovenian to the celebrations of the American ones; she talks about people of the same origin and maintains correspondence with the family and friends in Slovenia.

On the other hand, the narratives also confirmed that the experiences of negotiated identities in the context of migration are specific and different, even if women lived in the same migrant communities. Marlene Parrish, who was embarrassed by her Slovenian origin sixty years ago and claimed in school she was Austrian, says today:

> *My granddaughters now are black. My son married and adopted two little black children. I have a hilarious picture of me teaching my black granddaughter how to make potica. And I said, 'Traditions go on, I don't care what you are'.*[24]

[23] Alasuutari, The Discursive Construction, 3.

[24] All quotes without further reference in this section are from the narratives collected for the above-mentioned research project in the Cleveland, Pittsburgh, New York City, Washington, D.C., and Chicago areas between 2001 and 2004.

As a child, she was horrified because her cousin played accordion, but today she teaches her daughter-in-law of Thai origin how to dance polka. She said to her: "This will help you understand your husband, dear." What has changed in sixty years? Undoubtedly, the society in which the uncompromising Americanisation of the first six decades of the previous century was transformed into the worshiping of ethnicity in the 1970s, and afterwards into today's moderate tolerance for diversity as individual choice. My narrator had changed as well. The horror she experienced when thinking her school friends could find out that her cousin played an accordion vanished because of the different times, the personal re-evaluation of identity and the intimate reflections on what we are made of, which old age, experiences and nostalgia frequently bring. What she says today, namely that music is a strong connector and that she wishes to preserve the tradition she is familiar with, underlines the main point of her narrative: she thinks that in her entire life she has never been more Slovenian than she is now. And this illustrates the main point of the analysis of the women's narratives: the changing nature of identity. The narratives offer an exciting journey through given, rejected and intimately reconstructed ethnic identities, which is at the same time a personal experience of conflicting forces of ethnicity, identity and subjectivity.

Jean Pohar Ficek, who grew up in the 1930s, remembers the complex combination of reproduction and transformation of cultural traditions, which is a common theme in most of the narratives. The Slovenian language was almost forbidden because to know English was crucial. But on the other hand, she exclaimed: "Oh, everything was tradition! All our meals were always Slovenian food, always. Nothing was American". Mimi Mejac had a different experience growing up during the Depression in New York:

> *When I started school I didn't know any English at all. But then I learned so much that I skipped the second grade. So I can speak both. At home, my mother and sister talked only Slovenian and if we talked in English my mother said, 'I don't understand, speak Slovenian'.*

Here we can see culture as a field where identities, recognitions, fears, and curiosity are negotiated in a personal, intimate way. As Danquah mentions, "the dilemma of deciding how much of one's heritage and customs must be sacrificed to camouflage oneself as a member of mainstream society" is of utmost importance.[25] For the first and second Slovenian migration waves (before and after the Second World War) we can assume that every first generation immigrant tried to resolve it in her own way. However, for the second and third generations and for the contemporary Slovenian immigrant women in America the dilemma has changed. The issue now is how much heritage and custom must one preserve to still feel to be a member of a particular ethnicity. For Slovenian migrants and their descendants the turnaround was possible because in a period of one hundred years they had, like many other European ethnic immigrants, climbed from the status of "less civilized and culturally unsuitable" to the position of the American middle class of "the whites". They reached, in Jan and Leo Lucassen's words, "assimilation as the state in which immigrants

[25] Danquah, Becoming American, xv.

or their descendants do not regard themselves primarily as different from the native-born population and are no longer perceived as such".[26]

Slovenian women who come to America today are already middle class, well educated, independent, ambitious, clever, and, of course, white. For Slovenian women who moved to America in the last ten to twenty years, the question of identity and the choice of symbolic ethnic identification does not exist. They regard the problem of preserving the Slovenian cultural heritage and maintaining their ties with their home, language, parents and friends as solved to a large extent by having access to the Internet. As one of them defines it, her home is her briefcase and her laptop. Having an email address allows them to maintain daily connection with their parents, friends, even children; on their computer they keep their photos, albums, letters and other memorabilia; and on the internet they can check the situation in Slovenia, read books and newspapers, listen to the radio and TV programmes or join a chat group in Slovenian; if they feel like doing it, of course, because many times they do not. However, I often found that their views on the cultural heritage changed when they started a family and had children. Even those who felt strongly about preserving their cultural heritage had to face the questions of cultural and ethnic background, language and tradition in a much more definite way when they were addressing their children's future.

I try to use and explore the methodological approaches and analysis that fit into the new tradition of migration research. As Baily states, migration researchers today see

> [...] *a more complex, dynamic, and open-ended process that began in the village of origin and continued outward with migration, incorporation into the host society, and socio-cultural adjustment. They no longer assume a single outcome such as assimilation, the termination of the process after any given period of time, or the inevitability or irreversibility of specific patterns of interaction. Economic, social and political structures – as well as the cultures of the villages of origin – become an essential part of the explanation of what happened to individuals abroad. The sending and receiving communities are conceptually linked in a framework of analysis that enables these scholars to explore the simultaneous influence of cultural persistence and change.*[27]

What happened to the individual abroad was also individually experienced since migrants dealt with the new social and economic order in a unique, personal, and individual way. As Bodnar emphasises:

> *Immigrants were not clinging together as clusters of aliens or workers but were, in fact, badly fragmented into numerous enclaves arranged by internal status levels, ideology, and orientation. The important implication of group fragmentation is that the real dynamic which explained immigrant adjustment was not simply at the nexus of immigrant and American culture or at the point where foreign-born workers met industrial managers, but it was at all the points where immigrant families met the challenges of capitalism and modernity: the homeland, the neighbourhood, the school, the workplace, the church, the family, and the fraternal hall.*[28]

[26] Lucassen, Lucassen, Migration, Migration History, 23.
[27] Baily, Immigrants in the Lands of Promise, 10–11.
[28] Bodnar, The Transplanted, xvii.

Joyce Plemel described group fragmentation in the case of the Slovenian community. As a little girl in the 1920s she noticed that her Slovenian community in Cleveland was strictly divided into "the church people and the non-church people". This was a legacy from the old country and could also be called "Catholic and non-Catholic" or "the conservatives and the progressives", and around this schism cultural, artistic, supporting, editorial and social organisations were structured. Joyce Plemel told me that they lived separately "by streets, by a bridge" and even "didn't marry each other", and everything was double in the community. On the left side of the actual and political ideological bridge, there were choirs, theatre groups, fraternities, newspapers and publishers, national homes and recreational centres – and the same were on the other side.

However, the majority of the population in Slovenian communities experienced a life of connectedness and solidarity despite the ideological and political polarisation. On the one hand, there were unbridgeable differences, cemented by ideological, political and religious leaders, and on the other there was the unity of the majority of the community, despite the differences, even within them. The key element of the heterogeneous migrant communities (in addition to ideological differences) is the time in which the migration process started. If we consider the class, gender, education, age and generation aspects of a migration experience we must also take into account that the historic aspect is among the most important. Marie Gombach describes how terrible it was, when she arrived in Cleveland as a child with her family in 1935:

> *Nobody really cared, because nobody really wanted us here, nobody wanted us to come here. I remember when I sang with one of the children's groups. This was shortly after we came to this country. I remember at the concert I had a solo – 'Kje je moj mili dom'*[29] *– and I just broke up and the whole audience cried with me.*

Gombach's family left their native village in the Primorska region and landed in the United States in the midst of the worst economic crisis. The Slovenian community was not welcoming. The newcomers were simply extra mouths to feed and another pair of hands out of work. And yet they cried to the same folk song together.

Who came from where and when is important as well for other elements of the migration experiences. The historic context is most poignantly revealed by migrants who arrived after World War Two as 'displaced persons'. Their arrival changed the relationships within the Slovenian community although they amounted to no more than six to ten percent of the total Slovenian community. They came burdened with the traditional division of their ancestors; this time, however, it was tainted with the blood of the civil war. However, the relations had not changed merely because of this image of Slovenia they brought with them, the image Ivanka Antolin described as "split, bleeding Slovenia". They had left the so-called Communist Yugoslavia at the beginning of the Cold War and disembarked into McCarthy's communist witch-hunt, which marked the whole decade in the US.

[29] "Where is my sweet home", a sad Slovenian folk song.

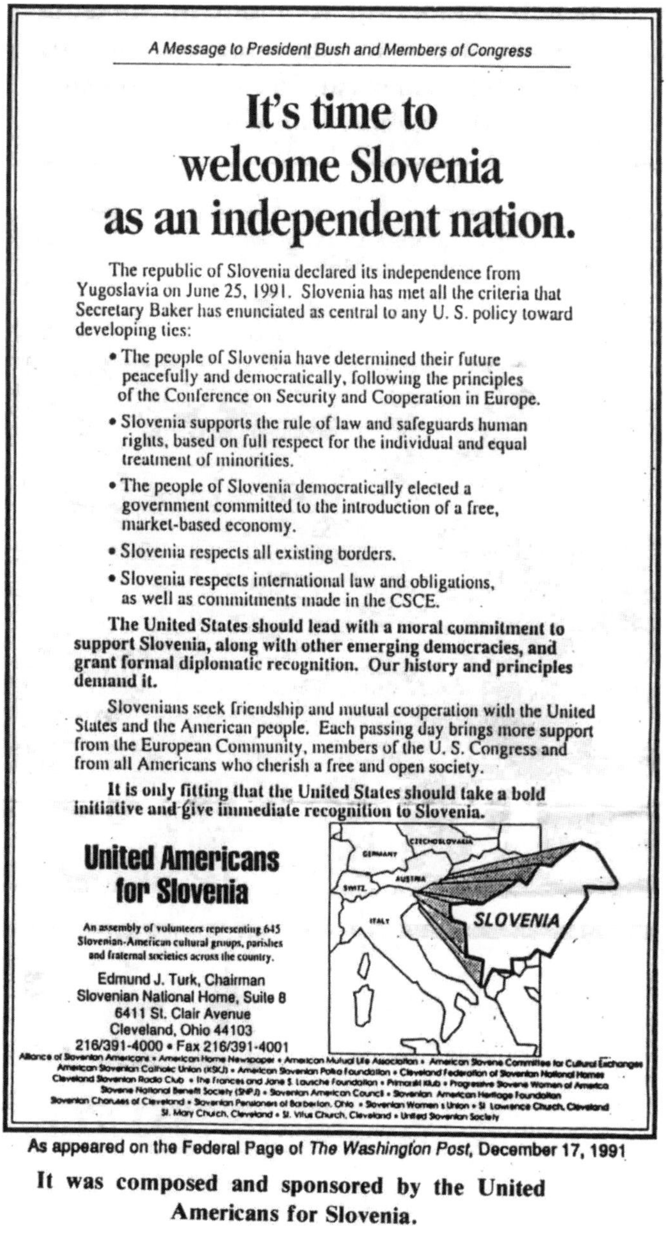

A Message to President Bush and Members of Congress

It's time to welcome Slovenia as an independent nation.

The republic of Slovenia declared its independence from Yugoslavia on June 25, 1991. Slovenia has met all the criteria that Secretary Baker has enunciated as central to any U. S. policy toward developing ties:

- The people of Slovenia have determined their future peacefully and democratically, following the principles of the Conference on Security and Cooperation in Europe.
- Slovenia supports the rule of law and safeguards human rights, based on full respect for the individual and equal treatment of minorities.
- The people of Slovenia democratically elected a government committed to the introduction of a free, market-based economy.
- Slovenia respects all existing borders.
- Slovenia respects international law and obligations, as well as commitments made in the CSCE.

The United States should lead with a moral commitment to support Slovenia, along with other emerging democracies, and grant formal diplomatic recognition. Our history and principles demand it.

Slovenians seek friendship and mutual cooperation with the United States and the American people. Each passing day brings more support from the European Community, members of the U. S. Congress and from all Americans who cherish a free and open society.

It is only fitting that the United States should take a bold initiative and give immediate recognition to Slovenia.

United Americans for Slovenia

An assembly of volunteers representing 645 Slovenian-American cultural groups, parishes and fraternal societies across the country.

Edmund J. Turk, Chairman
Slovenian National Home, Suite 8
6411 St. Clair Avenue
Cleveland, Ohio 44103
216/391-4000 • Fax 216/391-4001

Alliance of Slovenian Americans • American Home Newspaper • American Mutual Life Association • American Slovene Committee for Cultural Exchanges • American Slovenian Catholic Union (KSKJ) • American Slovenian Polka Foundation • Cleveland Federation of Slovenian National Homes • Cleveland Slovenian Radio Club • The Frances and Jane S. Lausche Foundation • Primorski Klub • Progressive Slovene Women of America • Slovene National Benefit Society (SNPJ) • Slovenian American Council • Slovenian American Heritage Foundation • Slovenian Choruses of Cleveland • Slovenian Pensioners of Barberton, Ohio • Slovenian Women's Union • St. Lawrence Church, Cleveland • St. Mary Church, Cleveland • St. Vitus Church, Cleveland • United Slovenian Society

As appeared on the Federal Page of *The Washington Post*, December 17, 1991

It was composed and sponsored by the United Americans for Slovenia.

Picture 2: Ad by the United Americans for Slovenia in the *Washington Post*, 17 December 1991.

The arrival of the displaced persons, who differed from the previous migrants in experience, class, cultural and educational level, fragmented the community along the traditional schisms, but in a different historic context. This context is well presented in the statement of the Slovenian-American politician Frank Lausche: "Better Trst [Trieste] in Catholic Italy than in godless Yugoslavia". Whether these are his exact words – as they assured me in Cleveland – and whether his opinion was up for consideration in the White House when the Allied forces allocated Trieste to Italy and not Yugoslavia, I cannot tell. But I can imagine what such a statement meant to Marie Gombach, Pepica Valencich and thousands of others who had to emigrate because of the discriminatory politics towards Slovenians in fascist Italy. Another statement, "Absolutely no help for communist Yugoslavia!" dates from this time, the time of the arrival of the displaced Slovenians. It deepened the gap between them and the people who helped the resistance movement in Slovenia throughout the war. The fact is that the schism in the Slovenian community deepened after 1945. Although it started to become less and less important already in the 1970s, it was only in 1991 that some sort of historic reconciliation occurred.

In July 1991, immediately after the Yugoslav People's Army attacked the newly independent Slovenia, the organisation "United Americans for Slovenia" was established. The committee of the United Americans for Slovenia represented 659 organisations and estimated one million Slovenian-Americans.[30] In July 1991 its members started to plan campaigns for United States recognition of Slovenia, which included: mailings to government leaders, petitions and 50,000 postcards to the White House, telephone call-in marathons to the White House, special editions of newspapers and radio programmes, fund-raising activities and meetings with political leaders. After Slovenia had been recognised, United Americans for Slovenia started to campaign for Slovenia to become a NATO member. Their representatives were invited to the White House for a briefing on United States acceptance of Slovenia as a NATO member in July 1997. This was the first time the White House directly addressed Americans of Slovenian heritage on an issue concerning the community. Again, thousands of postcards were sent to the president and another phone marathon to the White House was conducted.[31] The organisation managed to bridge all the differences and to unite people of Slovenian origin at a special and unique historical moment. Since the goal to help Slovenia to secure its independence and international recognition was accomplished, United Americans for Slovenia ceased to exist in 2006.

[30] These statements were made by Joseph Valencic, responsible for public relations at the United Americans for Slovenia, in an interview, Ljubljana, October 2006.

[31] Valencic, United Americans for Slovenia.

Robert Pichler

Migration, Architecture and the Imagination of Home(land). An Albanian-Macedonian Case Study

Introduction[1]

Any attentive traveller crossing the western part of the Republic of Macedonia will perceive a number of striking differences between the Macedonian and Albanian inhabited areas. These differences are particularly obvious in rural zones and in ethnically mixed towns like Gostivar, Kičevo/Kërçovë or Tetovo/Tetovë. Apart from the signs marking religious differences (churches and mosques), one might be impressed by the number and size of new houses in the areas inhabited by Albanians. Many of these new buildings are still under construction. The shells made of red bricks are lacking plaster and on the first and second floors, windows are often missing. In the Macedonian settlements on the other hand, one can also see houses under construction, but mostly on a more moderate level. Most of the private buildings here stem from the 1970s and 1980s, when the state economy was still in a relatively good condition. Private construction among Macedonians today focuses basically on the renovation of already existing houses; new buildings are rare.

The economic landscape offers a similarly divided picture. In the Albanian inhabited areas numerous small shops and private enterprises have been mushrooming for the last twenty years. The streets are crowded with young people walking or hanging around in cafés and restaurants. These Albanian areas are young and dynamic. In the Macedonian inhabited neighbourhoods on the other hand, street life is quieter, with only a few shops operating and fewer people strolling around. There is no dynamic visible such as in the Albanian parts.[2] In the villages these differences are even more pronounced. Macedonian villages are scarcely inhabited and then by old people only, whereas many Albanian villages have developed in number and in size from small hamlets into little towns in the course of the last fifty years.

1 This article is a further developed and extended version of a text I wrote together with Barbara Derler (Derler, Pichler, Migration und die topographische Imagination). The research for this article was carried out within the research project "Migration and Nationalism", which is funded by the Austrian Science Foundation (ASF). I am deeply grateful to Joel M. Halpern for his attentive reading of the draft version of this article and his very helpful comments.

2 See for this phenomenon also the report of the European Stability Initiative, Ahmeti's village.

When looking closer at ethnically mixed areas, one can further observe sharp social divisions between Albanians and Macedonians. Apart from the fact that Macedonians and Albanians do not intermarry, in mixed settlements the two ethnic communities live basically in segregated social worlds. The sharp social divisions among the children and youth are particularly striking. For example, the two ethnic groups attend separate classes at preschool, primary and secondary levels. In ethnically mixed schools, where all students study under the same roof, education is organised in shifting units. What is obvious in school can be observed in many other social spheres as well. Both ethnic groups are actively engaged in strengthening and maintaining their ethnic boundaries. Where ethnic divisions appear they are being reinforced by networks of intra-ethnic interaction.

The case study

In this article I want to draw attention to the relationship between migration and the imagination of home(land) as it is expressed in the architecture of domestic Albanian houses. The building boom among Albanians, who stay abroad for most of the year yet invest a lot of their money in new houses, has to be seen against the background of macro-political developments in Macedonia. This particular relationship will be analysed on the basis of a case study of Velešta/Veleshtë, an Albanian inhabited village in the region of Struga/Strugë in western Macedonia. The changing architectural landscape of the village and the forces that are behind this transformation of locality provide an intriguing insight into the transterritorial relationship of migrants towards their places of origin.

The village of Velešta/Veleshtë[3], which is situated in a fertile plain ten kilometres north of the famous lake Ohrid, in many ways reflects the overall developments of the last fifty years in those rural areas of Macedonia inhabited by Albanians. The village population was characterised by a rapid increase in size, by a high rate of labour migration to German speaking countries and by the establishment of close social networks which stretch across state borders. In order to understand the motives behind this private building boom and the way new houses are constructed in this village, one has to take a closer look at the social dynamics of interethnic relations during socialism and thereafter. Macedonians and Albanians were differently affected by socialist modernisation and nation-building. I will, therefore, in the first section provide an overview of some structurally decisive features of ethnically distinctive developments by putting them into their historical context. In doing so, I will draw on already established assessments concerning the different ways Albanians and Macedonians experienced the socialist and post-socialist transformations in the country, and I will try to relate some of these arguments to the main issue of this article.

Before I begin to explore interethnic relations and to lay out my empirical material, a note is necessary on the terminology used. I prefer the term *transterritorial* instead of *tran-*

3 In the following I will use only the Albanian name of the village, Veleshtë.

snational in order to denote the social links and practices of migrants directed towards their imagined home(land) and vice versa. The term *transnationalism* might be misleading in the Balkan context since it derives from the Anglo-American concept of the nation-state. In this particular "Western" notion, *nation* and *state* as well as *nationality* and *citizenship* are generally used as synonyms.[4] Albanian migrants by contrast imagine their nation as cut across the boundaries of state and citizenship. Even if they attain citizenship in the country of destination, their national longing remains strongly directed towards their ethnic homeland. The ethnic loyalty of Albanian migrants from Macedonia is not restricted to their ethnic community in Macedonia but includes Albanians in Kosovo and Albania as well. Thus, to consider oneself Albanian in Austria or in Switzerland is to understand oneself as belonging to the Albanian ethno-cultural nation, which encompasses persons with different citizenships living in different states that might be far away from the imagined ethnic territory. As a consequence, Albanian migrants are part of a transterritorial ethno-national community which stretches across states and territories, but not national boundaries. The feeling of ethno-national belonging is certainly not all encompassing and varies according to generation, gender, personal experiences and the level of integration or exclusion in the respective host country. It furthermore depends on political developments in the country of origin.

Apart from this conceptual framework, I also need to discuss the concept of *home(land)*. The term *home* is often used in an unspecific and metaphorical way. Indeed *home* can acquire very different and sometimes even contradictory meanings. It can relate to a place, a landscape or a territory as well as to memories of a lost past or wishful imaginations of an ideal future. *Homeland* certainly has a more concrete meaning since it refers to a given territory and often designates the state or the imagined ethnic space. But this imagination is imbued with political and cultural elements and can thus not be understood simply as a geographical place. In my research, *home* and *homeland* were among the most frequently used terms in conversations and interviews with people from the villages. This is not really surprising given that their migratory experience challenges the idea of *home(land)* in a substantial way. But what makes it useful for my approach is the fact that the idea of *home(land)* evokes a powerful imagination. I argue along with Torgovinick that *home* belongs to the few remaining utopian ideals, which need not be replaced by more analytical terms like *ethnicity, nationality* or *loyalty*.[5]

In this context, the semantic affinity between *home* and *house* is meaningful. In English and German *home (Heim)* and *house (Haus)* are symbolically closely related, though *house*

4 Jasna Čapo Žmegač prefers the concept of *translocality* instead of *transnationalism* in her studies on Croat labour migrants in Munich (Čapo Žmegač, Dva lokaliteta). *Translocality* is certainly appropriate to denote border-crossing practices by contemporary migrants from the Balkans, but in my view *locality* is too confined a concept to understand the relationship that migrants have to their home(land). The *territorial* component, which refers to the idea of an ethnic space and its political significance, is of utmost importance in the analysis of Albanian migrants from Macedonia.

5 Torgovinick, Slasher Stories, 133.

also has a very concrete meaning in terms of its material presence. Figuratively though, house can serve as a metaphor for home. In Albanian the term for *house* is *shtëpi*. An older term is *vatër*, which in a figurative sense means *fireplace* or *stove*.[6] Both terms, *shtëpi* and *vatër*, can acquire broader meanings. They designate *family* and the (social) place to where one belongs. Phrases like *kthim në shtëpi* (homecoming) or *mall për shtëpi/vendlindje* (homesickness) give evidence of this. An older term for *Heimat* is the Turkish noun *vatan*, which originally meant *the place of ones birth*, a localised place like a town or a village. By the second half of the 19th century, however, the word *vatan* had acquired the meaning of *motherland*. The modern Albanian equivalent for *vatan* is *vendlindje*, literally meaning also *the place where one is born*. More abstract and political understandings of *Heimat* in Albanian are the terms *atdhe* (fatherland) and *mëmëdhe* (motherland). Although these Albanian terms are etymologically not directly linked with each other, there are close semantic relations which have broader cultural and even political meanings. These links are particularly striking if we turn our attention to the actor-oriented perspective of migrants. For them the representations of *house*, *household* and *home(land)* are related to their migratory experience, which in most of the cases intensifies their desire for a stable physical centre, a safe and quiet place to leave from and to return to. Under particular political and cultural circumstances, *house* might also become a metaphor for the state, an ideal representation within which space and time are structured in a functional way.[7] The coordination of its members, the distribution of authority and the relations between genders and generations might serve as ideal examples for the community as a whole. Both *home* and *house* imply cultural norms of inclusion and exclusion, which are relevant for political discourse as well as for the process of decision making.

Causes and consequences of ethnically divergent paths of development

If we look at the roots of the ethnically divergent development paths in the former Socialist Republic of Macedonia (SR of Macedonia), two main aspects become apparent.[8] Firstly, we have to acknowledge the ambitious socialist project to modernise a country that was marked by economic and social backwardness. Secondly, the new political leadership in Yu-

6 This traditional understanding of *house* derives from Albanian customary law. In order to be entitled with elementary rights, a family had to have a building with an operating fireplace. If rising smoke was visible from outside, this condition was fulfilled (Godin, Das albanische Gewohnheitsrecht, 8).

7 Rapport, Dawson, Migrants of Identity, 6.

8 The concept of path analysis, as developed by Stark and Bruszt, emphasises the fact that post-socialist transformation cannot be understood as a standardised model but follows very different paths according to the respective history, culture, politics and economic structures of individual countries and even ethnic communities (Stark, Bruszt, Postsocialist Pathways).

goslavia faced the challenge of designing a constitutional model that would counterbalance the national conflicts that had characterised the first Yugoslavia and had come to the fore during World War II. One part of the solution was the creation of a separate Macedonian Republic.[9] This new political entity was endowed with a number of institutions that were designed to develop the Macedonian nation.[10] The foundation of the Republic and the creation of a distinctive nation thus went hand in hand. The Albanians, by far the largest minority in the Republic[11], were recognised as a nationality (*narodnost*) and gained a number of cultural rights.

Among the first steps of socialist transformation was the campaign for agricultural collectivisation, which began in 1948–1949.[12] This initiative aimed at making agriculture more productive and to set people free for the ambitious industrialisation and modernisation of the country.[13] While many Macedonian peasants entered agricultural cooperatives, either forced or voluntarily, Albanians in their majority refused to participate in such schemes and continued to practice agriculture on a private and autonomous basis. They also tended to stay in their villages. Brunnbauer rightly concludes that in these early years of socialist transformation, the structural pattern of a specifically ethnic division of labour was being established.[14] This ethnic division of labour was further enhanced by the prevailing policies of Macedonian nation-building. In line with these policies, leading positions in state institutions, administration and government were predominantly filled with people who were supposed to define themselves as Macedonians. For the recruitment of industrial labour, clientelistic networks based on ethnic affiliation also played an important role.[15]

Apart from the fact that Albanians did not have equal opportunities to participate in the project of socialist modernisation, they were also less eager to become part of it. Along with

9 In the interwar period the territory of present day Macedonia belonged to Serbia and was exposed to ruthless Serbianisation.

10 Institutions like the Institute of National History and the Institute for Macedonian Language were responsible for the formation of a distinctive national history and the creation of a Macedonian literary language. The Macedonian Orthodox church, which was founded in 1958 and declared its autocephaly from the Serbian Orthodox Church in 1967, was also important for the formation of a Macedonian national identity; on the formation of Macedonian national consciousness see Brown, In The Realm; Brunnbauer, Nationalgeschichte; Troebst, Makedonische Antworten; Voss, Sprach- und Geschichtsrevision.

11 In 1948, out of 1,115,000 inhabitants of the SR of Macedonia, 190,665 had declared themselves as Albanians (17.1 %). The Macedonian share of the total population was 68.5 % (763,775). Divergent demographic trends had led to a relative decrease of the Macedonian share in relation to the Albanian minority. The latest census of 2002 gives a share of 64.2 % to the Macedonians compared with 25.2 % to the Albanians (State Statistical Office, Census of Population).

12 The collectivisation campaign lasted until 1952–1953. In 1953, the government allowed farmers to leave the newly created cooperatives, which most of them did. Private farmers would thus dominate Yugoslav agriculture, although limits on private farming property were kept in place.

13 Brunnbauer, Fertility, Families and Ethnic Conflict, 580–1.

14 Ibid., 582.

15 Sandevski, Die Entwicklung der interethnischen Beziehungen, 29.

this social reality and the accompanying attitude of those who were in power, there was a pronounced Albanian mistrust towards all sorts of state interventions. In part, this situation was a heritage of the interwar period,[16] but it was also the consequence of enduring anti-Albanian hostilities due to their alleged collaboration with the Italian and German occupiers during the Second World War.[17] Another important aspect, which contributed to the marginalisation of Albanians in the SR of Macedonia, was their low educational standards. Albanians had had no schooling in their mother tongue prior to World War II; therefore in the 1940s and 1950s their rate of illiteracy was still very high. In addition, their attitude towards the socialist educational system was fuelled with reservations and distrust. Parts of the Muslim clergy, who were influential among the Albanians, regarded schools as a hostile element that brought evil moral values.

The Muslim and patriarchal milieu which dominated in the Albanian villages in these first two decades after World War II, left little room for female emancipation. While Macedonian households were exposed to rural-urban migration, resulting also in the weakening of patriarchal values and the increase of female employment, Albanian households remained stuck in their rural milieu with relatively low educational standards and almost no female waged labour. Whereas Macedonians were exposed to a continuing process of national integration, Albanians were only marginally affected by this process. In view of this, Albanians and Macedonians developed different relations towards the institutions and the symbolic representations of the state. Whereas for Albanians social networks on the family, kinship and village level remained the pre-eminent source of loyalty and trust, these ties were gradually replaced by more abstract relationships towards the institutions of the state and the symbolic representation of the nation for Macedonians.[18]

In political affairs, Albanians in Macedonia always looked towards Kosovo. Kosovo was regarded as the national heartland of the Albanians in Yugoslavia and almost all Yugoslav Albanian intellectuals gained their academic degrees in Prishtinë/Priština, where a university with Albanian as the language of instruction was established in 1970.[19] The growth of

16 In the interwar period the Albanians in Yugoslavia were particularly exposed to a policy of marginalisation. At that time, a distinctive Albanian national consciousness seems to have been lacking among ordinary people in the countryside. Five hundred years of Ottoman rule had had a strong impact on the self-definition of people along denominational categories. But efforts by the Serbian administration to assimilate these Muslims speaking a non-Slavic idiom turned out to be rather hopeless. As a consequence, the authorities in Belgrade pursued a policy of marginalisation and attempted to force non-Slavic Muslims to leave the country (see Edvin Pezo in this volume).

17 Most Albanians had welcomed the Axis occupation during WWII, which brought them the union of the Albanian inhabited territories of Kosovo and western Macedonia with the Albanian state for the first time. This behaviour became a burden for the Albanians in early socialist Yugoslavia. The attitude of the Yugoslav government towards the Albanian population in Kosovo and Macedonia deteriorated further after the Stalin-Tito break in 1948, when Albania's communist leader Enver Hoxha decided to side with the Soviet Union.

18 Pichler, Makedonien im Dilemma.

19 Kostovicova, Kosovo, 42.

Albanian nationalism in Kosovo consequently had repercussions among the Macedonian Albanians. In 1968, when demonstrations in Kosovo called for the status of the autonomous province to be upgraded to republic, demonstrators in Tetovo/Tetovë in Macedonia demanded the inclusion of the Albanian inhabited areas of Macedonia into one single "Albanian republic" in Yugoslavia. Similar demands were expressed in 1981, both in Kosovo and among Albanians in Macedonia. Questioning the territorial integrity of the Macedonian Republic mobilised deeply rooted anxieties among the Macedonians. Such demands would have endangered the very existence of the Republic. The authorities thus reacted fiercely against rising Albanian nationalism. Apart from severe observation and persecution of 'nationalistic elements', the authorities aimed at counteracting the 'cultural alienation' among Albanians by intruding into their cultural spheres. A provision, which aimed at curbing the birth rate of Albanians by cutting down on free medical treatment and social security services for families with more than two children, was accompanied by a law that restricted the ongoing sale of land to Albanians.[20] In the area of Tetovo/Tetovë and Gostivar, the Macedonian police raised the walls of large Albanian farmsteads to the ground in order to get a better purview and control of the seemingly inscrutable family networks.

The independence of the Republic of Macedonia in 1991 and the transition to democracy and a market economy brought about a new constellation in the power struggle between Macedonians and Albanians. The Macedonians, heavily challenged in their national self-consciousness by their neighbours,[21] regarded themselves as the founders and the sole 'owners' of the new state. In their ethnically designed concept of the state, Albanians figured simply as one minority among others which would be provided with minority rights in line with the new constitution. But Macedonians regarded the definition of the state and its symbolic and material resources as a 'national property' of their own. Albanians, on the other hand, did not accept being treated as a national minority any longer. They estimated their share of the total population to be between 30–40 percent[22] and demanded a constitutional upgrading to the status of the second constitutive people of the country. They also complained about widespread discrimination at all levels of the administration and economy and about structural disadvantages in the educational system. On the political level, since 1991 every government had been comprised of at least one of the major Macedonian and Albanian parties, which many observers took as a sign of peaceful multiethnic coexistence.

20 Poulton, Who are the Macedonians?, 126–7.

21 The very existence of the Macedonian nation was challenged by its neighbours. Bulgaria did not recognise the Macedonian language and the existence of a separate nation, the Serb Orthodox Church refused to recognise the Macedonian Orthodox Church, and Greece voiced strong opposition against the name of the new state ("Republic of Macedonia") and its symbols.

22 These estimates are certainly exaggerated. The 2002 census seems to give the correct picture of the demographic situation in Macedonia. According to this census, 64.2 % of the total population was Macedonian and 25.2 % Albanian (State Statistical Office, Census of Population).

But this image concealed the deep-rooted social, cultural and economic cleavages between the two major ethnic communities in Macedonia.

What made these cleavages even more pronounced was the dire economic situation of the country. But the economic crisis, in general, hit the Macedonians harder than the Albanians. This was due to the fact that Albanians were only scarcely employed in the industries and in state administration. Macedonians, on the other hand, were exposed to rapidly increasing unemployment and to a dramatic devaluation of the currency. They experienced a sharp decrease in their living standards, whereas Albanians with their strong transterritorial networks and their ability to improvise, combined with their extensive degree of private entrepreneurship (including smuggling), were seemingly better prepared to handle these economic difficulties.

The façade of peaceful coexistence came down when in 2001, Albanian guerrillas calling themselves the *National Liberation Army* (NLA), and inspired by the 'success' of their counterparts in neighbouring Kosovo (*Kosovo Liberation Army*, KLA),[23] started to attack Macedonian security forces. In the course of this military confrontation the NLA occupied large areas in the northwestern part of the country. In their official statements, representatives of the NLA employed an irredentist rhetoric which claimed dominance over an imagined national territory. Whenever the NLA took control over a village with an Albanian population they declared the area "liberated territory".[24] The situation almost escalated to all-out civil war when NLA units advanced to a village only twenty kilometres away from the capital, Skopje. The rebels threatened to attack the capital and to shell the international airport and the nearby oil refinery. Macedonians in the capital were extremely concerned by this aggressive approach. Their fear was intensified by the fact that Skopje is almost entirely surrounded by Albanian villages. The tall minarets of the numerous new mosques are visible from a long distance. This situation was perceived as a kind of siege from which it seemed impossible to escape in case of attack.[25]

These developments illustrate how demography, culturally marked settlements and land ownership patterns gained enormous political significance during and after communism. The purchase of land, the construction of houses and the expansion of Albanian settlements, their continued population increase[26] and the seemingly isolated cultural development of Albanians, roused anxieties among the Macedonians. In a climate of rising nationalism, cultural differences mattered because of their proximate political impact. Furthermore, Macedonians did not see the high birth rate among Albanians primarily as a consequence of

[23] In fact these two paramilitary organisations were closely linked with each other and the NLA would not have come into existence without the KLA's support.

[24] British Helsinki Human Rights Group, Macedonia in Crisis.

[25] Risteski, Is the Macedonian Knot Becoming a Dog's Knot?, 48–9.

[26] As Brunnbauer points out, fertility was the most important reason for the increase in the Albanian population in Macedonia. In 1981, the number of live births per 1,000 inhabitants among Albanians amounted to 30.0 in comparison to 17.8 among Macedonians (Brunnbauer, Fertility, Families and Ethnic Conflict, 569–70).

belated modernisation, but as a political tool that aimed at shifting the majority-minority relationship by a continuous demographic growth. Under these circumstances, the countryside became a contested territory upon which divergent claims and imaginations of 'homeland' were projected. The urbanised Macedonian population has developed an ambivalent relationship towards the countryside. On the one hand, it represents for them backwardness and rural lifestyles, which they had left behind during socialism. On the other hand, the countryside relates to their origin, which is still alive in the memory of older people. At the same time, rural life gained appreciation during the turbulent years of transition, since it was related to the idea of a morally better world. These mythologised imaginations of a 'lost home(land)' were seriously challenged by the demographic and territorial expansion of the Albanians in the rural areas of the country. Keith Brown emphasises this aspect when he states that the Muslim Albanians "were perceived as occupying the physical and imagined territory of the countryside from which Macedonians left in the time of socialist Yugoslavia".[27]

The social and economic topography of Veleshtë

Picture 1 shows a typical view of a road in the village of Veleshtë in 1962. One can see basic elements of 'traditional' Muslim Albanian villages, which manifest cultural values, economic circumstances and political positions. The walls, which surround the residential buildings and farmsteads, indicated the significance of protection and security for the people. This can further be seen by the fact that only a few windows were directed towards the road. The strict seclusion of the private sphere was also inspired by the idea to keep women away from the male dominated public sphere.

The picture was taken at a time when agriculture was still the main source of income for the people of Veleshtë. According to the official government census for 1961, 80 percent of the male village population was engaged in agriculture. Another six percent of the males worked in the construction industry. Only five men (0.7 percent) had a job in administration and four (0.6 percent) practiced a trade. Twenty-two persons (3.2 percent) were registered as skilled workers at that time, among them only one woman. The women generally were registered as housewives. The social topography of the village was based on the division into several quarters (*mahallë*) where members of the same agnatic kin-group (*fis*) lived together. These quarters were relatively segregated from each other. There were no thoroughfares but many corners with dead ends.

The household was the main source of social status and economic maintenance. Structurally the households were complex, comprising at least two married couples under one roof. It was common practice that sons stayed together with their parents even after marriage. The women consequently moved into the household of their father-in-law upon mar-

[27] Brown, In the Realm, 125.

riage. In Veleshtë, village endogamy was (and still is) widespread. According to the census of 1961, more than 90 percent of the married women were born in Veleshtë. The remaining ten percent came from neighbouring Albanian villages. As has been confirmed in several interviews, the family and communal life at that time were based on a strictly patriarchal authority. The position of individual members within a household depended on their kin-relationship, their age and their gender; the males were generally privileged against the females and the older against the younger household members. Loyalty towards ones own household was regarded a primary duty of everyone. Further important elements of the complex patriarchal household have been its particular labour organisation and inheritance practice. The principle that every male member had to contribute the same share to the wellbeing of the household was constitutive for its economic organisation. This share was not calculated in terms of income, but in terms of individual work. It was irrelevant whether someone contributed his share as a student, shepherd or worker – the share always remained the same. The head of the household, usually the father, administered the property. In case the household was divided – either through the wishes of the father or after his death – all sons were entitled to the same share of the property. The daughters were excluded from the heritage of immobile property.

Another important feature of households was its size, which was considered an indication of its position within the community. The more children a family had the higher was its status. This ideology derived from older times when infant mortality was high, hygienic conditions bad, deceases difficult to treat and when life, in general, was insecure because the neighbour and the state were possible threats. Male offspring were given preference to female according to the patrilineal kinship ideology. This 'traditional' attitude did not change significantly until the 1960s due to the limited extent to which Albanian villages in Macedonia were exposed to the social and economic transformations of socialism. What did change, though, were the introduction of free medical treatment and the improvement of hygienic conditions, although many women from the village still preferred to give birth to their babies not in a hospital but at home with the help of a midwife. Nevertheless, the overall death rate and infant mortality decreased significantly, while birth rates remained high, so the village population grew rapidly. The population increased from 2,304 in 1953 to 2,728 in 1961, which amounted to an annual growth rate of 2.13 percent. By 2002, the village had more than doubled its population (5,834).[28] Looking at the average size of households, one can see striking differences between Veleshtë and the Macedonian Or-

[28] It is difficult to get exact numbers for the actual size of the village population. The census of 1991 was boycotted by the Albanians, who also consider the internationally monitored 1994 census as manipulated. According to the unofficial registration of the village population carried out by activists from the local municipality, Veleshtë had 6,015 inhabitants in 1991. In 2002 the mayor again pursued an unofficial census which included all those who lived abroad. According to this count, Veleshtë had 6,600 inhabitants. The official census of 2002 listed 5,834 inhabitants for the village (Kaso, Vendbanimet me Popullsi, 351).

Picture 1: Village road in Veleshtë, 1962. *Source:* Joel Halpern, Halpern Collection, Department for Southeast European History at the University of Graz.

thodox segment from the neighbouring village of Labuništa/Labunishtë.[29] In Veleshtë the average household size was 8.91 members in 1961, in Labuništa/Labunishte it was 5.75 members.[30] In the meantime the average household size has decreased considerably in Veleshtë as well. In 1994 there were 904 households registered in the village with an average size of 5.6 persons.[31]

When village people talk about the 1960s, they emphasise the scarcity of housing space as a consequence of the population increase. Concomitant household divisions reduced the average size of farmed land to such a degree that many families could no longer sustainably

[29] Labuništa/Labunishtë is a mixed village. In 1961 the population consisted of 2,345 Macedonian-speaking Muslims – so-called *Torbeši* – and 380 Orthodox Macedonians.

[30] All this statistical data derives from the US anthropologist Joel Halpern, who did field work in Veleshtë and in Labuništa/Labunishtë in 1961. Halpern, in addition to collecting demographic data, carried out a number of interviews with villagers and took a lot of photographs, which are, in view of the scarcity of visual representations from that time, an important source for a historical-anthropological analysis. The Department for Southeast European History in Graz owes Joel Halpern a lot since he put this and many other important source materials at the disposal of its researchers. The evaluation of the census data could not have been done without the support of Anna Hausmaninger and Siegfried Gruber.

[31] These data come from the local Statistical Office in Ohrid.

depend entirely on agriculture. The purchase of additional land – a widespread strategy among Albanian households – could not compensate for this trend. Not many non-farming jobs were established either: although Veleshtë was the largest village in the area, there were no factories established in the immediate vicinity. Macedonian villages, on the other hand, obtained this economic advantage. In Labuništa/Labunishtë, for example, two small factories were built at that time. The same happened in Vevčani/Vevçen and Vraništa/Vranishtë, two settlements close to Veleshtë with a Macedonian majority population. Two former Albanian officials, both members of the League of Communists of Yugoslavia, explained this uneven relationship by arguing that their voices had not had the required weight in the assemblies.

Two causes seem important for the structural discrimination of Albanians: firstly, Albanians were often regarded as politically disloyal. The widespread resistance of Albanians against the communist takeover of power and their previous siding with the occupying forces during World War II continued to influence Macedonian authorities. But more decisive, according to these two interlocutors, was that politics from the very beginning was ethnically biased and Albanians were underrepresented at all levels. That Veleshtë was economically neglected in comparison with neighbouring Macedonian villages was not the result of a political master plan designed from above. The reason for this was that its own political influence on the local scene was too weak. "They had their people in the first ranks, and they were powerful. We didn't have this position; we were underrepresented and not strong enough to push through our demands."

'They', who had power, certainly has also an ethnic angle but if one looks deeper into the complex issue of power relations, ethnicity emerges as not the only criteria important in decision-making processes. What was also relevant at that time was the power position of individual people within the relevant committees. There were also Macedonian settlements without powerful representatives, which therefore lacked the support of the authorities. Not every Macedonian village in the area was equipped with the desired economic infrastructure. The position of individual power brokers and their patron-client networks, which in most cases were also based on ethnic affiliation, certainly played an important part in these processes.[32]

Due to these circumstances, Veleshtë was only furnished with a police station, not a factory. All the policemen stationed there were ethnic Macedonians. The lack of investment in the village infrastructure was evident also in other areas. Although important improvements were reached at a not particularly late date in comparison to similar villages, people nevertheless complained about the way in which these projects had been financed and carried

[32] The strong political influence that charismatic personalities could wield in socialist Yugoslavia appears to have been a widespread phenomenon. Carolin Leutloff-Grandits, for example, in her thorough field study in the region of Knin, points out that the successful development of infrastructure in the village of Biskupija was dependent on the popularity and political influence of the village leader, who managed to generate funds for the village from the municipal council (Leutloff-Grandits, Claiming Ownership, 76).

out. When electricity was brought to rural areas in the early 1960s, people in the village were concerned about the fact that the power poles were made out of cheap wood instead of iron like in the neighbouring Orthodox Macedonian village of Vevčani. In 1964 a new school building replaced the old one which could no longer satisfy the required standards in terms of space and equipment. Since the investment from the state was only limited, villagers contributed to this initiative by providing timber for the roof of the new building. In 1971 a piped water system was built mostly with money from the village community. But this system, which still operates, was never fully operative. The same happened with the roads in the village, which were partly asphalted between 1981 and 1984.[33]

As a rule such sorts of investments were realised with the financial support of the local inhabitants. Every household had to contribute a certain sum for such projects, in money or even in kind. The better a village community was incorporated into the local economy and linked to the political institutions of the state, the more financial means it had at its disposal to invest in the improvement of the local infrastructure. A corollary was that the local authorities became more interested in sustaining the infrastructure of those villages that were economically significant. This was certainly not the case for Veleshtë. The village was disadvantaged in this respect and villagers feel that public investments were held back for political reasons. The local infrastructure in fact remained very poor in comparison to neighbouring Macedonian villages, which were better off in terms of the diversity of their economy and in maintaining external political ties. This was true even though other villages had a smaller population.

Migration from the village

Since the beginning of the 19th century western Macedonia – along with the western borderlands of Bulgaria, southeast Serbia, Kosovo/a, southern Albania and northern Greece – had been a centre of labour migration in the Balkans. At first migration was confined to the mountainous areas, but during the 19th century seasonal migration spread to the lowlands, partly as a consequence of population growth, partly due to the fact that labour migration guaranteed a good income.[34] As far as ethnographic sources indicate, Veleshtë was only marginally affected by 'traditional' forms of labour migration: there were only a few members from the village community who made their living as construction workers in different regions of Yugoslavia during the interwar period and after World War II.

It was only in the 1960s, when Yugoslavia concluded recruitment treaties with various Western European countries, which regulated the temporary employment of Yugoslav workers in these quickly expanding lands, that labour migration became a widespread

[33] Qyra, Veleshta në Histori, 244.
[34] Palairet, The Migrant Workers, 23–5.

phenomenon in the village.[35] Since access to a state job was difficult, Albanians were more likely than Macedonians to look for jobs abroad once the opportunity of international labour migration emerged. In the following two decades, the Albanian labour migrants from Yugoslavia were overwhelmingly male.[36] Most of them left with the intention of returning to their native villages. The main objective of migrants was to earn as much money as possible in order to support their families and to improve the living conditions at home. Due to the rapid increase in the village population, the creation of new living space was among the foremost needs of many families. Remittances were therefore invested in extending existing houses or in constructing new ones. Money from abroad was also used to modernise the village infrastructure. Today, migrants often credit themselves with important improvements in the living conditions in the village.

As Parnreiter rightly points out, first-generation labour migrants made a distinction between their economic and social identities. Socially they remained attached to their families and friends at home, whereby their stay abroad had only one purpose, to work and to earn money.[37] Despite their spatial distance they maintained their social ties with their families. Living conditions abroad were very bad. This was due to the fact that the hiring companies only offered substandard accommodation, and migrants who organised private accommodation tried to keep their expenses as low as possible in order to save money. Three or four men often lived in one room without a kitchen or shower. A large part of their income, either from regular or irregular work, was transferred back home. As long as the native household was kept together, which in the 1960s and 1970s was more or less the rule, the head of the household administered the money flowing in from abroad.

In the 1970s and 1980s more and more Albanian men followed their relatives and friends abroad. This was caused, on the one hand, by continued economic hardship in the rural areas of Macedonia. On the other hand, emigration for many young men became a powerful imagination of an alternative life. Migration to Western Europe spurred expectations of social upward mobility, but also expressed the longing for a different life style inspired by Western (youth) culture. However, migration became a frustrating experience for many of those who left the village at that time, since Western countries had imposed stops on the recruitment of foreign labour during the oil crisis of the 1970s; therefore, many new labour migrants ended up in the shadow economy and those who had come earlier faced

35 As a consequence, the number of Yugoslav migrant workers in Western Europe increased dramatically between 1965 and 1971, from 14,000 to 660,000 according to official counts. In 1974 and 1975 some 130,000 migrants returned to Yugoslavia due to the economic crisis in the West, but after this short interruption the number of migrants towards Western Europe increased again (Baučić, Regional Differences).

36 In the Yugoslav average, female labour migration played an important part. In the official 1971 count of Yugoslav workers abroad, approximately 31 % of the total were female (Baučić, Regional Differences, 220). Women migrants formed a much higher share of the total migration from the 'developed' regions in the north, while labour migration from the 'underdeveloped' southern parts of Yugoslavia was overwhelmingly male, especially in Kosovo.

37 Parnreiter, Theorien und Forschungsansätze, 26–8.

unemployment. On the other hand, returning to the village in the immediate future, which had been the initial intention of many a labour migrant, proved to be illusionary. Although the future, which had been filled with promises of progress, liberation and emancipation, was soon darkened by the experience of economic insecurity and displacement in the host countries, the flow of migrants towards the West continued.

In the beginning of the 1970s there were only few households left that were not directly affected by migration. The growing intensity of migration dramatically increased the dependency of the village on remittances. However, close transterritorial ties were not confined to economic matters but included social and cultural transfers as well. The destiny of a family, its wellbeing, its social relations and its self-image vis-à-vis the outside world were strongly affected by transterritorial migration networks. At the same time, alienation from the Macedonian state was intensified. Dissatisfaction about the impossibility of making a living at home, precarious employment abroad, difficult living conditions in a culturally alien environment, and ongoing separation from the family fuelled the conviction among Albanians that the political circumstances in Macedonia were deliberately designed to make them leave the country.

Those migrants who left the village in the late 1970s and in the 1980s certainly had other ideas and expectations of life than their fathers. They did not isolate themselves any longer to the same extent in the host society like their parent generation had done. They often met each other at public places, in restaurants, cafés, or bars. They read newspapers, listened to the radio and participated in political debates. Some of them came in contact with Albanian migrants from Kosovo, who were already much better co-ordinated and linked with each other. Kosovo Albanian migrants also had a more developed political consciousness; many of them were radicalised due to the escalating conflict in the aftermath of the suppressed demonstrations in Kosovo in 1981.[38]

Architecture, family and the imagination of home(land)

After 1981, the political situation for Albanians also worsened in the SR of Macedonia. Migrants were deeply concerned about the events that took place in their homeland and observed the political developments with great attention. But this period was also marked by changing migration patterns. In the framework of family reunion schemes more and more men took their wives and children with them and decided to settle permanently in the host country.[39] These decisions were based on social and economic considerations in view of the difficult conditions at home. However, the process of loosening physical ties

[38] On Kosovo Albanian transnationalism see Hockenos, Homeland Calling; Andrees, Die Kosovo-albanische Diaspora.

[39] Albanians, in this respect, were latecomers in comparison to Croats or Serbs. In 1973, among the total number of *Gastarbeiter* from Yugoslavia in Austria, 32.6 % were women (Parnreiter, Migration und Arbeitsteilung, 132–3).

went hand in hand with an imaginary rapprochement from afar. This was expressed, among other things, by the increasing investments that migrants made in the village infrastructure and in new private houses. Now, solidarity with the village community was often seen as a sort of political statement. The incentive to 'modernise' the home village was also spurred by the powerful stereotype voiced by ethnic Macedonians that Albanians were incapable of escaping from their own backwardness. Albanian migrants today argue with pride that their village has undergone a rapid transformation in the last 20 years, whereas Macedonian settlements have fallen apart. Local modernisation due to private engagement was inspired by the idea of political emancipation that would bring Albanians from a heavily disadvantaged into a privileged position. But this process did not lead to integration into the wider society since it was based primarily on the intensification of transterritorial networks.

The flourishing economic activities of the last fifteen years have drastically changed the outlook of the village. On the main road that connects the town of Struga/Strugë with Veleshtë, a whole new village quarter appeared. Among the new businesses which settled in *Veleshta e re* (New Veleshta) are two petrol stations, an ice-cream factory, a mill, a car garage, a building contractor, a wood-processing company, a motel and two big hotels. The most 'famous enterprise' is certainly Hotel Diplomat, which is shown in Picture 2. The hotel is well known in the area for its huge dimension and its expensive furnishing. It has thirty rooms and thirteen apartments with a total capacity of 96 beds. There are two big halls in the hotel, one in the basement and the other one on the first floor, which provide space for 900 people. The terrace is large as well and provides space for another 300 people.

A Macedonian bus driver, an elderly man some sixty years of age, with whom I passed the village on the way to Struga/Strugë, expressed his indignation to me: "How can it be that *they* build a hotel like this?! It certainly costs two million Euro!" "They worked a lot abroad", I answered. "No!" he replied, "you cannot earn so much money in a hundred years!" He himself, he explained to me, receives a salary of 200 Euro per month and with that has to provide for himself and his sick wife. The bus driver's point is common opinion among Macedonians: the economic upswing of the Albanians cannot possibly be based on hard labour only, but depends also on crime such as prostitution, smuggling and other sorts of illegal activities. Albanians, whom I confronted with this view, did not deny the fact that criminal elements were active among them. But they immediately pointed out that crime is certainly not confined to members of their ethnic community. The most horrible criminals, they argue, are to be found among the politicians ruling this country for the last sixty years. Needless to say, the majority among them are of ethnic Macedonian origin. Albanians furthermore criticise the way Macedonians form their views about them. "They look at us, as if we came from a different world, from a dangerous and uncivilised one! They stay apart and form their opinion. But they don't have any idea about the way we organise our life here and abroad."

The degree of ethnic separation is indeed remarkable. Out of all the Macedonians I met in Ohrid, a town 25 kilometres away from Veleshtë, not one of them has ever visited this place or any other Albanian inhabited village in the vicinity. Whenever I told Macedonians

Picture 2: Hotel Diplomat, *New Veleshta*, 2003. *Source:* Barbara Derler, Visual Archive Southeastern Europe at the Department for Southeast European History at the University of Graz.

that I regularly go to, and work in Veleshtë, where I stay with Albanians, they were amazed and sometimes estranged. My proficiency in Albanian, a language competence totally lacking among Macedonians, even made me a bit suspicious for some of them. The ethnic distance between the two communities certainly contributes to the flourishing of mutual prejudices.

These deeply rooted negative images aside, the number and size of hotels in *New Veleshta* really is astonishing. Picture 2 above was taken in 2003. In the meantime another big hotel has been built in the immediate vicinity. Two further motels with big restaurants already existed and a third one is currently under construction. Although private economic activities increased during the last fifteen years and Lake Ohrid, a well developed tourist resort, is only ten kilometres away, the room capacity of the hotels far exceeds the existing demand for accommodation. A major rationale for the local business boom of hotels and restaurants is related to a local tradition which has experienced rapid intensification since the end of socialism: if one travels in the region during July or August, one might easily witness one of the lavish wedding ceremonies that take place in these locations.[40] The wedding season starts at the beginning of July and lasts until mid-August. This is the time when migrants

40 This is a widespread phenomenon among transterritorial migrants from former Yugoslavia, but also from Turkey, who return to their places of origin for their summer holidays. In Herzegovina, for instance, one can find huge restaurants which are designed for the wedding ceremonies of migrants.

return to the village for their summer holidays. They come from Switzerland, Austria, Germany, Sweden and even the USA.[41] Although the social networks have virtually expanded into the world, the tendency towards village endogamy is still pronounced. This is particularly true for women. Among the men there have been reported cases of 'out-marriage', particularly of those who went abroad and lived there alone for several years.[42] But this has only happened during the last two decades. On the other hand, there are also cases of couples that come together in the village after years of absence in different countries in order to marry.[43] In recent years marriage has also become a means of obtaining a visa for those who stayed behind and can see no other opportunity of leaving the country legally. This is partly due to stricter Western immigration politics. As a result, the number of divorces shortly after marriage has increased considerably.

Village endogamy despite migration also has to be seen as a sign of a strong communal identity and the maintenance of tight relations between the migrants and their places of origin. It can furthermore be seen as a mechanism of ethnic solidarity which is closely linked to the recent political developments and ethnic conflict. Close kinship relations and village endogamy serve as a means to keep the community ethnically 'pure' and to strengthen ties of ethnic solidarity. Wedding ceremonies usually include processions of cars where the wealth of migrants is displayed by using luxury vehicles. Sometimes processions lead through areas inhabited by Macedonians. These processions are expressions of strong national self-confidence, with loud music, honking horns and waving of the Albanian national flag. The public space thus becomes a stage where social polarisation is expressed in ethnic categories. The village in this way remains an important place of memory (*lieu de memoir*) for people who live scattered throughout Europe for most of the year; the wedding ceremonies are rituals which signify origin, social affiliation and ethnic community.

Picture 3 displays a typical example of a newly constructed residential building which includes a store on the first floor. The building is situated on the main road in *New Veleshta*. It obviously gives evidence of economic advancement and the expectation of a flourishing

41 The greatest number of migrants from Veleshtë lives in Switzerland and in Austria. According to a count of migrants from the village, which was taken in 1999, almost 40 % stay in Switzerland and 26 % in Austria, 15 % in Germany and 13 % in the USA. 5 % settled in Sweden (Qyra, Veleshta në Histori, 217–33). I could not get the exact numbers for those who are currently living abroad, but a reasonable estimate would be 2,700 migrants. This would mean that 46 % of the inhabitants of the village according to the official census now live abroad.

42 Instances of men who married foreign women are often downplayed in conversations with villagers. People typically stress "we don't know a lot about them since they don't return to the village any longer". According to the local historian Zejnulla Qyra, who is a notorious defender of the national cause, such people are "lost for the community". The same holds true, according to Qyra, for those who left the village for the US because only a few of them return regularly to the village.

43 Such cases are rare but they indicate that the parental influence on marriage arrangements is still rather strong. In most of the cases, however, the choice of marriage partners depends on the young men and women themselves.

Picture 3: A new building in the business area *New Veleshta*, 2003. *Source:* Barbara Derler, Visual Archive Southeastern Europe at the Department for Southeast European History at the University of Graz.

future. In architectural style, the house differs from earlier constructions in many respects. The protruding balconies, the many windows and the use of expensive building materials refer to recently achieved wealth. Only a few elements are reminiscent of the former architecture. The walls around the plot have almost disappeared and the former secluded private space has been replaced by transparency. This building is designed to be visible for both the members of the same ethnic group as well as for 'the others' who pass along the main road on the way to Debar/Dibër or Struga/Strugë. At a closer look, however, it emerges that the new visibility is rather the product of a desire for and the imagination of a 'modern way of living' than an ethnic statement. The size of the building is still committed to the traditional concept of the co-residence of at least two nuclear families. However, this imagined ideal contradicts the reality, since the families of the two brothers, who are supposed to live in this house, have been living abroad for many years already. Only during a couple of weeks in summer, when they return for holidays, are the second and third floors of the house inhabited. The probability that the brothers will return for good and settle in the village is very small. Nevertheless, both of them have invested a lot of their money in the construc-

Picture 4: New buildings in the village, September 2007. *Source:* Robert Pichler.

tion of the house. This is not a singular case, but a more or less widespread pattern in the village.

An additional striking fact is that during the year, only the basements of many of these huge houses, which are situated directly on the main road, are inhabited. This is where those family members who remain in the village all year long or who have already returned live. In many cases these are elderly people who live together with one of their married sons, mostly the youngest. This can be regarded as a remnant of the old system, in which the youngest son was expected to stay with his father after the division of the household. People thus still stick to a relatively secluded way of living, so that no one from outside can have a view into their private sphere. The basement offers this sort of seclusion and, in a way, replaces the former walls around the property. Asked about the seemingly paradox situation of why they do not move into the upper parts of the house, people point out that there, in the basement, they feel safe and can keep up an informal way of private intimacy which remains out of the public view.

The majority of the buildings in the village have been constructed during the last twenty-five years. There is hardly a family that did not replace its older building with a new one. The older ones, however, are not the same, as can be seen in Picture 1 from 1962. These original buildings have been replaced with new ones in the course of the 'first building boom' in the late 1960s and 1970s. At that time, the need for more living space was pronounced due to rapid population increase. A good part of the money earned by labour migrants abroad was invested in the purchase of land and in the construction of new houses. In many cases the decision to build new houses went hand in hand with the dissolution of large multiple households.

Picture 5: Çashif Istrefi and his grandchildren in front of one of the houses he built in 1970, July 2007. *Source:* Robert Pichler.

Picture 6: The houses of three brothers, August 2007. *Source:* Robert Pichler.

The division of complex households, however, was not always followed by a complete shift in the structure of family authority, as illustrated by the story of Çashif Istrefi (see Picture 5). He left Veleshtë in 1968 for Austria to work there for three years. In 1971 he returned and helped build four new houses for himself and his brothers. His father administered the income of all family members and led the building project. Even after the split of the household the father remained the head of the separated families and disposed of their income. His youngest son stayed with him in the old house. Only after the father's death in 1982 was the household really separated into five parts. The dissolution was carried out by Çashif's grandmother Selvije, whose decision it was to split the household. In the following years Çashif built two more houses, one for his own family and the other for his grandson. He built his own house in 1992 with the money he had earned in Germany, where he had been working between 1973 and 2005. Since 2005 he has been living as an old-age pensioner in the village, where he wants to stay for the rest of his life. He still possesses a small apartment in a private residential building in the German city of Mainz. The house for his grandson is being built in the nearby town of Struga/Strugë. Çashif had purchased land there and built the house on his own initiative and mostly with his own hands. The construction is almost finished now. It is Çashif's idea that his grandson moves to Struga/Strugë as soon as he has his own family. There, so Çashif hopes, he will have better chances than in the village of finding an appropriate job. His grandson is 17 years old today, and Çashif assumes that he will get married in three or four years.

The principle that all male heirs receive exactly the same shares of property upon inheritance, which was typical for most parts of the Balkans and Eastern Europe,[44] is still cherished in the village. The construction of new houses, therefore, in many cases is supervised and directed by the elderly men, who pay attention that no heir is being disadvantaged. Given this practice, it might seem paradoxical that the construction boom set in at a time when the trend of whole families emigrating significantly increased. The solution lies in the fact that the same period was characterised by the return of many of those who had left the village in the 1960s. Many of the first generation labour migrants decided to return home at least temporarily after they had retired. It is often in their interest to build new houses. Many of them had worked, at least on the side, in the construction industry. With this experience and the financial means at their disposal, they can use their time to engage in construction work, which gives them self-esteem and respect in the family and the local community. Apart from this, investment in houses is regarded as a security that no one should be able to endanger.

During the time of migration the migrants had often remained in a vague position between home and abroad. Their longing was always directed towards a return, but the economic circumstances and the political conditions at home jeopardised or delayed their plans to come home. Now, after retirement, their wishes for so many years finally come true. The wish to return is not limited to their individual future but in their imagination at least, pertains to all the male family members. This can best be seen in the way many of the new houses are built. They are designed for two or even three single families. The separate floors are constructed as individual apartments with kitchens and bedrooms. More recent architectural solutions of this design are displayed in Picture 6: here, every son even gets his own house, which is built in an almost identical way close to the houses of his brothers.

The deeply rooted desire for familial reunion, as expressed in the architecture, does not match the social reality. People are aware of this discrepancy, as they too are aware of the social dynamics of current emigration, which will most certainly continue in the near future. The construction of large houses, therefore, appears as a compensation for the loss of family co-residence and as a reaction to social and political insecurity. The ideal of a co-residential household community corresponds with the desire to bring together all those members of the family, who live scattered in different places far away from home. The house represents a place that is economically, socially and morally structured, similar to the ideal imagination of home(land), where the security of a familiar social environment is provided. The visual (architectural) manifestation of this ideal evinces the efforts to undo social and cultural changes, which have already been on the way for some time and are seen as threatening the social ideals. There are certainly a number of critical voices among the younger generation, but the majority of them share the beliefs of their fathers and maintain the investment of huge amounts of money in the construction of houses. Houses, even when uninhabited,

44 See Kaser, Macht und Erbe.

are and will remain signifiers of strong symbolic relations between family, origin and ethnic community.

Conclusion

Ethnically divergent migration flows have shaped the different social, economic and cultural development paths of Macedonians and Albanians in the Republic of Macedonia. This contributed to the development of different relations towards the common state. Albanians regard themselves mainly as victims of a politics of ethnic discrimination and social marginalisation. Macedonians, on the other hand, believe that Albanians, by way of politics, violence and cultural alienation, strive towards the disintegration of the country. The ongoing purchase of land by Albanians, their population increase and the extension of settlements are seen by Macedonians as expressions of the insidious 'Albanisation' of Macedonian territory. Emerging contesting topographic imaginations of home(land) thus play an important part in the interethnic conflict in the Republic of Macedonia.

The case study of the Albanian village of Veleshtë sheds light on the way migration contributes to the construction and imagination of locality. Migrants are moving regularly between places and form a transterritorial ethnic network. The migrants are caught in an interdependent relationship between physical absence, imagined adherence and the longing for home. A number of means of communication and rituals enable mutual contact and create spaces where the criteria of belonging are continuously disputed. In view of the concern for the home(land), migrants emphasise the adherence to localised and coherent communities. The ongoing construction of houses can be understood as one of the most fundamental expressions that mark affiliation to what can be regarded as home(land). Houses represent an idealised model of the co-residential family and, at the same time, the privation of an often lifelong absence from home. But they also symbolise the emergence of a new national self-confidence which wants to be perceived and respected.

Aleksandra Pavićević

Death in a Foreign Land. Entering and Exiting the Serbian Emigrant's World

Introduction

The question of migration is primarily connected with historical and political-economic processes, and only to a lesser extent with the problems of identity, identity processes and strategies. Nevertheless, the development of emigrant institutions, their methods of organisation and networking, their choice of cultural and ethnic models, and symbols and self-definition patterns of emigrant populations have already been the focus of ethnological and anthropological research. In this paper I will concentrate on identity discourses, focusing on one particular life event to which very little or no space has been dedicated in existing studies: death. I first studied this phenomenon in the context of the Serbian diaspora in European and overseas countries. However, for this paper I also made a short review of relevant data connected with the autochthonous Serbian minority in Southeast European countries.

When I decided to study this theme, my expectations were based on existing data and the established assumption that life cycle customs are an important and multi-functional means for forming and expressing identity under the conditions of life as an emigrant due to their peculiar symbolism.[1] On the one hand they represent temporary marks of gathering and integration of kindred, ethnic or vernacular communities, and on the other hand they are a symbolic, but conditional way of separating from the majority population or other groups. I use the term *conditional* because the conduction of traditional customs in the diaspora presumes the simplification of 'own' traditional rituals, the adoption of traditions from the dominant cultural environment and the attendance of members of the 'outside' network of social contacts, recruited from the emigrants' different spheres of interest. In the case of death, which by its nature is certainly an event packed with symbolism, it was logical to expect that it would find particularly characteristic expressions in the life of the emigrant population.

On the other hand, again due to the special nature of the event, the material collected in the course of my research often led me to question whether the subject of death or the subject of migrant identity would dominate my work. This was caused by the fact that iden-

1 Pavlović, Životni ciklus i etnicitet, 88.

tity discourses are mainly inclined to collective rather than individual identity (regardless of their logical conditionality), whereas death rituals, perhaps more than any other custom within the life cycle, more frequently appear as an event in which individual identity takes precedence over the social one. Of course, I do not mean that the community is excluded from this event, but in the context of this paper and the study of migration, the question arises of whether death is *ethnic* enough: is it revealed as a relevant element of ethnicity, which by definition is linked with the collective group identity?[2] I was relatively encouraged by what I found in Eriksen's work, which, summarising different observations concerning ethnicity, quotes Ebner Cohen, who states that ethnicity can be observed not just as a characteristic of inter-ethnic relations, but as a distinctive mark of inter-group relations as a whole, regardless of the nature of the group.[3] It would therefore follow that ethnicity can be seen as one characteristic of interpersonal relations, which includes both situational and common human determinations.

Therefore, when I began to write this paper, I was still not sure where it would lead me, or how I would succeed in answering the questions raised. I will attempt to show, through various examples, the role that both the event and the understanding of death occupy in the identity practice of the Serbian emigrant population, or ways, if any, in which death is 'used' as an important mark of ethnic identity.

Funeral places, epitaphs and obituaries

Although it would be logical to consider it at the last, the first association that actually came to mind in relation to death was cemeteries and gravestones – physical markers of space with symbolic messages aiming to 'overcome time'. Are Serbian emigrants buried in special cemeteries (in national-confessional ones or those reserved for foreigners) or in public burial sites of eternal rest? Do the epitaphs on their graves testify to vital indications of their identity and the identity of the community? The answer to my first question varies according to the organisation and size of the emigrant group and the time of their arrival. However, the nonexistence/existence of specially allocated cemeteries often discloses elements of the relation between the two groups, i.e. the relations between the natives of the host country and the immigrants. The question of whether feelings of mystic fear or matters of a political and economic nature predominate in this relation, often influences the issue of graveyards.

Of course, burial in special cemeteries or in special plots within public cemeteries is primarily characteristic of earlier stages of Serbian emigration to transoceanic countries, especially the United States. One of the first such cemeteries was a plot in Montrose Cemetery in Chicago, obtained for the needs of deceased Serbian emigrants in 1905 and initiated by the United Serbian Society. In 1981 they built a memorial stone on the site to all

2 Eriksen, Etnicitet i nacionalizam.

3 Ibid., 97.

their former members "who have gone to the Great Beyond".[4] In Chicago there is also a cemetery next to the New Gračanica monastery, in which, judging by newspaper obituaries, only prominent members of the Serbian emigrant population are buried. Bearing in mind that the Montrose site was essentially intended for the burial of United Serbian Society members, it is easy to conclude that death is often used for the internal hierarchy of Serbian emigrant communities. I should also mention that there are Serbian cemeteries in California – Jackson, San Francisco and Los Angeles – and Minnesota.

The older gravestones in all these sites, dating from the first half of the 20th century, are characterised by biographical entries of the deceased, e. g. place of birth, origin, and profession.[5] Cyrillic inscriptions predominate, although it is possible to find different examples, especially in family graves where one spouse was of a different nationality. After the Second World War the situation changed: biographical details are reduced, Cyrillic inscriptions become rarer, and the Serbian consonants 'č' and 'ć' are reduced to 'c' or 'ch'. On memorial stones built from the 1970s onwards, there is a tendency to write sentimental, emotional texts and to use religious terminology. In connection with these cemeteries, one interesting question arises: judging by data from Serbian church records and from cemetery sites, it appears that among the first generations of Serbian emigrants a large number were without family, or had left them behind in their native country. It becomes evident that epitaphs on stones in which the origin of the deceased is inscribed, were not directed towards his/her descendants but towards 'others'. They represent the confirmation of the deceased's unique emigrant identity, established through his/her life among 'strangers'.

Regarding Western European countries, I am only familiar with the situation in France. In the Thiais cemetery in Paris there are three plots for the burial of Serbs: two are for Serbian emigrants, while the third is for Serbian soldiers, who died in French hospitals in the First World War. Due to the limitation of available space and the uniqueness of new waves of emigrants (about which I will write later), the deceased have been buried in public cemeteries for the last few decades, their location dependant on the administrative district in which the deceased had lived.

The results of research into Serbian grave stone inscriptions in Southeastern Europe reveal interesting variations and divergences from the examples above, although in most of these cases emigrants, in the classical sense, are not an issue. Thus, epitaphs on gravestones in Serbian cemeteries in Hungary show the same manner of transformation as those in America: over time, Cyrillic inscriptions, along with the Serbian names and language are lost, and there are family tombs on which the names of spouses with different nationality are inscribed in a different alphabet.[6] However, during the last fifty years many Serbian cemeteries have been abolished in Hungary.[7] Here is not the place to discuss the motives and reasons for this development, but we should bear in mind the role which cemeteries are

4 United Serbian Society, 100th Anniversary, 21.

5 Drljača, Svedenost imigrantske potkulture Srba u SAD, 45; Pavlović, Srbi u Čikagu, 78.

6 Drljača, Groblja Srba u dijaspori, 70.

7 Lastić, O položaju Srba u Mađarskoj, 226.

given in constructing the historical memory of a people or nation. See for example the case of Albania, where in 1950, after Albania's break with Yugoslavia, the government ordered the demolition of the cemeteries of Serbian and Montenegrin soldiers killed in battles with the Ottomans, as well as the cemetery of the Serbian minority in the area of Shkodra.[8] Something similar occurred in Greece, where the mortal remains of Serbian soldiers buried along the Thessalonica Front of World War One were collected and laid in one place, the well-known cemetery of Zejtinlik.[9] The case of Slovenia is especially indicative for our topic, where members of the Serbian population still do not have their own burial site, regardless of their existence in large numbers there for many decades.[10] As long ago as 1921, the Ljubljana city council had received a request for a site to bury Orthodox Christians, but such an institution still does not exist. From the chronicles of the Orthodox Church of the Ljubljana municipality, it appears that until 1941, when the chronicle was closed, Serbs were buried either in public cemeteries or in sections of those cemeteries reserved for those of "*other*" faiths.[11] Today, according to the Serbian Orthodox Church parish priest there, all Serbs are buried in public cemeteries, and epitaphs do not include significant identifiers of ethnic origin.

Members of the most recent generation of Serbian emigrants to Greece, Slovenia or Cyprus do not show great interest in what will be inscribed on their gravestones, which will in any event be found in a cemetery outside the 'homeland'. This is undoubtedly related to the fact that the emigration only consists of young people, who do not think yet about their own death. At the same time, it reveals the specific identity crisis which characterises the emigrants that left from different parts of former Yugoslavia during the last decades of the 20th century. Thus, some of them feel that their name on a gravestone will be a sufficiently eloquent sign of their identity, while the attitude of others can be summarised by the announcement of a Serbian lady who, in 1995, moved from Belgrade to Cyprus: "This is how I imagine my epitaph: ZB, without faith, without homeland. She enjoyed life and others enjoyed it with her."

Questions concerning the burial place of the dead and the symbolism by which their identity is expressed lead to the further question – which is perhaps even more important – of the role that death plays in the identity of the living. What are the wishes of Serbian emigrants when choosing a burial place? In which ways are they testifying to both their symbolic and actual belonging? Where and how are those who await death in a 'strange land' buried?

The majority of migrations from Yugoslavia and Serbia during the 20th century were economically conditioned and these migrations were intended to be of a temporary nature, at least in the mind of the emigrants. This resulted in the fact that the identity of the emigrants became transnational – they practically lived their whole life in two cultures,

[8] Vlahović, Srpska i crnogorska manjina, 121, 126.

[9] Blagojević, Srbi u Grčkoj.

[10] Pavićević, Dva primera srpske emigracije.

[11] Majković, Letopis srpske crkvene opštine, 32.

'both here and there' or 'neither here nor there'. In most cases, an 'outer network' of social relations was developed only as much as was necessary, i.e. as much as the institutions of the host countries became functional in the everyday life of the immigrants. The 'inner network' of social relations was developed as a network of solidarity, but also as a symbolic presence of the homeland community, which was actualised on special occasions and fulfilled the special needs of its members. However, everyday conduct was either restricted to the strict family circle or to the solitary individual, whose life was generally characterised by the routine drudgery of work and aimed at accumulating savings. 'Real life' was reserved for short visits home.

This context explains the fact that most of the emigrants express their wish to be buried in their 'old country'. Fulfilment of such a wish depends on many parameters, above all economical ones, but also on the distance from home. Another important factor is the extent to which social networks are developed in the country of residence. Bearing these reasons in mind the desire to finally return home in the case of overseas emigrants was more part of the emigrants' rhetoric than their realistic expectation that it was going to happen. Research thus established that there were not many emigrants who left their last will and the necessary money for the realisation of their 'last trip'. If, however, the wish to be buried in the homeland is explicit, the solution is to cremate the remains, because in this case, travel is much easer and cheaper. However, this practice is not very common among the Serbian population.[12] But although Serbian emigrants are most often buried abroad, their final transition from the social community of the host country to their native community and vice versa might also happen on a symbolical level.[13] A case in point is a funeral oration held at a burial in Chicago, where it was said that "the soul of our dear and respected N.N. goes to the Serbian heaven, while his body rests in this hospitable American land".[14] According to Dunja Rihtman-Auguštin, the traces of such final transitions might also be found in newspaper death notices, which, emphasising the deceased's homeland, actually confirm his/her final leaving (the homeland) or return, if the deceased is buried in the place where s/he was born.[15]

However, there are cases when the deceased was buried in his/her birthplace regardless of the fact that there were no remaining kin there and that all the members of his or her immediate family (first, second, and even third generation of his/her descendants) were in a state of 'irreversible' acculturation in the country of destination where their parents had sought a better life many years before. The reason for such a choice is again related to the specific attitudes toward graves in their homeland, in which some other close family members are already buried. Thus, *Glas kanadskih Srba* ("The Canadian Serbs' Voice") informed its readers in July, 2004, of the death of D.P., born in 1912, whose body would

12 Blagojević, Srbi u Kalifornii, 188.

13 Krstanović-Lukić, Srbi u Kanadi, 187.

14 Pavlović, Životni ciklus i etnicitet, 88.

15 Rihtman-Auguštin, Etnologija naše svakodnevice, 180.

be transported to her native Herzegovina, to the village of Bjelač, where she will rest next to her early deceased husband.[16]

The situation for Serbian emigrants in West European countries is very different: the dead are more often buried in their native country, and there is also an institutional network to support such a practice. In the *Pariski poslovni podsetnik* ("Parisian Business Reminder"), a pocket book with telephones and addresses of various services that Serbian people might receive from their compatriots, as well as of the institutions that they most often use abroad, for example, we find several advertisements for funeral services which carry out the very complicated procedure of transporting the dead to Serbia, or to some of the other former Yugoslav republics. The following entry is an eloquent example:

> *Our only official authorised carrier, Mr. Žika Krstić, organises all formalities, facilities and transportation of the deceased to his eternal home. We are well acquainted with routes, people and customs. Žika Krstić is the fastest, the most efficient and the most economical carrier. Up to five accompanists and all luggage as well as all possibilities with regards to payment are possible.*[17]

However, the head of the Serbian Orthodox Church in Paris states that although everybody wants to be buried 'at home', it rarely actually happens. This is confirmed by the Internet newspaper *Srpska dijaspora* ("Serbian Diaspora") although its *In Memoriam* entries also reveal many who speak about burial in the homeland.[18] Sometimes magnificent graves wait for the deceased representing real monuments of their social reputation and 'success' achieved abroad.[19] This practice was particularly characteristic for emigrants who left Serbian villages for West European countries during the 1970s and 1980s.

According to parish priest of the Serbian Orthodox Church in Ljubljana, the choice of funeral venue is becoming increasingly more dependant on more rational considerations and attitudes to life and less on the unconditional 'adoration of the homeland'. He mentioned a case from the 1980s, in which it had been so expensive to transport a corpse from Slovenia to Bosnia-Herzegovina that a Serb from Banja Luka, the son of the deceased, decided to transport his dead father in his own car, disguised as a living-yet-sleeping passenger. "He put a hat on his head, while two others propped him up and thus they travelled to their final destination. But that was possible during the times when there were no borders between republics." In the last ten years, deceased Serbs have been transported less and less from Slovenia as a result of the extraordinarily high prices for the transportation of corpses, but also because the content of what 'homeland' used to be has changed with the political events and the war of the last two decades in the territory of the former Yugoslavia.

The process of homeland demystification is particularly evident in the representatives of the new wave of Serbian emigrants, mostly for the above reasons, but also due to the

16 *Glas kanadskih Srba*, 29 July 2004, 15.

17 Pariski poslovni podsetnik, 53.

18 *Srpska dijaspora*, 19 March 2004; 11 August 2002; 25 August 2002, see: <http://www.srpskadijaspora.info/vest.asp?id=4512>, last accessed: 24 October 2006.

19 Rihtman-Auguštin, Etnologija naše svakodevice, 163.

profile of this emigrant population. Nevertheless, out of the forty informants in Greece, in particular in Athens, who answered my question about the place where they would like to be buried, seventeen of them expressed their wish to be buried "at home". Ten claimed that they had not thought about this question, the same number wanted to be cremated (two of them expressing the wish that their dust be thrown into the sea), two responded that they would not die, and only one of them answered that his eternal home would be in Greece. Ten subjects from my survey – all Serbs living in Cyprus – did not take issue with the question. Although most of the responses reveal that many emigrants are inclined to 'return' to the homeland – no matter whether they would like to stand on their homeland soil or be covered by it – more than half of them did not use the terms *home, homeland*, or *old country*. The attitude that these emigrants have towards the question of 'home' is most concisely expressed in the answer of a young Serb from Bosnia-Herzegovina, who had moved to Greece after spending several years in Belgrade as a refugee: "Home?! What does home mean now? I cannot be buried at home any more... Home no longer exists."

It is interesting to also mention other ways, apart from graves, of 'investing in death' or 'for the soul', such as memorials, donations and church-building in the homeland, which carry a double message: one refers to the already mentioned double identity of emigrants, and the investment in graves or any other investment back home might be interpreted as a method of keeping certain positions in the social network and social relations back in the homeland. On the other hand, concerning the fact that such investments are often seen as a way of keeping the name of the investor or his/her kin from falling into oblivion, they might represent an attempt to symbolically bridge the gap between individual temporariness and the continuity of the social community, which represents a common human need and overcomes the classical subject of ethnicity studies. Such phenomena were characteristic for all generations of Serbian emigrants and are not related to and dependent on the country to which they emigrated. Thus a certain Tripo Runjevac, who died in the U.S. in 1944, built a monument devoted to his ancestors in 1912, 32 years before his death, in Petrovo polje, Herzegovina. Information about this kind of memorial represents an inevitable part of *In Memoriam* entries, for example one from the Canadian journal *Jedinstvo* ("Unity"), which, speaking about one of the deceased, gives information about the many donations he had made to different institutions in the homeland in memory of the dead.[20] Also the newspaper *Srpska dijaspora*, reporting about the death of a Serbian priest in Stuttgart, informs the readers that he built a church in Ljuljevci near the town of Gruža, which he devoted to St. John the Precursor.[21] Similar examples can even be found among the representatives of the latest Serbian emigration, as illustrated by a very successful sports coach with residence in Athens who sees the "crown" of his life in the building of a church in the Serbian town from which he comes.

20 *Jedinstvo*, 3 September 1971, 2.

21 *Srpska dijaspora*, 19 March 2004.

In Memoriam, *funerals and mourning*

The event of death, with its various associated customs, is far less marked by ethnic symbols than one would expect. Expressions of the ethnic belonging of the deceased are present above all in the different ways of announcing the death, especially *In Memoriam* texts, which are published in the press or on the Internet. Such articles are used by the members of a community to say farewell to the honoured deceased, while in the case of 'ordinary people' a public farewell is rare. These entries have more or less the same structure, and contain a notice of death, a short description of any illness suffered and finally a longer biography of the dead. The last states his/her birthplace, the year of and the reasons for emigration, and his/her merits in the expatriate community. The obituaries also state whom the deceased has left behind and give their names – usually renowned members of the community who were pall bearers at the funeral and made funeral addresses. Texts which announce the death of male members of the community characteristically emphasise their engagement in the foundation of their national associations or their achievements in the 'outer' social world.[22] Announcements of the death of honoured women typically praise their activities in charitable deeds directed towards the homeland, as well as their firm attitude in raising their own children in a national and patriotic spirit.[23] We often see women described as "the epitome of a Serbian wife and mother". Most of them gave birth to more than two or even three children. Apart from this, it is important to mention that the obituaries of deceased women present them, apart from their own biographic data, as the wife of an "honoured Serb".[24] Hence, these entries offer enough material for research into the gender dimensions of our topic.

In Memoriam texts as well as funeral speeches also represent important sources for learning about the political attitudes of the diaspora members. However, this particular topic exceeds the frame of this article and will therefore only be mentioned briefly. The identity strategies of Serbian emigrants have been changing during the last thirty years and are thoroughly connected to the political discourses and events in their home country. *In Memoriam* entries published in the *Jugoslovensko-kanadski tjednik* ("Yugoslav-Canadian Weekly") during the 1960s and 1970s are thus characteristic for not mentioning the nationality of the deceased. Only surnames or birthplaces gave possible hints as to which of the constitutive nations and nationalities of Yugoslavia the deceased belonged. Apart from this, these texts often emphasised the proletarian or communist attitudes of the dead. Such is, for example, the notice of death of M.S. in 1968, whose funeral was held "in a way which is appropriate for workers, without any church ceremonies".[25] In contrast to this, since the year 2000, the periodicals "The Canadian Serbs' Voice" and "Serbian Diaspora" have often published farewells from the community for the deceased, who were described as an "uncompro-

22 Examples in *Jedinstvo*, 19 April 1968, 2; *Srpska dijaspora*, 1 August 2002; 25 May 2002.

23 *Srpska dijaspora*, 24 August 2003; 19 March 2002.

24 E.g. *Glas Kanadskih Srba*, 30 January 2004, 14.

25 *Jedinstvo*, 19 April 1968, 2.

mising fighter for freedom from communist ideology", a "Serbian national fighter" and "Chetniks".[26]

Newspaper obituaries in the classical sense are hardly present in the newspapers of the diaspora. Where they occur, they often include only a eulogy or words of sadness, without any additional information (e. g. the birthplace of the deceased). This may stem from the fact that such newspapers are only published occasionally, so cannot be used as a method of informing friends and relatives about a death. The absence of death notices in these periodicals might be also interpreted as an indicator of the role that death plays in the wider, but still 'inner' community, where it does not appear as a relevant source of ethnicity. On the other hand, concerning the fact that information about the death of community members is usually given orally, death notices appear as a mechanism for the confirmation of the unity of the immediate group.[27]

As mentioned previously, the customs of emigrants are usually reduced to the basic tenets of the traditional practice and ritual, representing a mixture of old habits and those acquired and adopted in the new surroundings. Mirjana Pavlović maintains that customs related to death are the only ones that succeeded in maintaining their traditional form.[28] However, the analysis of my sources points to different conclusions, namely that the perseverance of the traditional ritual form, which underlines the more or less logical and only possible sequence of the ritual stages concerning the farewell to the dead (announcement, preparing the corpse, funeral, mourning), is not transferred in its content and even less in its meaning. Even in the sequence of the stages mentioned we might notice an obvious tendency to professionalise them as well as to shorten them (especially as regards the preparation of the dead and the time spent in mourning). However, it is clear that such a tendency is not exclusive to life in the diaspora but rather represents a common tendency in modern societies. Today, the preparation of the corpse is usually done in some funeral institution. *Srpska Diaspora* informs us that there is a Serbian funeral service even in Chicago, bearing the symbolic name *Sveta gora*.[29] Research among Serbian emigrants in California revealed that the local way of preparing burials for the deceased are often mentioned as the reason why people express the wish to be taken home or even cremated, because the deceased is subjected first to blood extraction and then to beautifying treatments, which makes the corpse apparently look better and younger than s/he did in life. Before condolences are conveyed to the family, the visitors pay the deceased compliments for the way he/she looks.[30]

The ethnic composition of the people present at a funeral testifies to the complex outer and inner social networks. According to the Serbian priests from Paris and Ljubljana, the specificity of certain customs often makes the representatives of 'outside groups' confused.

26 *Glas kanadskih Srba*, 29 May 2003, 14; 28 August 2003, 14; 30 October 2003, 14; *Srpska dijaspora*, 19 February 2005.

27 Pavlović, Srbi u Čikagu, 77.

28 Pavlović, Životni ciklus i etnicitet, 85.

29 "Mount Athos", *Srpska dijaspora*, 25 May 2002.

30 Blagojević, Srbi u Kalifornii, 187.

My respondents believe that this is the reason why families do not bring food and drinks to the grave, especially in Slovenia. Concerning overseas countries, this custom is even forbidden by administrative regulations. Therefore, wheat, *rakija* (brandy), bread and honey are usually served in the parish house, the Serbian club or restaurant, or, very rarely, in the place where the deceased lived. In recent years, the Serbian Orthodox Church has been inevitably present at funerals, functioning as the only stable and, at the same time, very important ethnic marker.[31] This includes performing the requiems – one in the chapel in which the deceased is exposed, the other at the grave. Apart from this, according to the protocol of St. Sava Church in St. Gabriel, California, it seems that the number of those who took communion on their deathbed increased during the 1980s.[32] In addition to this, the family stays awake the whole night and, similar to the custom still existent in Serbian villages, the deceased is exposed in an open coffin. 'Compatriots' who come to express their condolences often leave by the deceased something that he/she used to like – cigarettes, lighters, money, golf balls, beer cans and similar things.

It has been suggested that Slovenia is where such matters are the most difficult to organise, particularly in relation to the processional stages of the funeral. According to the administrative procedure of that country, it is obligatory to display the state flag of Slovenia during the funeral. Hoisting the national flag is also permitted. The priest from the Serbian Church in Ljubljana mentions that the Serbian flag has only appeared twice during the last twenty years at a funeral. On the other hand, the number of people wanting to be buried with an Orthodox funeral service is increasing, as well as the number of those wanting to be cremated. The funerals of atheists are often accompanied by Catholic priests, who are on duty at the cemetery and who conduct the funeral oration as a matter of course. There are also funerals at which priests of both Churches are present. In this case, the service is carried out by the Orthodox priest, while the Catholic one is just present. My informants mentioned that "the customs of the old region" were not carried out because it was "not necessary", or "in order to avoid confusion", and "because of children", who are obviously assimilated in the local culture and for whom the emphasis of any difference might appear problematic.

The period of mourning is the same for all regions researched – commemorations of the death are repeated after forty days, half a year and one year. This includes going to the grave, but without practising the traditional custom of bringing food and drink – wheat, round bread and *rakija*. All Souls' Day does not appear to be an important occasion for gatherings in overseas countries. The data from California suggest that not many people visit graves on this day. Those who do are usually older women, who keep the gravestone clean.[33] In France, however, the All Souls' Day of *Mitrovdan* (just before the day of St. Dimitrios, 8 November) appears as a day of mass gatherings in the Serbian community. In 2006, the Serbian Orthodox Church service in Paris on that day gathered around 2,000 people. It is

[31] Pavlović, Životni ciklus i etnicitet, 85.

[32] Blagojević, Srbi u Kalifornii, 186.

[33] Ibid., 189.

interesting that at funerals of Serbian emigrants in Paris, food appears at the grave, and most of the funerals are held with the participation of the Church.

Concerning wearing black and other markers of mourning, I only have information for Serbian emigrants in the U.S., in particular in California and Chicago. In these places, only the elderly women wear black, usually for forty days or half a year after the death of the deceased. Younger people only wear black, if at all, on the day of the funeral itself. The custom of isolating the family and temporarily breaking relations with the outer world, as well as not using TV, radio and music devices for a certain time, was, among the groups studied, only observed by one family from Herzegovina that lives in San Gabriel.[34]

Empty grave

Finally, I want to raise the question of how the community in the homeland perceives the death of its members abroad. The phenomenon of the so-called "*jabadžinski* grave", which has been recorded in traditional migrant worker places in Bulgaria, led me to such a question.[35] *Jabadžinski* grave means a collective grave for all migrant workers who died and were buried abroad. It is the place to which the family in the homeland comes to symbolically see off their dead, performing customs and rituals usual at a funeral. In Serbia, as well as all in other regions of the former Yugoslavia, we come across the phenomenon of the 'empty grave', which is reminiscent of the traditional Bulgarian custom mentioned above. Empty grave represents the place where the community symbolically buries all those who die far from their home.[36] In this way, the double identity of the emigrant is not only confirmed and transferred to eternity, but it becomes clear that the whole community – both the part that lives abroad, as well as those who stayed in the country – bears traits of symbolic dislocation in time and space.

In this extremely symbolic world, death abroad appears to also be a very convenient instrument for the (contemporary) political strategies of different groups in the homeland which, using mythological assumptions about the 'holiness of exile', try to confirm their own role as well as to sanctify that of the deceased. The most striking recent example for such a usage of death was when Slobodan Milošević died in the prison of the Hague Tribunal. This event served as the occasion for various political claims from parts of the Serbian diaspora, which found their place in the diaspora periodical *Srpska dijaspora.* From the day on which his death was announced, to the day of his funeral, articles were published which

[34] Ibid., 189.

[35] I express my gratitude to Petko Hristov from the Institute of Ethnography and Museum at the Bulgarian Academy of Sciences for providing me with this information.

[36] Kulišic, Petrović, Pantelić, Srpski mitološki rečnik, 139; Jovanović, Magija srpskih obreda, 211.

alluded to innocent suffering on an epic scale, discrimination and unjust stigmatisation.[37] Similar motives can be found in the discussion on the transfer to Serbia of the mortal remains of King Peter II Karađorđević as well as of other members of the royal family, who rest in peace in England and Scotland.[38] Although these cases are not related to migrant strategies of identification – the subject of this paper – I mention them as other revealing examples of the significance of death abroad.

Conclusions

In order to answer the questions posed at the beginning of this article and considering the empirical material just exposed, it is necessary to regard the phenomenon of death and its meaning in the life of emigrants on several levels: the individual; the closest circle of the social network, which consists of the family and the closest kin of the deceased; the wider circles of the inner social network, which includes the so-called 'patriotic community' (wider circle of friends, acquaintances, people from the same village, region and republic, politically like-minded persons, etc.); the outer social network, which is made up of all those people who are not included in the circles that I have just mentioned, but are directly related to the individual and his/her family.

Concerning the individual level, we have seen that death confirms a person's double identity. It often gives it a lasting, almost eschatological character. Facing death might also lead to a final decision about the choice between belonging to the emigrant community or the home country, either in a real or symbolical way. This also refers to the identity of the closest people who surrounded the deceased, because, as we have seen, the characteristics of double identity are transferred from the individual to the community – those who lived with the deceased and those who were left in the homeland.

On the next level of the closest social circle of the deceased, death has an integrative role both in the immediate emigrant surroundings and among relatives in the home country. The customs, which the family of the deceased obeys as emigrants, express and confirm their ethnic identity, but only to a certain extent. These manifest and confirm their belonging to the wider circles of the inner network, which on the other hand also affects the reduction of the ritual, because it does not represent the measure of differentiation between and within the groups. It is possible to say that in such a context, the role of death in the social structure hierarchy of the wider internal network is more important.

Concerning the place and identity of the group in the outer social surroundings, the importance of the event of death and the rituals that follow as an ethnic marker are limited and conditioned by the type, measure and extent of dependence and involvement of the

[37] Dimitrijević, O sudbini srpskih vladara. See also *Srpska dijaspora*, 11 March 2006; 19 March 2006; 22 March 2006.

[38] *Srpska dijaspora*, 15 March 2004; 11 September 2003.

deceased in the outer network of social relations. Therefore, the stronger and deeper these bonds, the lesser 'ethnicity' is contained in the farewell and funeral customs. This has caused a simplification of emigrants' customs.

It is possible to conclude that the attitudes and behaviour related to death, as well as death itself, represent important sources of the personal, individual identities of emigrants, in which the ethnic dimension occupies an important place. However, concerning the function of death in relation to the identity of the group, death appears as relatively functional only in the frame of the inner social network, while it does not appear as an important pillar of ethnicity in the context of the outer social network.

There are two reasons for this situation: first of all, death is not 'useful' for the confirmation and widening of the outer social network. It even represents a danger of extinction for the part of the network in which the deceased may have played an important or even irreplaceable role. In this situation, emphasising differences, or boundaries between groups, which ethnically coloured death rituals certainly do, is seen as a behaviour that might contribute to this process. On the other hand, such a 'dysfunctionality' of death mirrors the global process of the de-sacralisation of reality which, above all, underlines the removal of death from our day-to-day reality and the attempt to forget about it. Death is increasingly pushed into privacy and as an exclusively private event it loses its place and function in the life of the community.

The material presented demonstrates one more fact – the difference in attitudes between the old and new Serbian emigration. The indifference of new emigrants (above all those who left the area of the former Yugoslavia during the 1990s) regarding the question of funeral and death points to the relation and dependence between two parameters that influence the formation of their (ethnic) identity. The first refers to the reasons for these migrations that were conditioned by the disintegration of the state, exile, difficult life conditions, and the fact that the migrants' national identity was often deprived of any spatial coordinates. These facts, combined with the second parameter, the age structure of emigrants, as well as the aforementioned attitudes of modern society towards death, result in a situation where the level of 'ethnicisation' of death is low.[39] Such a conclusion can especially be drawn from my research among Serbian emigrants in Greece. In Slovenia, where I met emigrant groups with a more differentiated age, educational and professional composition, the results of my research confirmed the well-known rule that symbolic borders are less distinct in situations where two groups share a richer and more protracted history. This, however, does not necessarily point to processes of assimilation or to the mutual tolerance of groups. It rather reveals the fact that there is competition for the same resources, whether economic, political or cultural, which determines the selection of symbols by the groups concerned. This is also not a context in which death would appear as a relevant event in relation to the outer network.

We have seen that, contrary to my expectations, death is an event with limited symbolic value. Nevertheless, it appears to be a very interesting 'source' for revealing facets of the

[39] Pavićević, Ambiguity of Integration Processes, 104–5.

migrant experience which often remain beyond the reach of scholarly studies: the reading and interpreting of individual and micro-social realities and their relevance for the identity of the community.

Periodicals, Newspapers

Srpska dijaspora
Glas kanadskih Srba
Jedinstvo, jugoslovensko-kanadski tjednik
Vesti

Janine Dahinden

Understanding (Post-)Yugoslav Migrations through the Lenses of Current Concepts in Migration Research: Migrant Networks and Transnationalism

1. Introduction

> *I think everybody is sending remittances – all our people, particularly the older generation. We* [the Serbs] *have two households: one here* [in Switzerland]*, an apartment with everything, and a second one in Ranovac* [in Serbia].[1]

Nowadays, one would say that the man quoted above is involved in transnational practices: he is engaged simultaneously at two distant places on the globe, he participates in transnational networks, he sustains two households financially and he travels a few times a year between Serbia and Switzerland. However, a few decades ago, nobody would have used the notion 'transnational' to describe these practices. Migration research was for a long time a poor cousin in the European social sciences. This has, however, dramatically changed in the last two decades, and research institutes dedicated to migration studies and migration journals are spreading like mushrooms on a warm autumn day. Put bluntly, migration has become a hot topic not only in public and political discourse but also among scholars. Little by little, a colourful spectrum of new concepts and ideas has found its way into academic discourse – for instance the notion of 'transnationalism'. One sometimes wonders whether these concepts contribute to a better understanding of migration processes and their effects, or whether they are not perhaps more like 'old wine in new skins'.

The aim of this article is to concentrate on a few selected current concepts in migration theory: looking through the lenses of these ideas I shall elaborate what they potentially reveal about (post-)Yugoslav migration. I will discuss the concepts of migration networks, transnationalism and methodological nationalism, and look at their usefulness for the study of (post-)Yugoslav migration. My reflections are limited, however: they are based on my knowledge of just a small part of the emigration movements out of the region of former Yugoslavia – mainly in the Kosovo-Albanian and Serb context and the immigration of these nationals into Switzerland.

1 Participant in a focus group interview.

Janine Dahinden

2. Migrant networks and transnationalism: the need for differentiation

It is more than a decade since the idea of transnationalism was introduced into academic discourse. Nina Glick Schiller and her colleagues[2] apparently touched the *Zeitgeist*, as the concept has evolved into one of the most popular among migration scholars. From then on, this new perspective on migration phenomena put the accent on the modes of construction and reconstruction of networks by migrants in more than one society and on the ways in which transnational spaces are evolving – as the notion says – and crossing national boundaries. Generally speaking, the idea of transnationalism emerged from the insight that immigrants maintain ties with their countries of origin, making home and host society a single arena for social action by moving back and forth across international borders and between different cultures and social systems, and by exploiting transnational relations as a form of social capital for their life strategies.[3] A number of case studies showed how in the migration process, new interdependencies are built up and how migrants are involved in creative social, economic and political activities in transnational fields all over the world.[4]

Concomitantly to studies on transnationalism, we have witnessed a growing interest in the analysis of migration networks. Since the 1960s, 'network' has been a key word in the literature on migration: by studying the links between migrants and non-migrants as a complex web of social roles and interpersonal relationships, researchers have been emphasising that personal networks can be understood as conduits of information as well as social and financial assistance, thereby shaping and sustaining migration.[5] The central idea underlying the popularity of migration networks in recent studies (implicitly or explicitly) is their rendering of a pool of different kinds of resources. I would even argue that there exists something like a scientific *mot d'ordre* whereby migration networks constitute a form of social capital which enhances and facilitates migration by decreasing its costs and risks.[6] For instance, once started, emigration becomes self-sustaining due to well-established migrants' networks. Once they arrive in an immigration country, migrants can rely on their network for different forms of support; it is a kind of 'diasporic social capital', which allows the settled migrants to capitalize on the ethno-national resources of the established community in question. When speaking about 'circulatory' migration, meaning migrants circulating in fluid networks conducting economic exchanges between different cities, the social capital consists of the readiness and availability to be mobile by capitalizing on a transnational network of friends or family that is built on the basis of common entrepreneurial experiences.[7]

2 Schiller et al., Transnationalism: A New Analytic Framework.
3 Vertovec, Conceiving And Researching.
4 E. g. Pries, Transnationale Migration.
5 Boyd, Family and Personal Networks.
6 Bourdieu, Le capital social; Portes, Social Capital.
7 Morokvasic, Transnational Mobility; Tarrius, La mondialisation.

This perception of migration networks as a form of social capital also underlies assumptions about the existence of transnational social spaces.

Most scholars agree that transnationalism is not a new phenomenon as such, but should rather be understood as a new perspective on migration processes.[8] The historical perspective shows that migration processes have always been accompanied by long-distance practices: writing letters home or being involved in political activities in the former home country was also the rule for most European emigrants at the beginning of the twentieth century, for instance. However with enhanced globalization processes, the development of communication technologies and cheap transport, these transnational connections have certainly intensified. Much empirical research on transnationalism has helped to clarify some of its conceptual and theoretical issues. These studies have put ideas about transnationalism into perspective, sometimes even questioning the concept as a whole, and the initial euphoria has been replaced by a certain sobriety.[9]

The catch-word of 'network' has also come under fire: scholars have pointed to the fact that migration networks are complex and that more than a merely 'metaphorical approach' is needed in order to understand the evolution and composition of migration networks, as well as the constraints and potentials growing out of them. When investigating migrant networks it can, for instance, be valuable to look for ties of different qualities, for fleeting and dynamic elements of network as well as strong and family ties, as these ties of different nature have different outcomes with regard to human action. Ties cannot be reduced to a narrow dichotomous view in which someone has a (transnational) relation to another person or not, for this view fails to reveal whether or not this relation has social relevance and in which situation the relation is of importance.[10]

One of the main benefits of the idea of 'transnationalism' is, without doubt, that it allows to overcome and connect the bi-polar approach of classical migration theory: until recently one group of researchers has been analysing the causes of migration (often reduced to push-pull-factors and economically motivated rational-choice approaches); a second group of scholars has been occupied with the effects of migration, analysing assimilation or integration processes of 'uprooted' migrants in their new environment. The transnational perspective allows us to bring together emigration, immigration, integration, and return as they are perceived as being steps in one and the same process taking place in a transnational space. Most social scientists in the field would agree that migration is often circular in nature rather than irreversible. Social relations are not bound to fixed places and migration decisions are not separated from processes of adaptation to a new environment. This allows us for instance – and this is of importance for this article – to think about (post-)Yugoslav migration while at the same time taking into account the conditions in the region of origin and places of immigration of these migrants.

8 E. g. Levitt et al., International Perspectives on Transnational Migration.

9 Al-Ali, Koser, Transnationalism, International Migration; Waldinger, Fitzgerald, Transnationalism in Question.

10 Dahinden, Prishtina – Schlieren; Gurak, Caces, Migration Networks.

3. 'Missing' transnationalism among (post-)Yugoslav migrants? Attempts at an explanation

Some voices have been insisting lately that the notion of transnationalism – notwithstanding its usefulness – needs more differentiation: certain empirical studies show, for instance, that only a minority of, and by no means all, migrants are involved in transnational activities. A study conducted in the USA revealed that the ones who are engaged in stable transnational practices as transnational entrepreneurs or in the political arena were mainly well-educated and integrated male migrants. Furthermore, even if migrants do practise a kind of occasional transnationalism this does not mean that stable transnational practices will develop in the future.[11] In other words, the question arises whether transnational ties maybe do not have the weight that could have been expected from the early studies, when transnationalism was celebrated as a new form of life of all migrants.

Two empirical studies on migration from the (post-)Yugoslav region not only underscore these results, but can also contribute to explaining these facts. In a recently completed study, we were interested in a specific form of transnational practice, concretely in the remitting behaviour of Serbian migrants in Switzerland.[12] A survey[13] among Serb households showed that remitting behaviour is not the same for all but rather mirrors the heterogeneity of these people's biographies and their socio-economic status in Switzerland. Research suggests that not all Serbs remit – a quarter did not remit money and/or goods in the past twelve months – and that different factors influence their involvement in this specific transnational practice: the better educated and the higher the household income of the Serbs, the more likely they are to remit, and the larger the amounts transferred. Furthermore, Serbs who have become naturalized Swiss citizens are more likely to send more remittances. We might say that the economically best integrated (males) in Switzerland are the ones who are most involved in transnational economic activities. Another important result is that there is almost nothing of what we call *stable* economic transnationalism among the Serb migrants in Switzerland: first, members of the second generation are overrepresented among the non-remitters, raising serious questions about the future stability of these monetary flows. Second, the study shows that transnational ethnic businesses between Serbia and Switzerland are rare: only a small minority of the respondents in Switzerland own a business or at least

11 E.g. Guarnizo et al., Assimilation and Transnationalism; Portes, Conclusion: Theoretical Convergences.

12 Lerch et al., Remittance Behaviour.

13 The remittance behaviour was approached by two different methodologies: first, a telephone survey (in Serbian) among 600 Serb migrants was launched: 500 interviews with citizens of Serbia and Montenegro (excluding Kosovars and Montenegrins) living in Switzerland holding a resident or settlement permit, and 100 interviews with recently naturalized Serbian migrants were conducted. Second, focus groups with migrants, ethnic business holders and informal remittance service providers were organised. The study was mandated and financed by the Swiss Secretary of State for the Economy.

do business in Serbia. To put it differently, there are almost no transnational entrepreneurs, and those who are, are the best educated and economically best off. This example illustrates the need to distinguish between different forms of transnationalism, for instance between occasional and more stable forms.

A similar pattern emerges from a second study where we were interested in the personal social networks of Albanian-speaking persons originating from former Yugoslavia living in the German-speaking part of Switzerland.[14] Transnational relations have very little importance within the social support networks of these Albanian-speaking migrants and transnational social spaces are almost non-existent. Data suggest that on the level of everyday life and daily interaction, Albanian migrants have developed a strong local orientation and we discovered highly localized networks. Over three quarters of the persons in the personal networks of the interviewees lived in Switzerland, mostly even in the same canton. The networks however displayed a strong ethnic homogeneity: Albanian-speaking immigrants rely on other Albanians when they need general advice about professional or family affairs, economic or emotional support. Leisure is also spent with other Albanian speakers. In addition, Albanians turn to other Albanians to find a job or an apartment. On the basis of the results of this study, the picture emerges of an 'Albanian community' which is almost hermetically closed and – at least regarding the first generation of migrants – quite disconnected from Swiss society; but this 'community' is not at all of a transnational nature.

With regard to practices of political transnationalism a similar picture emerges: not all Albanians maintain and participate in transnational political activities. There is a specific group who is engaged in Albanian migrant associations and political parties, mainly refugees who are well-educated males. Albanians having arrived in Switzerland as *Fremdarbeiter* and also women are only rarely engaged in political transnationalism. Finally, similar to the results of the study on the Serbs, stable transnational practices among Albanian speakers are almost entirely absent in the economic realm. This does not alter the fact that Albanian migrants support their relatives in the country of origin whenever they have the financial means to do so by sending remittances. Nonetheless, there are no specific transnational and ethnic businesses of a sustainable nature, either in the national or in the transnational context.[15]

From these two empirical studies we can conclude that stable transnational spaces between Serbian or Albanian-speaking migrants in Switzerland and their place of origin are rare and fragmented. What are, then, the reasons for the limited transnational participation of these immigrants in Switzerland? Scholars have argued that certain conditions have to be fulfilled to allow for the creation of transnationalism. These conditions are dependent on the legal, social, political and economic factors prevailing in the countries of immigration, as well as the countries of emigration. Transnational practices are not free from the

14 DAHINDEN, Contesting Transnationalism?

15 There might be transnational economic practices of illegal or illicit character, but I did not investigate these (see below).

constraints and opportunities imposed by the local context.[16] If we take a closer look at the case studies presented, it becomes clear that the explanations for 'missing' transnationalism are highly interwoven with the power relations and structural features of Swiss and former Yugoslav society.

It is the economically best integrated in the labour market and the naturalized Serbs who are able to build up a transnational space: they are the ones who have acquired specific resources in Switzerland. But conversely, the example of the Serbs illustrates that transnational practices are influenced – among other factors – by the local context in Switzerland. We can even ask if integration – meaning having access to the important resources of the host society and acquiring different forms of capital – might not be a precondition for the development of stable transnational spaces. The least integrated people – for instance unemployed persons – with low education are less likely to remit.

In this line of argument we could maintain, with regard to the second study, that the 'missing' transnationalism could – at least partially – be explained by the disadvantaged and under-privileged position of the Albanian migrants in Switzerland and by their limited personal resources, particularly in terms of cultural capital. It is well known that many Albanian immigrants in Switzerland face significant problems of marginalization and pauperization. They sometimes live in precarious circumstances and are often unemployed. In general, we might say that the socio-economic and professional status of members of this group is very low and mechanisms of exclusion based on discrimination can be observed.[17] For these reasons we assume that the social capital that Albanian migrants can mobilize through their networks is very weak. If a migrant's personal network mainly includes people with limited resources, the volume of social capital that this migrant is able to mobilize is quite limited. This could be a factor for Albanian migrants not being able to build up transnational social fields: they are mainly in contact with other Albanians, most of whom have limited personal resources. This argument goes even further: as social capital is mainly a local asset, it is very hard to transfer it from one country to another. We can therefore assume that immediately after immigration – at least if we defend the idea that a person does not migrate with all the persons of her/his personal network – part of the social capital of the migration network has to be constructed under the conditions of the new environment. If these conditions are of an under-privileged character – for instance lacking in social, political or economic possibilities, or discrimination – the opportunities for the manifestation of transnationalism will be very limited. Therefore, my argument is that transferability of social capital increases in parallel with the emergence of transnational social space. Conversely, low levels of transnationalism can – at least partially – be equated with low levels of social capital in networks.

However, it is not only the local context and the constraints of living in Switzerland that influence the development of transnational space, but also the other end of the transnational chain: the situation in post-war Serbia and above all in Kosovo is also not favourable

16 Al-Ali, Koser, Transnationalism, International Migration.

17 Fibbi et al., Le passeport ou le diplôme?; Wanner, Migration et integration.

for transnational practices, as economic and political stability are far from being a reality. In the eyes of the Serbs interviewed, it was the present bad economic situation in their country of origin and the unaccomplished democratic process, which kept them from investing in a transnational business because they feared the risks of losing money. Furthermore, they mentioned a lack of "business culture" and a lack of trust in the government as major determinants for the absence of transnational economic activities and investment behaviour. In short, the general conditions in former Yugoslavia are not very favourable for economic transnational activity, which impedes the evolution of transnational spaces.

To put it differently, neither of the two poles of the transnational chain offers the necessary resources and it seems logical that stable transnational practices will not develop. From the case studies presented, transnationalism thus appears to be just another outcome of immigrant adaptation to the receiving society. Adaptation in the receiving country parallels the development of a stable transnationalism: the cultivation of strong networks with the country of origin and the implementation of economic and political initiatives based on dense networks may mirror the fact that immigrants have gained access to important resources in the receiving society during the assimilation process. A few years ago, Thomas Faist developed a typology of different types of transnational social spaces arising from international migration.[18] The one described here could be classified as transnational kinship groups where the primary resource in social ties is reciprocity.

Neither the Serbs nor the Albanian speakers could be labelled as transnational communities. However, the question arises whether there might not be other forms of transnationalism among these groups which could not be gathered through the conducted studies, because grasping these forms would require differently designed research. I am speaking about circulating transnational entrepreneurs active somewhere between formal and informal economies: a question which arises – but cannot be answered here – is that it would be interesting to see whether these specific contexts in former Yugoslavia and Switzerland might give rise to an economic transnationalism of a circulatory nature and whether, secondly, this is more likely to be of illicit character. Among the migrants from former Yugoslavia there are illegal and violent networks working in a transnational way, for instance networks engaged in drugs and human trafficking, but also networks operating at the border between the formal and informal economies, such as smugglers (see below).

There may be yet another factor that contributes to 'missing' transnationalism among the settled migrants of this origin in Switzerland: I will argue the premise that nationalism has some serious implications for migrants which both enhance and prevent the development of different transnational activities. In the next section I will look more closely at this issue

[18] Faist, Transnationalization in International Migration.

3.1 The premises of nationalism and migration

It is clear that 'nation' is a very important concept in migration research. We find the concept in the notion of 'trans*nation*alism' as well as in the concept of 'methodological nationalism'. Reflections about these concepts can give valuable insight when it comes to understanding migration from (post-)Yugoslav space to Western European countries.

The idea that the world was naturally divided into nation-states and that these states were the units for analysis had the effect of blinding not only politicians but also researchers. The concept of methodological nationalism has been put forward in order to describe this weakness of social science: the critique refers to the unquestioned transfer of boundaries, categories and variables of the national view into the scholarly perspective, and to the excessive weight of the nation-state as a category of reference, even among social scientists.[19] Ernest Gellner showed in his works how the supposedly natural congruence between national, territorial, political, economic and social boundaries actually emerged in due course from nationalism and nation-building processes.[20] For Gellner, nationalism is primarily a political principle which holds that political and national units should be congruent, so having a nation with its people and culture is not an inherent attribute of humanity, but has come to appear as such.[21] This is what he called the premises of nationalism. Methodological nationalism, in this line of thinking, has been defined by Wimmer and Schiller as "the assumption that the nation/state/society is the natural social and political form of the modern world".[22]

It therefore does not come as a surprise that although migration is a structural element of human history, the control of migration has preoccupied policy makers since the formation of the modern nation-state: as nationalist concepts of people and society took hold, the conception of immigrants began to change and free circulation of humans was replaced by historically new forms of border control. With the creation of the modern nation-state, belonging to a specific ethnic or national group started not only to be naturally given, but furthermore to determine access to the territory, rights and – later on with the establishment of the welfare state – services the modern state is supposed to guarantee to its citizens.[23] It became necessary for a person to have a permit to enter a country and reside there, creating the differentiation between nationals who did belong to the polity and 'foreigners' who did not. Wimmer and Schiller showed convincingly how immigrants must appear as anomalies to these premises of nationalism by destroying the isomorphism between people, sover-

[19] Beck, Macht und Gegenmacht, 84–94.

[20] Gellner, Nations and Nationalism.

[21] Ibid., 6.

[22] Wimmer, Schiller, Methodological Nationalism, 302.

[23] Mackert, Kampf um Zugehörigkeit. It is obvious that methodological nationalism not only has its impact on the perception of migrants, but also on the perception of 'national minorities': this is without doubt of high importance in the case of former Yugoslavia. For the relation between ethnicity/nationality/citizenry, see Allcock, Explaining Yugoslavia; Denich, Unmaking Multiethnicity.

eign and citizenry, but also between people and nation and between people and solidarity group.[24] Immigrants are an exception to the rule of sedentariness within the boundaries of nation-states.[25] It follows that living as foreigners in a 'host nation' means not having the same rights as other citizens and being deprived of a set of specific resources, both material and symbolic.

Nation-states have the sovereignty to define which citizens from other states are admitted with which rights to their territory. Conversely, states also have the sovereignty to define which parts of their national population should or should not leave the territory of the state; they can try to regulate not only immigration but also emigration. To come back to the idea of trans*nation*alism: it shows that this notion only makes sense since the establishment of a world naturally divided into endless nation-states. I propose that these ideas allow us to better understand the process of migration from the (post-)Yugoslav region. I will therefore look more closely at the premises of nationalism and how they shaped emigration out of Yugoslavia, but also immigration into Switzerland, as well as the 'side effects' they had.

3.2 Out-migration from socialist Yugoslavia

Migration out of socialist Yugoslavia was, from the very beginning, highly influenced by these premises of nationalism. During the first years of socialist Yugoslavia's existence (1945–early 1960s), the country was – like other socialist countries in the Balkans, Eastern Europe and the Soviet Union – a closed country in terms of outward migration. Yugoslav economic emigration to Switzerland, as well as to other countries, started in the early 1960s. The Yugoslav Federation's political decision to open up its borders for emigration was associated with the launching of liberal (national) economic reforms in 1965.[26] Whereas internal population movements (from the less developed southern regions to the northern ones) had already started after World War Two, the north-western parts of the country were the first to be affected by mass labour emigration. In the 1960s the majority of Yugoslav migrants in Europe, and in Switzerland, were Croatian. At the beginning of the 1970s, however, the regional pattern of emigration progressively changed, affecting the south-eastern parts of the country with increasing intensity.[27] This temporary economic migration, which has been "subject to state organisation since 1965", was considered to be a form of "demographic management" in order to export labour surplus and to stabilize the economy through the inflow of currencies from the returnees.[28] Yugoslav migration policy was ideologically (and socially) justified on the basis of the assumption that migration was only temporary, and that migrants still formed an integral component of the so-called Yugoslav working class.

24 Wimmer, Schiller, Methodological Nationalism.
25 Ibid., 309–10.
26 Schierup, Former Yugoslavia.
27 Mesic, External Migration.
28 Molnar, The Sociology of Migration, 110.

Their positions in the receiving countries as well as their return were therefore not merely of their own concern, but the responsibility of the whole socialist and national community. This social concern of the Yugoslav state about its migrants led to the signing of employment contracts, the establishment of social security conventions (with Switzerland in 1964), the designation of diplomatic-consular representatives who, besides their standard consular functions, were given the task to "protect" the interests of Yugoslav migrants, and the encouragement of migrants to join clubs and associations for a better "social-organization".[29]

3.3 In-migration into Switzerland: categorizing migrants

The norms of nationalism were not only mirrored by the Yugoslav emigration policy and the socialist state of Yugoslavia, but also by Swiss immigrant admission policy: through the 'ethno-national sorting' of its admission policy Switzerland created different categories of migrants. In 1931 it implemented for the first time a law controlling immigration and defining the rights of the 'foreigners' on its territory, thereby ending a phase of liberal circulation. After the Second World War, Switzerland needed foreign labour: former Yugoslavia was, after Italy and Spain as from the 1960s, a central recruitment region for Switzerland's so-called *Fremdarbeiter* ("alien workers"). Interestingly enough, while in Germany migrant workers were called 'guest workers', in Switzerland they were labelled from the outset by their 'otherness', i.e. *Fremdarbeiter*. This fact mirrors the logic of the nation-state described above in seeing immigrants as 'natural' others. With a shift in immigration policies, specifically with the implementation of the so-called 'three-circles' model in 1991, the recruitment of workers from former Yugoslavia was no longer possible. They were soon categorized as members of the 'third' circle and had no chance of obtaining a work permit anymore.[30] People from the third circle have been seen as "culturally the most distanced" – meaning that by their 'otherness' they produce xenophobia in Switzerland and they can only be integrated with great difficulty.[31] At this point, the nexus between the two policy fields of migration and integration became strong and inextricable, and both are impregnated with the premises of nationalism: nationality is not only seen as naturally linked to a certain territory, but also as a kind of backpack that the migrants carry with them. In this backpack one finds not only the nationality but also a corresponding culture that dictates the behaviour of the nationals in question. Furthermore, culture has been conjugated with geographical distance with the result that the further away people live, the larger their assumed cultural distance to the Swiss.

29 Baletic, International Migration; Mesic, External Migration. These practices could be equated with transnationalism as well, even though they might never have been looked at in this light. See Dahinden, Moret, Transnationale Aktivitäten.

30 Swiss Federal Council, Bericht des Bundesrates (1991).

31 Hoffmann-Nowotny, Chancen und Risiken.

For most Swiss citizens it may be obvious that 'the Swiss' are far from being a homogenous group with an overarching collective identity; in fact they are plural and diverse on different levels. But with regard to immigrants, ethnic or national groups are seen as invariable and group formation of immigrants along ethnic lines is taken for granted; and we witness the habit of referring to such groups as "Turks", "Yugos" or "Albanians", as though they were homogeneous and clearly circumscribed and as though their members formed a unitary collective with a common purpose and a common culture. This thinking entails the phenomenon, for which Rogers Brubaker coined the word "groupism": the tendency to take discrete, sharply differentiated, internally homogeneous, and externally bounded groups as basic constitutes of social life to which interests and agency can be attributed.[32] Each of these groups is defined in national or ethnic terms and each group is said to have its own culture, which is responsible for the behaviour of the members of the group in question.[33] It even seems, if I may put this in a slightly ironic way, that these ethnic or national groups form a kind of extended arm of their 'naturally' and territorially defined ethnic or national origin. In this way, ethnic groups or communities are transformed into transnational ethnic groups.[34] The further away these groups are from their original national territory, the greater their 'cultural distance' from the Swiss is perceived to be.[35]

Going back to the process of categorizing migrants we can summarize that through the shift in immigration policy in 1991, people from former Yugoslavia were classed among the most 'culturally different' – placed in the third circle: from this moment on, they could only immigrate to Switzerland through family reunification or by seeking asylum (Switzerland implemented its first law of asylum in 1979, again producing a new category of migrants). In other words, the category of asylum seeker was not only a product of the 'ethnic conflicts'[36] in former Yugoslavia, but also of the Swiss nation-state finding new ways of categorizing people along ethno-cultural lines. The civil wars within the different republics of former Yugoslavia led to a phase of mass emigration to Switzerland, either through family reunification or asylum. It should be said, however, that many of the asylum seekers returned after the wars.

From 1998 onwards, Switzerland adopted a dual admission policy – in line with most European countries – which is still based on the premises of ethno-national categories and cultural distance, but which introduced a different logic in the categorizing process. Mean-

32 Brubaker, Ethnicity without Groups, 35.

33 It is obvious that the notion of culture which is underlying these debates is highly problematic and, from a social science perspective, démodé (Hannerz, When Culture is Everywhere; Wicker, From Complex Culture to Cultural Complexity). Contemporary notions of culture highlight the capability of human beings to interpret interaction and give sense to the world. Culture in this way has to be analysed, as 'having a culture' does not exist (Dahinden, Was heißt schon interkulturell?).

34 Dahinden, Deconstructing Mythological Foundations.

35 See Castles, La sociologie et la peur.

36 That the conflicts in former Yugoslavia have been 'ethnically framed' is also closely related to the norms of nationalism.

while the right was created for European Union (EU) and European Free Trade Association (EFTA) citizens and residents of its member states to move and settle within Europe on a free basis. On the other hand, Switzerland as well as most EU states developed restrictive and defensive immigration policies to keep out migrants from outside the EU/EFTA, among others also from former Yugoslavia. For non-EU/EFTA citizens, the new policies offer educational and work opportunities exclusively to highly qualified foreigners. Semantically, ethno-national categories have been linked more and more with a strong hierarchization between desired and unsolicited migrants. One could bring these processes together under the category of the wanted travellers on the one side – the highly skilled migrants who are supposed to be easily integrated into the host societies, as is the common hypothesis – and the remaining migrants on the other side. For the non-solicited and non-invited migrants new and increasing barriers have been erected and for them, national boundaries and borders and the sovereign right of states to decide on admission of non-nationals have gained importance.[37]

4. Effects: processes of social exclusion?

It is important to note that these processes of categorization which seem 'natural' have important consequences for the lives of migrants from former Yugoslavia. First, people of this origin can no longer come legally to Switzerland unless they are highly qualified or through family reunification. Interestingly enough, among the wanted travellers we incidentally find a new incoming flow of well-qualified persons from the regions of former Yugoslavia.[38] However, all other post-Yugoslav migrants entering Switzerland are criminalized, as their entries are illicit. Furthermore, these processes based on cultural 'otherness' have some effects at which we shall look in the next section.

It seems obvious that, with a spiralling pattern of new measures to restrict and control migration among the Western European states, 'innovative' new forms of immigration, new actors and new dynamics will also develop. First, immigration is increasingly being criminalized, which has specific effects, also with regard to migrants from former Yugoslavia: tougher regulation has by definition led to more illegality and irregularity, creating opportunities for new actors like smugglers and traffickers. At least we can confidently state that the new migration policy has created another important category of migrants: *sans papiers* as they are commonly called in Switzerland, or undocumented migrants, meaning migrants living and working in Switzerland with no legal residence and working permit.[39]

37 Pennix, Introduction.

38 Gross, Immigration to Switzerland.

39 Irregular migration is a complex and diverse concept that requires careful clarification, which cannot be done here. It is important to recognise that there are a variety of routes into irregularity: irregular migration includes people who enter a country without the proper authority (for example through clandestine entry and entry with fraudulent documents); people who

The phenomenon of undocumented, and hence illegal, migrants has also started to bother the Swiss government, which mandated a study in order to measure the scale of the *sans papiers*.[40] This and other research in this field showed that among the irregular migrants living and working in Switzerland, there is a consistent proportion of people from former Yugoslav countries. Hence, we are witnessing a criminalization of migrants of that origin.

Moreover, during the 1990s, the phenomenon of undocumented migrants linked to human trafficking – defined here as the facilitation of illegal entry to states for profit – has gained a lot of attention in the international arena. Meanwhile, European states have accorded highest priority to the fight against undocumented migrants and human trafficking. On the other side, social scientists have started to differentiate: in the public debate there is widespread 'moral panic' linking trafficking to organised crime, to threats to sovereignty and the internal security of states, and to the exploitation of human beings, all intensifying the picture of the 'enemy immigrant', which is predicated upon the norms of nationalism. However, social scientists found little evidence for claims that organized crime is involved in human smuggling.[41] They suggest that many smuggling operations take place within the respective ethnic community or within family and acquaintances.

As long as Yugoslav migrants were liberally admitted to Europe, smuggling and *sans papiers* were subordinate issues. However, with the introduction of the distinction between wanted and un-wanted migrants and the categorization of migrants, smuggling has acquired a certain normality: Efionayi-Mäder et al. showed, based on interviews with Kosovo-Albanians, Iraqis and Sri Lankans in Switzerland, that all these persons who requested asylum in Switzerland in the 1990s had been smuggled at some point along the trajectory that brought them to that country.[42] In short, we witness new trajectories and categories of migrants also among the ones originating from former Yugoslavia.

The production of new categories of migrants on the basis of national criteria and 'cultural distance' had yet another side effect which I want to discuss briefly: it seems obvious that the way from creating a mosaic of nationally defined and internally homogenous and bounded immigrant groups to a hierarchization of these groups is now far advanced: up to the 1980s Yugoslav immigrants remained relatively unnoticed by the Swiss public, although they were the *Fremdarbeiter* – the alien workers. But in parallel to the reinforcement of 'otherness' in Swiss immigration law through the model of circles of cultural distance, the Yugoslavs have come under fire from the media and in public: drug dealing, violence, pa-

remain in a country in contravention of their authority (for example by staying after the expiry of a visa or work permit, through sham marriages or fake adoptions, as bogus students or fraudulently self-employed); or people moved by migrant smugglers or human trafficking (Efionayi-Mäder, Cattacin, Illegal in der Schweiz; Koser, Irregular Migration). There were *sans papiers* in Switzerland already in the 1970s, however with the increasingly restrictive policy the phenomenon has grown considerably.

40 Longchamp, Sans Papiers in der Schweiz.

41 Laczko, Data and Research; Van Liempt, Doomernik, Migrant's Agency.

42 Efionayi-Mäder et al., Asyldestination Europa.

triarchal culture and family structure, crime, and high unemployment are the catchwords, which are today connected with this section of the population. There has been an increasing tendency to explain the observed social exclusion of some of the immigrants of these origins by stressing their cultural peculiarities and differences – or even their cultural 'incompatibility' as some right-wing parties did.

At the same time, the 'ethnic framing' of the conflicts in former Yugoslavia produced the effect that the group in question was split up along the same ethno-national lines. The Yugoslav *Fremdarbeiter* changed semantically from hard-working "Yugos" to Serbs, Albanians, Bosnians and Croats: again a hierarchization of these groups took place, with some of them even becoming 'culturally' more different than others. Croats were now considered Europeans; Albanians were – culturally speaking – the most distanced persons. That this kind of categorization process can result in exclusion seems logical: recently, a study showed that young people having an Albanian name are highly discriminated against when looking for work.[43] When in 2006 thirteen youngsters – six naturalized Swiss of Yugoslav and Turkish origins, two Serbs, two Macedonians, one Bosnian, one Italian and one person from the Dominican Republic – violated a thirteen year old girl in Zurich, the explanations heard in public for this horrible offence were all culturally tinged, as though it were their culture which rendered them dangerous, and some political parties were demanding processes of de-naturalization of the youngsters. It is obvious that in the public imagination the premises of nationalism are fixed and unmovable: nobody would speak about de-naturalization of Swiss-born boys who had committed the same offence and nobody would explain their behaviour by their cultural background. Although some of the offenders have acquired Swiss nationality, in the national imagination, they still do not belong to this state, but are guided in their actions by their backpack from their ancestral homeland, even though they may never have lived there. This is a concrete example of how the premises of nationalism create strong hierarchization and processes of exclusion which are difficult to counter, as they seem to be 'natural'.[44]

It comes as no surprise, however, that we find the same tendency to frame and categorize themselves in essentially ethno-national categories among the immigrants from former Yugoslavia in Switzerland: if going abroad involves escaping repression by another 'national' or 'ethnic' group, as was the case, for instance, for the Albanian-speaking migrants who left Kosovo in the 1980s or 1990s, and if it involves being able to be 'more Albanian' in the new host country, capitalizing on the ethnic connection is a logical behaviour. The growing nationalism and politicization of ethnicity in the Balkans has also had its effect on established diasporic communities in immigration contexts, contributing to a growing consciousness and essentialization along ethnic lines within immigrant communities. From this perspective, the ethnic homogeneity of immigrants is therefore also, but not only, directly linked –

43 Fibbi et al., Le passeport eu le diplôme?

44 Just to be clear: there is no apology for this offence, but the reasons why some persons do commit this kind of offence are obviously more complex.

in a highly interwoven world – to events taking place in geographically quite distant places, underscoring methodological nationalism and also being *transnation*

5. By way of conclusion: TransNationalism

I would maintain that the transnational perspective allows us to understand migration phenomena in greater depth by widening our horizons. This is, however, only the case if we differentiate between different and specific morphologies of transnational practices and if we take seriously the '*nation*' part in the notion of transnationalism. Methodological nationalism and the premises of nationalism not only shape the conception of migration – emigration as well as immigration and processes of assimilation – but they also strongly influence the politics of states and public perception as well as the self-description of migrants. These ideas have far reaching effects as they are directly linked to processes of exclusion.

However, one might have to distinguish carefully between different practices of transnationalism: (post-)Yugoslav migration was and is transnational in character and has developed different forms of transnationalism. Still, we need more research in order to understand the different transnational morphologies in greater depth. Furthermore, I hope to have shown that the nation-state had and still has a major impact, not only on emigration from former Yugoslavia, but also on immigration into Switzerland.

Jasna Čapo Žmegač

Family Dispersal Across National Borders: A Strategy for Betterment

Tamo i ovamo
Svako ko je 'vamo ima nekog tamo
pa čas je ovamo, čas odlazi tamo,
muči se ovamo da pomogne tamo
glavom je ovamo a srcem je tamo.
Sve bi dao 'vamo da je bolje tamo
i čeka ovamo kad će bolje tamo,
da napusti 'vamo da se skrasi tamo.[1]

This is an excerpt from a song that was given to me in 2004 by the Bosnian-Herzegovinian consul to Munich, Mr. Jerić, who had downloaded it from the Internet. In its entirety, the song talks about bifocality – the here and the there – experienced by Croatian migrants to Germany: about the fact that they live in one place and look at what is going on in the other, exchanging one for the other for periods of time, striving for betterment in one so that it can have effect on the other.

In this article I will focus precisely on this parallelism in the lives of migrant families, on the here and there that Croatian families originating from Croatia and Bosnia-Herzegovina have been practising in their everyday lives for over thirty years. Moving, going back and forth, living in and commuting between two or more places in two or more states appears to be the central theme of the existence of migrant families whose members are divided across international borders.

Migrant families

The editor of a book published in Germany under the title *Die ausländische Familie: Ihre Situation und Zukunft in Deutschland* ("The Foreign Family: Its Situation and Future in

1 Translation: *Here and there* – Everybody who is here, has somebody there / So he is at moments here, at moments there / He struggles here to help there / With his head he is here, with his heart he is there / He would give everything here that it be better there / He waits here that things get better there / To leave here, to settle there.

Germany")[2] introduced the contents by situating the term "foreign family" in the sociological literature of the 1960s. Some of the characteristics of the "foreign family" that took shape in Germany at that time include elements such as unsuitable lodgings, unsatisfactory hygienic conditions, economic need, language problems, confrontation with unfamiliar educational requests, ambivalence between a need for integration and keeping up one's own sociocultural identity, etc.[3] The author notices that such an image of the "foreign family" has not changed in the public discourse and that the stereotype has not acknowledged the manifold changes which the foreign family underwent through the decades since its elaboration as a concept.[4] Besides being petrified in the notion, which emerged some forty years ago, this view is also specific in that it sees the migrant family from the aspect of the receiving society.

Parallel to this, approaches to the migrant families were developed in the former Yugoslavia, as the country of emigration, which treated them primarily from the viewpoint of their twofold spatial embeddedness. Multi-placement was identified as an important characteristic of Croatian migrant families by Croatian sociologists writing about their forms and experiences almost simultaneously or immediately after the peak in migration of various nationals from Yugoslavia to Western European countries in the 1960s and 1970s. These scholars have left us invaluable material and analyses of migration in its early phase.[5] In a study of a sample of 1,807 pupils from emigrant families published in 1978, Vjeran Katunarić was among the first to speak of "bilocal families" in Croatian and, more generally, in the Yugoslav sociological literature.[6] At a period when this vocabulary was rare and migrant families were considered in some way "incomplete" or "deficient", and the migrants "up-rooted",[7] Katunarić rectified this image and pointed out the rootedness of migrants in their milieus of origin, thus anticipating the so-called transnational paradigm in migration studies by at least ten to fifteen years.[8]

In this article I will look into the modalities in which Croatian economic migrant families in Germany have dispersed across space. I shall address the questions of why spatially dispersed families come into being and whether the separation of family members leads to unstable relations and emotional detachment among its members. What kinds of relationship arise in the spatially dispersed migrant families, especially between the parents and the children and the siblings among themselves? How do the migrants judge their split lives and family arrangements? In an effort to answer these questions, I rely on migrant biographies

2 Lajios, Die ausländische Familie.

3 Lajios, Die allgemeine Situation ausländischer Familien, 13.

4 Ibid., 15.

5 Baučić, Porijeklo i struktura radnika; Katunarić, Vanjske migracije; Nejašmić, Povratak jugoslavenskih vanjskih; Morokvašić, Jugoslawische Frauen.

6 Katunarić, Vanjske migracije.

7 Quoted in ibid., 11.

8 Cf. among others: Glick Schiller, Basch, Blanc-Szanton, Transnationalism; Faist, The Volume and Dynamics of International Migration; Guarnizo, Smith, The Locations of Transnationalism.

which recount family experiences over time.[9] The longitudinal dimension will enable an analysis of family living arrangements in the migratory situation as a process over the life course of the family.[10]

This text is based on ethnography of the particular,[11] on several family biographies recounted by Croatian migrants in Munich. Three migrant families are from Croatia, one is from Bosnia-Herzegovina, and one is of mixed Croatian-Bosnian origin. They have been chosen among fifty migrant family histories that I gathered during fieldwork in Munich because they exhibit changing family arrangements and the multi-placement of different family members.

The remainder of the text is divided into three parts: short migrant families' biographies, focussing on the changing living arrangements of family members, are presented in the first part. The second part discusses their similarities and differences. In the final section it is argued that the changing migrant families' living arrangements are dependent as much on macro-structural policies regulating migration as on the entire migration biography, their plan of return, and the phase in the (migratory) life course of the family.

Migrant families' stories

Case 1

Marija[12] (b. 1941) came to Germany with her husband in 1970. Their son, then nine years old, stayed at home in Croatia because the parents left with the plan to return soon. As if to seal this plan, they bought a house in the husband's natal town in Slavonia, in which they would live once they returned. However, the husband did not live long enough to return. After her husband died, Marija decided to stay in Germany until she reached retirement

[9] The research for this article was enabled by a fellowship from the Alexander von Humboldt Foundation, Bonn, Germany, in 2002–2003, and by funding of the No. 0189001 project by the Croatian Ministry of Science, Education and Sports, 2002–2006.
The migrant family biographies have been reconstructed based on interviews which I conducted among Croatian labor migrants in Munich in 2002 and 2004. They are thus the result of a methodological technique that gathers individuals' narratives about themselves and their experiences. The limited scope of such a data source stems from the side effects of narrative data, for any narration about the self is unavoidably a self-construction and self-presentation (to the researcher and to oneself) and cannot be taken at face value (for more on this point see Čapo Žmegač, Strangers Either Way). It should also be noted that although the families who agreed to talk to me (about their life in migration) may have lived through periods of hard work and scarcity, they represent relatively "successful" migrants (in terms of economic standing and good family relations), who have precisely for that reason self-selected themselves as my interlocutors.

[10] Hareven, Cycles, Courses and Cohorts; ibid., Recent Research on the History; Klimt, European Spaces.

[11] Cf. Abu-Lughod, Writing against Culture.

[12] The name of this and other migrants are pseudonyms.

age; she will have earned her retirement in Germany after thirty-three years spent working in the textile industry and in the kitchen.

At the time of our conversation Marija was about to retire and leave for Croatia. She did not have much to take for she has lived all her life in Germany in a rented apartment, modestly furnished with used pieces that she would occasionally find via newspaper ads.[13] After having lived for more than thirty years in Germany, Marija states that her life and that of her husband was a "normal life". Her only sorrow is that she left her son when she and her husband went to Germany:

> *How shall I put it, it was difficult, because my child was down there in Croatia. We were actually separated. Hmm, I don't know if I had had such an opportunity, if we had had an opportunity, maybe it would have been better down there* [in Croatia] *than here. Firstly, when the family is divorced, I mean when you are not with your child, that is not easy. And then, we bought a house in N. and then we always used to say, still only one more year and we shall return. And this is how it happened, my husband did not return.*

The nine-year-old son remained with Marija's mother and brother, and later on, during his studies, lived with his mother's sister. Since they were separated by a distance of approximately 1,000 kilometres, the parents did not visit the child more than three or four times a year: for Easter, Christmas, and their annual vacation. Before telephones became standard in Croatian villages, the dispersed members of the family communicated mainly via letters. Marija states that she had no "problem" with the son due to the fact that he was growing up without her and his father. During the time before migration she had taught the child working and hygienic habits, and appealed to him to "finish schooling" so that he would have an easier life. The son fulfilled his mother's wish, and graduated from the University of Zagreb. At a certain point the couple wanted to bring the child to Germany, but, allegedly, he refused: he was already in his teens and did not want to part from his friends. Summing up her relationship with her son, Marija said:

> *We have a very good mother-son relationship; we have very close relations and good ones. He takes care; he takes immense care of me. When his father died it was a catastrophe for him, and if anything happened (to me) I think that he... he would not let me go to an old people's home ... neither would my daughter-in-law. I feel safe. They want to have a house built, and it is planned that they have an apartment for me, next to theirs, under the same roof, so that I have mine and they have theirs. This will be fine, if I live to enjoy it.*

Case 2

Joža (b. 1946) is a Croat from central Bosnia, who left his home village at the age of twenty to work in Germany. For almost thirty years he was working in the construction industry, and then found an easier job as a janitor in a *Spielsalon* (amusement arcade) in Munich. For

13 She had ambivalent feelings about going back: on the one hand, she had been living in Germany for over thirty years and claimed to have got used to living there. On the other hand, the return seemed attractive because of her son and his family, who are a source of joy to her, and from whom she did not wish to be separated any longer.

the first seven years he lived and worked in Frankfurt, but after he had married a woman from his native village, he moved to the south, to Munich, in order to be closer to his family, who lived in Bosnia.

Joža did not complain about hard work in the construction industry; he liked this job for two reasons: on the one hand, the pay was good and he managed to save a lot; on the other, it enabled him to spend longer periods in Bosnia during the winter season. Besides these longer stints spent at home, Joža often travelled home to Bosnia, sometimes twice a month. Not only was his family growing – in a period of just over ten years he had fathered four children – but he was also heavily investing in his house and property in Bosnia and his presence was needed. Commuting every second weekend or so was quite exhausting, but he did it since he was indispensable for supervising the investments. Joža speaks of himself as the "main family axis" because he was needed on the farm and because he was financing everything that was being implemented in the household and on the farm. Since his plan was to stay in Germany for a short period – until he earned enough for a house – his family joining him was never a question. However, he kept postponing his return. He gives a somewhat ironic, even caricatured portrayal of how his stay was prolonged (see below).

The war, which broke out in his native country in 1992, marks a big break in his and his family's life. In order to protect his family from the war Joža brought them to Munich. The family reunion brought tensions and even conflict into the, until then, well-functioning family. It was hard for Joža and his wife to get used to living together after almost twenty years of separate lives. It was difficult, especially at the beginning, when they lived in the one-bedroom apartment that Joža had been living in for years. The wife spoke of other difficulties, including her not knowing German and how, for the first time in her lifetime, she had started to work outside the household.

Joža thought once again that this was a temporary move and that the family – like himself in the previous period – would not stay in Munich for good. It occurred to him that the return to Bosnia would perhaps not be possible because of the war and he felt that he needed to secure another retreat for the family in case anything "developed badly" in Germany. Therefore, like many other Bosnian Croats forced out of their homeland by the 1992–1995 war, he bought land in the surroundings of Zagreb and started to build a four-apartment house. The construction of the house was interrupted, and only one apartment was finished because at some point Joža realised that he better invest in Munich. So a two-bedroom apartment was purchased with a bank loan. The entire family lives in Germany at the moment. The daughters married and left the joint household. Although both sons earn their own living, they live with their parents.

Case 3

Draga came to Germany in 1971 at the age of eighteen with no intention of staying there. The encounter with her future husband, a Croat from Bosnia, who had lived in Germany since the late 1960s, was decisive for Draga's life trajectory. The couple married in Germany, had two children and lived there for the first six years of their life together. However,

Draga was dissatisfied with her life and wanted to return to Croatia. After the couple had bought a house in a small town near Zagreb, in spite of her husband's disapproval, Draga moved there in 1981 with her two daughters, precisely at the moment when one of them was about to start elementary education. The mother and daughters lived in Croatia for six years, while the father remained in Germany, because the couple judged that his return would significantly lower the family's standard of living. The period spent in Croatia has remained in very good memory to both Draga and her daughters. In order to be closer to the family, whom he visited every two or three weeks, the father moved to Munich. According to Draga, the girls did not miss their father, for he visited them regularly and was closely involved in monitoring their life in Croatia. However, according to one daughter, Tonka, the father's absence made life in Croatia less appealing.

Tonka has vivid memories of her childhood in Croatia: of the little town in which the family settled, of their house that she does not allow her mother to sell even today,[14] of their yard, of the walks in the nearby woods, of herself and her sister playing in the streets of what they called their "territory". They pursued several extra-curricular activities: folklore and judo lessons, religious and organ instructions. In short, Tonka describes the period spent in Croatia in two words – freedom and independence.

After six years of split lives, the parents decided to reunite and the female part of the family returned to Germany. Fifteen years later, Draga cannot say precisely what made them take such a decision: "There was no specific cause, but [...] a person always evaluates, reflects..." The girls had lost much of their knowledge of German. Re-learning German was no simple matter, and Tonka is still somewhat bitter when she recalls the difficulties she encountered, and the derisive attitude shown towards her by her teacher at the time when she still had not mastered the German language. In spite of these initial difficulties, Tonka finished Gymnasium and was studying Macroeconomics in Munich at the time I encountered her.

Shortly after the family reunited in Germany, the husband/father died in a car accident. Draga decided to stay in Germany with her two daughters, and take advantage of the benefits offered to her by the German social system. She completed medical school, and is still working part-time as a registered nurse at a clinic. One daughter moved out of the family household, while Tonka stayed on with her mother during her studies.

Since Draga only works part-time, and since her girls have become more independent, she has organised her life in such a way that, after about two weeks of working in Germany, she travels to Croatia for a two-week stay. When in Croatia, she does not stay in her own house, which she has partly rented out, but lives with her parents in a nearby mountain village. She describes her life in two locations in two countries as "changing gears": when she goes to Croatia she excludes and forgets her life in Germany, and vice versa. Apart from attending to family business (for example, caring for her parents) or matters connected

[14] "I would like this house to continue to be mine: it was my childhood, *Erinnerung* (memories); there is something positive in relation to this house, there we were *frei* (free)", says Tonka.

with property, Draga largely uses her stay in Croatia for recreation. This nature-lover takes advantage of the location of her birthplace, a mountain village that has few inhabitants now, for almost daily excursions in the mountains.

Case 4

Kata (b. 1952) and Martin (b. 1944), then a young couple from the Međimurje region in Croatia, came to Germany in 1969, first to Hannover and two years later to Munich. Both had jobs as factory workers. Since they moved to Munich, Kata has been working as a cook in the same establishment, while Martin has had several job changes (working as a construction worker, driver, and then janitor). Their initial plan was to stay for five years:

> *We came to Germany; you know how it was then. Five years, that was it at the most we said, five years and that's it. Then, we shall go home to work in farming. Now those five years have become thirty-six years.*

Parallel to their work in Germany, for the first fifteen years of migration they were also working in Croatia, helping the husband's aging parents till the land. With time it became more difficult to continue working on two fronts, but it took almost fifteen years before they made a decision on where they would definitely settle down. According to Martin, the husband:

> *We were in a dilemma: here or there? And the longer we were here, the more accustomed to it we became. It was more difficult to decide, for here it was safe, I had a safe job, and we could exist with the money we earned. Farming the land on the other hand, I did not know how that would go.*

In the mid-1980s when the situation in the former Yugoslavia started to deteriorate, and after the wife had spent some months at home with her newborn child, they finally made the decision not to return.

Kata and Martin have four children: the elder two were born in Croatia, the younger two in Germany. They took the first-born daughter with them when they first came to Germany. But when their second daughter was born a year later the couple decided to leave both girls with their grandparents in Croatia, since they had just moved to Munich and thought they could not take care of two small children. After having settled in Munich they wanted to bring the children to live with them but, Kata claims, her mother would not let them go. With the birth of the third child, the decision was different: at first the child – a son – lived with them, but when he was six they sent him to Croatia to school, because they were still planning to return and wanted to spare the child language difficulties once they returned. Their son was already attending the seventh grade of elementary school in Croatia when the couple finally made up their minds and decided they would stay in Germany. At that point they resettled the son to live with them. In the meantime, a fourth child had been born, whom the couple kept with them in Munich. For the two older daughters it was already too late to seek permission for family reunion in Germany.

Today, Kata and Martin feel sorry that they lived apart from their two older children and that they sent the third one to school to Croatia. They speak of very emotional farewells from the children, whom Kata was visiting regularly every two weeks. They blame the family separation on their plan to return and the fact they constantly postponed it. On the other hand, they claim not to have had any "problems" with the children: they were under the firm supervision of Kata's mother. Today, the older daughters, who live in Croatia, are married and have children of their own. One has graduated from the University of Zagreb; the other one has finished a four-year professional school. After returning to Germany, at the age of thirteen, the son had language problems, but was able to finish an apprenticeship as a mechanic; the youngest daughter is finishing a professional school to become an *Industriekauffrau* (industrial sales representative). The son has married and moved out to a house near Munich, which the family helped him buy, while the youngest daughter is living with her parents. They claim that they are all on good terms and feel happy when they meet in Germany or in Croatia for family gatherings or weddings.

Case 5

Jela (b. 1959) is an economist with secondary school qualifications and married to a man (b. 1950) who has lived in Germany since the 1970s. The couple did not live together after their marriage, not even after the birth of their son and, several years later, daughter: seeking construction work, her husband changed his place of residence in Germany fairly frequently, while Jela and the children lived and worked in a smallish town in northern Croatia. They exchanged visits relatively regularly, with either the husband coming to Croatia during the winter season, or with Jela and the children travelling to Germany during the holidays and vacations. Only exceptionally did she leave the children with her mother, because, as she says:

> *I am surprised generally by those parents, all those parents who left their children with grandmothers, whom you could trust. Just imagine, my mother! She raised them better than I did and everyone always fussed over them. But why did all those parents leave their children with their mothers and mothers-in-law? That's the way our women are, taking care of everyone, but how did they manage ... When I look at it today, well I did it too, I left them for a couple of months straight, not even as much as that, but I found even that difficult.*

In the summer of 1991, just when war broke out in Croatia, Jela found herself with her children in Germany. Because of the feverishness of war and out of fear, she decided to give notice in Croatia and to stay in Germany. Thanks to her husband's German descent, the entire family already had dual nationality at that time – German and Croatian (Yugoslavian until 1991) – and there were no administrative obstacles whatsoever to their remaining there. Describing her life in Germany at that time, Jela said:

> *How did we live? We were constantly involved in Croatian issues. We concentrated on the problems in Croatia.* [...] *We spent those three years in Germany thinking about Croatia. Refugees started to arrive. On the whole, everything was reduced to those stories about Croatia.*

They socialised with other Croats and various other foreigners who had settled in the small western German township in which they lived. The children went to school and mastered the German language, while Jela, despite certain difficulties with the language, found her feet and organised their joint family life, but she did not work. During their life in Germany, she and the children often spent prolonged periods in Croatia. Eventually, her husband's inconstant employment and concern for the children led her to return to Croatia with the children and to find a job, after three years spent in Germany:

> *I did not regret returning, not even once, because I realised that I had to work for my existence, simply for a living existence. And that in that struggle for a living existence I had to raise my children, to ensure that they obtained an education, and I have ensured them a top education.*[15]

Since then, and until her husband's early retirement, the children and their mother lived separately from their father, while reasonably often visiting each other as they had done in the period prior to their settlement in Germany. Constant travelling does not seem to have been wearing for Jela: "It was strenuous, but it was also interesting, because you were constantly going home, or going there. It wasn't a strain. People find everything a strain nowadays. To me then, it wasn't." She liked going to Germany, while she considers the fact that the children learnt the German language well and became familiar with German culture to have been a great advantage. Still, she does also mention a certain tension and alienation that arose between the children and their father and/or between her and her husband.

After her husband's return to Croatia and the resumption of joint family life on a daily basis, problems ensued in the family. Being used to organising her life and that of the children alone, Jela would not accept her husband's desire for authority:

> *He came from Germany. He wanted to identify himself as a great returnee, a big boss, and he said, "I'm your boss here. I shall tell you how and what...".*

Multi-placement of migrant families: a comparison

The five families have had both similarities and dissimilarities in their life trajectories in Germany and Croatia or Bosnia-Herzegovina. Except for Jela and her husband (case five), who came to Germany in the 1980s and lived without any specific plan, other migrants had a plan that would keep them in Germany for only several years.

The macro-structural factors that influenced the migrants' plan for a short-term stay are rather well known. Above all, it was the German policy of foreign labour rotation in the 1960s and 1970s. The term *Gastarbeiter* (guest worker) was coined at the time to denote that temporary and changeable labour force, which mostly consisted of men below the age of forty.[16] The state of Bavaria efficiently supported the rotational recruitment of foreign labour through its cultural policy – the development of bilingual education aimed at the retention of migrant cultural identity.[17] Therefore, maintaining ties with the country of

15 Both children are university students today.

16 Kolinsky, Non-German Minorities; Lapeyronnie, Les politiques locales; Bougarel, Allemagne: Assimilation; Münz, Where Did They all come from?

17 Lapeyronnie, Les politiques locales; Bougarel, Allemagne: Assimilation.

origin and, moreover, leaving wives and/or children in the country of origin, was in direct correlation with German and Bavarian migration policy at the time. Croats were reaching Bavaria (and other parts of Germany) with the aim of returning to their country of origin after their labour contract expired and their immediate financial plans were realised. Therefore, the plan to return – moreover, the plan to return as soon as possible – was an inherent part of their coming to Germany in the first place. However, the people featuring in this text did not return, even after thirty years had elapsed from the time of resettlement.

My interlocutors recount quite candidly, sometimes with self-irony, how the plan to return kept changing and ended up in an unintended sojourn in Germany of over thirty years. Joža's recital perhaps best expresses the process of postponing the return:

> *You know, I built a house. Then* [I thought], *if I could only arrange it so that I have everything that I need in the house: furniture, bathrooms, everything. When I arranged that… then I opened a shop on the ground floor; now I need to take care of it. I made an arrangement with Upi* [a grocery store] *to work there when I came back. I thought one hundred percent I would return. When I return I will work there in person. Eeh, I told myself, I will have a job in my own house. And then I settled that. Now,* [I thought] *if I could save a little bit, to have some money when I go there* [he laughs]. *This is how it was.* […] *Then, I told myself I should buy a small truck, for transportation. And then, I told myself, a little bit more savings. Then I bought a tractor, various other equipment, bought land* [he laughs]. *I told myself, to have it all when I retire. When all of this was achieved, finished, then I said, a little bit more savings, then we will… I needed sheds and a garage … when you have a tractor and a car.* […] *Everything, when I fixed everything, it started … It started to tremble, politics started to change everything.* […] *I say, I had not even taken a rest from all that I had done, when the war broke out.*

For others it was not the war that triggered a postponement of the plan to return; for Kata and Martin (case four) it was the difficulty of living parallel lives in two places located in two states, and the dissatisfaction with life in Croatia, that made them stay in Germany. For Marija and her husband (case one), there seems to have been no key event that made them stay so long in Germany – they just kept postponing the return, judging that their savings were not enough to live from if they returned. Draga (case three) and Jela (case five) did return after having lived several years in Germany, each under very different circumstances. Both took their children and went to live in Croatia whereas the husbands stayed in Germany: this marked the beginning of a six-year long period of rather comfortable life without work for Draga and the beginning of an "existential fight" for Jela.

Because of the pending return, which was planned to be effected after several years had elapsed from the time of migration, and a concomitant need to economise as much as possible during the time spent abroad, these people had made various arrangements leading to families dispersed over international borders. In two of these cases, both husband and wife migrated leaving the child/children in the care of the grandparents. Thus, they gave precedence to the conjugal over the filial relationship. In one case, it was the husband who migrated abroad while the wife and the children stayed at home. In case three and five, after having lived in one location for several years, the family split in such a way that the mother-children relationship was given precedence over the conjugal one. In materialising the transnational living arrangements in which parents lived separately from their children, my interlocutors relied on their extended families. Children in the fourth migrant biography were quite mobile in the earlier stages of their lives, living at some point with their parents in Germany, at another with their matrilineal or patrilineal kin in the home country.

It was the plan to return and the children's schooling that determined the children's mobility and the change of caregivers in the cases in which both parents migrated. Except for short periods at an early age, the mobility of Kata and Martin's older daughters was confined to *intra*-national mobility. Their brother, however, alternated longer periods of living in the two countries; after having spent the first six years with his parents in Germany, the parents – who at the time were still forging plans to return and wanted to avoid their son having language problems on their return – sent him to elementary school in Croatia under the care of his maternal grandmother; seven years later, when he was thirteen, they brought him back to Germany. His last move was determined by his parents giving up their plan to return and not by better schooling opportunities. Had schooling considerations been dominant in determining this last move, his parents would probably have not resettled him at the time when he was approaching the end of elementary school in Croatia. When they brought him back to Germany, his language skills were judged insufficient for him to be enrolled in an adequate grade and school in Munich. Therefore he attended a bilingual school, which restricted his schooling opportunities later on. This case demonstrates that parental international mobility and the split family arrangement entail children's mobility, even when they are left at home at the beginning of migration. However, these cases do not demonstrate that children's schooling is of primary importance in deciding family and children's movements.[18]

The primary factor influencing the mobility of family members seems to lie in the changing project of the migrants' return. It is decisive for family separation and reunion. The changing plan of return could also influence the temporary return of one (with or without children) or both partners to the country of origin, without, however, the returnees severing ties with Germany. This is the case in the third family, which was locationally united until a certain time. It split temporarily between two countries and its members lived dispersed lives until the final decision was made as to whether everybody would return or whether those who had returned would re-emigrate. This family chose the latter solution and reunited in Germany.

Although the parents in cases one, four and five knew that their children were in the safe hands of grandparents, physical separation from the children was not easy for them. As soon as they settled in Munich and had the means to afford it, or realised that the return would not occur soon, they tried to reunite with their children. These efforts were not successful, for, according to the migrants, either the children or the extended family in the country of origin opposed such a move. In no case did the part of the family living in Germany decide eventually to return and thus reunite its members. With their four children, couple four

[18] Cf. Schiffauer, Migration und Selbstverständnis; Şimşek-Çağlar, German Turks in Berlin.

claims to have striven for family reunion over almost fifteen years. At times they succeeded, so that they lived with all of their children at some phases in their life course and with some of them at others. However, they also lived without any of them at other periods. This family, then, experienced various living arrangements throughout its migration history. They were a function of the stages in their migration course, which were determined by the extent to which the migrants were settled in Germany, by the currently valid plan for return and by the age of the children.[19] Both the wife and the husband express sorrow that they did not succeed in reuniting the entire family for good; both wish they could somehow have divided themselves in order that they simultaneously lived with all of their children, on both sides of the border. The fact that they were often paying visits to the children in the country of origin for the first fifteen years does not compensate for this painful separation.

In cases three and five, the physical separation of family members seems to have been problematic for both the children and the father in spite of the father's frequent visits. In distinction to other parents, the Bosnian migrant (case two) does not mention having had emotional difficulties because of the long-lasting separation from his children and wife. To my question whether he had any difficulties stemming from family separation he answered: "You know how it is when you are alone: you have to cook for yourself, and wash." He also mentioned that frequent visits home were exhausting, and that after the family reunited in Germany he could finally have a rest. He finds satisfaction in what he perceives to be his very successful role as bread-winner and caretaker and takes pride in the way he fulfilled his parental duties, which he primarily sees as catering for his family's material welfare and security (in terms of securing a refuge for them in case a need should arise). He pursues this goal, even in the period when his children have grown up, live on their own, and are financially independent. This demonstrates a cultural system in which the father's physical absence from the family household is accepted and the parental (paternal) role fulfilled in securing a house and general material welfare for the family.

In the latter case, family reunion seems not to have been pursued by either of the parents. The break-up of Yugoslavia and the war that struck Joža's native land had an immense impact on this family and served as a catalyst for the family reunion – in Germany – after twenty years of spatially separated life. Had he known what would happen, claims Joža today, he would have brought the family to Germany earlier. However, since the family lived very well in Bosnia with the aid of his earnings from Germany he saw no reason to resettle them there. The war also led to family reunion in the fifth case. Unlike Joža's family, Jela's family was at an early stage of the family life cycle when she came with her two youngsters to live with her husband in Germany. Their reunion was interrupted shortly afterwards, when this resolute woman with a wilful personality left for Croatia to seek economic betterment for herself and her children. Their reunion was reinstated about ten years later when the

19 Under the German migration law only children under age sixteen are allowed to enter the country upon request for family reunion. This explains why the couple could not bring over the two older daughters once they decided to stay in Germany.

husband/father returned to Croatia. In the meantime, for over ten years, the members of this family lived separately in two states. Jela asserts that theirs was not a "tight community", but that they "pooled their forces for their common benefit".

Except perhaps in the latter case, it does not follow from the migrant narratives that the transnational family arrangements caused estrangement or any particular difficulties in either parent-parent, parents-children or sibling relations. The parents living in Germany underlined their very good relations with their child/children in Croatia or Bosnia-Herzegovina. The youngest daughter of Kata and Martin, who lives in Germany, assured me of her very good and close relationship with her elder siblings and their families who live in Croatia. Joža's elder son mentioned no traumatic events in relation to his former life without his father in Bosnia. A daughter of yet another couple, who has lived all her life in Croatia with her paternal grandparents, while her parents and her younger brother have lived in Germany, adamantly insisted that in spite of international dispersal theirs was a functioning family, and that she was brought up by her mother and father (living in Germany) and not by the grandparents with whom she lived all year round, except for the annual two-month holiday she spent with her parents in Germany. If anything, she reproaches her parents for not having let her younger brother live with her in Croatia. However, this woman, today in her mid-thirties, does admit a past phase of conflicts in her relationship with her parents. This came about in her somewhat turbulent adolescence, and she could not dissociate the effect of family separation from the effect this had on her and her parents' relationship.

In spite of these allegedly harmonious intra-familial relations, the explored case studies demonstrate that a migrant family is not necessarily a uniform entity in terms of language acquisition, educational achievement or citizenship.[20] Due to diverse migration histories and experiences of family separation and reunion, children and parents within any one family speak German and/or Croatian to a varying degree of fluency; some are monolingual, some bilingual, some speak better German, some Croatian, while some only speak the dialect of the region of origin and not the standard Croatian language. The education of children within any one family is also diverse. It appears that those who remained in the homeland, in the care of their grandparents, received a better education – some even earning academic degrees – while those who lived partly or entirely in Germany sometimes did not do so well in the German schooling system. In part, this can be explained by the fact that they arrived in Germany at an advanced age (late teens), with practically no (e. g. family two) or little (e. g. families three and four) command of the German language. Whatever the reasons for this might be, it appears that separation from the parents did not negatively impact the schooling of those who were left in Croatia or in Bosnia-Herzegovina,[21] but it might have had an impact on those children who had more mobile trajectories and were resettled once or several times in order to join their parents. Another element of internal

[20] Cf. Erel, Reconceptualizing Motherhood.

[21] This is in tune with earlier findings that success at school for children from migrant families is not dependent on the presence of parents (Katunarić, Vanjske migracije, 75).

family differentiation was citizenship, when e.g. all or some of the children decided to take up German citizenship, while the parents and the other children did not. This was the case in family three, in which the mother wanted to retain Croatian citizenship while the daughters applied for German citizenship.

Tentative conclusions

In spite of the fact that several decades had elapsed since their migration, it is difficult to only locate Croatian migrant families in the places to which they had migrated. On the one hand, not all family members migrated and they lived all or part of their lives in the places of origin. These families have thus had a double location in physical space, in places far apart (600 to 1,000 kilometres) located in different states. From a macro-structural point of view, multi-placement and transnational family arrangements were enabled by German labour migration policies and Bavarian cultural policies vis-à-vis resident foreigners at the time of migration of the people under review here. On the one hand, these policies encouraged contractually limited employment, short-term stays of the foreign labour force and its rotation, and offered opportunities for schooling in the language of origin. On the other hand, they contributed to fostering the plan to return among the labour migrants. As I have argued elsewhere,[22] the plan to return was not a purely rhetorical figure among Croatian economic migrants in Munich. It was real and actually influenced migrant family arrangements, living standards, and investments in and perceptions of Germany and the homeland. Within the limits set by the society of settlement, realisation and/or deferral of return were, however, individual family decisions, made on the basis of concrete circumstances in the life of the migrant family and on the basis of the opportunities in the countries of origin and settlement, and perceptions thereof.[23]

The transnational family arrangement was satisfactory for some families (case two), and had it not been for wider political processes in the country of origin, it would have probably been a durable living modality of this family. However, in other cases it was probably a less satisfactory pattern, since family members claim to have striven for reunion. In case four, this striving was occasionally successful and resulted in changeable family arrangements, i.e. in shorter or longer periods of separation followed by reunion of all or some family members who crossed borders in one or another direction. Some of the family members were particularly unstable in a locational sense, even "volatile",[24] as, for example, some children who changed the place of living several times over their life course. Families three and five also experienced changeable living arrangements, in one case finally reuniting in Germany, in the other in Croatia.

22 Čapo Žmegač, Trajna privremenost.
23 Ibid., Dynamik der Beziehungen.
24 Cf. Bryceson, Vuorela, Transnational Families in the Twenty-first Century.

There is another reason why some of these migrant families cannot be unambiguously located in one bounded physical place: those who migrated have never really taken leave of their places of origin.[25] Especially in the first decade or even for two decades after migrating, migrants were not only regularly visiting and monitoring the lives of those family members who were left behind (the children in particular, but also grandparents), but they were also engaging in diverse economic activities in those places; they were actually living parallel lives in two places located in two countries, their "here" and "there" were interwoven into a common field. Even after it had become clear that they would not be returning soon, their places of origin were not entirely abandoned because they had children who lived there. Their bilocality led to bifocality[26] throughout their migration history, with periods of more or less intense physical presence and transnational activities in both places.[27]

These two characteristics of migrant families – the cross-sectional, bilocal placement of diverse family members with some members living bifocal lives on the one hand, and longitudinal changes in the geographic location of individual family members resulting in changing family arrangements over time on the other – render impossible any attempt to precisely and uniformly locate them in only one physical space over time and characterise them in any essentialist terms. It follows from the analysis of these cases in a diachronic perspective that, rather than being a temporary phase aimed at reintegration of the family at a higher economic level,[28] bilocality and transnational family arrangement might be viewed as a more or less continuous family configuration and the way of life of migrant families.[29] This results from a synergic effect of a particular family time (the stage in the family and migration course) and the related decision-making on the one hand, and historical time and the constraints that it brings about on the other.[30]

In spite of their physical separation, these migrant families claim to have retained a network of good relations and emotional attachment.[31] As evidenced in two cases (families two and five), it is family reunion rather than family dispersal that brings about tensions and conflicts inside the family. Analysing transnational families in the context of USA-Mexico

25 Cf. Herrera Lima, Transnational Families: Institutions.

26 Cf. Rouse, Making Sense of Settlement.

27 Cf. Čapo Žmegač, Dynamik der Beziehungen, for an analysis of the ebbs and flows of transnational activities at various stages of migration.

28 Katunarić, Vanjske migracije, 43 passim.

29 There are, of course, also families who have not practiced bilocality and whose members have lived together throughout their entire migration history. Why some chose one or another family arrangement can be explained only within particular migratory contexts.

30 For the concepts of family and historical time, see Hareven, Cycles, Courses and Cohorts; ibid., Resent Research on the History.

31 This should not be generalised as relating to the entire migrant population, for, as mentioned in Footnote 9, the families that in some way suffered from the geographic separation of their members or were not doing well in economic terms were usually not willing to share their experience. Family five also points out some tensions in the conjugal as well as in the filial relationship.

transmigration, Fernando Herrera Lima argued that, instead of conceptualizing dispersed migrant families as unstable and unviable units, we can conceptualise a type of family reconfiguration with translocal and transnational dimensions.[32] This hypothesis seems to be applicable to the cases under review here. However, the insistence of my interlocutors (except in case five) on there having been firm and harmonious relations between dispersed nuclear family members – with occasional problems – should not be taken at face value. It might point to a prevalent family ideology and a narrative family reconfiguration. In other words, it might be hypothesised that precisely because it is dispersed across long distances the family needs to construct its unity (emotional if not physical) and therefore presents itself as integrated and reconfigured. This point is worthy of further examination and comparative analysis of particular cases.

Finally, these migrant cases demonstrate that by maintaining multi-placement, migrants kept open their options for a better and secure life. They took advantage of it in the past when the immediate lives of their family members were in danger, for example, when the war broke out in Croatia and Bosnia-Herzegovina (families two and five). Having decided it was better to live in Germany, another couple could reunite with at least one of their offspring precisely because of almost fifteen years of intensive transnational activities (family four), and a wife with children joined her husband (family three). Options also remain open whether to stay in Germany or return to the country of origin. This illustrates very well the ability of transnational migrant families to "reconstitute and redefine themselves over time contingent on spatial practicality and emotional and material needs",[33] and their strategic use of bilocal (or multilocal) transnational family arrangements.[34]

32 Herrera Lima, Transnational Families.

33 Bryceson, Vuorela, Transnational Families in the Twenty-first Century, 3.

34 A version of this paper was published in the journal *Migracijske i etničke teme* (Čapo Žmegač, Spanning National Borders).

Pascal Goeke

From Ubiquitous to Specific Networks. Social Change and the Relevance of Networks in Migrant Families

Labelling the world

How to depict and label the social world are two of the classic questions in the public sphere as well as in the social sciences.[1] In doing so, the labels and metaphors used in these areas by no means develop independently: every *zeitgeist* requires its own mode of representation; hence we are now familiar with a wide range of various narrations. Evolutionary ideas with biological connotations, as well as cybernetic systems with rectangular links between functional terms, may come to mind. A more recent concept is the idea of networks. Quite often networks dominate our thinking, form our terms, nourish our metaphors and shape our observations and conceptions of the world. Along with the concept of transnationalism, the term 'network' has become one of the key labels in migration studies in the last two decades. Yet what is behind this enormous surge in usage of a simple metaphor? The explanations are manifold and often multilayered, especially since the label 'network' is used in various disciplines and for different phenomena. The presumption that everybody who is using the term has something very different in mind and is tackling very different problems is well founded but does not account for the popularity of the term.

Two major and complementary routes of explanation are possible to elucidate the continuous boom of 'network' in the social sciences. The first attempt is to look for more general reasons within the social sciences or academia. Without doubt, sociologists of science are able to explain the widespread use of 'network' with reference to modes of distinction and career ambitions. They might also point to the attractiveness of the newly developed techniques of magnetic resonance imaging, which enable neuroscientists to offer fascinating insights into the human brain, which can also be portrayed as a network. The occasional wish to stick with the winners fosters the import of these ideas and images into other areas of scientific endeavour. This sort of explication, however, will be left aside in this article and the second major route will be taken instead.

[1] I am indebted to Peter Linder, who made valuable comments on the first draft of this paper and helped to clarify some nebulous lines of thought. I also thank the participants at the conference '(Post-)Yugoslav Migration. State of Research, New Approaches and Comparative Perspectives' for their comments.

The paper seeks to explain the upswing of networks from the perspective of a general social theory,[2] i.e. with reference to the so-called external world, to the environment of the social sciences, or to 'reality'. It will be asserted that social change, more precisely the ongoing process of social differentiation, fosters the emergence of very specific networks which can be understood as a second order or parasitic social form. References to the social world or to reality should not be mistaken for naïve and simplistic understandings of the world. The underlying assumption is that the environment unfolds its social relevance only in the moment of communication, which requires some sort of indication. Communication is conceived as the synthesis of three selections: information (what is communicated), utterance (how and why it is communicated), and understanding the difference between utterance and information. Since understanding is required, communication is an emergent phenomenon that is not attributable to a single individual: at least two individuals are presupposed.[3] Hence it is science, a differentiated world within the social world, which tries to classify the world 'out there' without ever being able to model a positive copy of the world, but offering more or less useful and compatible 'negative' descriptions of the world – like a key in the keyhole.

As mentioned above, almost every discipline uses the term 'network' differently and tries to grasp different phenomena through it. It even can be argued that the fuzziness of terms like 'network' fulfils a very specific task, i.e. the task of building bridges and offering connections between the disciplines. A narrow and concise definition would thus contradict the interdisciplinary and international spirit of migration research, where my attempt becomes even more precarious. To lean on a highly abstract and somehow autistic theory like Luhmann's system theory, (which is always a risky endeavour), becomes even riskier: the positioning of the term 'network' in a special corpus of social theory runs the risk of cutting the ties with adjacent disciplines.[4]

Besides the tension between a tight conceptual construct on the one hand and loosely defined metaphors on the other hand, a second tension runs through this paper. For a long time the assessment that "the deepest canyon separates social scientists from historians" held true.[5] This paper does not seek to fill the gap between the searches for "distinctive locational patterns" on the one hand and "universalistic claims" on the other (a distinction made by Klaus Bade);[6] yet it proceeds from the conviction that interdisciplinarity only makes sense if prior to the exchange, some sort of disciplinary specialisation has taken place. Otherwise migration research would become an interdisciplinary endeavour without discipline(s).[7] Since it can also be argued that the canyon is not as wide as it is often depicted to be, the paper will suggest how the notion of a network can be adopted more powerfully – an argu-

2 Drawing mainly on Luhmann, Die Gesellschaft der Gesellschaft.
3 Baraldi, Corsi, Esposito, GLU. Glossar zu Niklas Luhmanns Theorie, 89.
4 See Goeke, "It Ain't Interdisciplinarity".
5 Lucassen, Lucassen, Migration, Migration History, 10.
6 Bade, Sozialhistorische Migrationsforschung.
7 Cf. Bommes, Maas, Interdisciplinarity in Migration Research.

ment which will unavoidably both restrict and strengthen the concept. The theoretical suggestion will be made with reference to social change in general and to the change of family structures, especially within the migration process, in particular.

Network: metaphor, method and theory

Michael Bommes and Veronika Tacke argue that social networks are ubiquitous and there is no domain in society where networks are absent.[8] Indeed, it is easy to think of the social world in the form of a single or multiple networks; networks in which individuals or organisations as nodes are linked with each other or with machines and computers. Networks are so omnipresent that moral judgements can place them on every single place on the scale from good to evil. Good networks of friends and kinship are desired, and corrupt or criminal networks are condemned.[9] The broad application and evocation of the term 'network' demonstrates that virtually no social field is free of networks. Even in areas where social interaction is severely restricted (e. g. in the case of prisoners at Guantanamo, or Carthusian monks due to their vow of silence), it is still possible to think of these rare interactions in form of networks. Only the complete absence of interaction – and thus the end of society – would allow us to deny the existence of networks, but then the question would be to whom such a finding might be told. The crucial point is clear: the tricky and general problem while using the term 'network' is its opaque meaning and diverse application. If everything is described as a network, the term itself looses its discriminatory function and fails to designate the specificity of any certain network.

Therefore, it seems helpful to differentiate between three broad usages of the term:[10] First and foremost, 'network' is used as a trope. Such a usage does not in itself pose a problem, though joyful metaphors are hard to exploit for theoretical purposes. The value of metaphorical descriptions can thus primarily be seen in their capacity to complicate established and seemingly fixed knowledge. At such a point it would also be counterproductive to fix the term into a narrow corset, since semantic ambiguity has its own very specific function.

A second usage of the term 'network' refers to the method of network analysis.[11] Since networks are ubiquitous phenomena of the social world it is not a big surprise that the method of network analysis can be applied almost everywhere. Especially with the rise of new software packages like UCINET, network analysis has become an interesting tool in social research. The software with all its components allows the processing of large amounts of data with a reasonable amount of effort. According to the above-mentioned understanding of a network as built out of interactions or communications, it becomes possible to visualise

8 Bommes, Tacke, Das Allgemeine und das Besondere, 38.

9 Holzer, Netzwerke.

10 See also Mitchell, The Concept and Use of Social Networks; van Loon, Network; Holzer, Netzwerke.

11 Jansen, Einführung in die Netzwerkanalyse.

the structure of all these social events.[12] However, the results and graphs of network analysis hardly say anything substantial about the world. The demonstration that everything within the world is linked is of little value. Or to put it another way: representational networks visualise otherwise invisible relations, but the graphs themselves fail to differentiate between the general and the specific; interpretation is required.

From this point of view a third domain of usage becomes even more interesting, i.e. the theoretical implications. In sociology a general theoretical framework for networks has existed since the 1970s,[13] with some predecessors dating back to the mid-1950s.[14] The concept can be classified as a structural theory of action.[15] According to that concept, actors refer in their action to other concrete actors, i.e. they step into social relations in which their action is embedded and in which they embed their action respectively.[16] The mutual constitution of social action and social relations implies that networks are regarded as the last or basic unit of sociality. This poses the problem that networks cannot be distinguished from other social forms, such as organisations, interactions or, more generally, social systems. The technical reason for such an unsatisfying situation is the identity of the theoretical key term with the problem under consideration. To phrase it within the deductive-nomological model, the two constituents of the explanation – *explanandum* (the phenomenon to be explained) and *explanans* (sentences which are apt to account for the phenomenon) are identical and thus overstressed. Of course, network theorists are able to describe networks with their rich and useful vocabulary. They describe the meshes of networks as more or less dense, the links as weaker or stronger and the nodes as more central or more peripheral. The result of these descriptions might be that some networks are more similar than others or that some are more successful than others. But since network theory hardly says anything about borders, it remains all too often unclear whether the chosen border is the analytical one (maybe due to limits on the research capacity) of the researcher or whether it is an observable one, which is independent of the researcher's eye and has a function itself. Some relief might be found in James Clyde Mitchell's often cited definition of a social network as "a specific set of linkages among a defined set of persons, with the additional property that the characteristics of these linkages as a whole may be used to interpret the social behaviour of the persons involved".[17]

12 See also the gallery of networks at <http://www-personal.umich.edu/~mejn/networks/>, last accessed: 22 May 2007.

13 Burt, Structural Holes; Granovetter, The Strength of Weak Ties; ibid., Economic Action.

14 Mitchell, The Concept and Use, 1.

15 Bommes, Tacke, Das Allgemeine und das Besondere, 39.

16 Granovetter, Economic Action.

17 Mitchell, The Concept and Use of Social Networks, 2. It is presumably not by coincidence that network concepts are rooted in anthropology. This Western science was regularly confronted with the problem that Western categories were useless in the societies or regions which gave legitimacy to the discipline. It was thus required to search for new terms and concepts – this thought, however, will have to be immediately left behind, for the current paper is primarily

Yet the general problem remains: as Bommes and Tacke argue, the development of a sufficiently general network terminology which is able to grasp the similarities of the – by the way very different – networks has failed. What is needed is a general term or terminology that must be applicable and specifiable for the different societal contexts in which networks occur.[18]

Networks in general social theory

The identified shortcomings lead to the necessity of developing a framework which allows the designation of the specificity of networks as a social form. Systems theory as elaborated by the German sociologist Niklas Luhmann offers a variety of useful conceptual tools.[19] Additionally, Veronika Tacke and Michael Bommes recently outlined how systems theory might integrate the empirical findings of both network research and analysis.[20] Thus they provide the basis for further theoretical development and specification as attempted in this paper.

It is commonplace to describe systems theory as being both complex and circular. Both characteristics obstruct easy access. Yet at the same time access is possible from various vantage points. To cut a long story short, the most basic assumptions can suffice to support the argument. We take as given that society consists solely of communication as defined above. Communication is the only social element we know and without communication society will not emerge. As a matter of course, in order to perpetuate communication, (and thus society), people are required, even though is it quite evident that both people and society would collapse without communication. Within such a concept the external border of society is identical with the border of communication. This is the reason why systems theory conceptualised society from the very beginning as a world society. There might be two or even more societies yet as long as we do not know anything about them it does not matter to us.[21] The internal form of the world society is not regarded as predefined. The forms must be generated by communication. The borders as known and experienced by individuals are generated borders within society. Borders are drawn, fixed, condensed, confirmed and often kept under fierce surveillance, but as we all know, they are not fixed for eternity and always subject to change.

Still on a very abstract level Luhmann suggests that social systems do exist and that every form can be addressed as a social system. A system is defined as the unity of difference between the system and its environment. Social forms or systems are imprinted in mediums.

concerned with contexts and regions which fit more or less into the very Western concept of modernisation and development.

18 Bommes, Tacke, Das Allgemeine und das Besondere, 38.

19 Luhmann, Soziale Systeme; ibid., Die Gesellschaft der Gesellschaft.

20 Tacke, Netzwerk und Adresse; Bommes, Tacke, Das Allgemeine und das Besondere.

21 Luhmann, Die Weltgesellschaft.

There are ephemeral forms like interactions or more formalised and lasting social systems like organisations or functional systems.[22] Modern world society is – at least in the so-called Western sphere – characterised by the primacy of functional differentiation, i.e. differentiation in functional systems like economy, law, politics, education and science, religion, etc. In the words of modernisation theory we have witnessed the transformation from organic solidarity to mechanic solidarity.

Network theories ignore the fact that the transition from stratified societies – e.g. societies with nobility at the top and serfs at the bottom – to functional differentiated societies, involves a radical shift of modes of inclusion.[23] Functional differentiation is based on the possibility that individuals adopt more than one or two roles in the social structure. In stratified societies, by contrast, persons and role expectations were almost identical. Status-role sets were attached to individual persons, whereas in modern society status-role sets are increasingly subject to discussion and deconstruction. The expectations attached to status-role sets are replaced by expectations attached to specific functional roles. This implies that henceforth the context is decisive as to whether individuals are addressed for the continuation of communication or not. Typically we will find asymmetrical role allocations: teacher-pupil, doctor-patient, vendor-vendee, employer-employee, etc. But these roles depend on the context and are hardly transferable: even the professor has to queue behind his or her students if they meet in a shop. In stratified societies individuals bore their same role – their status – in different contexts.

The crucial point of this description is not the proclamation of an ideally free or egalitarian society. What can be observed, instead, is the fact that values like liberty and equality are now widely spread and that reality is measured against these norms and values. Of course, people are different. But if, for example, a person has the ability to pay for goods and services or has the cognitive capacity to study, or if a person is sick it appears as unfair or unjust if they are prevented to buy and to study or if they do not receive medical treatment. Although people are different they are regarded as equal in relation to the modes of communication within each functional system. The fact that the transfer of role advantage from one sphere into others is under strict surveillance is evidenced by the talk about corrupt networks: the politician, for example, must not instruct his or her brother or sister to build a new school without tender. If, however, the politician does so, he or she has to have very good reasons for it.

On an abstract level it can be argued that the process of differentiation follows the primacy of the problem and not the primacy of the social dimension. This sheds a first light on the specificity of networks in modern society. Even though the genesis of networks can start in various social contexts, e.g. kin, ethnicity, fraternities, sororities, etc., the continuation and stabilisation of specific networks rely on the combination of addresses across the borders of social systems, especially across the borders of functional systems and more im-

22 Luhmann, Soziale Systeme. Grundriß.
23 Tacke, Netzwerk und Adresse, 297.

portantly, organisations. The addressing and mobilisation of individuals in networks does not follow the primacy of the problem but the primacy of the individual address. The addressing, of course, is a precarious endeavour: you never know whether the addressed person is willing to help you. To sum up: a network theory, but not network analysis, makes sense only under the condition that social relations are not predetermined by societal structures, but are understood as being reflexively producible.[24] In the next section of the paper, this idea will be transferred to the family and social change.

The zadruga: *a segment embedded in strata*

Arguing that some networks can be understood as specific networks, and that the amount of networks that can be subsumed under such a specific category is growing, implies automatically that the social world is changing. Such a general change will now be exemplified alongside the change of families. With regard to the Balkans the classical buzzword is undoubtedly the *zadruga*. Yet our knowledge about the zadruga is very diverse and depends apparently on such factors like disciplinary background, regional variation and the time in question, to name but a few. On top of these differences the zadruga, whatever it has been or still is, underwent an ideological career and was as such challenged for its ideological misuse.[25] Leaving these considerable differences behind, basic principles still occur – principles and approved knowledge which are sufficient for the argument.

Originally, the South Slavic word zadruga was not used to designate a family form, yet it existed "in its adjectival form (zadružen, zadrugarski, etc.), meaning communal, united, joint, corporative, and the like, and would be used to describe 'work', 'relations' and so on. The first time it appears as a noun used, as it is later, to designate a certain family type is in Vuk Karadžić's Serbian dictionary, published in Vienna in 1818."[26] Whether it was an ideological cliché or an apt description of the prevailing family form is at this point less relevant. What can be taken from the literature is the definition of the zadruga as a residential kin unit composed of at least two nuclear families. Other relatives were often included as well; the zadruga, however, was taxed as a single household. The families jointly owned their means of livelihood and commonly regulated the control of the household property, labour, and livelihood.[27] A less charged expression for the label zadruga would be the German word *Großfamilie* or the French *frérèche*. The latter is a type of multiple family, which consists of two or more married brothers and their families constituting a single household. Such family forms occurred in places where families did not want to divide their farm for economic reasons.

[24] Bommes, Tacke, Das Allgemeine und das Besondere, 41.
[25] E.g. Todorova, Myth-Making.
[26] Ibid., 38.
[27] Halpern, Kerewsky Halpern, A Serbian Village, 17.

Debates about the decisive characteristics of the zadruga are occasionally fierce. Thus it might ease the tension if the prevailing pre-modern families in the Balkans are characterised more abstractly as patrilineal groups of descent, varying in size and divided into subgroups. Subgroups and family members are committed in a corporative manner to each other. Exogamy is predominant and assets like pastures are shared. A common name for the group and forms of ancestor worship are also characteristic.[28] Needless to say, these characteristics are neither unique to the Balkans nor apply to all parts of it.[29]

The family should not be considered in isolation. It is equally important to look at its relation to society in general. It will soon become clear that families as economic units were embedded in a system of serfdom or, more abstractly, in social strata. Exclusion from the family was almost the equivalent to exclusion from society. Without being a member of a family the chances of survival were pretty low, partly because labour markets were small (if they existed at all).[30] Non-existent labour markets are just a small example of the characteristics of society that were present before the process of functional differentiation set in and profoundly altered the modes of inclusion and exclusion. There might be quarrels about how to grasp this transformation and which processes are the more important (e. g. democratisation, juridification, colonisation of the life-world, marketisation or others) but the general trend is rarely challenged.[31] The outcome of these transformations is, among others, that exclusion from the modern family has less severe consequences for the individual than in stratified societies.

At this point it is useful to distinguish between the semantics of self-description, which accompanied the family on the one hand, and the things which actually happened within the families on the other. The semantics of self-description are likely to gloss over the latter. It is thus not surprising that a gap between the self-described ideal family and the facts will occur. Such as present-day organisations prioritise rationality over intuition, families, or more precisely spouses, privilege love over economic reasons for their marriage. The clear relations between the medium love and marriage, between organisations and rationality or, for example, the legal system and equality, are questionable and yet, in comparison to pre-modern societies, the linkages today are more clear-cut than in former times due to processes of differentiation.

Although the pre-modern family cannot be linked to a single mode of communication, it can be argued that the family was a model for the long run, in which the individual and its decisions were subjugated by the collective unit. Economy, affection, care, religion, etc. all had their place in the family, but the fundamental dimension was time, and plans were

28 Kaser, Familie und Verwandtschaft, 28.

29 For exceptions see for example Brunnbauer, Die Berge und die Familien.

30 Serious doubts exist whether the borders were really under strict surveillance. To maintain the continuity of the family the rules were broken – suddenly patrilineal rules could become less important.

31 Schimank, Volkmann, Gesellschaftliche Differenzierung; Nassehi, Die Theorie funktionaler Differenzierung.

made primarily for the family with consequences for individual tasks. Also investments in individuals were made under the premise of family well being. The reasons for this are manifold and they might appear cruel from our point of view, but with regard, for example, to life expectancy, the primacy of the family was a quite understandable strategy. Although people could also reach quite an old age in those days, death occurred 'in the course of life': sometimes only fifty percent of a birth cohort reached the age of forty and nobody could predict who would be getting old and who would not (although individual life expectancy was heavily dependent on the social stratum one belonged to). A simple appendicitis could mean the end. The expectation that one could live until an old age has, with high regional differences, only existed for the past hundred years.[32] In combination with other changes, the growing predictability of individual careers also altered the prevailing forms of providence for the families. The family as a model for the long run, which means for more than two generations, has – if at all and only partly – survived in two areas: first in the sorrow for farmyards and second in the tradition of noble families and later families of industrialists in which the organisation and the increase of assets were the prime target. An extended family meant both a lack of freedom and at the same time a safe harbour.

What can be learned from this in relation to the discussion on transnationalism in migration research, where it is continuously argued that migrants and migrant families are increasingly transnationally dispersed, and the difficulties of such a kind of organisation are described?[33] We have sufficient reason to assume that in the extended family of the past the absence of an individual was evaluated differently and probably less problematic than it is today. Indeed the absence of one or more male family members was quite common. He worked far away or abroad and contributed to the general household income. The migrant could be almost sure that decisions made in his/her absence were in the interest of the household.[34] The classic intervention against such an argument can probably be found in many diaries: complaints about disregard or disrespect and stories of unjust enrichment of individual family members. And yet these complaints or anomalies were measured against the norm that the family was the basic social and conceptual unit. The closeness of family life and work caused the incalculability of mutual services and benefits and thus rendered a high degree of reciprocity.

A closer look at migrant families in the twentieth century in the Balkans reveals that even though the zadruga had come to an end, the concept of extended family in which mutual help was self-evident was still alive. Especially in rural areas it was quite common that parents left their children behind while working abroad. They somehow continued the *pečalba* tradition; a migration tradition of mainly male family members leaving their village or town in order to find seasonal work in other regions. This kind of migration did not automatically evoke disentanglement from the family or the region of origin. The migration

32 Kohli, Die Institutionalisierung des Lebenslaufes, 4–5.

33 Glick Schiller, Basch, Blanc, Transnationalism: A New Analytic Framework; Lutz, Leben in der Twilightzone.

34 See Oberpenning, "People were on the move".

process was seasonal and the *pečalbari* perpetually returned back to their home.[35] Some of the migrants who left their children behind would probably not even dare to describe the situation in these terms. The idea that they had actually left their children behind would not come into their mind, since their sisters and brothers, aunts and uncles or grandmothers and grandfathers were looking after the kids.

From this perspective the findings of studies about Yugoslav "guest workers" and their children are not surprising. They show that children in rural areas suffered less from the absence of their parents than children in cities.[36] Apparently and not astonishingly, the family structures in rural areas are more resistant to social change than in the cities. Without fixation on the nuclear family the absence of the parents is less dramatic. Since the receiving countries focussed on the nuclear family and only allowed family unification of the closest relatives, the dissolution of the extended family was accelerated in the migration process.[37] It should also now be evident that the description of these families as transnational is misleading, since families can hardly be defined along national borders. For them, national borders only matter if they interfere and disturb the family unit – be it an economic unit or a modern family. In the 1970s only twenty-three percent of the Yugoslav families in Germany were completely living in Germany: seventy-five percent of the children lived in Yugoslavia and were raised by relatives – a relatively high number in comparison with other countries of emigration.

So far the description of migrant families has been without the idea of a network. As mentioned above a societal network theory makes sense only under the condition that social relations are not predetermined by societal structures, but are understood as reflexively producible. Without a doubt, it is possible to use network analysis to describe the relations within pre-modern families in more detail. It is also possible to adopt important insights from network theory to pre-modern societies, such as that relations rather than individuals are in the focus of analysis and that power, for example, is neither a property of the individual nor can it be directly influenced by an individual. Changes at certain nodes in the network are thus able to alter the position for other remote nodes and their relations. And yet it is the sociology or anthropology of the family that offers more insights into family structures than modern network theory. It is also general social theory that provides the framework in which network analysis unfolds its analytical surplus. Looking at the family as an economic unit differs markedly from the modern concept of a family, which renders significantly different necessities for network building and maintenance.

35 Morokvašić, Jugoslawische Frauen, 59.

36 Katunarić, Vanjske migracije i promjene, 89.

37 Stölting, Die Zweisprachigkeit jugoslawischer Schüler, 33; Pusić, Gegenwärtige Entwicklung der Familie, 34.

The modern nuclear family: a segment with links to functional systems

What makes modern families so different except that they are smaller? To talk about modern families means talking about an old word with a young meaning. Most notably this statement becomes clear with respect to the appraisal of the family by the Catholic Church. The current plaudit of the family was absent at the beginning of ecclesiastical history and is a product of the nineteenth century, when the Church adapted itself to the primacy of functional differentiation. It is only then that the Catholic Church started to privilege marriage and family as a divine institution, and to propagate that children are the most valuable godsend for married couples.[38] As mentioned above the family as a social system can still be addressed as a system which is differentiated by segmentation, though then and now society was and is not compounded of families.[39] The absence of a single family would not unhinge the world; the absence of a functional system (e.g. law, economy, education) would probably cause troubles such as in former times, when the absence of a social stratum would have had severe consequences. The difference between the pre-modern and the modern family lies in its embeddedness. In pre-modern times the family was embedded in a social stratum and membership of a certain family determined the role in society. Nowadays families have lost their all-embracing determining power. They are no longer embedded in the social strata, but loosely coupled with other social systems. It has become impossible to order functional systems along families. This entails that families have lost their general instance of inclusion in society. Certainly, well-educated, smart and rich parents or relatives increase the probability of their youngsters performing well at school, and they might help if it comes to searching for a job. Yet, and this is equally important, too much networking – and the term is used deliberately – is not appreciated and might even be regarded as corrupt or at least unfair. Thus the probability of being included in many or even all functional systems via the family status is rather low.

Whereas the functionally specialised systems of society are always only partly interested in individuals and thus address them mainly in one single dimension of their personality (e.g. science addresses somebody as a good scientist but not as a good mother, or as a brilliant student but not as a good player, etc.), the social system family is interested in the whole person and thus includes him or her completely – *in toto*: everything which affects a family member, all acts and experiences, including those made beyond the family, are of potential interest for the communication within the family and can become a subject for discussion.[40] If everything is relevant to everybody within the nuclear two-generation family, and if secrets can be kept only to a limited extent (e.g. in diaries, letters, e-mails, etc.) then intimate relations will grow. Now that the ideal is claimed, it has to be modified.

38 Fresacher, Moderne Familien.
39 Luhmann, Die Gesellschaft der Gesellschaft, 634f.
40 Baraldi, Corsi, Esposito, GLU, Glossar zu Niklas Luhmanns Theorie, 56.

Most importantly a difference between the parents as a social system and their children as another social system has to be made. The imperative of frankness applies first and foremost to couples. It applies also to parents and their children but with a marked difference. Whereas children allow themselves to lie to their parents, they get mad if their parents lie to them. The asymmetry clarifies that even though communication within the family is often marked by the medium love, a clear link between the family and love or intimacy is missing; as opposed to the economy, for example, which knows the clear link of the medium money.

The possibility of intense and intimate relations within families has only become possible due to the dominance of functional differentiation. Only if a certain share of interactions is regulated anonymously, can individuals gain the capacity to intensify some of their social relations. The rise of love as passion and the romantic concept of marriage are some results of these developments.[41] The medium love is supplemented by a high amount of reciprocal interactions. At the same time monetary market mechanisms are excluded. Reciprocity guides interactions both in cooperation and in conflict and sets rules for exchange and revenge. The closer and nearer a relationship is lived, like in a household, the more unspecific becomes the relation of donation and requital and the more inadequate becomes the summation and clearing.[42] The fact that divorce rates are increasing, that domestic violence is an ongoing problem and that other evils continue to survive within the family are no counter-arguments, for all these ugly things destroy the family, or if these things occur hardly anybody dares address the family as family.

The difficulties for migrant families and the threat against the continuity of the family within a transnational situation now become clear. To fulfil the normative claim that the world of 'alter' must be taken into account if 'ego' decides, becomes increasingly difficult if 'alter' is absent. It also becomes easier to hide something from other family members. Means of instant communication might substitute the lack of physical co-presence but it is unlikely that they stop or change the basic process of differentiation. The rule that the amount of secrets must be limited is hard to supervise, if 'alter' lives far away.[43] In the case of regulated labour migration, at least from Yugoslavia to Germany, another point worth noting is that the initial costs of migration were relatively low. Of course, there were friends and relatives who gave small loans to ease the start abroad or who encouraged people to move, but with the coming into effect of the bilateral treaty on the recruitment of workers between the FRG and SFRY in 1969, initial costs became a negligible obstacle. Article 12 of the treaty even regulated who was to pay for lunch during the workers' travel from Yugoslavia to Germany, which today seems really odd.[44] Emphasising these low financial hurdles is important since the opposite is more often the case in migration processes, i.e. relatives put money aside

41 LUHMANN, Liebe als Passion.
42 LUHMANN, Die Gesellschaft der Gesellschaft, 653.
43 Cf. GOEKE, Transnationale Migrationen, 138 passim.
44 See the bilateral convention between the Federal Republic of Germany and the Socialist Federal Republic of Yugoslavia about the control of the interposition of Yugoslav employees to Germany and their occupation in Germany, *Bundesgesetzblatt*, II, 1969, 1107–1115.

in order to one day fund the migration of one person. This creates completely different normative claims.[45]

This theoretical outline leaves no doubt that network analyses can be applied to modern families, but scepticism, nevertheless, is advisable. Network analyses might deliver apt and instructive descriptions of the family itself but as long as they restrict themselves only to the social system family, it is likely that they will fail to denominate the specific characteristics of families within a changing society. They also ignore the fact that specific modern networks are networks across the boundaries of social systems. In combination with general social change it becomes clear that the zadruga, even though it survived semantically, has changed dramatically in the Balkans. This development has different roots and dimensions: collectivisation of agriculture and industry, urbanisation, emancipation and the spread of matrilineal elements in families, the access and adoption of modern principles of the state in Yugoslavia and in its successor states as well as in other South East European states – not to mention other changes.[46]

Establishing specific networks: boundary spanning in a functionally differentiated society

Finally the various thoughts and arguments shall be illustrated by an empirical example. The case will demonstrate that family borders are drawn through the medium of love and that they are based on the idea that the amount of secrets is under surveillance. It makes clear that families have lost their all-encompassing inclusionary power in the process of modernisation. Regardless of the observation that families might serve as the initial foundation for network creation, the example shows that the actual specificity of networks lies in their boundary-spanning capacities.

This case example is of Dina Kertész.[47] I met and interviewed her during my field research in Germany while she was spending a few months there; usually she lives and studies in Serbia. We were talking about her foreign connections and she told me that both an uncle and an aunt of hers were living abroad. The uncle migrated to Germany and the aunt to Australia. She considers her uncle as a 'guest worker' even though she doubts whether this is a concise denomination, since he will not come back to Serbia. Her aunt, by contrast, she considers an emigrant. Dina loves her aunt more than her uncle and gives reasons for her appraisal. She says that her aunt is always sending letters with pictures of her and her children. Her aunt also asks after Dina and her family in Serbia. Her uncle has never sent letters let alone pictures of his son: "He has never spoken about him [his son/my cousin]. It is as if he was excluded from our lives." So far the story is not surprising. This corresponds with the

45 Cf. Müller-Mahn, Ein ägyptisches Dorf.
46 Denich, Urbanization and Women's Roles; Kaser, Familie und Verwandtschaft.
47 For the case in all its details see Goeke, Transnationale Migrationen, 273 passim.

claim that everything should be of interest to other family members and with the ban on having too many secrets. Other elements of her description are more startling. She has seen her aunt only two or three times in her life, but her uncle on an annual basis. Additionally it is her uncle and not her aunt who regularly sends money back home, and it is Dina who benefits from the money because it allows her to study more comfortably in Belgrade. For the purpose of this study, the intentions of aunt and uncle can be neglected; I also abstain from evaluating the gender relations. From Dina's point of view it is love and trust that are missing in the relation to her uncle and only this is decisive. It can be concluded that financial transfers are important but by no means sufficient to maintain the inclusion of a person within a family. Without love and with too many secrets no family will survive – remittances then become an annoying burden.

When I met Dina, she had been considering moving to Germany. The legal possibilities for her were rather limited and she did not dare ask her uncle or cousin for help – neither for information nor for a personal security. This is crucial. From her narration it became clear that they hardly belonged to her family, even though they might have had a different status from her mother's perspective. Within a family favours should not be a problem but here the potential request can be characterised as a boundary-spanning process. Within the framework of network language, the tie to her uncle can be classified as a weak tie as opposed to a strong one. Although it was shown that in some contexts, better jobs and opportunities can be gained through such weak ties,[48] Dina's weak tie was apparently useless for her purposes. Her weak tie, i.e. a tie which crosses homogeneous horizons of meaning, knowledge and possibilities, was, from her point of view, hardly exploitable for her further plans. What can be seen in this particular situation is that the initial claiming of benefits is a precarious step. Not necessarily because 'alter' might refuse the request – for whatever reasons – but because of the potential asymmetry in the request. Formulated as a question: will I, or some of my acquaintances, ever be able to do a favour for him? Dina gave a negative answer to this question and the situation was even more precarious, since the expected asymmetry had already existed for a long time. She had been benefiting for years from his remittances without giving anything back. The network fell through. Her uncle was not considered as a part of her family thus it required some sort of boundary spanning to address him; such networks are probably the specific networks of modern times, i.e. networks which combine a variety of addresses with various backgrounds. These networks can thus be labelled as a specific new form, which has become necessary and extremely useful within the ongoing process of (functional) differentiation.

The claim that the specificity of modern networks lies in their boundary-spanning capacity can be supported by other observations, but firstly the objection that boundary spanning is an everyday phenomenon has to be opposed: the functional system education, for example, is linked with the economy via school reports or diplomas; the economy is coupled through taxes with the political system and through the constitution with the legal system

[48] GRANOVETTER, The Strenght of Weak Ties.

and so on. But all these linkages and connections work without particular individuals – unlike networks, which are dominated by the primacy of the individual address.

The transformation period in Eastern and Southeastern Europe is thus an interesting process. Which role did networks play during this time? It has often been argued and shown in various studies that networks were decisive and beneficial for some individuals but less so for the countries in total. These networks were classified as some sort of nepotism and considered to be major obstacles in the modernisation and democratisation process.[49] But what are the implications of such findings? It is obvious that the moral quality of networks is measured against modern norms and ideals. It is only in this context that some networks are as such remarkable. Kin networks, formerly rather known as extended families, are now under suspicion since they are no longer accepted as a principle of social order and rule. Even though the modern social order in functional systems is as contingent, i.e. not logically necessary, as kin or other networks are, the latter are nowadays viewed with scepticism and considered to be changeable, whereas functional systems hide their contingency.[50]

Conclusion

The theoretical draft and short analyses have shown how and when networks as a specific social form might become relevant and grow in size and number. There is no doubt that network analysis provides a powerful tool to analyse networks, which range from corrupt and terrorist networks, over inter- and intra-organisational networks of reputation, to nice networks of friendship and help.[51] But the argument at stake in this paper differs slightly from such general or broad applications. With reference to systems theory and to networks related to families, it was shown that networks as a specific and unique social form rely on the functional differentiation of society. As such the talk about specific networks only makes sense if addressees can be combined freely and reflexively. By separating *explanans* and *explanandum* it becomes possible to understand that networks should be better seen as secondary and dependent forms. General social theory not only offers a theoretical position for networks but also a concept of society, which helps to control claims about social change.

By discussing the transformation of the family it became clear that the family is no longer an economic unit but a place where love and intimacy should thrive. This shift has

[49] E. g. see studies on the role of networks in Bulgaria in Brunnbauer, Kaser, Vom Nutzen der Verwandten.

[50] Accordingly the paper does not object to the importance of networks, for example in migrant families (as shown by Čapo Žmegač, Transnacionalizam, for example). Whether these 'networks' are specifically modern networks or whether the interactions within families should better be described in other terms is questionable. I prefer a more restricted usage due to the arguments made above.

[51] E. g. Krebs, Mapping Networks of Terrorist Cells; Glückler, Reputationsnetz; Müller-Mahn, Ein ägyptisches Dorf in Paris.

become possible thanks to the primacy of functional differentiation. It also requires more individual networking, since the family or other social systems as all-embracing social forms of inclusion have lost their inclusionary power. Thus networks which follow and primarily combine various addressees with each other have not come to the forefront of social research by accident. Such a limited conception of networks renders the concept a powerful analytical and descriptive category – not only with regard to families or social change but also with regard to modern societies on a more general scale.

Bibliography

Abu-Lughod, Lila: Writing against Culture, in: Richard G. Fox (ed.): Recapturing Anthropology: Working in the Present. Santa Fe, New Mexico: School of American Research Press 1991, 137–162.

Adamic, Louis: The Land of Promise, *Harpers Magazine* (1931), no. 153 (October), 618–619.

Adamović, Mirjana / Silva Mežnarić: Migration of Young Croatian Scientists, *AEMI Journal* (2006), no. 4–5, 81–92.

Åkerman, Sune: Towards an Understanding of Emigrational Processes, in: William H. McNeill / Ruth S. Adams (eds.): Human Migration. Patterns and Policies. Bloomington, London: Indiana University Press 1978, 287–306.

Akrap, Anđelko: Migracije Hrvata u posljednjem desetljeću 20. stoljeća, in: P. Josip Klarić (ed.): Hrvatska dijaspora u crkvi i domovini. Frankfurt/M. 2003, 23–55.

Al-Ali, Nadje / Khalid Koser: Transnationalism, International Migration and Home, in: Nadje Al-Ali / Khalid Koser (eds.): New Approaches to Migration? Transnational Communities and the Transformation of Home. London, New York: Routledge 2002, 1–14.

Alasuutari, Pertti: The Discursive Construction of Personality, in: Amia Lieblich / Ruthellen Josselson (eds.): The Narrative Study of Lives, vol. 5. London, New Delhi, Sage Publications 1997, 1–3.

Allcock, John B.: Explaining Yugoslavia. London: Hurst & Company 2000.

Alund, Aleksandra: Teoretski okvir za istraživanje dvostruke polujezičnosti kod manjinskih grupa, *Rasprave o migracijama* 20 (1975), 39–45.

Anderson, Kathryn / Dana C. Jack: Learning to Listen. Interview Techniques and Analyses, in: Robert Perks / Alistair Thompson (eds.): The Oral History Reader. London, New York: Routledge 1998, 157–171.

Andrees, Beate: Die kosovo-albanische Diaspora zwischen Krieg und Frieden, *WeltTrends* 9 (2001), no. 32, 59-76.

Anić de Osona, Marija: Die erste Anerkennung der DDR. Der Bruch der deutsch-jugoslawischen Beziehungen 1957. Baden-Baden: Nomos Verlagsgesellschaft 1990.

Anić, Josip: Tradicija migracija u Imotskoj krajini, *Migracijske teme* 5 (1989), no. 4, 269–286.

Anić, Josip / Sonja Podgorelec, Psihičke tegobe prognane i izbjegle djece, *Migracijske teme* 8 (1992), no 3–4, 217–229.

Anteby-Yemini, Lisa / William Berthomière / Gabriel Sheffers (eds.): Les diasporas, 2000 ans d'histoire: issu du colloque tenu les 14, 15 et 16 février à Poitiers. Rennes: Presses universitaires de Rennes 2005.

Antić, Ljubomir: Arhiv Jugoslavenske Narodne Obrane – Glavno vrelo za istraživanje povijesti iseljeništva u južnoj americi, *Migracije* 12 (1981), no. 10, 444–447.

Antić, Ljubomir: Prilog istraživanju austrijske iseljeničke politike i zakonodavstva kao činilaca masovnog iseljavanja iz dalmacije pred prvi svjetski rat, *Zadarska revija* (1985), no. 2–3, 242–254.

Bibliography

Antić, Ljubomir: Naše iseljeništvo u Južnoj Americi i stvaranje jugoslavenske države 1918. Zagreb: Stvarnost 1987.

Antić, Ljubomir: Iseljenička politika stare jugoslavenske države, in: Nusret Šehić et al. (eds.): Migracije i Bosna i Hercegovina. Sarajevo: Institut za istoriju, Institut za proučavanje nacionalnih odnosa 1990, 229–236.

Antić, Ljubomir: Hrvati i Amerika. Zagreb: Hrvatska sveučilišna naklada, Hrvatska matica iseljenika 2002.

Austin, John L.: How to Do Things with Words. London: Oxford University Press 1971.

Avdić, Avdija: Jugoslovensko turski pregovori o iseljavanju muslimanskog stanovništva u periodu između dva svetska rata, *Novopazarski zbornik* 15 (1991), 112–125.

Avdić, Hakija: Položaj Muslimana u Sandžaku: 1912–1941. Sarajevo: Biblioteka Ključanin 1991.

Avramovski, Živko: Prilog pitanju italijansko-albanske iredentističke propagande na Kosovu i Metohiji u vreme minhenske krize i okupacije Albanije, *Istorijski glasnik* (1964), no. 2–3, 123–140.

Bade, Klaus J.: Migration in European History. Oxford: Blackwell Publishing 2003.

Bade, Klaus J.: Sozialhistorische Migrationsforschung, in: Michael Bommes / Jochen Oltmer (eds.): Sozialhistorische Migrationsforschung. Osnabrück: V & R unipress 2004 [1988], 13–25.

Baily, Samuel L.: Immigrants in the Lands of Promise. Italians in Buenos Aires and New York City, 1870 to 1914. Cornell: Cornell University Press 1999.

Baily, Samuel L. / Franco Ramella (eds.): One Family, Two Worlds. An Italian Family's Correspondence across the Atlantic, 1901–1922. New Brunswick, London: Rutgers University Press 1988.

Bajrami, Hakif: Konventa jugoslavo-turke e vitit 1938 për shpërnguljen e shqiptarëve, *Gjurmime albanologjike. Seria e shkencave historike* 12 (1982), 243–271.

Baletic, Zvonimir: International Migration in Modern Economic Development. With special Reference to Yugoslavia, *International Migration Review* 6 (1982), no. 4, 736–756.

Baletić, Zvonimir: Međunarodne migracije u modernom ekonomskom razvitku, *Ekonomski pregled* 32 (1982), no. 3–4, 125–135.

Banac, Ivo: The National Question in Yugoslavia: Origins, History, Politics. Ithaca, London: Cornell University Press 1984.

Banović, Branimir: Emigracijska Politika Austro-Ugarske i Iseljavanje iz Hrvatske u razdoblju 1867–1914, *Migracijske teme* 3 (1987), no. 3–4, 313–323.

Baraldi, Claudio / Giancarlo Corsi / Elena Esposito (eds.): GLU. Glossar zu Niklas Luhmanns Theorie sozialer Systeme. Frankfurt/M.: Suhrkamp 1997.

Barbič, Ana / Inga Miklavčič-Brezigar: Domestic Work Abroad: A Necessity and an Opportunity for Rural Women from Goriška Borderland Region of Slovenija, in: Janet Henshall Momsen (ed.): Migration and Domestic Service. London: Routledge 1999, 164–177.

Bartulica, Milostislav: Iseljenička konferencija u Splitu. Zagreb: Savez organizacija iseljenika u Zagrebu 1929.

Bartulica, Milostislav: Iseljenički kongres u Sarajevu. Zagreb: Savez organizacija iseljenika u Zagrebu 1933.

Basch, Linda / Nina Glick Schiller / Cristina Szanton Blanc: Nations Unbound: Transnational Projects, Postcolonial Predicaments, and Deterritorialized Nation-States. New York: Gordon and Breach 1994.

Baskin, Mark Allan: Political Innovation and Policy Implementation in Yugoslavia: the Case of Worker Migration Abroad. PhD dissertation, University of Michigan 1986.

Baučić, Ivo: Porijeklo i struktura radnika iz Jugoslavije u SR Njemačkoj. Zagreb: Institut za geografiju Sveučilišta u Zagrebu 1970.

Bibliography

Baučić, Ivo: Socijalno-ekonomske posljedice vanjskij migracija radne snage iz Jugoslavije, *Geografski glasnik* 33–34 (1971–1972), 25–59.

Baučić, Ivo: The Effects of Emigration from Yugoslavia and the Problems of Returning Emigrant Workers. The Hague: Martinus Nijhoff 1972.

Baučić, Ivo: Neka suvremena obilježa i problemi vanjskih migracija jugoslavenskih radnika, *Sociologia* 15 (1973), no. 2, 183–216.

Baučić, Ivo: Radnici u inozemstvu prema popisu stanovništva Jugoslavije 1971. Zagreb: Radovi Instituta za geografiju sveučilišta u Zagrebu 1973.

Baučić, Ivo: Die Auswirkungen der Arbeitskräftewanderung in Jugoslawien, in: Reinhard Lohrmann / Klaus Manfrass (eds.): Ausländerbeschäftigung und internationale Politik. Zur Analyse transnationaler Sozialprozesse. Munich, Vienna: R. Oldenbourg Verlag 1974, 171–206.

Baučić, Ivo: Regional Differences in Yugoslav External Migration, in: Huey Louis Kostanick (ed.): Population and Migration Trends in Eastern Europe. Boulder, Co. 1977, 218–243.

Baučić, Ivo: Stanje vanjskih migracija iz Jugoslavije krajem sedamdesetih godina. Zagreb: Centar za istraživanje migracija 1979 (Rasprave o migracijama, 57).

Baučić, Ivo: Regional Differences in Yugoslav External Migration, in: Huey Louis Kostanik (ed.): Population and Migration Trends in Eastern Europe. Boulder: Westview Press 1997, 217-244.

Baučić, Ivo / Bernd Gross: Rückkehr und Reintegration jugoslawischer Arbeitnehmer aus der BRD. Dt.-jugosl. Untersuchung der Zukunftspläne jugoslawischer Arbeitsmigranten und ihre Realisierung nach der Rückkehr. Bonn: Bundesminister für Arbeit und Sozialordnung 1987.

Beck, Ulrich: Macht und Gegenmacht im globalen Zeitalter. Neue weltpolitische Ökonomie. Frankfurt/M.: Suhrkamp Verlag 2002.

Becket Ian F.: The Great War, 1914–1918. Harlow: Pearson Education Limited 2001.

Benko Grado, Artur: Razvitak naše državne iseljeničke službe, *Jutarnji list* 28 (8 October 1939), no. 9952, 21.

Bessel, Richard: Mobilizing German Society for War, in: Roger Chickering / Stig Förster (eds.): Great War, Total War. Cambridge, Washington: Cambridge University Press and German Historical Institute 2000, 437–452.

Bigo, Didier: Globalized In-security: The Field of the Professionals of Unease Management and the Ban-opticon, *Traces: A Multilingual Journal of Cultural Theory* 4 (2005), 109–157.

Bilandžić, Dušan: Historija Socijalističke Federativne Republike Jugoslavije: glavni procesi 1918–1985. Zagreb: Školska knjiga 1985.

Blagojević, Gordana: Srbi u Kaliforniji. Belgrade: Etnografski institut SANU 2005 (Posebno izdanje, 54).

Blagojević, Gordana: Srbi u Grčkoj u 20. veku: transformacija identiteta. Belgrade: Etnografski institut SANU, forthcoming.

Bodnar, John: The Transplanted, A History of Immigrants in Urban America. Bloomington: Indiana University Press 1985.

Boeckh, Katrin: Von den Balkankriegen zum Ersten Weltkrieg: Kleinstaatenpolitik und ethnische Selbstbestimmung auf dem Balkan. Munich: Oldenbourg Verlag 1996 (Südosteuropäische Arbeiten, 97).

Böhning, Roger W.: Elements of a Theory of International Economic Migration to Industrial Nation States, in: Mary M. Kritz et al. (eds.): Global Trends in Migration: Theory and Research on International Population Movements. Staten Island, New York: Center for Migration Studies 1981, 28–43.

Bojnički, Artur Benko: Smjernice emigracione politike, *Socijalni preporođaj* (1925), no. 1–2, 35-36.

Bojnički, Artur Benko: Koje bi smjernice trebalo dati našoj emigracionoj politici, *Socijalni preporođaj* (1925), no. 4, 215.

Bibliography

BOKUN, Petar: Faktor migracija u genezi suicida, *Rasprave o migracijama* 63 (1980), 79–86.

BOMMES, Michael / Utz MAAS: Interdisciplinarity in Migration Research: On the Relation between Sociology and Linguistics, in: Michael BOMMES / Ewa MORAWSKA (eds.): International Migration Research: Constructions, Omissions and the Promises of Interdisciplinarity. Aldershot: Ashgate 2005, 179–202.

BOMMES, Michael / Veronika TACKE: Das Allgemeine und das Besondere des Netzwerkes, in: Betina HOLLSTEIN / Florian STRAUS (eds.): Qualitative Netzwerkanalyse. Wiesbaden: Verlag für Sozialwissenschaften 2006, 37–62.

BOUGAREL, Xavier: Allemagne: Assimilation ou préservation des spécificités, in: Didier LAPEYRONNIE (ed.): Immigrés en Europe: Politiques locales d'intégration. Paris: Harmattan 1992, 19–54.

BOURDIEU, Pierre: Le capital social. Notes provisoires, *Actes de la recherche en sciences sociales* 31 (1980), no. 2–3.

BOURDIEU, Pierre: Ce que parler veut dire, L'économie des signes linguistiques. Paris: Fayard 1982.

BOURDIEU, Pierre / John B. THOMPSON: Language and Symbolic Power. Cambridge, Mass.: Harvard University Press 1991.

BOYD, Monica: Family and Personal Networks in International Migration: Recent Developments and New Agendas, *International Migration Review* 23 (1989), no. 3, 638–670.

BOŽIĆ, Saša: Posljednja avantura: umirovljeničke migracije, klima i "ugodnosti", *Migracijske i etničke teme* 17 (2001), no. 4, 311–326.

BOŽIĆ, Saša: Nacionalizam – nacija, "transnacionalizam" – "transnacija": mogućnosti terminološkog usklađivanja, *Revija za sociologiju* 35 (2004), no. 3–4, 187–204.

BOŽIĆ, Saša: Strengthening Cross Border Cooperation in the Western Balkans Regarding Migration Management, in: Vladimir PETRONIJEVIĆ (ed.): Migration Flows in Southeastern Europe. A Compendium of National Perspectives. Belgrade: Sinag 2007, 13–42.

BOŽIĆ, Saša: Integration of Migrants: Political Models and Social Reality, 2008, <http://www.hgk.hr/wps/wcm/resources/file/eb9e0e0e7de8d0d/useljenicka_politika_program_EN.pdf>, last access: 8.7.2008.

BOŽIĆ, Saša / Ivan BURIĆ: Migracijski potencijal Hrvatske – mikroanalitički aspekti, *Migracijske i etničke teme* 21 (2005), no. 1–2, 9–33.

BRANDT, Willy: Begegnungen und Einsichten. Die Jahre 1960–1975. Hamburg: Hoffmann und Campe 1976.

BRATIĆ, Dobrila / Miroslava MALEŠEVIĆ: Kuća kao statusni simbol, *Etnološke sveske* 4 (1982), 144–152.

BRECELJ, Aleš: Nekaj podatkov o izseljevanju iz Slovenskega primorja v Južno Ameriko, predvsem v Argentino, *Annales* 7 (1997), no. 10, 215–236.

BRETTELL, Caroline B.: Theorizing Migration in Anthropology, in: Caroline B. BRETTELL / James F. HOLLIFIELD (eds.): Migration Theory: Talking across Disciplines. New York, London: Routledge 2000, 97–135.

BRETTELL, Caroline B.: Anthropology and Migration. Essays on Transnationalism, Ethnicity and Identity. Walnut Creek: Alta Mira Press 2003.

BRITISH HELSINKI HUMAN RIGHTS GROUP: Macedonia in Crisis. Report. 29.6.2001, <http://www.bhhrg.org/CountryReport.asp?ReportID=147&CountryID=15>, last access: 10.1.2008.

BROWN, Keith: In the Realm of a Double-Headed Eagle: Parapolitics in Macedonia 1994–1999, in: Jane K. COWAN (ed.): Macedonia. The Politics of Identity and Difference, London: Pluto Press 2000, 122–139.

BRUBAKER, Rogers: Nationalism Reframed: Nationhood and the National Question in the New Europe. Cambridge: Cambridge Univ. Press 1996.

BRUBAKER, Rogers: Ethnicity without Groups, in: Andreas WIMMER et al. (eds.): Facing Ethnic Conflict. Toward a New Realism. Oxford: Rowman & Littlefield Publishers 2004, 34–52.

BRUNNBAUER, Ulf: Die Berge und die Familien: Haushaltsstrukturen unter Muslimen und Christen in den Rhodopen (19. und 20. Jahrhundert), in: Ulf BRUNNBAUER / Karl KASER (eds.): Vom Nutzen der Verwandten. Soziale Netzwerke in Bulgarien (19. und 20. Jahrhundert). Vienna: Böhlau 2001, 219–251.

BRUNNBAUER, Ulf: Nationalgeschichte als Auftrag. Die makedonische Geschichtswissenschaft nach 1991, *Jahrbücher für Geschichte und Kultur Südosteuropas* 4 (2002), 165-203.

BRUNNBAUER, Ulf: Fertility, Families and Ethnic Conflict. Macedonians and Albanians in the Republic of Macedonia, 1944–2002, *Nationalities Papers* 32 (2004), no. 3, 565-598.

BRYCESON, Deborah / Ulla VUORELA: Transnational Families in the Twenty-first Century, in: Deborah BRYCESON / Ulla VUORELA (eds.): The Transnational Family: New European Frontiers and Global Networks. Oxford, New York: Berg 2002, 3–30.

Bundesamt für Migration und Flüchtlinge: Migration, Asyl und Integration in Zahlen. Nürnberg 2006.

BURT, Ronald S.: Structural Holes. The Social Structure of Competition. Cambridge, London: Harvard University Press 1995.

ČAČIĆ, Jadranka: Francuzi, Jugoslaveni ili nešto treće?, *Migracijske teme* 4 (1988), no. 3, 249–264.

ČAČIĆ-KUMPES, Jadranka: Multiculturality in Croatian Education, in: Milan MESIĆ (ed.): Perspectives of Multiculturalism – Western and Transitional Countries. Zagreb: Faculty of Philosophy Press; Croatian Commission for UNESCO 2004, 315–329.

ČAČIĆ-KUMPES, Jadranka / Josip KUMPES: Etničke manjine: elementi definiranja i hijerarhizacija prava na razliku, *Migracijske i etničke teme* 21 (2005), no. 3, 173–186.

ČAČIĆ-KUMPES, Jadranka / Ivo NEJAŠMIĆ: Social Changes, Migration and Ethnic Structure: Case Study of Petrinja (Croatia), *Društvena istraživanja* 10 (2001), no. 1–2, 253–277.

ÇAĞAPTAY, Soner: Citizenship Policies in Interwar Turkey, *Nations and Nationalism* 9 (2003), no. 4, 601–619.

CANNISTRARO, Philip V. / Gianfausto ROSOLI: Fascist Emigration Policy in the 1920s: An Interpretative Framework, *International Migration Review* 13 (1979), no. 4, 673–692.

ČAPO ŽMEGAČ, Jasna: Constructing Difference, Identifying the Self: A Case of Croatian Repatriates from Serbia, in: Bojan BAŠKAR / Irena WEBER (eds.): Mediterranean Ethnological Summer School. Ljubljana: Univerza v Ljubljani 2002, 135–148.

ČAPO ŽMEGAČ, Jasna: Dva lokaliteta, dvije države, dva doma: transmigracija hrvatskih ekonomskih migranata u Minchenu, *Narodna umjetnost. Hrvatski časopis za etnologiju i folkloristiku* 40 (2003), no. 2, 117–131.

ČAPO ŽMEGAČ, Jasna: Transnacionalizam, lokalitet, rod: hrvatske migrantske obitelji u Münchenu, *Traditiones – Inštitut za slovensko narodopisje* 32 (2003), no. 2, 179–192.

ČAPO ŽMEGAČ, Jasna: Trajna privremenost u Njemačkoj i povratak hrvatskih ekonomskih migranata, in: Dražen ŽIVIĆ / Nenad POKOS / Anka MIŠETIĆ (eds.): Stanovništvo Hrvatske – dosadašnji razvoj i perspektive. Zagreb: Institut Ivo Pilar 2005, 255–273.

ČAPO ŽMEGAČ, Jasna: Dynamik der Beziehungen der Migranten zum Herkunftsland: biographische Perspektive, *Schweizerisches Archiv für Volkskunde* 102 (2006), no. 1, 1–20.

ČAPO ŽMEGAČ, Jasna: Strangers Either Way: The Lives of Croatian Refugees in Their New Home. New York: Berghahn Books 2007.

ČAPO ŽMEGAČ, Jasna: Encounters in the Transnational Social Space, in: Rajko MURŠIČ / Jaka REPIČ (eds.): Places of Encounter. In Memoriam Borut Brumen. Ljubljana: Univerza v Ljubljani 2007, 277–290.

ČAPO ŽMEGAČ, Jasna: Spanning National Borders: Split Lives of Croatian Migrant Families, *Migracijske i etničke teme* 23 (2007), no. 1–2, 33–49.

CASTLES, Stephen: La sociologie et la peur de "cultures incompatibles": commentaires sur le rapport Hoffmann-Nowotny, in: Marie-Claire CALOZ-TSCHOPP et al. (eds.): Europe: montrez patte blanche! Les nouvelles frontières du "laboratoire Schengen". Genève: Centre Europe-Tiers Monde 1994, 370–384.

CASTLES, Stephen / Mark MILLER: The Age of Migration: International Population Movements in the Modern World. New York: Guilford Press 1993.

ČEPIČ, Zdenko: Razvoj prebivalstva, in: Jasna FISCHER (ed.): Slovenska novejša zgodovina. Ljubljana: Mladinska knjiga 2005, 816–823.

ČERNELIĆ, Milana: Istraživanje tradicijske baštine, identiteta i etnogeneze primorskih Bunjevaca, *Senjski zbornik: prilozi za geografiju, etnologiju, gospodarstvo, povijest i kulturu* 30 (2003), 407–424.

CHASE, Susan E. / Coleen S. BELL: Interpreting the Complexity of Women's Subjectivity, in: Eva M. MCMAHAN / Kim Lacy ROGERS (eds.): Interactive Oral History Interviewing. New Jersey: Lawrence Erlbaum Associates 1994, 63–81.

CHMELAR, Hans: Höhepunkte der österreichischen Auswanderung. Die Auswanderung aus den im Reichsrat vertretenen Königreichen und Ländern in den Jahren 1905–1914. Vienna: Österreichische Akademie der Wissenschaften 1974 (Studien zur Geschichte der österreichisch-ungarischen Monarchie, 14).

ČIČAK-CHAND, Ružica: Ethnic and Cultural Identity of Muslim Immigrants in Western Europe, *AEMI Journal* 2 (2004), 106–118.

ČIČAK-CHAND, Ružica: Multikulturne politike i međuetnički odnosi: Kanada, *Migracijske i etničke teme* 21 (2005), no, 1–2, 55–68.

ČIČAK-CHAND, Ružica / Josip KUMPES (eds.): Etničnost, nacija, identitet: Hrvatska i Europa. Zagreb: Institut za migracije i narodnosti 1998.

ČIZMIĆ, Ivan: O iseljavanju iz Hrvatske u razdoblju 1880–1914, *Istoriski zbornik* 27/28 (1974/75), 27–47.

ČIZMIĆ, Ivan: Doseljavanje, struktura i položaj naših iseljenika u prekomorskim zemljama. Zagreb: Centar za istraživanje migracija 1976.

ČIZMIĆ, Ivan: Emigration from Yugoslavia Prior to World War II, in: Ira A. GLAZIER / Luigi DE ROSA (eds.): Migration across Time and Nations: Population Mobility in Historical Contexts. New York: Holmes & Meier 1986, 255–267.

ČIZMIĆ, Ivan: Jugoslavenski socijalisti u Sjedinjenim Američkim Državama u prvom razdoblju svoga djelovanja (1894–1910), *Migracijske teme* 4 (1988), no. 1–2, 79–87.

ČIZMIĆ, Ivan: Emigration from Croatia, 1880–1914, in: Julianna PUSKÁS (ed.): Overseas Migration from East-Central and Southeastern Europe 1880–1940. Budapest: Akadémiai Kiadó 1990, 143–167.

ČIZMIĆ, Ivan / Vesna MIKAČIĆ: Neki suvremeni problemi iseljeništva iz SR Hrvatske, vol. 1. Zagreb: Centar za istraživanje migracija 1974 (Teme o iseljeništvo, 12).

ČIZMIĆ, Ivan / Marin SOPTA / Vlado ŠAKIĆ: Iseljena Hrvatska. Zagreb: Golden Marketing 2005.

CLEWING, Konrad: Mythen und Fakten zur Ethnostruktur in Kosovo: Ein geschichtlicher Überblick, in: Jens REUTER / Konrad CLEWING (eds.): Der Kosovo Konflikt. Ursachen – Verlauf – Perspektiven. Klagenfurt et al.: Wieser Verlag 2000, 17–63.

CLEWING, Konrad / Edvin PEZO: Jovan Cvijić als Historiker und Nationsbildner: Zu Ertrag und Grenzen seines anthropogeographischen Ansatzes zur Migrationsgeschichte, in: Markus KRZOSKA / Hans-Christian MANER (eds.): Beruf und Berufung. Geschichtswissenschaft und Nationsbildung in Ostmittel- und Südosteuropa im 19. und 20. Jahrhundert. Münster: Lit Verlag 2005, 265–297 (Studien zur Geschichte, Kultur und Gesellschaft Südosteuropas, 4).

CLIFFORD, James: Diasporas, *Cultural Anthropology* 3 (1994), no. 9, 302–338.

COHEN, Robin: Global Diasporas: an Introduction. Seattle: University of Washington Press 1997.

Colic-Peisker, Val: Croatian and Bosnian Migration to Australia in the 1990s: Gender, Ethnicity and Belonging, in: C. Lange (ed.): Being Australian Women: Belonging, Citizenship and Identity. Nedlands: Centre for Western Australian History 2000, 117–136.

Colic-Peisker, Val: "Ethnic" and "Cosmopolitan" Transnationalism: Two Cohorts of Croatian Immigrants in Australia, *Migracijske i etničke teme* 22 (2006), no. 3, 211–230.

Condon, Richard: The Manchurian candidate. New York, N.Y.: Armchair Detective Library 1991 [1958].

Connolly, William E.: Essentially Contested Concepts in Politics, in: William E. Connolly (ed.): The terms of political discourse. Lexington, Mass: Heath 1974, 10–44.

Čoralić, Lovorka: Na drugoj obali Jadrana: Migracije iz Slavonije u Mletke od 15. do 17. stoljeća, *Migracijske i etničke teme* 19 (2003), no. 1, 97–110.

Čović, Bože (ed.): Izvori velikosrpske agresije. Rasprave, dokumenti, kartografski prikazi. Zagreb: August Cesarec 1991.

Crampton, Richard Ben: Atlas of Eastern Europe in the Twentieth Century. London: Routledge, 1996.

Crnković-Pozaić, Sanja: Buduće potrebe na tržištu rada. Možemo li bez imigracije?, in: Hrvatska gospodarska komora (ed.): Međunarodna konferencija Useljenička politika u funkciji razvoja hrvatskoga gospodarstva. Zagreb 2008, 21–28.

Dahinden, Janine: Contesting Transnationalism? Lessons from the Study of Albanian Migration Networks from Former Yugoslavia, *Global Networks. A Journal of Transnational Affairs* 5 (2005), no. 2, 191–208.

Dahinden, Janine: Prishtina – Schlieren. Albanische Migrationsnetzwerke im transnationalen Raum. Zürich: Seismo 2005.

Dahinden, Janine: Was heisst schon interkulturell? Mediation in den Zeiten der Globalisierung, in: Alex Von Sinner / Michael Zirkler (eds.): Hinter den Kulissen der Mediation. Kontexte, Perspektiven und Praxis der Konfliktbearbeitung. Bern: Haupt 2005, 101–114.

Dahinden, Janine: Deconstructing Mythological Foundations of Ethnic Identities and Ethnic Group Formation: Albanian-Speaking and New Armenian Immigrants in Switzerland, *Journal of Ethnic and Migration Studies* 34 (2008), no. 1, 55–76.

Dahinden, Janine / Joelle Moret: Transnationale Aktivitäten serbischer und kosovarischer Migrantenorganisationen in der Schweiz, in: Denise Efionayi-Mäder / Gérard Perroulaz / Catherine Schümperli Younossian (eds.): Schweizerisches Jahrbuch für Entwicklungspolitik: Migration und Entwicklung: Eine Zweckallianz. Genf: The Graduate Institute 2008, 235-248.

D'Amato, Gianni / Brigitta Gerber / Martina Kamm: Menschenschmuggel und irreguläre Migration in der Schweiz. Neuchâtel: Schweizerisches Forum für Migrations- und Bevölkerungsstudien 2005 (SFM-Forschungsbericht, 37).

Daniels, Roger: Coming to America. A History of Immigration and Ethnicity in American Life. New York: Perennial 2002.

Danquah, Meri Nana-Ama (ed.): Becoming American. Personal Essays by First Generation Immigrant Women. New York: Hiperion 2000.

Dăržaven vestnik: Zakon za emigracijata, *Dăržaven vestnik* 10 (14. January 1908), 2–5.

Definitivni rezultati popisa stanovništva od 31 januara 1921 god. Sarajevo: Državna štamparija 1932.

Deisinger, Mitja: Prepoved razširjanja, in: Lenart Šetinc (ed.): Omejitve javne besede. Ljubljana: Gospodarski vestnik 1989, 111–119.

Denich, Bette S.: Urbanization and Women's Roles in Yugoslavia, *Anthropological Quarterly* 49 (1976), no. 1, 11–19.

DENICH, Bette S.: Unmaking Multiethnicity in Yugoslavia. Media and Metamorphosis, in: Joel M. HALPERN / David A. KIDECKEL (eds.): Neighbors at War. Anthropological Perspectives on Yugoslav Ethnicity, Culture, and History. University Park, Penn.: The Pennsylvania University Press 2000, 39–55.

DERLER, Barbara / Robert PICHLER: Migration und die topographische Imagination von Heimat. Eine albanisch-makedonische Fallstudie, in: Klaus MÜLLER-RICHTER / Ramona URITECU-LOMBARD (eds.): Imaginäre Topographien. Migration und Verortung. Bielefeld: Transcript 2007, 213-236.

DEŽELIĆ, Berislav Đuro: Naša emigracija u Njemačkoj. Zagreb: Jugoslovenska Štampa 1931.

DIKIĆ, Božidar: Intervju Vili Branta "Politici". Nadamo se da će politički dijalog s Beogradom doprineti da se prebrodi podeljenost kontinenta, *Politika* (14 March 1968), 3.

DILLINGHAM, William P.: Dictionary of Races and Peoples. Reports of Immigration Commission, V. 5, 61st, Congress, 3rd Session, Document 16.748. Washington: Government Printing Office 1911.

DIMIĆ, Ljubodrag: Kulturna politika Kraljevine Jugoslavije: 1918–1941, vol. 1: Društvo i država. Belgrade: Stubovi kulture 1996.

DIMITRIJEVIĆ, Bojan: O sudbini srpskih vladara, *Srpska dijaspora,* 12.2.2006, <http://www.srpskadijaspora.info/index.asp>, last access: 26.2.2009.

ĐORĐEVIĆ, Obren: Osnovi državne bezbednosti: opšti deo. Belgrade: Visa skola unutrasnjih poslova 1985.

DODER, Milenko: Jugoslovenska neprijateljska emigracija. Zagreb: Centar za informacije i publicitet 1989.

DOLANC, Stane / Zoran VEJNOVIĆ: Snage, sredstva i metodi spoljnog ugrožavanja bezbednosti SFRJ. Belgrade: Odbrana i zaštita 1985.

DOLENEC, Ivan (ed.): Izbrani spisi, vol. 4. Celje: Družba sv. Mohorja 1933.

DRLJAČA, Dušan: Svedenost imigrantske potkulture Srba u SAD, in: Dušan DRLJAČA (ed.): Zbornik radova Etnografskog instituta SANU, vol. 20. Belgrade: SANU 1985, 45–56.

DRLJAČA, Dušan: Groblja Srba u dijaspori, Etno-antropološki problemi, vol. 7. Belgrade 1985, 67–73.

DRNOVŠEK, Marjan: Pot slovenskih izseljencev na tuje. Od Ljubljane do Ellis Islanda – Otoka solza v New Yorku, 1880–1924. Ljubljana: Založba Mladika 1991.

DRNOVŠEK, Marjan: The Attitude of the Slovene Catholic Church to Emigration to the United States of America before 1914, *Slovene Studies* 14 (1992), no. 2, 169–184.

DRNOVŠEK, Marjan: Mass Emigration and Slovenes, *Dve domovini / Two Homelands* 5 (1994), 19–36.

DRNOVŠEK, Marjan: Slovene Immigrants in Belgium before 1940, *Archives et bibliothèques de Belgique* 68 (1997), no. 1–4, 357–389.

DRNOVŠEK, Marjan: Usodna privlačnost Amerike: pričevanja izseljencev o prvih stikih z novim svetom. Ljubljana: Nova revija 1998.

DRNOVŠEK, Marjan: Slovenian Emigrants and Europe: Their Dispersal in the European Area in the Past Two Centuries, in: John MORISON (ed.): Ethnic and National Issues in Russian and East European History. Houndmills, New York: MacMillan Press Ltd. and St. Martin's Press 2000, 323–330.

DRNOVŠEK, Marjan: Izseljenec: življenjske zgodbe Slovencev po svetu, in: Monika Kokalj KOČEVAR (ed.): Izseljenec: življenjske zgodbe Slovencev po svetu. Ljubljana: Muzej novejše zgodovine Slovenije 2001, 9–26.

DRNOVŠEK, Marjan: Kuharica Liza v New Yorku, in: Monika KOKALJ KOČEVAR (ed.): Izseljenec: življenjske zgodbe Slovencev po svetu. Ljubljana: Muzej novejše zgodovine Slovenije 2001, 43–46.

DRNOVŠEK, Marjan: The Standpoint of the Communist Party of Slovenia Towards the Political Emigration up to 1991, *Dve domovini / Two Homelands* 19 (2002), 21–36.

DRNOVŠEK, Marjan: Izseljevanje je rak rana na telesu našega naroda, in: Metoda KOKOLE / Vojislav LIKAR / Peter WEISS (eds.): Historični seminar, vol. 4. Ljubljana: ZRC SAZU 2003, 7–33.

DRNOVŠEK, Marjan: Izseljevanje Kočevarjev v Združene države Amerike, *Dve domovini / Two Homelands* 21 (2005), 7–34.

DRNOVŠEK, Marjan: Jugoslovansko-nemška sporazuma o sezonskem delu med svetovnima vojnama, *Prispevki za novejšo zgodovino* 46 (2006), no. 1, 219–234.

DRNOVŠEK, Marjan: L'Europe et les Émigrants Slovènes, in: Marie PISLAR FERNANDEZ (ed.): Slovenci v železni Loreni (1919–1939) skozi družinske pripovedi / Slovènes en Lorraine du fer (1919–1939) à travers des récits de familles. Ljubljana: Založba ZRC 2006, 137–151.

Družbeni razvoj SR Slovenije 1947–1972. Ljubljana: Zavod SR Slovenije za planiranje, Zavod SR Slovenije za statistiko 1974.

DUFOIX, Stéphane: Notion, concept ou slogan: qu'y a-t-il sous le terme de "diaspora"? Paper presented at the Colloque 2000 ans de diasporas, Poitiers, France, February 2002.

DUFOIX, Stéphane: Généalogie d'un lieu commun, "diaspora" et sciences sociales, *Actes de l'Histoire de l'Immigration* 3 (2003), <http://barthes.ens.fr/clio/revues/AHI/articles/preprints/duf.html>, last access: 26.2.2009.

DUFOIX, Stéphane: Les Diasporas. Paris: P.U.F. 2003.

EFIONAYI-MÄDER, Denise et al.: Asyldestination Europa: eine Geographie der Asylbewegungen. Zürich: Seismo 2001.

EFIONAYI-MÄDER, Denise / Sandro CATTACIN: Illegal in der Schweiz. Eine Übersicht zum Wissensstand. Discussion Paper 12/2002. Neuchâtel: Schweizerisches Forum für Migrations- und Bevölkerungsstudien 2002.

Ekonomska politika: Teorija i život o radu van granica. Belgrade 1964.

ERCEG, Heni: Bojim se za Hrvatsku (Interviuj s Mirkom Tripalom), *Feral Tribune* (1994), no. 11/01, 4–5.

EREL, Umut: Reconceptualizing Motherhood: Experiences of Migrant Women from Turkey Living in Germany, in: Deborah BRYCESON / Ulla VUORELA (eds.): The Transnational Family: New European Frontiers and Global Networks. Oxford, New York: Berg 2002, 127–146.

ERIKSEN, Thomas Hilan [Hylland]: Etnicitet i nacionalizam. Belgrade: XX vek 2004.

European Stability Initiative (ESI): Ahmeti's Village. The Political Economy of Interethnic Relations in Macedonia. Brussels: ESI 2002, <http://www.esiweb.org/pages/rep/rep_mac_mac_02.htm>, last access: 10.1.2008.

European Stability Initiative (ESI): Cutting the Lifeline. Migration, Families and the Future of Kosovo. Brussels: ESI 2006, <http://www.esiweb.org/index.php?lang=en&id=156&document_ID=80>, last access: 11.8.2008.

FAIST, Thomas: The Volume and Dynamics of International Migration and Transnational Social Spaces. Oxford: Clarendon Press 2000.

FAIST, Thomas: Transnationalization in International Migration: Implication for the study of Citizenship and Culture, *Ethnic and Racial Studies* 23 (2000), no. 2, 189–222.

FELSHTINSKY, Yuri: The Legal Foundations of the Immigration and Emigration Policy of the USSR, 1917–27, *Soviet Studies* 34 (1982), no. 3, 327–348.

FERENC, Mitja 1993: Kočevska: Izgubljena kulturna dediščina kočevskih Nemcev. Ljubljana: Zavod Republike Slovenije za varstvo naravne in kulturne dediščine.

FIBBI, Rosita / Bülent KAYA / Etienne PIGUET: Le passeport ou le diplôme? Etude des discriminations à l'embauche des jeunes issus de la migration. Rapport de recherche 31/2001. Neuchâtel: Forum Suisse pour l'étude des migrations et de la population 2003.

FISCHER, Jasna: Migracije, in: Enciklopedija Slovenije, vol. 7. Ljubljana: Mladinska knjiga 1993, 122–125.

FISCHER, Jasna: Prebivalstvo, in: Enciklopedija Slovenije, vol. 9. Ljubljana: Mladinska knjiga 1995, 250–252.

FOUCAULT, Michel: Naissance de la biopolitique: Cours au Collège de France (1978–1979). Paris: Gallimard, Seuil 2004.

FOUCAULT, Michel: Sécurité, territoire, population: Cours au Collège de France (1977–1978). Paris: Gallimard, Seuil 2004.

FRESACHER, Bernhard: Moderne Familien: Modelle und Trends, in: Josip P. KLARIĆ (ed.): Hrvatska obitelj u pokretu = Die kroatische Migrantenfamilie. Pastorale Jahrestagung, Bergisch Gladbach, 9.–12.10.2000. Frankfurt/M.: Kroatenseelsorge in Deutschland 2001, 137–158.

FRIDENSON, Patrick: The Impact of the First World War on French Workers, in: Jay WINTER / Richard WALL (eds.): The Upheaval of War. Family, Work and Welfare in Europe 1914–1918. Cambridge, New York: Cambridge University Press 1988, 235–248.

GABACCIA, Donna: From the Other Side: Women, Gender, and Immigrant Life in the U.S., 1820–1990. Bloomington, Indianapolis: Indiana University Press 1994.

GABACCIA, Donna: When the Migrants are Men. Italy's Women and Transnationalism as a Working-Class Way of Life, in: Pamela SHARPE (ed.): Women, Gender and Labour Migration. Historical and Global Perspectives. London, New York: Routledge 2001, 190–208.

GAČEŠA, Nikola: Radovi iz agrarne istorije i demografije. Novi Sad: Matica Srpska 1995.

GAGNON JR., Valère Philip: The Myth of Ethnic War, Serbia and Croatia in the 1990s. Ithaca, London: Cornell University Press 2004.

GANTAR GODINA, Irena: Slovenski izobraženci iz Prage na Hrvaško, *Dve domovini / Two Homelands* 22 (2005), 197–218.

GAŠIĆ, Ranka: Beogradska politička i vojna elita u svetlu nemačkih i britanskih izvora pred drugi svetski rat, *Istorija 20. Veka* 3 (2006), no. 1, 63–80.

GELLNER, Ernest: Nations and Nationalism. Oxford: Blackwell 1983.

GERAY, Cevat: Türkiye'den ve Türkiye'ye göçler ve göçmenlerin iskanı (1923–1961). Ankara: Ankara Üniv. Siyasal Bilgiler Fak 1962 (Maliye Enst. Türk iktisadi gelişmesi arastırma projesi, 9).

GERBER, David A.: Epistolary Masquerades: Acts of Deceiving and Withholding in Immigrant Letters, in: Bruce S. ELLIOTT / David A. GERBER / Suzanne M. SINKE (eds.): Letters across Borders. The Epistolary Practices of International Migrants. New York, Hampshire: Palgrave Macmillan 2006, 141–157.

GESTRIN, Ferdo: Slovanske migracije v Italijo. Ljubljana: Slovenska matica 1998.

GILROY, Paul: Diaspora, *Paragraph* 17 (1994), no. 1, 207–212.

GLAMOČAK, Marina: Koncepcije Velike Hrvatske i Velike Srbije u političkoj emigraciji. Užice: KPZ 1997.

GLAMOČAK, Marina: La genèse de l'émigration politique serbe et croate, *Balkanologie* 2 (1998), no. 1, 37–61.

GLICK SCHILLER, Nina / Linda BASCH / Christina SZANTON BLANC: Transnationalism: A New Analytic Framework for Understanding Migration, in: Nina GLICK SCHILLER / Linda BASCH / Cristina BLANC-SZANTON (eds.): Towards a Transnational Perspective on Migration: Race, Class, Ethnicity and Nationalism Reconsidered, *Annals of the New York Academy of Sciences* 645 (1992), 1–24.

GLICK SCHILLER, Nina / Georges FOURON: Terrains of Blood and Nation: Haitian Transnational Social Fields, *Ethnic and Racial Studies* 22 (1999), no. 2, 340–366.

Gliederung der Bevölkerung des ehemaligen Jugoslawien nach Muttersprache und Konfession nach den unveröffentlichten Angaben der Zählung von 1931. Vienna: Selbstverlag der Publikationsstelle 1943.

GLÜCKLER, Johannes: Reputationsnetze. Zur Internationalisierung von Unternehmensberatern. Eine relationale Theorie. Bielefeld: Transcript 2004.

GODIN, Marie Amelie Freiin von: Das albanische Gewohnheitsrecht, *Zeitschrift für vergleichende Rechtswissenschaft* 57 (1954), 1–81.

GOEKE, Pascal: "It Ain't Interdisciplinarity if it Ain't Got Disciplines": On the Relation Between Geography and History in the Case of Transnational Migration Research, in: Patrick MANNING (ed.): World History: Global and Local Interactions. Princeton: Markus Wiener 2005, 149–165.

GOEKE, Pascal: Jugoslawische Arbeitswanderer in West-, Mittel und Nordeuropa seit dem Ende des Zweiten Weltkriegs, in: Klaus BADE et al. (ed.): Enzyklopädie der Migration. Munich: Schöningh 2007, 731–735.

GOEKE, Pascal: Transnationale Migrationen. Post-jugoslawische Biografien in der Weltgesellschaft. Bielefeld: Transcript 2007.

GOFFMAN, Erving: Frame analysis: an essay on the organization of experience. New York: Harper & Row 1974.

GOLUB, Branka: Neki aspekti potencijalnog odliva znanstvenika u inozemstvo, *Revija za sociologiju* 23 (1992), no. 1–2, 91–100.

GOMBAČ, Jure: Esuli ali optanti? Zgodovinski primer v luči sodobne teorije. Ljubljana: Založba ZRC 2005.

GOSAR, Anton: Obseg, vzročnost in karakteristika slovenskega izseljevanja v tujino, in: Ivan ČIZMIĆ et al. (eds.): Iseljeništvo naroda i narodnosti Jugoslavije i njegove uzajamne veze s domovinom. Zagreb: Zavod za migracije i narodnosti 1978, 144–159.

GOVORCHIN, Gerald G.: Americans from Yugoslavia. Gainesville, Fl.: University of Florida Press 1961.

GRANOVETTER, Mark: The Strength of Weak Ties, *American Journal of Sociology* 78 (1973), no. 6, 1360–1380.

GRANOVETTER, Mark: Economic Action and Social Structure: The Problem of Embeddedness, *American Journal of Sociology* 91 (1985), no. 3, 481–510.

GRBIĆ, Jadranka: Identitet, jezik, razvoj. Istraživanje o povezanosti etniciteta i jezika na primjeru hrvatske nacionalne manjine u Mađarskoj. Zagreb: Institut za etnologiju i folkloristiku 1994.

GREČIĆ, Vladimir / Mihailo JOVANOVIĆ: Osnovne komponente pretvaranja privremene ekonomske emigracije u iseljeništvo, in: Ivan ČIZMIĆ et al. (eds.): Iseljeništvo naroda i narodnosti Jugoslavije. Zagreb: Zavod za migracije i narodnosti 1978, 273–286.

GREEN, Nancy L.: The Politics of Exit: Reversing the Immigration Paradigm, *The Journal of Modern History* 77 (2005), no. 2, 263–289.

GREEN, Nancy L.: The Comparative Method and Poststructural Structuralism: New Perspectives for Migration Studies, in: Jan LUCASSEN / Leo LUCASSEN (eds.): Migration, Migration History, History. Old Paradigms and New Perspectives. Berlin, Vienna: Peter Lang 1999, 57–72.

GREEN, Nancy L. / François WEIL (eds.): Citizenship and Those Who Leave. The Politics of Emigration and Expatriation. Urbana, Chicago: University of Chicago Press 2007.

GROSS, Dominique M.: Immigration to Switzerland. The Case of the Former Republic of Yugoslavia. Washington/DC: World Bank, Development Research Group, Trade Team 2006 (Policy Research Working Paper, 3880).

GUARNIZO, Luis Eduardo / Alejandro PORTES / William HALLER: Assimilation and Transnationalism: Determinants of Transnational Political Action among Contemporary Migrants, *American Journal of Sociology* 108 (2003), no. 6, 1211–48.

GUARNIZO, Luis Eduardo / Michael Peter SMITH: The Locations of Transnationalism, in: Michael Peter SMITH / Luis Eduardo GUARNIZO (eds.): Transnationalism from Below. New Brunswick, London: Transaction Publishers 1998, 3–34.

GURAK, Douglas T. / Fe CACES: Migration Networks and the Shaping of Migration Systems, in: Mary M. KRITZ / Lin Lean LIM / Hania ZLOTNIK (eds.): International Migration Systems: A Global Approach. Oxford: Clarendon Press 1992, 150–176.

HABERL, Othmar Nikola: Die Abwanderung von Arbeitskräften aus Jugoslawien: zur Problematik ihrer Auslandsbeschäftigung und Rückführung. Munich: Oldenbourg 1978.

HADŽIĆ, Senad: Titos "Gastarbeiter". Hintergründe und Ursachen des Anwerbeabkommens zwischen der Bundesrepublik Deutschland und Jugoslawien, in: Dietmar NEUTATZ / Volker ZIMMERMANN (eds.): Die Deutschen und das östliche Europa. Essen: Klartext Verlag 2006, 103–114.

HALPERN, Joel M.: Some Perspectives on Balkan Migration Patterns (with particular reference to Yugoslavia), in: Brian M. DU TOIT / Helen I. SAFA (eds.): Migration and Urbanisation. Models and Adaptive Strategies: The Hague, Paris: Mouton Publishers 1975, 77–115.

HALPERN, Joel M. / Barbara KEREWSKY HALPERN: A Serbian Village in Historical Perspective. New York et al.: Holt, Rinehart and Winston 1992 [1967].

HANNERZ, Ulf: When Culture is Everywhere: Reflections on a Favorite Concept, *Ethnos* 58 (1993), no. 1–2, 95–111.

HANNERZ, Ulf: Kokoschka's return: Or, the Social Organization of Creolization, in: Ulf HANNERZ: Transnational Connections: Culture, People, Places. London, New York: Routledge 1996, 65–78.

HAREVEN, Tamara K.: Cycles, Courses and Cohorts: Reflections on Theoretical and Methodological Approaches to the Historical Study of Family Development, *Journal of Social History* 12 (1978), no. 1, 97–109.

HAREVEN, Tamara K.: Recent Research on the History of the Family, in: Michael DRAKE (ed.): Time, Family and Community: Perspectives on Family and Community History. Oxford: Blackwell Publishers 1994, 13–43.

HARVEY, George: Effects of the War upon Immigration, *North American Review* 100 (1915), no. 1, 667–671.

HATTON, Timothy J. / Jefrey G. WILLIAMSON: The Age of Mass Migration. New York, Oxford: Oxford University Press 1998.

HATTON, Timothy J. / Jefrey G. WILLIAMSON: Global Migration and the World Economy. Cambridge, London: The MIT Press 2006.

HERBERT, Ulrich: Geschichte der Ausländerpolitik in Deutschland. Munich: Verlag C. H. Beck 2001.

HERRERA LIMA, Fernando: Transnational Families: Institutions of Transnational Social Space, in: Ludger PRIES (ed.): New Transnational Social Spaces: International Migration and Transnational Companies in the Early Twenty-First Century. London, New York: Routledge 2001, 77–93.

HERŠAK, Emil: "Druga generacija migranata" i utjecaj sociolingvističkih procesa na materinski jezik migranata, *Migracijske teme* 1 (1985), no. 2, 23–38.

HERŠAK, Emil (ed.): Leksikon migracijskog i etničkog nazivlja. Zagreb: Institut za migracije i narodnosti 1998.

HERŠAK, Emil (ed.): Etničnost i povijest. Zagreb: Institut za migracije i narodnosti 1999.

Heršak, Emil: Drevne seobe: prapovijest i stari vijek. Zagreb: Školska knjiga 2005.

Heršak, Emil / Ružica Čičak-Chand, Kanada: Multikulturalizam, *Migracijske teme* 7 (1991), no. 1, 13–28.

Heršak, Emil / Milan Mesić: L'espace migratoire de Yougoslavie: historique des migrations yougoslaves, *Revue Européenne des Migrations Internationales* 2 (1990), no. 6, 27–64.

Historical Statistics of the United States. Colonial Times to 1970. Washington, DC: US Bureau of the Census 1979.

Hockenos, Paul: Homeland Calling. Exile Patriotism and the Balkan Wars. New York: Cornell University Press 2003.

Hoffmann-Nowotny, Hans-Joachim: Chancen und Risiken multikultureller Einwanderungsgesellschaften. Bern: Schweizerischer Wissenschaftsrat 1992.

Holjevac, Većeslav: Hrvati izvan domovine. Zagreb: Matica Hrvatska 1967.

Holzer, Boris: Netzwerke. Bielefeld: Transcript 2006.

Höpken, Wolfgang: Flucht vor dem Kreuz: Muslimische Emigration aus Südosteuropa nach dem Ende der osmanischen Herrschaft (19./20. Jahrhundert), *Comparativ* 6 (1996), no. 1, 1–24.

Horvat, Dražen: Tko nam dolazi u Hrvatsku, in: Hrvatska gospodarska komora (ed.): Međunarodna konferencija Useljenička politika u funkciji razvoja hrvatskoga gospodarstva. Zagreb 2008, 29–34.

Horvat, Lazar: Naše iseljeničko pitanje ili šta nam je Amerika dala i donela. Zagreb 1912.

Hrabak, Bogumil: Džemijet. Organizacija muslimana Makedonije, Kosova, Metohije i Sandžaka 1919–1928. Belgrade 2003.

Hranilović, Nada: Iseljenička politika i služba u Jugoslaviji između dva rata, *Migracijske teme* 3 (1987), no. 3–4, 325–334.

Hudelist, Darko: Banket u Hrvatskoj. Zagreb: Globus International 1999.

Hudelist, Darko: Tuđman je "norvalcima" obećao jedno ministartstvo a Šušak je postao ministar slučajno, umjesto Belje, *Globus* 474 (2000), no. 07/01, 61–93.

Hudelist, Darko: Tuđman, biografija. Zagreb: Profil international 2004.

Human Rights Watch: Croatia's Democracy Deficit, a Preelectoral Assessement, 1999, <http://www.hrw.org/reports/1999/croatia2/>, last access: 5.6.2006.

Huntington, Samuel: The Erosion of American National Interests, *Foreign Affairs* 76 (1997), no. 5, 28–49.

Ipsen, Carl: The Organization of Demographic Totalitarianism: Early Population Policy in Fascist Italy, *Social Science History* 17 (1993), no. 1, 71–108.

Ivanović, Vladimir: Obnavljanje diplomatskih odonosa između Socialističke Federativne Republike Jugoslavije i Savezne Republike Nemačke, *Istorija 20. Veka* 2 (2005), 129–144.

Jakir, Aleksandar: Dalmatien zwischen den Weltkriegen: Agrarische und urbane Lebenswelten und das Scheitern der jugoslawischen Integration. Munich: Oldenbourg Verlag 1999 (Südosteuropäische Arbeiten, 104).

Janjetović, Zoran: Deca careva, pastorčad kraljeva: Nacionalne manjine u Jugoslaviji 1918–1941. Belgrade: Institut za noviju istoriju Srbije 2005 (Biblioteka: Studije i monografije, 29).

Janjetović, Zoran: Od Auschwitza do Brijuna. Pitanje odštete žrtvama nacizma u jugoslavenskozapadnonjemačkim odnosima. Zagreb: Srednja Europa 2007.

Jansen, Dorothea: Einführung in die Netzwerkanalyse. Opladen: Leske + Budrich 2003.

Jarman, Robert L. (ed.): Yugoslavia. Political Diaries 1918–1965, vol. 1: 1918–1926. Slough: Archive Editions 1997.

Jelić, Milosav: Iseljavanje Turaka, *Politika*, 21 August 1923, 1.

Jonjić, Pavao: Identifikacija "gastarbeitera", *Migracijske teme* 4 (1988), no. 3, 285–291.

Jonjić, Pavao / Jasna Blažević: Baza podataka "Djeca građana Hrvatske u europskim i prekomorskim zemljama i nakon povratka", *Migracijske teme* 7 (1991), no. 3–4, 227–234.

Jovanović, Bojan: Magija srpskih obreda. Novi Sad: Svetovi 1993.

Jovanović, Nadežda: Politički sukobi u Jugoslaviji 1925–1928. Belgrade: Rad 1974.

Jovanović, Vladan: Jugoslovenska država i Južna Srbija 1918–1929: Makedonija, Sandžak, Kosovo i Metohija u Kraljevini SHS. Belgrade: Institut za noviju istoriju Srbije 2002 (Biblioteka: Studije i monografije, 23).

Jovanović, Vladan: Interministerijalna konferencija Kraljevine Jugoslavije o iseljenju "neslovenskog elementa u Tursku" (1935), *Prilozi* 35 (2006), 105–124.

Just, Michael: Ost- und südosteuropäische Amerikaauswanderung. Wiesbaden, Stuttgart: Franz Steiner 1988.

Kalc, Aleksej: Prekooceansko izseljevanje skozi Trst 1903–1914, *Zgodovinski časopis* 46 (1996), no. 4, 479–496.

Kalc, Aleksej / Aleš Brecelj / Inga Miklavčič Brezigar et al. (ed.): Poti in usode: selitvene izkušnje Slovencev z zahodne meje. Koper, Trst: Zgodovinsko društvo Slovenija, ZRS RS Koper, Narodna in študijska knjižnica Trst 2002.

Kaplan, Carla (ed.): Zora Neale Hurston. A Life in Letters. New York, London, Toronto: Doubleday 2002.

Karpat, Kemal H.: The Ottoman Emigration to America, 1860–1914, *International Journal of Middle East Studies* 17 (1985), no. 2, 175–209.

Kasapović, Mirjana: Znaju li uopće koliko glasova košta jedan mandat?, *Globus* 440 (1999), no. 14/05, 10–11.

Kasapović, Mirjana (ed.): Hrvatska politika 1990.–2000.: izbori, stranke i parlament u Hrvatskoj. Zagreb: Fakultet politickih znanosti Sveucilista 2001.

Kaser, Karl: Macht und Erbe. Männerherrschaft, Besitz und Familie im östlichen Europa. Vienna, Cologne, Weimar: Böhlau 2000.

Kaser, Karl: Familie und Verwandtschaft in Bulgarien. Historische und anthropologische Perspektiven, in: Ulf Brunnbauer / Karl Kaser (eds.): Vom Nutzen der Verwandten. Soziale Netzwerke in Bulgarien (19. und 20. Jahrhundert). Vienna: Böhlau 2001, 13–40.

Kaso, Sherafedin S.: Vendbanimet me Popullsi Musliman në Maqedoni. Skopje, Prishtina, Tirana: LOGOS-A 2005.

Kastoryano, Riva: Vers un nationalisme transnational. Redéfinir la nation, le nationalisme et le territoire, *Revue française de science politique* 56 (2006), no. 4, 533–555.

Katić, Žarko: Postojeće zakonske regulative i prijedlozi za prilagodbu, in: Hrvatska gospodarska komora (ed.): Međunarodna konferencija Useljenička politika u funkciji razvoja hrvatskoga gospodarstva. Zagreb 2008, 47–52.

Katunarić, Vjeran: Vanjske migracije i promjene u porodici. Zagreb: Centar za Istraživanje Migracija Zagreb 1978 (Vanjske migracije, 7).

Klemenčič, Matjaž: Slovenci v ameriški statistiki v 19. in 20. Stoletju, *Celovški zvon* 2 (1984), no. 4, 23–31.

Klemenčič, Matjaž: Images of America among Slovene and Other Yugoslav Migrants, in: Dirk Hoerder / Horst Rössler (eds.): Distant Magnets: Expectations and Realities in the Immigrant Experience, 1840–1930. New York: Holmes & Meier 1993, 199–221.

Klimt, Andrea: European Spaces: Portuguese Migrants' Notions of Home and Belonging, *Diaspora* 9 (2000), no. 2, 259–285.

Kodrič, Majda: Slovene Emigration to the United States and the Establishment of Ethnic Communities, in: Walter Hölbling / Reinhold Wagnleitner (eds.): The European Emigrant Experience in the U.S.A. Tübingen: Gunter Narr Verlag 1992, 149–169.

KOHLI, Martin: Die Institutionalisierung des Lebenslaufes: Historische Befunde und theoretische Argumente, *Kölner Zeitschrift für Soziologie und Sozialpsychologie* 37 (1985), no. 1, 1–29.

KOLAR-DIMITRIJEVIĆ, Mira: Djelovanje jugoslavenskih komunista među radničkom emigracijom zapadne Europe u međuratnom razdoblju, *Migracijske teme* 4 (1988), no. 1–2, 5–12.

KOLINSKY, Eva: Non-German Minorities in Contemporary German Society, in: David HORROCKS / Eva KOLINSKY (eds.): Turkish Culture in German Society Today. Providence: Berghahn Books 1996, 71–111.

KORENČIĆ, Mirk:, Naselja i stanovništvo SR Hrvatske 1857–1971. Zagreb: JAZU 1979.

KOS, Lucijan: Rijeka kao slobodna luka u razdoblju od 1719–1939, *Anali Jadranskog instituta* 4 (1968), 341–400.

KOSER, Khalid: Irregular Migration, State Security and Human Security. A Paper prepared for the Policy Analysis and Research Programme of the Global Commission on International Migration. Geneva: Global Commission on International Migration 2005, <http://www.gcim.org/attachements/TP5.pdf>, last access: 31.1.2009.

KOSTOVICOVA, Denisa: Kosovo. The Politics of Identity and Space. New York: Routledge 2005.

KREBS, Valdis E.: Mapping Networks of Terrorist Cells, *Connections* 24 (2002), no. 3, 43–52.

KRESAL, France / Jurij PEROVŠEK: Slovensko narodno ozemlje in razvoj prebivalstva, in: Neven BORAK / Zdenko ČEPIČ / Vida DEŽELAK BARIČ et al. (eds.): Slovenska novejša zgodovina. Ljubljana: Mladinska knjiga 2005, 17–21.

KRESER, M.: Gustoća žitelstva Kraljevine Hrvatske i Slavonije. Zagreb 1917.

KRISTAN, Ivan: Ustavni okviri javne besede, in: Lenart ŠETINC (ed.): Omejitve javne besede. Ljubljana: Gospodarski vestnik 1989, 57–66.

KRSTANOVIĆ-LUKIĆ, Miroslava: Srbi u Kanadi. Belgrade: Etnografski institut SANU 1992 (Posebno izdanje, 36).

KRSTIĆ, Đorđe: Južna Srbija i iseljenički problem, *Izseljeniški magazin* (November 1927), 18.

KRSTIĆ, Đorđe: Kolonizacija u Južnoj Srbiji. Sarajevo 1928.

KULIŠIĆ, Špiro / Petar PETROVIĆ / Nikola PANTELIĆ: Srpski mitološki rečnik. Belgrade: Etnografski institut SANU 1998.

KÜNNE, Wilfried: Die Außenwanderung jugoslawischer Arbeitskräfte. Ein Beitrag zur Analyse internationaler Arbeitskräftewanderungen. Königstein: Hanstein 1979.

KUŠAN, Jakša: Bitka za Novu Hrvatsku. Rijeka: Otokar Keršovani 2000.

La Législation Turque. Recueil des Lois, Décrets et Règlements de la République de Turquie, vol. IV (2e legislature: 3e session novembre 1925-octobre 1926). Constantinople 1926.

LACZKO, Franz: Data and Research on Human Trafficking, *International Migration* 43 (2005), no. 1–2, 5–16.

LAJIĆ, Ivan: Hrvatske migracije početkom 21. Stoljeća, *Migracijske i etničke teme* 18 (2002), no. 2–3, 135–149.

LAJIOS, Konstantin: Die allgemeine Situation ausländischer Familien in der Bundesrepublik Deutschland, in: Konstantin LAJIOS (ed.): Die ausländische Familie. Ihre Situation und Zukunft in Deutschland. Opladen: Leske + Budrich 1998, 13–23.

LAJIOS, Konstantin (ed.): Die ausländische Familie. Ihre Situation und Zukunft in Deutschland. Opladen: Leske + Budrich 1998.

LAKATOŠ, Josip: Narodna statistika. Zagreb 1914.

LAMPE, Evgen (ed.): III. slovenski katoliški shod dne 26., 27. in 28. avgusta 1906. Ljubljana: Katoliška bukvarna 1907.

LAPČEVIĆ, Dragiša: Iseljavanje muslimana, *Politika* (24 August 1923), 1.

Lapeyronnie, Didier: Les politiques locales d'intégration des immigrés en Europe, in: Didier Lapeyronnie (ed.): Immigrés en Europe: Politiques locales d'intégration. Paris: Harmattan 1992, 5–17.
Lastić, Petar: O položaju Srba u Mađarskoj, in: Vojislav Stanovčić (ed.): Položaj i identitet srpske manjine u Jugoistočnoj Evropi. Belgrade: SANU 2005, 187–235.
Laušić, Ante: Venezuela i Hrvati. Zagreb: Institut za migracije i narodnosti, Hrvatska matica iseljenika 2007.
Lazarević, Branko: Jugoslovenske potporne organizacije u Americi, *Nova Evropa* 2 (21 March 1921), no. 1, 15–20.
Le Bras, Hervé: L'invention des populations. Paris: Odile Jacob 2000.
Leković, Ananije: Ugroženi identitet. Belgrade: Pres Kliping 1981.
Lerch, Mathias / Janine Dahinden / Philippe Wanner: Remittance Behaviour of Serbian Migrants Living in Switzerland. Neuchâtel: Swiss Forum for Migration and Population Studies 2007 (SFM-Studies, 51).
Leutloff-Grandits, Carolin: Claiming Ownership in Postwar Croatia. The Dynamics of Property Relations and Ethnic Conflict in the Knin Region. Berlin: Lit Verlag 2006.

Levitt, Peggy / Josh DeWind / Steven Vertovec: International Perspectives on Transnational Migration: An Introduction, *International Migration Review* 37 (2003), no. 3, 565–575.
Lipoglavšek-Rakovec, Slava: Slovenski izseljenci, *Geografski vestnik* 22 (1950), no. 1–58.
Lohrmann, Reinhard: Politische Auswirkungen auf die Bundesrepublik Deutschland, in: Reinhard Lohrmann / Klaus Manfrass (eds.): Ausländerbeschäftigung und internationale Politik. Zur Analyse transnationaler Sozialprozesse. Munich: R. Oldenbourg Verlag 1974, 101–140.
Longchamp, Claude: Sans Papiers in der Schweiz: Arbeitsmarkt, nicht Asylpolitik ist entscheidend. Bern: gfs.bern 2005.
Lucassen, Jan / Leo Lucassen: Migration, Migration History, History: Old Paradigms and New Perspectives, in: Jan Lucassen / Leo Lucassen (eds.): Migration, Migration History, History. Old Paradigms and New Perspectives. Berlin, Vienna: Peter Lang, 2nd edition, 1999, 9–40.
Luhmann, Niklas: Die Weltgesellschaft, in: Niklas Luhmann (ed.): Soziologische Aufklärung 2. Aufsätze zur Theorie der Gesellschaft. Opladen: Westdeutscher Verlag 1991 [1971], 51–71.
Luhmann, Niklas: Soziale Systeme. Grundriß einer allgemeinen Theorie. Frankfurt/M.: Suhrkamp 1991 [1984].
Luhmann, Niklas: Liebe als Passion. Zur Codierung von Intimität. Frankfurt/M.: Suhrkamp 1994 [1982].
Luhmann, Niklas: Die Gesellschaft der Gesellschaft. Frankfurt/M.: Suhrkamp 1998.
Lukšič-Hacin, Marina: Mass Emigration from the Slovene Ethnic Area With Emphasis on the Situation of Slovene in Sweden, in: Vojislav Likar (ed.): Zgodbe in pričevanja. Ljubljana: Založba ZRC 2001, 325–348.
Lutz, Helma: Leben in der Twilightzone. Migration, Transnationalität und Geschlecht im Privathaushalt, in: Jutta Allmendinger (ed.): Entstaatlichung und Soziale Sicherheit. Verhandlungen des 31. Kongresses der Deutschen Gesellschaft für Soziologie in Leipzig 2002. Opladen: Leske + Budrich 2003, 254–267.

Macartney, Carlile Aylmer: The Habsburg Empire, 1790–1918. London: Weidenfeld & Nicolson 1968.
Mackert, Jürgen: Kampf um Zugehörigkeit: nationale Staatsbürgerschaft als Modus sozialer Schließung. Opladen: Westdeutscher Verlag 1999.
Majković, Bogdan: Letopis srpske crkvene opštine u Ljubljani. Ljubljana, unpubl. manus., 1941.
Makale, Manfred: Zadnji popis pučanstva u Dalmaciji. Vienna 1912.

Makuc, Dorica: Aleksandrinke. Gorica: Goriška Mohorjeva družba 2006.
Malačič, Janez: Labor Migration from Former Yugoslavia, in: Heinz Fassmann / Rainer Münz (eds.): European Migration in the Late Twentieth Century: Historical Patterns, Actual Trends, and Social Implications. Aldershot, Brookfield: E. Elgar; Laxenburg: IIASA 1994, 207–219.
Malcolm, Noel: Kosovo. A Short History. London: Macmillan 1998.
Manfrass, Klaus: Die Beziehungen zwischen der Bundesrepublik und den einzelnen Herkunftsländern im Zeichen der Arbeitskräftewanderung. Das Entstehen neuer Beziehungsstrukturen im staatlichen und gesellschaftlichen Bereich, in: Reinhard Lohrmann / Klaus Manfrass (eds.): Ausländerbeschäftigung und internationale Politik. Zur Analyse transnationaler Sozialprozesse. Munich: R. Oldenbourg Verlag 1974, 255–334.
Marković, Predrag: Verloren in der Transmigration? Der Einfluss der serbischen „Gastarbeiter" auf das Alltagsleben in Serbien, in: Klaus Roth (ed.): Arbeitswelt – Lebenswelt. Facetten einer spannungsreichen Beziehung im östlichen Europa. Berlin: LIT Verlag 2006, 239–256.
Marković, Živko / Miodrag Milenović: Neka pitanja vezana zu reintegraciju radnika u domovini i pitanje usmjeravanja kapitala i tehnologije prema radnicima, in: Ivo Baučić (ed.): Problemi povratka radnika migranata. Zagreb: Centar za istraživanje migracija 1975 (Rasprave o migracijama, 18), 27–34.
Matica Iseljenika Hrvatske: Izvještaj o Radu Matice Iseljenika Hrvatske (od 15.4.1956 do 23.11.1958). Zagreb, Drustvo Matica Iseljenika Hrvatske 1958.
Mattes, Monika: „Gastarbeiterinnen" in der Bundesrepublik. Anwerbepolitik, Migration und Geschlecht in den 50er bis 70er Jahren. Frankfurt/M.: Campus-Verlag 2005.
Mesić, Milan: Vanjske migracije i društveni razvitak. Zagreb: Institut za migracije i narodnosti 1991.
Mesić, Milan: External Migration in the Context of the Post-War Development of Yugoslavia, in: John B. Allcock / John J. Horton / Marko Milivojević (eds.): Yugoslavia in Transition. Choices and Constraints. New York, Oxford: Berg 1992, 171–198.
Mesić, Milan: Osjetljivi i ljuti ljudi: hrvatske izbjeglice i prognanici. Zagreb: Institut za migracije i narodnosti Sveučilišta u Zagrebu 1992.
Mesić, Milan: Socijalna obilježja i povratak hrvatskih prognanika i izbjeglica, in: Dubravka Hrabar (ed.): *Zbornik pravnog fakulteta u Zagrebu* 43 (1993), no. 2–3, 167–179.
Mesić, Milan: Međunarodne migracije: tokovi i teorije. Zagreb: Filozofski fakultet, Zavod za sociologiju 2002.
Mesić, Milan: Globalizacija migracije, *Migracijske i etničke teme* 18 (2002), no. 1, 7–22.
Mesić, Milan: Harmonizacija europske migracijske politike: Neuspjeh politika imigracijske kontrole sedamdesetih i osamdesetih godina 20. Stoljeća, *Migracijske i etničke teme* 19 (2003), no. 4, 343–361.
Mesić, Milan: Multikulturalizam. Društveni i teorijski izazovi. Zagreb: Školska knjiga 2006.
Mesić, Milan: Ekološke migracije, *Socjalna ekologija: časopis za ekološku misao i socjologijska istraživanja okoline* 1 (2006), no. 2, 167–177.
Mesić, Milan: Metodološki kozmopolitizam versus metodološki nacionalizam, *Revija za sociologiju* 38 (2007), no. 1–2, 71–83.
Mesić, Milan et al.: Vanjske migracije i društveni razvitak. Zagreb: Institut za migracije i narodnosti Sveučilišta u Zagrebu 1991.
Mesić, Milan / Emil Heršak: Evropa, integracije i (jugoslavenska) migracija, *Migracijske teme* 5 (1989), no. 1, 5–20.
Meštrovic, Mate: U vrtlogu hrvatske politike: kazivanje Peri Zlataru. Zagreb: Golden marketing 2003.
Mežnarić, Silva: Jugoslavenska sociologija (vanskih) migracija – pokušaj sistematizacije. In: *Migracijske teme* 1 (1985), no. 1, 77–96.

MEŽNARIĆ, Silva: Osvajanje prostora prekrivanje vremena / Migracije umjesto razvoja. Zagreb: Sociološko društvo Hrvatske 1991.

MEŽNARIĆ, Silva: Migracije, prinudne migracije, izbjeglištvo: građa za konceptualizaciju, *Revija za sociologiju* 26 (1995), no. 1–2, 35–42.

MEŽNARIĆ, Silva: Europa i Hrvatska u njoj: kultura adaptacije, in: Jadranka ČAČIĆ-KUMPES (ed.): Kultura, etničnost, identitet. Zagreb: Institut za migracije i narodnosti 1999, 115–120.

MEŽNARIĆ, Silva: Migracijske aktualnosti: stanje, problemi, perspektive paradigmi istraživanja, *Migracijske i etničke teme* 19 (2003), no. 4, 323–341.

MEŽNARIĆ, Silva: Migracije u Hrvatskoj: što očekivati, in: Hrvatska gospodarska komora (ed.): Međunarodna konferencija Useljenička politika u funkciji razvoja hrvatskoga gospodarstva. Zagreb 2008, 53–64.

MEŽNARIĆ, Silva / Ivan GRDEŠIĆ: "Odljev mozgova" iz Jugoslavije, *Politička misao* 27 (1990), no. 4, 136–163.

MIKULIĆ, Branislav: Vanjske migracije i razvoj Jugoslavije. Sarajevo: Ekonomski institut 1991.

MILARDOVIĆ, Anđelko: Neokonzervativizam, nove desnice, desni radikalizam i stranci u zapadnoj Europi, *Migracijske teme* 3 (1987), no. 3–4, 261–274.

MILARDOVIĆ, Anđelko: Politika njemačke vlade spram stranih posloprimaca, *Migracijske teme* 7 (1991), no. 3–4, 251–258.

MILARDOVIĆ, Anđelko: Novi val ksenofobije u zapadnoj Europi: Politologijski okvir promatranja, *Migracijske teme* 9 (1993), no. 2, 153–163.

MILARDOVIĆ, Anđelko: Demografske dimenzije globalizacije i vrijednosne promjene, in: HRVATSKA GOSPODARSKA KOMORA (ed.): Međunarodna konferencija Useljenička politika u funkciji razvoja hrvatskoga gospodarstva. Zagreb 2008, 65–74.

MILETIĆ, Aleksandar R.: Iz Memoara dr. Ninka Perića, *Tokovi istorije* (2003), no. 1–2, 141–61.

MILETIĆ, Aleksandar R.: Unutrašnja trgovina u Kraljevini SHS 1919, *Tokovi istorije* (2003), no. 3–4, 7–20.

MILETIĆ, Aleksandar R.: Afera Turn-Taxis, in: Aleksandra BULATOVIĆ / Srdjan KORAĆ (eds.): Korupcija i razvoj moderne srpske države. Belgrade: Centar za menadžment i Institut za kriminološka istraživanja 2006, 89–93.

Ministarstvo socijalne politike: Pažnja iseljenicima, *Cicvarićev beogradski dnevnik*, 2 August 1923.

MIRKOVIĆ, Mijo: Ekonomska struktura Jugoslavije 1918–1941. Zagreb: Nakladni zavod Hrvatske 1950.

MIŠETIĆ, Roko: Aktualno demografsko stanje i projekcije stanovništva Republike Hrvatske do 2050. godine, in: Hrvatska gospodarska komora (ed.): Međunarodna konferencija Useljenička politika u funkciji razvoja hrvatskoga gospodarstva. Zagreb 2008, 75–84.

MITCHELL, Brian R.: International Historical Statistics. The Americas 1750–2000. New York: Palgrave Macmillan 2003.

MITCHELL, James Clyde: The Concept and Use of Social Networks, in: James Clyde MITCHELL (ed.): Social Networks in Urban Situations. Analyses of Personal Relationships in Central African Towns. Manchester: Manchester University Press 1969, 1–50.

MOCH, Leslie Page: Moving Europeans: Migration in Western Europe since 1650. Bloomington, Ind. et al.: Indiana Univ. Press, 2nd edition, 2003 [1992].

MOLNAR, Iren Gabrity: The Sociology of Migration from the Former Yugoslavia. *New Community* 23 (1997), no. 1, 109–122.

MOROKVAŠIĆ, Mirjana: Jugoslaveni u Francuskoj. Istraživanja veze između predstave o nacionalnoj pripadnosti i adaptacije stranaca na novu sredinu, *Sociološki pregled* 4 (1970), no. 1, 89–104.

MOROKVAŠIĆ, Mirjana: Žene iz Jugoslavije na radu u Evropi, *Sociološki pregled* 16 (1982), no. 4, 21–33.

Morokvašić, Mirjana: Jugoslawische Frauen: Die Emigration – und danach. Basel: Stroemfeld, Roter Stern 1987.

Morokvasic, Mirjana: Transnational Mobility and Gender: A View from Post-Wall Europe, in: Mirjana Morokvasic / Umut Erel / Kyoko Shinozaki (eds.): Crossing Borders and Shifting Boundaries. vol. 1: Gender on the Move. Opladen: Leske + Budrich 2003, 101–133.

Mrnjavac, Željko: Problem migracija s aspekta ljudskih resursa privrede Mediterana, *Radovi Ekonomskog fakulteta Sveučilišta u Splitu* 9 (1993), no. 3, 19–26.

Müller, Dietmar: Das „lange 20. Jahrhundert" der „ethnischen Säuberungen" in Südosteuropa, *Jahrbücher für Geschichte und Kultur Südosteuropas* 7 (2005), 33–52.

Müller, Dietmar: Staatsbürger auf Widerruf: Juden und Muslime als Alteritätspartner im rumänischen und serbischen Nationscode. Ethnonationale Staatsbürgerschaftskonzepte 1878–1941. Wiesbaden: Harrassowitz 2005 (Balkanologische Veröffentlichungen, 41).

Müller-Mahn, Detlef: Ein ägyptisches Dorf in Paris. Eine empirische Studie zur Süd-Nord-Migration am Beispiel ägyptischer 'Sans-papiers' in Frankreich, in: Michael Bommes (ed.): Transnationalismus und Kulturvergleich. Osnabrück: IMIS 2000 (IMIS-Beiträge, 15), 79–110.

Münz, Rainer: Where Did They all Come From? Typology and Geography of European Mass Migration in the Twentieth Century. Berlin: Humboldt-Universität zu Berlin 1995 (Demographie aktuell, 7).

Naredba o likvidaciji Generalnog iseljeničkog komesarijata prenošenjem njegovih ingerencija na Iseljeničko odeljenje Ministarstva socijalne politike u Beogradu, *Službene novine KSHS*, 3 April 1923.

Naredba o stupanju u dejstvo Uredbe od 21. maja 1921, *Službene novine KSHS*, 14 July 1921.

Naredba ministra socijalne politike sporazumno sa ministrom unutrašnjih poslova [...] o izdavanju pasoša, *Službene novine KSHS*, 1 August 1921.

Nassehi, Armin: Die Theorie funktionaler Differenzierung im Horizont ihrer Kritik, *Zeitschrift für Soziologie* 33 (2004), no. 2, 98–118.

Nedeljković, Milorad: Iseljeničke uštede, *Izseljeniški magazin* (November 1927), 19–20.

Nejašmić, Ivica: Povratak jugoslavenskih vanjskih migranata i njihovo uključivanje u gospodarski i društveni život zemlje. Zagreb: Centar za istraživanje migracija 1981.

Nejašmić, Ivica: Iseljavanje iz Hrvatske u evropske i prekomorske zemlje od sredine 19. stoljeća do 1981. godine-pokušaj kvantifikacije, *Migracijske teme* 6 (1990), no. 4, 511–526.

Nejašmić, Ivica: Iseljavanje iz Hrvatske. Brojčani aspekt stoljetnog procesa, in: Ivan Crkvančić (ed.): Političko-geografska i demografska pitanja Hrvatske. Zagreb 1991, 61–81.

Nejašmić, Ivo: Hrvatski građani na radu u inozemstvu: razmatranje popisnih podataka 1971., 1981. i 1991, *Migracijske teme* 10 (1994), no. 2, 139–156.

Niedermüller, Peter: Arbeit, Identität, Klasse. Der Sozialismus als Lebensentwurf, in: Klaus Roth (ed.): Arbeit im Sozialismus – Arbeit im Postsozialismus. Munich 2004 (Forost Arbeitspapier, 20), 19–31.

Nikolić, Goran: Kurs dinara i devizna politika Kraljevine Jugoslavije 1918–1941. Belgrade: Stubovi kulture 2003.

Nikolić, Miloje: Neke karakteristike jugoslovenske migracije, *Jugoslovenski pregled* 16 (1971), no. 1, 1–8.

NL 1966: Schüsse in Stuttgart, *Die Zeit* 13 (9 September 1966), no. 37.

Obadić, Alka: Makroekonomika tranzicijskog tržišta rada. S posebnim osvrtom na Hrvatsku. Zagreb: Politička kultura 2005.

Obadić, Alka: Ocjena stanja hrvatskog tržišta rada i njegova mobilnost, in: Hrvatska gospodarska komora (ed.): Međunarodna konferencija Useljenička politika u funkciji razvoja hrvatskoga gospodarstva. Zagreb 2008, 97–110.

Oberpenning, Hannelore: “People were on the move”. Wanderhandelssysteme im vor- und frühindustriellen Europa, in: Hannelore Oberpenning / Annemarie Steidl (eds.): Kleinräumige Wanderungen in historischer Perspektive. Osnabrück: IMIS 2001 (IMIS-Beiträge, 18), 123–140.

Obradović, Milovan: Agrarna reforma i kolonizacija na Kosovu (1918–1941). Priština: Progres 1981.

Oklobdžija, Mirjana: Promjene u obitelji i specifični problemi migrantica, *Migracijske teme* 6 (1990), no. 4, suppl., 39–46.

OSCE: Statement: Presidential Election in the Republic of Croatia. 15 June 1997, <http://www.osce.org/item/1536.html>, last access: 15.3.2006.

Palairet, Michael: The ‘New’ Immigration and the Newest Slavic Migrations from the Balkans to America and Industrial Europe since the Late Nineteenth Century, in: Thomas C. Smout (ed.): The Search for Wealth and Stability. Essays in Economic and Social History presented to M. W. Flinn. London: McMillan 1979, 43–65.

Palairet, Michael: The Migrant Workers of the Balkans and their Villages (18th Century – World War II), in: Klaus Roth (ed.): Handwerk in Mittel- und Südosteuropa. Mobilität, Vermittlung und Wandel im Handwerk des 18. bis 20. Jahrhunderts. Munich: Südosteuropa Gesellschaft 1987, 23–46.

Pariski poslovni podsetnik. Paris 2000.

Parnreiter, Christof: Migration und Arbeitsteilung. AusländerInnenbeschäftigung in der Weltwirtschaftskrise. Vienna: Promedia 1994.

Parnreiter, Christof: Theorien und Forschungsansätze zu Migration, in: Karl Husa / Christof Parnreiter / Irene Stacher (eds.): Internationale Migration. Die globale Herausforderung des 21. Jahrhunderts? Frankfurt/M.: Brandes & Apsel 2000, 25–52.

Pavićević, Aleksandra: Ambiguity of Integration Processes: the Serbs in Greece. National Identity of New Imigrants, *Ethnologia Balkanica* 8 (2004), 103–115.

Pavićević, Aleksandra: Dva primera srpske emigracije – Slovenija i Grčka, in: Vojislav Stanovčić (ed.): Položaj i identitet srpske manjine u Jugoistočnoj Evropi. Belgrade: SANU 2005, 421–434.

Pavlinić-Wolf, Andrina: Obrazovanje i zaposlenost djece migranata, *Migracijske teme* 1 (1985), no. 2, 39–55.

Pavlović, Mirjana: Srbi u Čikagu (Serbs in Chicago). Belgrade: SANU 1990 (Posebna izdanja, 32).

Pavlović, Mirjana: Životni ciklus i etnicitet Srba u Čikagu, in: Radost Ivanova / Valentina Vaseva / Evgenija Krăsteva-Blagoeva (eds.): Životni ciklus. Referati bugarsko-srpskog naučnog skupa, 12–16. juna 2000. Sofia 2000, 82–88.

Pederin, Ivan: Arhivske vijesti o iseljavanju iz Dalmacije, Bosne i Hercegovine početkom XX. Stoljeća, *Migracijske teme* 12 (1996), no. 3, 219–225.

Pejović, Đorđe: Iseljavanje Crnogoraca u XIX veku. Titograd: Istorijski institut Narodne republike Crne gore 1962.

Pennix, Rinus: Introduction, in: Rinus Pennix / Maria Berger / Karen Kraal (eds.): The Dynamics of International Migration and Settlement in Europe. A State of the Art. Amsterdam: Amsterdam University Press 2006, 7–18.

Perić Kaselj, Marina / Simona Kuti: Croatian Immigrants in Chile, *AEMI Journal* 4–5 (2006), 93–106.

Peričić, Marijana et al.: Review of Croatian Genetic Heritage as Revealed by Mitochondrial DNA and Y Chromosomal Lineages, *Croatian Medical Journal* 46 (2005), no. 4, 502–513.

Perovšek, Jurij: Razvoj prebivalstva, in: Neven Borak / Zdenko Čepič / Vida Deželak Barič et al. (eds.): Slovenska novejša zgodovina. Ljubljana: Mladinska knjiga 2005, 177–182.

Petković, Simka: Osnovni faktori odlaska jugoslovenskih radnika na privremeni rad u inostranstvo, *Ekonomika poljoprivrede* 34 (1987), no. 1–2, 25–34.

Petrović, Jelenko: Pečalbari, naročito iz okoline Pirota. Belgrade 1929.

Pichler, Robert: Makedonien im Dilemma ethnisch divergierender Entwicklungsprozesse. Über die Schwierigkeit, auf der Basis des Ohrider Rahmenabkommens eine sozial gerechte Ordnung zu etablieren, in: Michael Daxner et al. (eds.): Bilanz Balkan. Vienna, Oldenburg: Verlag für Geschichte und Politik 2005, 68–100.

Pirjevec, Jože: Slovenci v Italiji, in: Enciklopedija Slovenije, vol. 11. Ljubljana: Mladinska knjiga 1997, 260–294.

Pirraku, Muhamet: Kulturno-prosvetni pokret Albanaca u Jugoslaviji (1919–1941), *Jugoslovenski istorijski časopis* 17 (1978), no. 1–4, 356–370.

Pislar Fernandez, Marie (ed.): Slovenci v železni Loreni (1919–1939) skozi družinske pripovedi / Slovènes en Lorraine du fer (1919–1939) à travers des récits de familles. Ljubljana: Založba ZRC 2006.

Portelli, Alessandro: The Death of Luigi Trastulli and Other Stories. Form and Meaning in Oral History. Albany: State University of New York Press 1991.

Portes, Alejandro: Social Capital: Its Origins and Applications in Modern Sociology, *Annual Review of Sociology* 24 (1998), 1–24.

Portes, Alejandro: Conclusion: Theoretical Convergences and Empirical Evidence in the Study of Immigrant Transnationalism, *International Migration Review* 37 (2003), no. 3, 874–892.

Poulton, Hugh: Who are the Macedonians? Bloomington, Indianapolis: Indiana University Press 2003.

Pravilnik o izvršenju Zakona o iseljavanju, *Službene novine KSHS*, 1 September 1922.

Pries, Ludger (ed.): Transnationale Migration. Baden-Baden: Nomos Verlagsgesellschaft 1997.

Prpic, Jure: The Croatian Immigrants in America. New York: Philosophical Library 1971.

Purić, Božidar: Naši iseljenici. Belgrade: Knjižarnica S. B. Cvijanovića 1929.

Pusić, Petar: Gegenwärtige Entwicklung der Familie in Jugoslawien, *Informationsdienst zur Ausländerarbeit* (1929), no. 2–3, 31–35.

Puskás, Julianna: From Hungary to the United States (1880-1914). Budapest: Akadémiai Kiadó 1982.

Qyra, Zejnulla: Veleshta në Histori. Tirana: Edlor 2000.

Radusinović, Pavle: Stanovništvo Crne Gore do 1945. godine. Belgrade: SANU 1978.

Ragazzi, Francesco / Igor Stiks: Croatian Citizenship: From Ethnic Engineering to Inclusiveness, in Rainer Bauböck / Wiebke Sievers / Bernhard Perchinig (eds.): A call to kinship? Citizenship and migration in the new member and accession states of the E.U. Amsterdam: University of Amsterdam Press 2009 (forthcoming).

Ranković, Aleksander: Domovina je odprla vrata na stežaj, in: Zima Vrščaj / Mila Šenk (eds.): Slovenski izseljenski koledar 1962. Ljubljana: Slovenska izseljenska matica 1961, 46–47.

Rapport, Nigel / Andrew Dawson (eds.): Migrants of Identity. Perceptions of Home in a World of Movement. Oxford, New York: Berg 1998.

Ratia, Camille: Le dixième département: entre pratiques des migrants et institutionnalisation de la diaspora haïtienne. Paper presented at the annual convention of the French Association of Political Science (AFSP), Lyon, 2005.

Republic of Croatia: The Constitution of the Republic of Croatia. Zagreb: Narodne novine 1998 [1991].

Reuter-Hendrichs, Irena: Jugoslawische Außenpolitik 1948–1968. Außenpolitische Grundsätze und internationale Ordnungsvorstellungen. Cologne et al.: Carl Heymanns Verlag KG 1976.

Richmond, Anthony: Sociological Theories of International Migration. The Case of Refugees, *Current Sociology* 36 (1988), no. 2, 7–26.

Richter Malabotta, Melita: Feminizacija migracijskih tokova i aspekti integracije na području Trsta Iiregije Furlanija-Julijska krajina, *Migracijske i etničke teme* 18 (2002), no. 4, 365–381.

Rihtman-Auguštin, Dunja: Etnologija naše svakodnevice. Zagreb: Školska knjiga 1988.

Risteski, Ljupčo: Is the Macedonian Knot Becoming a Dog's Knot?, *EthnoanthropoZoom. Journal of the Department of Ethnology (Skopje)* (2003), no. 3, 48–89.

Roksandić, Drago: Vojna Hrvatska – La Croatie Militaire. Zagreb: Školska knjiga 1988.

Römhild, Regina: Jenseits der deutschen Integrationslogik: Kulturanthropologische Perspektiven für die Einwanderungsgesellschaft, in: Christoph Köck / Alois Moosmüller / Klaus Roth (eds.): Zuwanderung und Integration: Kulturwissenschaftliche Zugänge und soziale Praxis. Munich: Waxmann 2004, 163–175.

Rouse, Roger: Making Sense of Settlement: Class Transformations, Cultural Struggle, and Transnationalism among Mexican Migrants in the United States, in: Nina Glick Schiller / Linda Basch / Cristina Szanton Blanc (eds.): Towards a Transnational Perspective on Migration: Race, Class, Ethnicity, and Nationalism Reconsidered. New York: The New York Academy of Science 1992, 25–52.

Roux, Michel: Les Albanais en Yougoslavie. Minorité nationale territoire et développement. Paris: Ed. de la Maison des Sciences de l'Homme 1992.

Safran, William: Diasporas in modern societies: myths of homeland and return, *Diaspora* 1 (1991), no. 1, 83–93.

Sandevski, Tome: Die Entwicklung der interethnischen Beziehungen in Mazedonien 1945-2002. Unpublished M. A. thesis, Free University of Berlin, 2004.

Savezni zavod za statistiku: Lica na privremenom radu u inostranstvu. Prema popisu stanovništva i stanova 1971. Belgrade 1971 (Statistički bilten, 679).

Schierup, Carl-Ulrik: Houses, Tractors, Golden Ducats. Prestige Game and Migration. A Study of Migrants to Denmark from a Yugoslav Village. Field Report. Århus: Institut for Etnografi og Socialantropologi Moesgård, Århus Universitet 1973.

Schierup, Carl-Ulrik: Migration, Socialism and the International Division of Labour. The Yugoslavian Experience. Aldershot et al.: Ashgate 1990.

Schierup, Carl-Ulrik: Former Yugoslavia: Long Waves of International Migration, in: Robin Cohen (ed.): The Cambridge Survey of World Migration. Cambridge: Cambridge University Press 1995, 285–288.

Schiffauer, Werner: Migration und Selbstverständnis: Biographische Untersuchungen zum Prozeß der Moderne. Frankfurt/M.: Johann Wolfgang Goethe Universität 1991.

Schimank, Uwe / Ute Volkmann: Gesellschaftliche Differenzierung. Bielefeld: Transcript 1999.

Schnapper, Dominique: De l'Etat-nation au monde transnational (Du sens et de l'utilité du concept de diaspora), *Revue Européenne des Migrations Internationales* 17 (2001), no. 2, 9–36.

Schönwälder, Karen: Einwanderung und ethnische Pluralität. Politische Entscheidungen und öffentliche Debatten in Großbritannien und der Bundesrepublik von den 1950er bis zu den 1970er Jahren. Essen: Klartext Verlag 2001.

Scott, James C.: Seeing Like a state: How Certain Schemes to Improve the Human Condition Have Failed. New Haven: Yale University Press 1998.

Searle, John R.: The Construction of Social Reality. London: Allen Lane 1995.

SHARPE, Pamela (ed.): Women, Gender and Labour Migration. Historical and Global Perspectives. London, New York: Routledge 2001.
SHEFFER, Gabriel: Modern Diasporas in International Politics. London: Croom Helm 1986.
SHEFFER, Gabriel: Diaspora Politics: at Home Abroad. Cambridge, U.K., New York: Cambridge University Press 2003.
ŠIDAK, Jaroslav et al. (eds.): Povijest Hrvatskog Naroda. Zagreb: Udžebenici Sveučilišta u Zagrebu 1968.
ŞIMŞEK-ÇAĞLAR, Ayse: German Turks in Berlin: Migration and Their Quest for Social Mobility. PhD dissertation, University of Montréal, Department of Anthropology 1994.
ŠKAFAR, Ivan: Prekmurski sezonski delavci v Slavoniji, *Izseljenski vestnik* 9 (1939), no. 3, 34–36.
SKRBIŠ, Zlatko: Long-Distance Nationalism: Diasporas, Homelands and Identities. Brookfield, Singapore, Sidney: Ashgate 1999.
SKUPNJAK-KAPIĆ, Sunčanica: Globalni migracijski trendovi i međunarodna iskustva u provođenju useljeničkih politika, in: Hrvatska gospodarska komora (ed.): Međunarodna konferencija Useljenička politika u funkciji razvoja hrvatskoga gospodarstva. Zagreb 2008, 117–124.
ŠKVORC, Boris: Nekoliko napomena o broju Hrvata, hrvatskom jeziku, školama i hrvatskim medijima u Australiji, *Društvena istraživanja* 7 (1998), no. 1–2, 189–206.
ŠKVORC, Boris: Australski Hrvati Mitovi i stvarnost. Zagreb: Hrvatska matica iseljenika 2005.
SMITH, Michael Peter / Luis Eduardo GUARNIZO (eds.): Transnationalism from Below. New Brunswick, London: Transaction Publishers 1998.
SMITH, Tony: Foreign Attachments. London: Harvard University Press 2000.
SOYARIK-ŞENTÜRK, Nalan: Legal and Constitutional Foundations of Turkish Citizenship: Changes and Continuities, in: Emin Fuat KEYMAN / Ahmet İÇDUYGU (eds.): Citizenship in a Global World. European Questions and Turkish Experiences. London, New York: Routledge 2005, 124–143 (Routledge Studies in Governance and Change in the Global Era, 3).
STANKOVIĆ, Đorđe / Ljubodrag DIMIĆ: Istoriografija pod nadzorom. Belgrade: Službeni list 1996.
STARK, David / László BRUSZT: Postsocialist Pathways. Cambridge: Cambridge University Press 1998.
State Statistical Office: Census of Population, Households and Dwellings in the Republic of Macedonia, 2002, Final Data 2003, <http://www.stat.gov.mk/english/glavna_eng.asp?br=18>, last access: 10.1.2008.
Statistical Yearbook of the Republic of Croatia. Zagreb: Državni zavod za statistiku 2007.
Statistički godišnjak Kraljevina Hrvatske i Slavonije 1905. Zagreb: Kr. zemaljski statistički ured 1913.
Statistički godišnjak Kraljevina Hrvatske i Slavonije 1996–1910. Zagreb: Kr. zemaljski statistički ured 1917.
Statistički godišnjak Kraljevine Jugoslavije 1929. Belgrade: Državna Štamparija Kraljevine Jugoslavije 1932.
Statistički godišnjak Kraljevine Jugoslavije 1938/39. Belgrade: Državna Štamparija Kraljevine Jugoslavije 1940.
STEINDORFF, Ludwig: Kroatien. Regensburg: Pustet 2001.
Stenografički zapisnici Sabora Kraljevina Hrvatske, Slavonije i Dalmacije 1897–1902. 15. siečnja do 24. veljače 1900. Svezak 4, dio 1, 1900. Zagreb.
Stenografički zapisnici Sabora Kraljevina Hrvatske, Slavonije i Dalmacije 1908–1913. 12. ožujka do 23. svibnja 1910. Svezak 1. 1910. Zagreb.
STÖLTING, Wilfried: Die Zweisprachigkeit jugoslawischer Schüler in der Bundesrepublik Deutschland. Wiesbaden: Otto Harrassowitz 1980.
STRACHAN, Hew: The First World War. New York: Viking Penguin 2004.

Štulhofer, Aleksandar / Zora Raboteg-Šarić / Lovorka Marinović: Trafficking in Women and Children for Sexual Exploitation. Zagreb: Center for Transition and Civil Society Research, International Organization for Migration 2002.

Šumrada, Janez: La Slovénie, carrefour de l'Histoire et des cultures, *Les arts en Slovénie, L'oeil* (1995), no 473, 26–27.

Sundhaussen, Holm: Jugoslawisch-deutsche Beziehungen zwischen Normalisierung, Bruch und erneuter Normalisierung, in: Othmar Nikola Haberl / Hans Hecker (eds.): Unfertige Nachbarschaften. Die Staaten Osteuropas und die Bundesrepublik Deutschland. Essen: Reimar Hobbing GmbH Verlag 1989, 133–151.

Sundhaussen, Holm: Unerwünschte Staatsbürger: Grundzüge des Staatsangehörigkeitsrechts in den Balkanländern und Rumänien, in: Christoph Conrad / Jürgen Kocka (eds.): Staatsbürgerschaft in Europa. Historische Erfahrungen und aktuelle Debatten. Hamburg: Ed. Körber-Stiftung 2001, 193–215.

Sundhaussen, Holm: Wirtschaftsgeschichte Kroatiens im nationalsozialistischen Großraum 1941–1945. Das Scheitern einer Ausbeutungsstrategie. Stuttgart: DVA 1983.

Švob, Melita: Migracije jugoslavenski žena. In: *Migracijske teme* 6 (1990), no. 4, Supplement, 3–11.

Svoljšak, Petra: Soča, sveta reka: italijanska zasedba slovenskega ozemlja (1915–1917). Ljubljana: Nova revija 2003.

Swiss Federal Council: Bericht des Bundesrates zur Ausländer- und Flüchtlingspolitik vom 15. Mai 1991. Bern: EDMZ 1991.

Szabo, Agneza: Socijalna struktura Slovenaca u Kraljevini Hrvatskoj i Slavoniji između 1880. i 1910. godine, in: Vera Kržišnik-Bukić (ed.): Slovenci v Hrvaški. Ljubljana: Inštitut za narodnostna vprašanja 1995, 85–105.

Tacke, Veronika: Netzwerk und Adresse, *Soziale Systeme* 6 (2000), no. 2, 291–320.

Tanić, Živan: Ekonomska emigracija: Klasno odredenje i svest, *Sociologija* 14 (1972), no. 3, 441–457.

Tanić, Živan: Seljaci na evropskim raskrsnicama. Analiza ekonomskih migracija. Belgrade: Institut društvenih nauka 1974.

Tanić, Živan: Povratak radnika iz inozemstva i zapošljavanje, *Ekonomski pregled* 27 (1976), no. 11–12, 941–950.

Tanner, Marcus: Croatia: A Nation Forged in War. London: Yale University Press 1997.

Tarrius, Alain: La mondialisation par le bas. Les nouveaux nomades de l'économie souterraine. Paris: Balland 2002.

Tarrow, Sidney: Power in movement: social movements and contentious politics. Cambridge: Cambridge University Press 1998.

Telišman, Tihomir: Statistički pokazatelji o iseljavanju naših ljudi s posebnim osvrtom na Hrvatsku, in: Ivan Čizmić et al. (eds.): Iseljeništvo naroda i narodnosti Jugoslavije. Zagreb: Zavod za migracije i narodnosti 1978, 130–143.

Thompson, Paul: The Voice of the Past. Oral History. Oxford, New York: Oxford University Press 1988.

Tilly, Charles: Migration in Modern European History, in: William H. McNeill / Ruth S. Adams (eds.): Human Migration. Patterns and Policies. Bloomington, London: Indiana University Press 1978, 48–72.

Tilly, Charles: Popular contention in Great Britain, 1758–1834. Cambridge, Mass.: Harvard University Press 1995.

Timmer, S. / Jeffrey G. Williamson: Racism, Xenophobia or Markets? The Political Economy of Immigration Policy Prior to the Thirties. Cambridge: National Bureau of Economic Research 1996 (Working Paper, 5867).

Tkalčević, Mate: Povijest Hrvata u Australiji. Melbourne: Hrvatski svjetski kongres u Australiji, Cross Color Printing 1999.

Todorova, Maria: Myth-Making in European Family History: The Zadruga Revisited, *East European Politics and Societies* 4 (1989), no. 1, 30–76.

Tölölyan, Kchachig: Rethinking Diaspora(s): Stateless Power in the Transnational Moment, *Diaspora* 1 (1996), no. 5, 3–36.

Torgovnik, Marianna: Slasher Stories, *Journal of Culture/Theory/Practice (The Question of 'Home')* 17 (1992), 133–145.

Torpey, John: The Invention of the Passport. Surveillance, Citizenship and the State. Cambridge, UK, New York: Cambridge University Press 2000.

Toš, Niko / Peter Klinar: A System Model for Migration Research, in: Anthony Richmond (ed.): International Migration and Adaptation in the Modern World. Toronto: SAGE 1976, 80–113.

Tripalo, Miko: Hrvatsko Proljeće. Zagreb: Globus 1989.

Troebst, Stefan: Makedonische Antworten auf die „Makedonische Frage" 1944–1992: Nationalismus, Republiksgründung, Nation-Building, *Südosteuropa* 41 (1992), no. 7–8, 423-442.

Tuđman, Franjo: Poruka Predsjednika Republike Dr. Franje Tuđmana Hrvatskim Iseljenicima, in: Ministarstvo povratka i useljeništva (ed.): Vodić za povratnike u Hrvatsku. Zagreb: Ministarstvo povratka i useljeništva 1997, 7–8.

United Serbian Society: United Serbian Society. 100th Anniversary. Chicago: United Serbian Society 1981.

Uputstvo o postupanju pri zapošlavanju u inostranstvu, *Službeni list* 42, 23 Oktober 1963.

U.S. Immigration Commission: Reports of the Immigration Commission (1907–1910), vol. 41. Washington, DC 1911.

Valenčič, Joseph: United Americans for Slovenia Make a Difference, *American Home – Special Edition, Freedom Section* (Fall 1992), no. 1–2B.

Valenčič, Vlado: Izseljevanje Slovencev v tujino do druge svetovne vojne, *Dve domovini/Two Homelands* 1 (1990), 43–82.

Valenčič, Vlado: Izseljevanje Slovencev v druge dežele Habsburške monarhije, *Zgodovinski časopis* 44 (1990), no. 1, 49–71.

Van Liempt, Ilse / Jerome Doomernik: Migrant's Agency in the Smuggling Process. The Perspectives of Smuggled Migrants in the Netherlands, *International Migration* 44 (2006), no. 4, 165–190.

van Loon, Joost: Network, *Theory, Culture & Society* 23 (2006), no. 2–3, 307–314.

Vertovec, Steven: Conceiving and Researching Transnationalism, *Ethnic and Racial Studies* 22 (1999), no. 2, 447–462.

Vidović, Mirko: Što je Hrvatsko Narodno Vijeće? Sydney: Knjižnica MO HNV-a "Kralj Tomislav" 1984.

Vijeće BK za hrvatsku emigraciju: Crkva i hrvatsko iseljeništvo. Zagreb: Kršćanska sadašnjost 1982.

Vinski, Ivo: Wirtschaftliche Schwierigkeiten, Arbeitslosigkeit und Auswanderung, *Osteuropa* 19 (1969), no. 11, Archive.

Vinski, Ivo: Ljudski kapital i neto produkt savremene jugoslovenske emigracije, *Ekonomski pregled* (Zagreb) 23 (1972), no. 3–4, 117–130.

Vlahović, Petar: Srpska i crnogorska manjina u Albaniji, in: Vojislav Stanovčić (ed.): Položaj i identitet srpske manjine u Jugoistočnoj Evropi. Belgrade: SANU 2005, 121–129.

Vodopivec, Peter: Temno in svetlo ogledalo zgodovine, in: Andrej Blatnik et al. (eds.): Samopodoba Slovencev. Ljubljana: Slovenski PEN 2001, 58–63.

VOLOSHINOV [BAKHTIN], Valentin. N.: Marxism and the Philosophy of Language. New York: Seminar Press 1973.

VOSS, Christian: Sprach- und Geschichtsrevision in Makedonien. Zur Dekonstruktion von Blaže Koneski, *Osteuropa* 51 (2001), no. 8, 953–967.

VOSS, Christian: Irredentismus als historischer Selbstentwurf. Wissenschaftsdiskurs und Staatssymbolik in der Republik Makedonien, *Osteuropa* 53 (2003), no. 7, 949–962.

VUKAS, Budislav: The Legal Status of National Minorities in the Republic of Croatia, in: Zlata DRNAS DE CLÉMENT (ed.): Estudios de derecho internacional en homenaje al profesor Ernesto J. Rey Caro. Córdoba: Drnas-Lerner 2002, 887–891.

VUKUŠIĆ, Bože: Tajni rat Udbe protiv hrvatskoga iseljeništva. Zagreb: Klub hrvatskih povratnika iz iseljeništva 2002.

WALDINGER, Roger / David FITZGERALD: Transnationalism in Question, *American Journal of Sociology* 109 (2004), no. 5, 1177–1195.

WANNER, Philippe: Migration et intégration. Populations étrangères en Suisse. Recensement fédéral de la population 2000. Neuchâtel: Office fédérale de la statistique 2004.

WEBER, Rolf: Problematische Jugoslawen, *Der Arbeitgeber* 21 (1966), 651–652.

WERTHEIMER-BALETIĆ, Alica: Stanovništvo i razvoj. Zagreb: Mate 1999.

WHELPLEY, James Davenport: The Problem of the Immigrant. London: Chapman & Hall 1905.

WICKER, Hans-Rudolf: From Complex Culture to Cultural Complexity, in: Pnina WERBNER / Tariq MODOOD (eds.): Debating Cultural Hybridity. Multi-Cultural Identities and the Politics of Anti-Racism. London, New Jersey: Zed Books 1997, 29–45.

WIMMER, Andreas / Nina GLICK SCHILLER: Methodological Nationalism and Beyond: Nation-State Building, Migration and the Social Sciences, *Global Networks* 2 (2002), no. 4, 301–334.

WIMMER, Andreas / Nina GLICK SCHILLER: Methodological Nationalism, the Social Sciences and the Study of Migration: an Essay in Historical Epistemology, *International Migration Review* 37 (2003), no. 3, 576–611.

WOHINZ, Kacin Milica / Nevenka TROHA (eds.): Slovensko-italijanski odnosi 1880–1956, poročilo slovensko-italijanske komisije / I rapporti italo-sloveni 1880–1956: relazione della commissione storico-culturale italo-slovena / Slovene-Italian Relations 1880–1956: Report of the Slovene-Italian Historical and Cultural Commission. Ljubljana: Nova revija 2001.

WOODWARD, Susan L.: Socialist Unemployment: the Political Economy of Yugoslavia, 1945–1990. Princeton, NJ: Princeton Univ. Press 1995.

WÖRSDÖRFER, Rolf: Südosteuropa an Rhein und Ruhr. Die „westfälischen Slowenen“ 1880–1941, in: Ulf BRUNNBAUER / Andreas HELMEDACH / Stefan TROEBST (eds.): Schnittstellen. Gesellschaft, Nation, Konflikt und Erinnerung in Südosteuropa. Festschrift für Holm Sundhaussen zum 65. Geburtstag. Munich: R. Oldenbourg 2007, 95–110.

Zakon o iseljavanju od 30. decembra 1921, *Službene novine KSHS*, 21 February 1922.

Zakon o taksama. Belgrade: Državna štamparija Kraljevine Srbije 1911.

ZIMMERMANN, William: Open Borders, Nonalignment, and the Political Evolution of Yugoslavia. Princeton: Princeton University Press 1987.

ZLATKOVIĆ WINTER, Jelena: Imigracijske politike zemalja prijema hrvatskih vanjskih migranata u prošlosti i sadašnjosti, in: Ante LAUŠIĆ (ed.): Hrvatske iseljeničke teme. Zagreb: IMIN 1997, 63–84.

ŽUNEC, Ozren / Darko DOMIŠLJANOVIĆ: Obavještajno-sigurnosne službe Republike Hrvatske: stanje i načela preustroja za razdoblje konsolidacije demokracije. Zagreb: Naklada Jesenski i Turk 2000.

Zürcher, Erik J.: Turkey. A Modern History. London, New York: I.B. Tauris & Co Ltd, 2nd edition, 1998.

Zwitter, Fran: Nacionalni problemi v Habsburški monarhiji. Ljubljana: Slovenska matica 1962.

List of Tables, Figures, Maps, and Pictures

Tables and Figures

Maps

Pictures

List of Contributors

Ulf Brunnbauer, Professor for Southeast and East European History at the University of Regensburg and Director of the Institute for Southeast European Studies (Südost-Institut), Regensburg, Germany.

Janine Dahinden, Professor for Transnational Studies, Center for Understanding of Social Processes (MAPS), University of Neuchâtel, Switzerland.

Jasna Čapo Žmegač, Professor at the Institute for Ethnology and Folklore Research, Zagreb, Croatia.

Marjan Drnovšek, Research Adviser at the Slovenian Migration Institute of the Scientific Research Centre of the Slovenian Academy of Sciences and Arts in Ljubljana, Slovenia, and editor-in-chief of the journal *Dve domovini / Two Homelands*.

Pascal Goeke, Lecturer at the Department of Human Geography, Goethe-University, Frankfurt/Main, Germany.

Karolina Novinšćak, Researcher at the Chair for the History of Southeastern and Eastern Europe, University of Regensburg, Germany.

Aleksandar Miletić, PhD student at the European University Institute Florence, Italy, and researcher at the Institute for the Recent History of Serbia, Belgrade, Serbia.

Mirjam Milharčič Hladnik, Senior Research Fellow at the Slovenian Migration Institute of the Scientific Research Centre of the Slovenian Academy of Sciences and Arts in Ljubljana and lecturer at the University of Ljubljana and University of Nova Gorica, Slovenia.

Aleksandra Pavićević, Scientific research fellow at the Ethnographic Institute of the Serbian Academy of Sciences and Arts, Belgrade, Serbia.

Edvin Pezo, Lecturer at the Chair for the History of Southeastern and Eastern Europe, University of Regensburg, Germany.

Robert Pichler, Researcher at the Department of Southeast European History, University of Graz, Austria.

Francesco Ragazzi, PhD Student at the University of Chicago, Ill., and at the Institute for Political Studies in Paris, France.